FUNDAMENTALS OF ENERGY REGULATION

Jonathan A. Lesser, Ph.D.

Leonardo R. Giacchino, Ph.D.

2007
Public Utilities Reports, Inc.
Vienna, Virginia

© Public Utilities Reports, Inc. 2007

All rights reserved. No part of this publication may be reproduced, stored in a retrieval system, or transmitted in any form or by any means, electronic, mechanical, photocopying, recording, or otherwise, without the prior written permission of the publisher.

This publication is designed to provide accurate and authoritative information in regard to the subject matter covered. It is sold with the understanding that the publisher is not engaged in rendering legal, accounting, or other professional service. If legal advice or other expert assistance is required, the services of a competent professional person should be sought. (From a *Declaration of Principles* jointly adopted by a *Committee of the American Bar Association and a Committee of Publishers.*)

First Printing, August 2007

Library of Congress Cataloging-in-Publication Data
Lesser, Jonathan A.
 Fundamentals of energy regulation/Jonathan A. Lesser, Leonardo R. Giacchino
  p. cm.
 Includes bibliographical references and index.
 ISBN 978-0-910325-19-6
 1. Energy industries – Government policy – United States. I. Giacchino,
  Leonardo R. II. Title.

HD9502.U52L47 2007
333.790973 – dc22

2007024399

Printed in the United States of America

In memory of
Shimon Awerbuch
Colleague, Mentor, Friend

Table of Contents

Preface xi

Part I: Principles 1

    Chapter 1: A Brief History 3
        1.1   Introduction 3
    Chapter 2: Economic Concepts of Regulation 15
        2.1   Introduction 15
        2.2   The Fundamental Economic Goal of Regulation 17
        2.3   The Competitive Ideal 18
        2.4   Factors that Preclude a Competitive Outcome 21
        2.5   Profit Maximization Under Monopoly 26
        2.6   The Contestability of Markets 28
        2.7   The Regulator's Pricing Challenge 29
        2.8   Other Complicating Factors 32
        2.9   How Deregulation Can Lead to More Regulation 36
        2.10 Chapter Summary 38
    Chapter 3: The Role of the Revenue Requirement 39
        3.1   Introduction 39
        3.2   Meeting the Regulatory Challenge 40
        3.3   Key Regulatory Principles 41
        3.4   Why Revenue Requirements Underlie <u>All</u> Regulatory Structures 44
        3.5   Revenue Requirement Components 51
        3.6   Other Issues 58
        3.7   Chapter Summary 61
    Chapter 4: Alternative Regulatory Structures 63
        4.1   Introduction 63
        4.2   Common Aspects of Regulatory Structures 64
        4.3   Cost Differences and Operating Environments 66
        4.4   Cost of Service 67
        4.5   Performance-Based Regulation 69
        4.6   Yardstick Competition 73
        4.7   Comparing Different Regulatory Regimes to Set Tariffs 74
        4.8   Chapter Summary 76

Chapter 5: Cost Measurement ... 77
- 5.1 Introduction ... 77
- 5.2 Why Regulators Measure Costs ... 77
- 5.3 Estimating and Regulating Operating Costs ... 84
- 5.4 Estimating and Regulating the Rate Base ... 99
- 5.5 Estimating the Regulated Rate of Return ... 108
- 5.6 Deferred Costs and Regulatory Assets ... 122
- 5.7 Chapter Summary ... 123
- APPENDIX: Depreciation Mechanics ... 124

Chapter 6: Cost Allocation ... 135
- 6.1 Introduction ... 135
- 6.2 Cost Functionalization ... 136
- 6.3 Cost Classification ... 139
- 6.4 Cost Allocation ... 141
- 6.5 Chapter Summary ... 149

Chapter 7: Rate-Setting Principles and Procedures ... 151
- 7.1 Introduction ... 151
- 7.2 Billing Determinants ... 153
- 7.3 Tariff Design ... 161
- 7.4 Alternative Design Structures ... 162
- 7.5 Tariff-Setting Methods ... 168
- 7.6 Pricing and Social Policy ... 180
- 7.7 Electric Restructuring and Default Service ... 182
- 7.8 Chapter Summary ... 184

Chapter 8: Rate and Tariff Adjustment Mechanisms ... 185
- 8.1 Introduction ... 185
- 8.2 Pass-Through Mechanisms ... 185
- 8.3 Inflation Adjustments ... 187
- 8.4 An Alphabet Soup of Adjustment Factors ... 188
- 8.5 Shared-Savings and Off-Ramps ... 195
- 8.6 Chapter Summary ... 196

Chapter 9: Market Power in the Electric and Natural Gas Industries ... 197
- 9.1 Introduction ... 197
- 9.2 Defining Market Power ... 199
- 9.3 Dominant Firms ... 201
- 9.4 Horizontal and Vertical Market Power ... 202
- 9.5 Remedies for Market Power ... 210
- 9.6 The Essential Facilities Doctrine ... 213
- 9.7 Chapter Summary ... 214

Part II: Extensions and Applications **217**
   Chapter 10: Dealing With Uncertainty 219
      10.1 Introduction 219
      10.2 Key Issues 219
      10.3 Making Investment Decisions Under Uncertainty 222
      10.4 Measuring Price Volatility 236
      10.5 Nonmarket Uncertainties 239
      10.6 Chapter Summary 242
   Chapter 11: Environmental Regulation of the Energy Industry 245
      11.1 Introduction 245
      11.2 Environmental Costs and Environmental Externalities 247
      11.3 Regulatory Responses 249
      11.4 Measuring Environmental Costs and Benefits 257
      11.5 Environmental Costs and Energy Prices 260
      11.6 Externality Adders 261
      11.7 Current Regulatory Policies: Renewable Energy and Global Climate Change 263
      11.8 Chapter Summary 268
   Chapter 12: Regulating Electric System Reliability 269
      12.1 Introduction 269
      12.2 Direct Current Circuits 270
      12.3 Alternating Current Circuits 274
      12.4 Defining Reliability 275
      12.5 Reliability and Installed Capacity Markets 278
      12.6 International Capacity Markets 284
      12.7 Chapter Summary 286
   Chapter 13: Regulation and Reform in International Markets 287
      13.1 Introduction 287
      13.2 Transition Mechanisms 288
      13.3 Alternative Privatization Arrangements 289
      13.4 Establishing the Regulatory Framework 291
      13.5 Renegotiation and Change 292
      13.6 International Arbitration 293
      13.7 Chapter Summary 294
   Chapter 14: The Future of Economic Regulation in the Electric and Natural Gas Industries 297
      14.1 Introduction 297
      14.2 The Regulatory Clash of Politics and Economics 298
      14.3 The Future of U.S. Regulation 300
      14.4 Concluding Thoughts 303
   Select Bibliography 305
   Index 315

List of Figures

Figure 2-1: Individual and Industry Equilibrium—Perfect Competition 18
Figure 2-2: Consumer's and Producer's Surplus 20
Figure 2-3: Natural Monopoly 24
Figure 2-4: The Monopolist's Output Decision 27
Figure 2-5: The Regulatory Challenge 30
Figure 2-6: One Regulatory Solution: Average Cost Pricing 30
Figure 2-7: Pricing When Average Costs Are Increasing 32
Figure 2-8: Regulation When AC Is Uncertain 34
Figure 2-9: Effect of Regulatory Policies on a Firm's Cost Structure 35
Figure 4-1: Three Sets of Rules to Determine Regulated Rates 64
Figure 5-1: The Framework for Developing Regulated Services and Prices 78
Figure 5-2: The Five-Step Procedure to Calculate Regulated Prices 79
Figure 5-3: The Three Sets of Books 82
Figure 5-4: Data Envelope Analysis 88
Figure 5-5: OLS and COLS 90
Figure 5-6: Stochastic Frontier Analysis 91
Figure 5-7: Effect of Depreciation Rate on Revenue Requirement 98
Figure A.5-1: Percentage Equipment Surviving Over Time 125
Figure A.5-2: Stub Survivor Curve 126
Figure A.5-3: Derived Stub Survivor Curve 131
Figure A.5-4: Iowa "L3" Survivor Curve and its Derivative Curves 133
Figure 6-1: Cost Functionalization 137
Figure 6-2: Cost Classification 140
Figure 6-3: Cost Allocation 143
Figure 7-1: Determining Prices 152
Figure 7-2: Observed Temperature Distribution 159
Figure 7-3: The Pricing Dilemma 161
Figure 7-4: Two-Part Tariff Pricing 163
Figure 7-5: Block Rate Design 164
Figure 7-6: Block Rate Design Under Increasing Marginal Costs 165
Figure 7-7: Selected International POLR Experience 183
Figure 9-1: Diagram of Market Power in the Electric Industry 205
Figure 9-2: Optimal Supply Curve Under Imperfect Competition 212
Figure 10-1: The Future Price of Electricity 225
Figure 10-2: Value of Option to Invest 227
Figure 10-3: Increased Price Uncertainty 227
Figure 10-4: A Decision Tree and Outcomes 229
Figure 10-5: Extended Decision Tree with Additional Information 230

Figure 10-6: Coal Plant Decision Tree 234
Figure 10-7: Henry Hub Daily Average Closing Natural Gas Prices (2005). 237
Figure 10-8: Comparing Multiple Projects—Probability Distribution of NPV 242
Figure 11-1: Inefficiency in Private Production. 250
Figure 11-2: Effects of an Output Tax 253
Figure 11-3: Determination of the Optimal Emissions Tax 254
Figure 12-1: A Simple Electric System 271
Figure 12-2: Impact of Higher Voltage. 273
Figure 12-3: Load Duration Curve and Generating Resources 279
Figure 12-4: NYISO Locational Capacity Demand Curves 283

List of Tables

Table A.5-1: Surviving Equipment Over Time—Original Group Method 124
Table A.5-2: Summary of Plant Account Activity by Year 128
Table A.5-3: Annual Exposures and Retirements. 129
Table A.5-4: Observed Life Table 130
Table 6-1: Typical Accounts for an Electric Utility. 138
Table 6-2: Sample Natural Gas Distribution System Plant and Expense Accounts .139
Table 6-3: Natural Gas Distribution Company—Estimation of Customer and Energy Allocators (2006 Test Year) 146
Table 6-4: Electric Distribution Company—Estimation of Demand Allocators (2006 Test Year). 148
Table 8-1: X Factors in Values and Methods in Selected Countries 191
Table 9-1: Delivered Price Test 208
Table 10-1: Distribution Planning Costs. 223
Table 10-2: Expected Costs of Alternative Investment Strategies 223
Table 10-3: Decision Matrix. 229
Table 10-4: Critical Event Matrix—Joint Probability Thresholds. 240
Table 11-1: Types of Environmental Policy Instruments. 251
Table 13-1: Increase in Average Maximum Tariffs for Mexican Natural Gas Distributors 291

PREFACE

As the title suggests, this book presents the fundamental "hows" and "whys" of regulation of the energy industry. That may seem odd, given the degree to which energy markets have been deregulated over the past 20 years. Energy markets continue to provide a fascinating—if sometimes disheartening—lure for regulators who have often lurched hurly-burly from one policy "solution" to another, all the while as the "invisible hand" of the underlying markets imposed often high costs on those who ignored basic economic principles. Moreover, in fairness (after all, we are economists), it is not just noneconomists who have made mistakes. A number of economist-inspired regulatory regimes have also failed miserably, in part because the underlying theory failed to conform to market realities.

We have not attempted to write an all-encompassing treatise on the economic and legal underpinnings of energy regulation. Such a book would be unwieldy, if not unreadable. Instead, our aim is far more modest: to provide readers with a strong foundation for further exploration in those areas most useful to them. Finally, although our focus is geared towards the structure of the electric and natural gas industries in the United States, we also present key rate concepts that are used internationally.

We owe a great debt to a number of individuals who encouraged us to write this book, and who have toiled to turn an idea into reality. At Public Utilities Reports, Inc., Phillip Cross encouraged us to take on the task and provided support in all phases of the writing and production. Diane Boiler provided eagle-eyed editing and saved us from more embarrassment than we would otherwise deserve. Jean Cole ably coordinated the production and marketing end. We were also greatly assisted by individuals at Bates White. Guillermo Israilevich helped greatly in the drafting of Chapter 9 and returned comments and suggestions for the other chapters. Our colleagues, Collin Cain, David DeRamus, Nicholas Marinakis, and Spencer Yang, provided many valuable comments and suggestions, clarified concepts, and saved us from errors. InBum Chung designed the book with his usual flair for elegance. Finally, we owe a special debt of thanks to Cindy Monroe, who worked tirelessly, first by reviewing and editing multiple drafts, and then by shepherding our manuscript into a published textbook. Without her, there would be no book. Of course, the errors and omissions that remain are ours, not theirs.

–Jonathan A. Lesser and Leonardo R. Giacchino, July 2007

PART I: PRINCIPLES

Part I focuses on the basic economic principles that underlie rate regulation, the mechanics of that regulation, and the broader regulatory issues that can affect rates. An understanding of these principles can help attorneys better serve their industry clients. Industry personnel can apply these principles to gain new insights into daily operations. Regulators, law students, and graduate students in business and economics can garner a more complete understanding of economic principles (including the practicalities of regulation) in two major industry segments (electricity and natural gas).

Because we can best understand the present only if we understand the past, we begin in Chapter 1 by exploring the antecedents of the current-day environment. We cover the important legislative, industry, and economic developments (and missteps) that began in the late 1800s and which continue to have an impact today (as indeed they will in the future).

In Chapter 2, we explore the fundamental economic principles that underlie energy regulation today. In doing so, we assume readers are familiar with basic concepts of supply and demand. Noneconomists may be surprised that there are really only a few core principles, which are ultimately designed to achieve what economists call "efficient" outcomes. Chapter 2 is the most purely "economic" chapter in the book, focusing on different outcomes when markets are competitive, and when they are not.

Chapter 3 begins our discussion of the economic concepts behind establishing regulated costs. We introduce the concept of revenue requirements, which underlies all forms of regulation—from traditional "cost-of-service" regulation to various types of "incentive" and performance-based regulation. Under all of these forms of regulation, establishing the baseline of revenues a regulated firm requires to operate successfully is crucial. Understanding the components of revenue requirements requires understanding a number of different operational aspects, since regulators must address a firm's investment costs, the risks it faces, and its operating costs. In Chapter 4, we review these different regulatory structures and explore how they work.

Chapter 5 discusses the principles that underlie the establishment of regulated rates. We discuss how cost components are measured and verified: in particular, we explain how the prudence of regulated investments is established, how the rate base is measured (including the role of cost depreciation), and how the regulated rate of return is determined.

In Chapter 6, we examine how costs are allocated between different customer groups. We review a number of methods that are used to allocate fixed and variable costs, as well as so-called "joint" costs. We also discuss the approaches that are used to establish the different customer groups themselves.

In Chapter 7, we consider rate setting principles and procedures. We analyze how to estimate billing determinants and how to design tariffs. We then consider the different methods used to determine tariffs, including the differences between short-run and long-run marginal costs, which often determine the overall structure of regulated rates (called the "tariff structure"). Following the economic concepts presented in Chapter 2, we discuss conflicts between pricing for efficiency and pricing for equity, as well as broader "social policy" price goals. We will discuss how "ready-to-serve" charges are established and the use of multipart price tariffs.

Chapter 8 discusses tariff adjustment mechanisms. We discuss different "pass-through" mechanisms that are designed to allow regulated companies to automatically adjust regulated rates in response to changes in cost components over which they have no control. We also review the different types of inflation adjustments, as well as other factors that adjustment formulae include, such as for productivity, investment, service quality, and exogenous factors. Finally, we review shared-savings and off-ramps.

Chapter 9 focuses on market power and addresses why it is important in these two industries. Firms with excessive market power can increase prices and harm consumers, raising regulators' concerns that deregulating previously regulated activities will not improve consumers' welfare and, indeed, may make consumers worse off. This is of particular concern, because once a market is deregulated, reregulation is impractical—much like stuffing a genie back into the bottle.

In Part II, readers can look forward to discussions of these basic principles extended to contemporary issues, controversies, and future applicability both in the United States and in other countries.

CHAPTER 1
A BRIEF HISTORY

1.1 Introduction

The regulatory structure that exists today, and which continues to evolve, is the result of a long and remarkable process of transformation. Deregulation of the electric industry, in particular, remains an unfinished canvas in the United States. Whether it will be finished, put aside, or rubbished is not clear. As a result, a number of countries, including Australia, New Zealand, and Great Britain, to name a few, have proceeded further down the path of market deregulation of their electric industries than has the United States. (We discuss regulatory approaches used internationally throughout the book.) Other countries, however, maintain traditional regulated structures for both electricity and natural gas, including, in many cases, government-owned monopolies. Thus, while our focus is U.S. regulation, the economic changes that have taken place in the electric and natural gas industries are equally relevant in many other countries.

Even where they have taken place, deregulation and restructuring have not eliminated the need to apply "traditional" regulatory methods to those aspects of the electric and natural gas industries that remain firmly regulated, notably, many transmission and local distribution functions. Moreover, deregulation has created a need for new regulatory methods to ensure that emerging unregulated markets are, in fact, competitive. As a result, regulations designed to combat market power and anticompetitive abuses have taken on new importance.

Historians are apt to argue that a better understanding of electric and natural gas regulation today—and perhaps insights into its direction tomorrow—can be gained by understanding how the two industries developed. Thus, we begin with a brief summary of the history of these two industries in the United States, from their inception, to the market and regulatory upheavals of the 1970s; and we continue with an exploration of developments in the 1980s and 1990s.

Charging Ahead

In 1879, the city of San Francisco built and operated the first electric generating station, which was used to power the city's arc lamps.[1] In that same year, Thomas Edison developed the incandescent light bulb and invented a commercially viable lighting system. A few years later, a generating station in New York City was built to provide power for 400 of Edison's lamps. At the time, there was no regulation of electric companies whatsoever. Instead, different companies competed to supply electricity to consumers, and each company would string its own set of electric lines, resulting in spider webs of distribution lines running along wooden poles.

The turning point for the electric industry came in 1886, when George Westinghouse developed a system that could transmit power using alternating current. Electricity became more readily available and its cost decreased. Although the number of electric firms kept growing for the next 20 years, economies of scale in power production and greater accessibility to electricity led to massive consolidation in the industry, especially through the growth of huge holding companies. Holding companies were able to skirt existing state regulation with impunity, because the states did not have jurisdiction over the <u>interstate</u> transmission of electricity or over the rates at which wholesale companies sold electricity to local retail distributors—and there was no corresponding federal regulation.[2,3]

To correct the competitive abuses, Congress passed the Public Utility Act in 1935. Title I of the act was called the Public Utility Holding Company Act (PUHCA), and it quickly and effectively ended the market abuses that had occurred. It gave the Securities and Exchange Commission (SEC) veto authority over the purchase and sale of holding company assets and imposed a "death sentence clause" that eliminated many holding companies. Moreover, it effectively limited mergers and acquisitions to contiguous areas and required joint electric and natural gas utility combinations to be economically justified.[4]

---

[1] The brief history of the electric and natural gas industries presented here is based on the far more detailed presentation in Charles F. Phillips, *The Regulation of Public Utilities: Theory and Practice*, 3d ed. (Arlington, VA: Public Utilities Reports, 1993), Chapters 13 and 14, and references therein.

[2] The states did have the power to regulate <u>intrastate</u> transactions and local rates. That regulation began with some states regulating railroad rates as early as the 1850s. A key legal case was *Munn v. Illinois*, 94 U.S. 113 (1877), in which the U.S. Supreme Court ruled that states could regulate the prices charged by businesses "affected with the public interest." In that particular case, the business was grain elevators. The first reference to *just and reasonable* rates, which, as we discuss in later chapters, is one of the most fundamental aspects of rate regulation, appeared in the Georgia Constitution, in 1877. For additional discussion, see Leonard S. Goodman, *The Process of Ratemaking*, Volume I (Vienna, VA: Public Utilities Reports, 1998), 13–20.

[3] Samuel Insull was the best known of the holding company barons.

[4] In 2005, PUHCA was repealed as part of the Energy Policy Act of 2005, allowing additional latitude for electric utility mergers.

Title II of the Public Utility Act amended the Federal Water Power Act (which was enacted in 1920) and granted authority to the Federal Power Commission (FPC) to regulate interstate transmission and sales.[5] In essence, wherever the individual states lacked regulatory authority, Congress granted that authority to the FPC.[6] However, in practice, the FPC was not particularly active, despite having authority over almost 30% of all electric production in the country. It was not until the 1960s that the FPC began to review wholesale power rates with any regularity.[7]

For the next three decades, until the 1973 OPEC oil embargo, the electric industry was perhaps distinguished only by its dullness; it was an industry that prided itself on its "widow-and-orphan" investment stability and safety.[8] Regulation of electric utilities was, in many respects, mechanical. The demand for electricity increased steadily, and, as it did, utilities constructed new plants to meet that demand; the costs were passed on to uncomplaining consumers. In fact, for most of that time, the real inflation-adjusted price of electricity continued to fall as economies of scale were realized in building larger and larger generating plants. The goal of greater size culminated with the utilities' embrace of nuclear power, the "fuel of the future." Construction and planning for new nuclear power plants began in earnest in the 1960s and engendered a regulatory legacy that continues four decades later, owing to construction cost overruns and plant cancellations, "stranded" cost estimates, and environmental concerns.

Burning Bright

The U.S. natural gas industry did not emerge until the 1920s. Prior to that, natural gas was either burnt off (flared) as a by-product of petroleum production or used by a few local industries. Instead of natural gas, there was a well-established "manufactured gas" industry that had been supplying light to cities for streetlights since the early 1800s.[9] By the 1850s,

---

[5] The FPC was created in 1920 under the Federal Water Power Act for the purpose of regulating construction and operation of nonfederal hydroelectric projects. In 1977, when the U.S. Department of Energy was created, the FPC became the Federal Energy Regulatory Commission (FERC).

[6] Congress also granted FERC responsibility to approve the rates charged by the five federal power marketing agencies: Alaska Power Administration, Bonneville Power Administration, Southeastern Power Administration, Southwestern Power Administration, and Western Power Administration. These agencies' primary role is to sell electricity generated by federal hydroelectric projects, such as Grand Coulee Dam, Hoover Dam, and so forth.

[7] The FPC also created the "Uniform System of Accounts" that is a critical component for allocating costs, as we discuss in Chapters 5 and 6.

[8] Historically, "widow-and-orphan" investments were so named because of their large dividends and price stability.

[9] Manufactured gas was made from coal and left an environmental legacy in the form of waste sites of coal tar. The U.S. Environmental Protection Agency (EPA) designated many of these sites as so-called "Superfund" sites. One of the most controversial issues in cleaning up these sites has been the allocation of cleanup costs between utility ratepayers and shareholders.

there were almost 300 separate gas companies supplying cities with a combined population of five million people. By the end of the nineteenth century, there were about 1,000 manufactured gas companies in the United States. However, once Edison's incandescent lamp system and Westinghouse's alternating current transmission system became well established, electricity became a viable option in the lighting business. This new competitor forced the manufactured gas industry to evolve, and these companies began to sell gas furnaces, water heaters, and ranges (for cooking).

Because the natural gas industry was so competitive, regulation was not an issue until the industry consolidated, beginning in the 1920s. But, whereas states were able to regulate local natural gas distribution, they could not regulate transmission rates for the few interstate pipelines that existed. That changed in 1938 when Congress passed the Natural Gas Act, which gave the FPC authority to regulate interstate transmission and sales.

The Natural Gas Act regulated only transmission rates, and not wellhead prices. By the end of World War II, as drilling and pipeline transmission technology improved, the natural gas industry began to grow rapidly. By 1954, the U.S. Supreme Court had ruled that the FPC should also regulate natural gas production and gathering.[10] So, having previously regulated only a relatively small number of interstate pipelines, the FPC now had to regulate the prices charged by thousands of independent natural gas producers. In July 1954, the FPC froze wellhead prices. This action started a two-decade long slide into an eventual natural gas supply "crisis," which was exacerbated by the turbulence of energy markets in the 1970s and regulatory zeal to correct it.

The 1970s: Regulation and Economics Diverge

While the decade of the 1960s is remembered for widespread societal upheaval, the decade of the 1970s is remembered for widespread turmoil in energy markets. The first OPEC oil embargo occurred in 1973. The oil-price shocks that followed the embargo directly affected the electric industry, because oil-fired generating plants were still relatively common. But a far more important legacy of that first embargo was that it set in motion a broad swath of federal regulatory efforts in the late 1970s. Those efforts spawned even more regulation in the decades that followed to correct what turned out to be economically misguided efforts.

---

[10] *Phillips Petroleum Co. v. Wisconsin*, 347 U.S. 672 (1954). For additional discussion, see Phillips, *supra* note 1, at 488–90.

Because wellhead natural gas prices were capped, supplies (not surprisingly) began to decrease as production from existing wells declined. Growth of the natural gas industry came to a standstill because there was little economic incentive to undertake new exploratory drilling efforts. Estimated reserves peaked in 1967 and then began to fall steadily, as did total U.S. production. Shortages developed, and service curtailments began, especially for industrial consumers. Even though imports from Canada replaced some of the domestic production losses, prices increased rapidly, since U.S. regulators obviously could not regulate Canadian prices. For the natural gas industry, predictions of complete supply exhaustion were common: the "spigot would run dry," many said, within the next decade. By the mid-1970s, the situation had become critical. To address concerns over looming energy shortages, Congress passed a broad series of bills collectively known as the National Energy Legislation of 1978. The primary goals of this legislation were to promote energy conservation and to increase production and use of domestic fuels. However, a number of the policies enacted by Congress paid little heed to basic economics.

The National Energy Legislation contained a number of key acts affecting both the electric and natural gas industries:[11]

- **The Public Utility Regulatory Policies Act (PURPA)**, whose goal was to encourage energy conservation and mandate that utilities purchase electric power from "qualifying" independent wholesale producers

- **The Powerplant and Industrial Fuel Use Act**, which was designed to encourage utilities and large industrial consumers to use coal instead of natural gas

- **The National Energy Conservation Policy Act**, which was designed to promote energy conservation by mandating that electric and natural gas utilities promote energy efficiency by customers, including programs for financing conservation investments through utility bills

- **The Energy Tax Act**, which provided a smorgasbord of tax incentives for energy conservation, renewable energy, and a "gas-guzzler" tax on low-MPG automobiles

- **The Natural Gas Policy Act (NGPA)**, which unlike some of the other legislation, actually addressed the impact of price controls on exploration and development and set a timetable for deregulating wellhead natural gas prices

---

[11] *Public Utility Regulatory Policies Act*, Pub. L. No. 95-617, 92 Stat. 3117 (1978); *Powerplant and Industrial Fuel Use Act*, Pub. L. No. 95-620, 92 Stat. 3289 (1978); *National Energy Conservation Policy Act*, Pub. L. No. 95-619, 92 Stat. 3206 (1978); *Energy Tax Act*, Pub. L. No. 95-618, 92 Stat. 3174 (1978); *Natural Gas Policy Act*, Pub. L. No., 95-621, 92 Stat. 3350 (1978).

1980s and 1990s: Natural Gas Deregulation

Not surprisingly, at least for economists, natural gas price decontrols worked wonders, and the dire predictions of the "spigot running dry" were never realized. In fact, the natural gas "glut" of the early 1990s had its genesis in the 1980s, when the Federal Energy Regulatory Commission (FERC) implemented a series of measures that reshaped the natural gas industry. Beginning in the late 1980s, new regulations severed the connections between producers in the field, the interstate pipelines that transported natural gas, and the local distribution companies that delivered natural gas to retail consumers. By the 1990s, a vibrant wholesale natural gas market was fully established.

Deregulation of the natural gas market in the United States took many years to accomplish. Different industry segments were dealt with separately and at different times. The end result is a marketplace with unbundled companies in healthy competition. Whereas market reforms began with the NGPA, it took passage of the Natural Gas Wellhead Decontrol Act of 1989 to abolish all remaining federal price controls on natural gas. Thus, 15 years after the NGPA was passed, wellhead prices were fully deregulated as of January 1, 1993.

In addition to Congressional action, FERC implemented a number of landmark orders addressing interstate pipeline deregulation. The result was (and still is) one of the most competitive natural gas markets in the world. The most important of these orders included:

- **Order No. 380 (1984)**, which eliminated local distribution companies' minimum bill requirements and made it feasible for many local distribution companies (LDCs) to switch natural gas suppliers
- **Order No. 436 (1985)**, which implemented voluntary *open access* on U.S. pipeline companies
- **Order No. 500 (1987)**, which dealt with economic problems arising from long-term take-or-pay contracts between producers and local distributors[12]
- **Order No. 636 (1992)**, which *unbundled* transportation from marketing activities and made pipeline-affiliated companies sell their natural gas before entering into the transmission system[13]

---

[12] *Associated Gas Distributors v. FERC*, 824 F.2d 981 (D.C. Cir. 1987). Order 500 was subsequently challenged and modified a number of times, with the Commission issuing modified orders 500-A through 500-K. See Phillips, *supra* note 1, at 712–13, for a more detailed discussion and case citations.

[13] Some pipeline companies were giving their marketing affiliates preference (contractual terms and conditions) in the transportation of their own natural gas as a result of the implementation of Order No. 436.

- **Order No. 637 (1999)**, which was designed to further improve the efficiency of the market, while continuing to protect against pipelines' exercising market power[14]

In addition to these FERC orders, Order No. 888, issued in 1996, also affected the natural gas industry, albeit indirectly. Order No. 888 was designed to deregulate electric transmission by requiring "open access" to high-voltage transmission lines, much in the same way that the Commission had required open access to natural gas pipelines. In doing so, FERC created additional economic incentives to develop more independently owned gas-fired generation capacity.

Power Struggle

Although it was affected by the OPEC oil embargoes, the electric industry was arguably more impacted by the tremendous cost overruns experienced by utilities building nuclear power plants. Talk of deregulation of the electric industry was more than a decade away. Instead, the National Energy Legislation set in motion a greater role for state utility regulators, many of whom became energy and environmental policy advocates, rather than simply guarantors of "just and reasonable" rates.

Under PURPA, individual states were to encourage new generating resources from so-called "qualifying facilities" (QFs)—essentially any generator under 80 megawatts (MW) of capacity that used something other than fossil fuels, or a cogenerator (typically, industrial facilities that used waste heat to generate electricity)—by requiring electric utilities to purchase all of the generation produced by those QFs at what were called "avoided costs." Avoided costs were not based on market prices, since there were no wholesale electric markets, but were set by state utility regulators. Those prices were, in essence, "but-for" forecasts of prices, i.e., predictions of what utilities themselves would have spent to develop new generating resources. By encouraging independent power generation, utilities "avoided" their own generation costs. Hence, under PURPA, it made sense to compensate independent generators at the same level.

There were several problems with this approach. First, forecasting future "avoided" power costs, much like forecasting the weather, was fraught with uncertainty and error. Regulators forecast avoided costs and required utilities to enter into contracts at those costs, only to discover that the contractual prices had little relation to market realities. Second, regulators

---

[14] Under Order No. 637, the Commission waived price ceilings for short-term released capacity for a two-year period and permitted pipelines to file for peak/off-peak and term-differentiated rate structures.

established a *cost-effectiveness* yardstick, rather than a *cost-benefit* one.[15] By failing to provide any incentives to independent power producers to innovate and provide electricity at a lower cost, PURPA forced ratepayers to enter into long-term contracts under which, years later, costs rose higher than actual market prices.

The 1990s to the Present: Electric Deregulation Comes of Age

In the early 1990s, Congress passed new legislation that encouraged still more independent development of generation. Under the Energy Policy Act of 1992 (EPAct), Congress created a new type of wholesale supplier, called an "Exempt Wholesale Generator" (EWG). Moreover, Congress set in motion mechanisms to allow those generators to sell the power they produced to regulated utilities. These new incentives for independent supply development were put into place when the United States was in the midst of an economic recession. The demand for electricity stagnated because of reduced economic activity and higher costs that were passed on to retail customers as a consequence of nuclear plant cost overruns. As a result, the amount of surplus generating capacity grew.

Large industrial customers, many of whom were reeling from price increases, saw a way out: if they could only contract directly with wholesale generators, they could bypass their local electric utilities and, essentially, avoid paying the share of those cost overruns they had been allocated. In 1994, electric industry restructuring was born; California introduced sweeping legislation to transform its electric industry. Those transformations continue to this day, although the path the industry has taken is far different than what was likely envisioned at the time.

Despite deregulation and restructuring, both the electric and natural gas industries continue to be affected by federal and state regulators. Domestic and international demand for natural gas has soared. As a result, market prices have been increasing significantly, as has price volatility. In addition to creating hardships for natural gas customers, the changes in natural gas markets have created problems for the electric industry. In the 1990s, the electric industry turned almost exclusively to natural gas as the fuel of choice for new generating capacity. This was a reaction, in part, to the supply "glut," but there were additional reasons that natural gas became a more attractive option. The development of other types of baseload (i.e., "round-the-clock") generating resources like coal and nuclear was stalled, the

---

[15] Many state utility regulators also required utilities to develop energy efficiency programs that included all conservation measures until the <u>average</u> cost of such programs equaled the forecast (avoided) costs. Not only did this violate basic economic principles (reviewed in the next chapter), but, in the extreme, provided no savings to ratepayers.

victim of increasingly stringent environmental and siting regulations and general "not-in-my-backyard" opposition to development. Moreover, nuclear power was stymied by fears of catastrophic plant accidents and a lack of permanent waste storage facilities.

Retail prices driven higher by the increasing price of natural gas further complicated the restructuring of the electric industry. Utilities, legislators, and regulators in many states had entered into agreements that would compensate utilities for the "stranded" costs of their generating plant investments in exchange for multiyear retail price caps to shield ratepayers from price increases. Not only did this prevent ratepayers from experiencing market prices and the consumption signals that prices send, but it also exacerbated the effects arising from the "days of reckoning," when those price freezes would expire. Coupled with price increases and greater volatility in natural gas markets, many states confronted massive retail price increases, which created a political backlash against electric industry restructuring. As a result, some politicians began calling for reregulation of the electric industry, although it is far from clear how the deregulation "genie" can ever be stuffed successfully back into its bottle. As a result, regulators, politicians, utilities, and customers have all confronted wrenching market changes and coped with the inevitable hardships.

Where this will all eventually lead in terms of an ultimate electric industry structure in the United States is uncertain. Some states have moved to reregulate their electric industries.[16] Of course, some of the difficulties confronting policymakers in the electric industry have been self-inflicted, for the simple reason that ignoring basic economic principles is a fool's errand. For example, a price freeze may "protect" consumers in the short term but impose greater long-term costs caused by market distortions. Similarly, constantly changing regulations creates tremendous financial uncertainty, which makes firms more reluctant to invest and banks less inclined to provide financing.

Other difficulties were caused by bad timing. Some of the price freezes, for example, expired on the heels of a "perfect storm" of events, including extensive damage to the natural gas collection and gathering infrastructure along the U.S. Gulf Coast caused by Hurricanes Katrina and Rita in 2005, which led to a subsequent spike in natural gas prices.

In still other cases, the difficulties confronting new market designs have been formidable. Establishing market incentives for the development and construction of new generating and transmission system capacity, so as to ensure "reliable" electric supplies, has in some

---

[16] For example, in April 2007, the governor of Montana signed legislation to reincarnate Montana Power Corporation (known otherwise as Northwestern Corporation at the time). As a result of the state's 1997 divestiture law, the then CEO of Montana Power decided to convert the utility into an Internet-based telecommunications firm. This was a strategic and financial disaster. Northwestern purchased the electric and natural gas distribution assets in 2002, but declared bankruptcy one year later.

cases pitted "elegant" economic theories against the sometimes "ugly" specter of political realities and classic "free-rider" behavior.[17] And creating markets for many of the "ancillary" services that ensure electric system reliability remains a challenge.

New Challenges for Natural Gas

After wellhead natural gas prices were fully deregulated, production and supplies exploded. New technologies enabled offshore natural gas drilling in deeper water, and large fields were discovered along the U.S. Gulf Coast. Drilling technology was leading to new discoveries in the Rocky Mountains; and Canadian production, especially in the West, was ramping up. New interstate pipelines were constructed to ship this natural gas to expanding markets.

Low natural gas prices, development of an independent wholesale power market, technological improvements, and growing environmental concerns about coal-fired generation, led to new, substantial investments in gas-fired generating capacity to meet growing electric demand. Natural gas became the "fuel of choice," not only for electric generation, but also for direct consumption. The shortages and dire predictions of the 1970s had given way to forecasts of plenty by the end of the 1990s.

Alas, times have changed. Today, the natural gas industry again faces challenges. However, despite significant price increases, and unlike electricity, there is no talk of regulating natural gas prices. Beginning in 2002, natural gas prices quickly increased in response to greater demand and rapid increases in oil prices. Overreliance on "the fuel of choice" for electric generation has exacerbated local supply shortages brought about not by a lack of natural gas itself, but by an insufficient pipeline infrastructure. And environmental challenges to continued offshore drilling, as well as to drilling on federal lands, have slowed the development of new conventional supplies.

At the same time, opportunities for new, "unconventional" natural gas supplies have increased, especially as the result of higher market prices. Liquefied natural gas (LNG), which first contributed to domestic supplies in the early 1970s, has the potential to be a significant supply source if environmental and safety fears over development of coastal unloading facilities can be overcome. Coal-bed methane (CBM) may also become a significant resource.[18] Thus, while there are market challenges for natural gas, in contrast to the electric industry, the natural gas market itself is well established. Regulatory challenges will likely

---

[17] We discuss capacity market design in more detail in Chapter 12.

[18] An exhaustive discussion of natural gas supplies can be found in reports produced by the Potential Gas Agency, Mineral Resources Institute, Colorado School of Mines Foundation.

be focused on development and siting of new infrastructure and, potentially, ensuring that vertical market power concerns are addressed so as to avoid anticompetitive impacts in downstream electric markets.[19]

As the electric and natural gas industries go forward, regulation will continue to play an important role. Not only will rate regulation remain important, especially for transmission and distribution functions that will continue to possess characteristics that do not lend themselves to true competition, but regulatory policy will almost certainly continue to evolve. So, whereas the structure of regulation in the future will, no doubt, differ from that of the past, rate setting in one or more forms will continue for the foreseeable future.

---

[19] Because of the role of natural gas as a fuel for electric generation, especially for peaking units, natural gas-fired generation is increasingly "on the margin" and sets wholesale electric prices. Thus, anticompetitive impacts in the natural gas industry can affect downstream electric markets. We address these and other market power issues in Chapter 9.

CHAPTER 2
ECONOMIC CONCEPTS OF REGULATION

2.1 Introduction

In the broadest sense, almost all businesses and markets are "regulated." Whether it is the hairdresser who must be licensed, the drugs manufacturer whose medicines must be tested for safety, or the fisherman who can only catch fish on specific days of the year, few markets are devoid of any regulation whatsoever. The purposes of such regulations vary. For example, to safeguard the public's health, there are countless regulations governing the *practices* of fast-food restaurants with respect to food storage and preparation. But, when it comes to prices, McDonald's is free to set whatever price it wants for a Big Mac.

In the natural gas and electric industries, things are quite different; regulations are mostly concerned with the prices customers pay for services. The current regulatory framework in the United States has a legal rationale based on the idea that certain industries are "affected with the public interest."[1] Policymakers determined early on that the operation of natural gas and electricity markets could not be left to the vagaries of the free marketplace; these industries were "too important" to be allowed to operate unfettered. In regulating industries affected with the public interest, the courts had to consider constitutional limitations, specifically, the "Due Process" clause of the Fourteenth Amendment of the U.S. Constitution, which limits the degree to which government can meddle in the affairs of private firms. To get around this limitation, industries so deemed were (and still are) defined as *public utilities:* private, for-profit firms whose operations were strictly controlled so as not to jeopardize the public interest.

The government (either individual states or the federal government, depending on the industry) regulated key elements of those industries, including who could enter (and exit) the market, the prices participants would be allowed to charge, the extent and quality of the services they could provide, and the "obligation to serve" all customers. The list of industries that were "affected" grew over time to include not only grain elevators and railways (the latter the subject of *Munn v. Illinois*), but also stockyards, water suppliers, electric and

---

[1] The U.S. Supreme Court first used the term "affected with the public interest" in *Munn v. Illinois,* 94 U.S. 113 (1877). For an extended discussion of the legal rationale for regulation and how broadly "affected with the public interest" was interpreted, see Alfred Kahn, *The Economics of Regulation*, vol. I (New York: Wiley, 1970), 3–11. *See also,* Charles F. Phillips, *The Regulation of Public Utilities* (Arlington, VA: Public Utilities Reports, Inc., 1993), Chapter 3.

natural gas companies, telephones, banks, airlines, and even dairies supplying milk, butter, and cheese. Today, the number of industries classified as public utilities is far smaller. The electric, and to a lesser extent, natural gas industries, are now the most pervasive public utilities.

In exchange for this control, public utilities were provided with certain guarantees, such as reasonable opportunities to recover their costs and earn a fair rate of return on their investment. This *quid pro quo* formed the basis of an unwritten "regulatory compact" between firms and government regulators that, ostensibly, exists today and forms the basis for regulating a number of components of the electric and natural gas industries.

So what do we mean by "regulation"? When we speak of regulation, we generally refer to the *direct* regulation of prices, which really lies at the heart of public utility regulation today.[2] Of course, prices are also *indirectly* affected by the regulation of underlying supply and demand conditions. We will discuss some of these types of regulation as they relate to the electric and natural gas industries in later chapters. In the electric industry, regulation of service quality and reliability has taken on greater importance over time as a result of a number of widespread blackouts and an inability or unwillingness to build sufficient new generating or transmission capacity.

As economists, we would like to believe that regulation hinges solely on the underlying market structures of the electric and natural gas industries, but our egos must give way to reality. Regulation occurs for many reasons: some of those are based on fundamental economic principles, and others stem from what can be charitably termed "political expediency." In this chapter, we will limit ourselves to the economic concepts that underlie regulation of the prices consumers pay for natural gas and electricity. Our goal is to explain the economic basis for regulating the electric and natural gas industries. We will describe the economic conditions that must exist for "successful" deregulation, which is an especially contentious issue for an electric industry that is fraught with so many problems, both in the United States and elsewhere.

---

[2] Kahn, *supra* note 1, vol. I, at 21.

2.2 The Fundamental Economic Goal of Regulation

The underlying economic concepts for regulation of the electric and natural gas industries are easily lost amid a myriad of state and federal regulatory proceedings, legislative rules, and court decisions. Yet, despite the complexities of actual regulation in these industries, the underlying economic concepts are relatively straightforward. *It is their application in practice that can be difficult.* In this chapter, we review these economic concepts and explain some of those practical difficulties.

The fundamental economic goal of regulation is straightforward: *to mimic a competitive market outcome, even when the underlying market is not competitive.* In other words, purely economic regulation strives to achieve outcomes that capture the benefits of competitive markets when those markets are themselves not competitive.

In practice, things are not so simple, for a number of reasons. First, regulatory goals can often include "noneconomic" factors, such as achieving outcomes that are "fair" and "just." After all, "the public interest" can include a number of attributes. Congress passed the Rural Electrification Act of 1936, for example, with the goal of providing universal access to electricity. Up to that point, most urban consumers had electricity, and most rural consumers did not. The costs of stringing electric lines hither and yon was too expensive. So, Congress established a means by which the federal government would pay to expand electric service. Today, electricity is truly a universal service, but rural customers are still subsidized by urban customers, since to do otherwise could jeopardize the provision of universal service.

Second, and this is a more recent phenomenon, regulators may want to promote specific policies they believe to be in customers' interests. A number of state utility regulators, for example, require local electric utilities—whether they are fully integrated (generation-transmission-distribution) or simply restructured local distribution companies—to obtain a minimum percentage of generation from renewable sources such as wind, hydro, and biomass. Or, regulators may have political goals that conflict with fundamental economic goals, such as shutting down generating plants or rerouting the location of transmission lines or natural gas pipelines to reduce the impacts on their constituents' property values.

Moreover, it is often the case that regulatory priorities tend to differ at the state and federal levels, and between states. Federal regulators tend to take a broader view of specific actions, such as a merger between firms, while state regulators may be more concerned with ensuring their state receives its "fair share" of the benefits.

2.3 The Competitive Ideal

Although this book is not intended to be an economics text, understanding the regulatory fundamentals of the electric and natural gas industries and the components that determine regulated prices requires an understanding of several economic concepts. To explain those concepts, economists are notorious for relying on charts, and we are no different.[3]

Most introductory economics courses begin with a stylized discussion of perfect competition, in which the actions of many buyers and sellers coincide and lead to the typical "supply equals demand" outcome that characterizes a purely competitive market. This is shown in Figure 2-1.

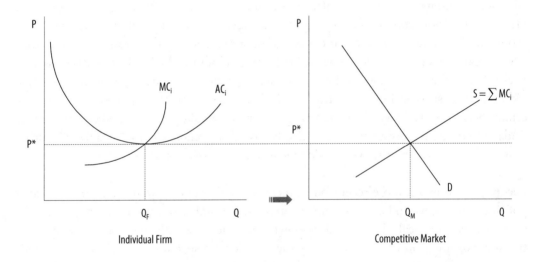

Figure 2-1: Individual and Industry Equilibrium—Perfect Competition

The left-hand side of Figure 2-1 shows the costs and market equilibrium production decision for a typical firm in an industry. This firm is characterized by its average cost (AC_I) and marginal cost (MC_I) curves. Average cost equals the firm's total costs (i.e., fixed plus variable), TC, divided by the total quantity of output produced, Q_i, that is, $AC_i = TC_i \div Q_i$.

A firm's *marginal cost*, however, is often more informative for economic decisions than its average cost. Marginal cost reflects the change in total cost associated with each incremental change in the firm's output. That is, $MC_i = \Delta TC_i \div \Delta Q_i$, where "$\Delta$" (the Greek letter delta)

---

[3] For those needing to brush up on basic economic principles, there are many useful references. One we like is N. Gregory Mankiw, *Principles of Economics*, 4th ed. (Mason, OH: South-Western College Publishing, 2006).

stands for "change."[4] Once a firm is operating, producing one more unit may be less expensive than the average cost of all the output produced, because capital and administrative expenses do not change with the additional unit produced. For an electric generator, producing an extra megawatt-hour (MWh) may just mean burning a bit more fuel. However, if the generator is running full tilt, the marginal cost may be astronomical (or just infinite), because additional output would require building an entirely new generating plant. This is also shown in Figure 2-1, in which marginal costs are below average costs at low production levels and eventually spike as the firm approaches full capacity.

An individual firm's supply curve is just its marginal cost curve. The reason is that the firm will be willing to supply more output up until the point where the market price just equals the marginal cost of production. In other words, if the market price is $10, the firm will be willing to sell (supply) output as long as it costs no more than $10 to produce each additional unit of output. Because we assume that all of the individual firms in this stylized market are the same size and have identical cost structures, each firm will produce the same quantity of output.

The right-hand side of Figure 2-1 illustrates the aggregate result of all of the firms' individual production decisions. There is an overall market demand curve, D, which equals the sum of all individual consumers' demand curves. Note that there is no demand curve on the left-hand side of Figure 2-1. The reason is that individual firms are assumed to be price takers; their individual production decisions are assumed to have no impact on the market price. That is an important assumption, because the main thrust of economic regulation is to address cases where an individual firm's production decisions <u>can</u> affect market price, and in the limiting case, the individual firm is a monopolist—the sole provider of the good or service in question in the relevant market. (As we shall see, one way to deal with a monopolist is to determine, like the U.S. Supreme Court did, that certain industries are "affected with the public interest," and then regulate the monopolist's behavior.)

The market supply curve, S, equals the sum of all of the individual firms' marginal cost curves, i.e., $S = \sum MC_i$. The intersection of the supply and demand curves determines the market equilibrium price, P*, and total market demand, Q_M. Each individual firm is a price taker, gauging its individual production decisions by what it sees as the market price. No firm can influence the market price by its production decisions, such as withholding supplies or "flooding" the market. It turns out, in the economists' perfectly competitive world, that the level of output produced by each individual firm will correspond to the point

---

[4] A note on terminology: in many cases, the term "incremental cost" is used interchangeably for "marginal cost." Although non-economists may be tempted to gloss over the definition, marginal cost is a critical concept in the regulated rate-setting process.

where each firm's average costs are minimum. Moreover, the minimum of the firm's average cost curve coincides with its marginal cost curve.[5] Here is why: Suppose demand increases (shifting the demand curve up and to the right). Increased demand leads to a higher market price, as anyone who buys gasoline in the summer realizes. Higher prices, however, mean that the firms already in the industry make additional profits. Those additional profits attract other firms. As those firms enter the market hoping to capitalize on higher prices, supplies increase and the market price falls; and the price will keep falling until there are no "excess" profits to be made.[6]

The equilibrium point where supply equals demand in Figure 2-1 represents the economist's competitive ideal, because the overall "value" of the market is a maximum at this point. This is the only point where consumers' willingness to pay (the demand curve) and producers' willingness to sell (the supply curve) exactly equal the market price, as shown in Figure 2-2.

Figure 2-2: Consumer's and Producer's Surplus

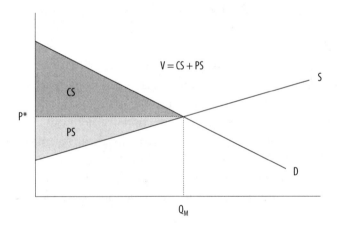

In Figure 2-2, we reproduce the competitive market outcome of Figure 2-1. The top, shaded triangle labeled "CS" represents what economists call *consumer's surplus*. This is the aggregate difference between what consumers would be willing to pay for the good or service in question and the price, P*, which they actually pay. The bottom, shaded triangle labeled

---

[5] By definition, a firm's marginal cost will always pass through the minimum of its average cost curve. This is simply a mathematical result of how average cost and marginal cost are defined. In Chapter 7, we discuss the crucial distinction between short-run and long-run marginal costs, since that distinction affects how rates may be set.

[6] "Real" markets, of course, never conform to economists' imaginary ideals, but some markets, such as many commodities markets, come close.

"PS" represents what economists call *producer's surplus*.[7] Producer's surplus is the difference between the market price and the price at which producers are willing to sell. The value of a market, V, is defined as the sum of consumer's and producer's surplus, that is, V = CS + PS. From the standpoint of pure economic efficiency, total value does not depend on who gets what. For example, it turns out that a monopolist who can perfectly price discriminate (i.e., charge different customers different prices based on their willingness to pay) will sell the same quantity, Q_M, that is sold in the perfectly competitive market shown in Figure 2-1. However, the monopolist will capture all of the consumer's surplus for himself. That is, under perfect price discrimination, CS = 0.

At the competitive equilibrium, the sum of producer's and consumer's surplus will be a maximum. For that reason, economists refer to the pure competitive market outcome as an *efficient market,* because the competitive market outcome is the point where the market's value is highest. Pure economic regulation seeks to mimic an efficient market outcome in situations where, in the absence of regulatory intervention, it would not otherwise occur.

2.4 Factors that Preclude a Competitive Outcome

If natural gas and electric markets were perfectly competitive, there would be no need to regulate the prices charged to consumers. There would be no need for rate cases or complex rate designs. (There would also be no need for this book.) Alas, electric and natural gas markets, at least some components of them, are not competitive and in fact have characteristics that preclude purely competitive outcomes in certain segments. As such, the prices charged in those market segments must be regulated if society is to improve the value of those segments. Two specific characteristics preclude robust competitive markets, especially in transmission and distribution: *natural monopoly* and high *barriers to entry.*

The simplest deviation from the competitive outcome, and the one that has traditionally served as the basis for regulation, is the presence of natural monopoly.[8] A natural monopoly is a firm characterized by average costs that decrease as the amount the firm produces in-

---

[7] More precisely, producer's surplus is the lump-sum amount that could be taken from an individual firm without affecting its production decision.

[8] As Kahn explains, historically, natural monopoly was used as a reason for regulation, so as to prevent "ruinous competition." Under this theory, competing firms would drive prices down to the level of their short-run marginal costs, and be unable to collect their fixed costs. As a result, they would not be able to survive. Alternatively, with only a few firms, sellers would have an incentive to refrain from "vigorous price rivalry," leading to higher prices for customers. In either case, there would be a case for regulating the industry. As Kahn further notes, these rationalizations for restricting competition have been vigorously disputed. Kahn, *supra* note 1, vol. I, at 1–3. For our purposes, we will avoid this debate, as it focused more on other industries (telephone, airlines, trucking, etc.) than electricity and natural gas.

creases. What this means is that it is less costly for one firm to produce all of the product demanded than for two or more firms combined to produce the same amount. There are two general reasons for this. First, production can be characterized by *economies of scale*. Second, production can also be characterized by *economies of scope*.

Economies of scale mean that, the more units of a good produced, the lower the per-unit production cost. A typical case occurs where the firm has high fixed costs, such as the cost to build an electric generating plant or an interstate natural gas pipeline. For the firm to prosper, it must be able to recover all of that construction cost over time. And, like a home mortgage payment, the cost is independent of the fraction of the year the house is lived in. As an example, suppose a firm spends $365 million to build a new pipeline with a maximum transmission capacity of one million cubic meters (meters^3) per day and that it must repay $36.5 million per year of that construction cost. Suppose it costs one dollar per meter^3 to operate the compressors that move the natural gas through the pipeline.

If the firm transports 100 meters^3 per day, the average annual cost per meter^3 of transport, AC, will equal:

$$AC = \$36.5 \text{ million} \div (100 \text{ meters}^3 \times 365 \text{ days}) + \$1 \div \text{meter}^3 = \$1,001 \div \text{meter}^3.$$

If the firm transports 1,000 meters^3 per day, AC will fall to $101 per meter^3, and so forth. Thus, the firm's average cost per meter^3 falls as the amount of natural gas transported increases, up to the point where the pipeline reaches its maximum capacity.

Another scale economy for a natural gas pipeline is that the average cost of building natural gas pipeline capacity also decreases as the size of the pipeline increases. This is a consequence of high school geometry: the volume of the pipeline increases geometrically as the diameter increases linearly.[9] This effect is another scale economy. Historically, increasing the size of electric generating plants also tended to reduce average costs per MWh of output, though this changed when plants, especially nuclear plants, became so large that the physical complexity of construction outweighed economies of scale.

---

[9] The construction cost of the pipeline is related to its circumference. Imagine you could slice the pipeline lengthwise and lay it out as a large cylinder. The size of the cylinder equals the length times circumference. The total amount of material needed equals length times circumference times thickness. However, as the diameter (and hence circumference) increases, the volume of the pipeline increases much faster. If we double the diameter of the pipeline, the circumference doubles, and so does the amount of material needed to construct it. But, the volume of the cylinder (cross-section) increases with the square of the diameter. Thus, doubling the diameter will increase the cross-section by four times. If the construction cost doubles, therefore, the average cost of transporting natural gas will be halved when the pipeline operates at capacity.

Economies of scope exist when it is cheaper for one firm to produce two or more goods than for firms to produce each good separately. For example, a combined electric and natural gas distribution utility can use one meter reader to determine a customer's consumption of both electricity and natural gas, whereas separate electric and natural gas distribution companies would require one meter reader each. Essentially, the meter reader is a common input to production for the distribution companies. With a combined distribution company, that common input is used to produce two different goods jointly, in this case bills for electric and natural gas customers. In general, economies of scope result when common equipment and facilities are used to produce different products.

Joint production can be an important regulatory issue, especially when a parent company has both regulated and unregulated subsidiaries. In those cases, regulators must determine what fraction of a firm's common costs should be allocated to the regulated side. If you allocate too many costs to the regulated side, the firm's regulated customers will pay too much, and other firms competing in the unregulated market will be placed at a competitive disadvantage because the firm's regulated customers are effectively subsidizing its unregulated business. (This is usually referred to as a *cross-subsidy,* which, as we will see in Chapter 9, has important consequences when addressing horizontal and vertical market power in markets.) If you assign too few costs to the regulated side, the firm's unregulated operations will be placed at a competitive disadvantage.

It is also possible for a firm not to be a natural monopoly, yet still be able to produce all of the output in a market at a lower cost than two or more firms combined. Or, a particular market may only support a few firms, again as a result of economies of scale and scope. Such outcomes raise competitive issues and the need for economic regulation for the simple reason that a firm having a natural monopoly will be able to set the market price itself. Thus, instead of being a competitive *price taker,* the firm can adjust its own production decisions to set the market price.

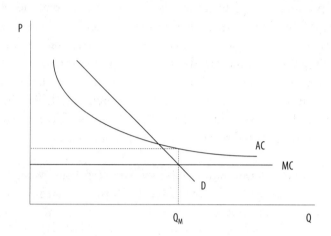

Figure 2-3: Natural Monopoly

To evaluate the effects of natural monopoly, consider Figure 2-3. In this figure, the market demand for the good or service is characterized by demand curve D. Suppose the firm has high fixed costs and a constant marginal cost. As the firm's output increases, its average costs decrease, because the fixed costs are spread over more units of output. What distinguishes a natural monopoly is that the individual firm exhibits economies of scale through the relevant range of market demand. So, although the firm's average costs will eventually increase, the level of market demand necessary for that to occur will be far greater than the observed market demand.

Thus, at the idealized competitive market price equal to marginal cost, MC, total demand would equal Q_M. At that level of demand, AC is still decreasing as a result of economies of scale and/or scope.

Historically, one of the reasons for regulating natural gas and electric utilities was their natural monopoly characteristics. Having competing local utilities, each stringing wires according to its own plan, would fail to exploit economies of scale. Moreover, because natural gas and electric utilities provided multiple products (production, transmission, and local distribution to ultimate customers), there were also significant economies of scope. There were other complexities that limited competition. For one, to serve natural gas and electric customers effectively, you have to have enough capacity to meet peak demands. So, a natural gas company would have to size its pipeline capacity to meet customer demands on the coldest day of the year, meaning that for the majority of the time some of that capacity would be unused. Similarly, an electric utility would need to build some generating plants just to meet electric demand on the hottest day of the year. Such plants would sit idle most hours.

Firms in most industries try to minimize excess capacity. Idle factories and employees are not sources of profits. Moreover, unlike electricity, most other goods can be inventoried cost-effectively.[10] Again, however, a competitive firm will want to keep inventory just high enough to meet anticipated demand over time. But, competing in a business *requiring* you to maintain a lot of excess capacity that remains unused most of the time is a tough competitive problem. And, despite all of the restructuring in the electric and natural gas industries, this is still a problem, as we shall see in Chapter 9.

A second historic reason for regulation has been the presence of *barriers to entry*, or just *market barriers*. Simply put, barriers to entry (and exit) make it easier for incumbent firms to charge prices above the competitive ideal.[11] In essence, incumbents can "get away with" high prices because the threat of entry is low. As a result, industries with high barriers to entry are more often subject to price regulation.

How are barriers to entry defined? Even though there is no single definition of market barriers, the "classic" operational definition used in economics is this: *any costs that must be borne by firms seeking to enter (or exit) an industry that are not borne by incumbent firms*.[12] The types of costs that fall under this definition will depend on the specific industry. For example, some economists consider economies of scale and large initial capital expenditures to be barriers to entry.[13] This is particularly relevant for wholesale electricity markets, because generation and transmission investments are highly capital-intensive and immobile. As a consequence, entry into wholesale electricity markets often requires a significant sunk investment, and the losses associated with unsuccessful market entry can be quite large.

More recently, economists have defined barriers to entry to include costs imposed on new entrants as a result of strategic behavior by incumbent firms. These barriers can be especially important if such strategic behavior by incumbents will significantly increase either the

---

[10] Electricity can be stored to a limited extent, such as batteries or even as water behind a hydroelectric dam. However, as yet, no cheap mass storage device for electricity exists.

[11] Regulators have also used presumed barriers to entry to pursue policies that may not be consistent with economic efficiency. For example, many state regulators subsidize demand-side management and renewable energy investments on the theory that, because they are more expensive than traditional electric generating resources, they face significant market barriers. This is nonsense, and stems from an erroneous understanding of what market barriers are, and are not. The fact that a Mercedes costs more to buy than a Ford does not mean that Mercedes faces barriers to entry.

[12] George Stigler, *The Organization of Industry* (Chicago: University of Chicago Press, 1968).

[13] Joe S. Bain, *Barriers to New Competition* (Cambridge, MA: Harvard University Press, 1956).

magnitude of the losses suffered by the new entrant or the probability that the new entrant will be ultimately unsuccessful.[14] As we discuss in Chapter 9, such strategic considerations may arise in considering whether incumbent firms have significant market power in a given market.

> **Regulation vs. Nationalization**
>
> One question that arises is whether an industry that is "affected with the public interest" should not only be regulated, but in fact also should be run by the government. For example, there has been an ongoing debate as to whether investor-owned electric utilities are preferable to municipally owned electric cooperatives, with the latter touting their lack of profit motive as "better" for consumers. It is not uncommon for cities and towns to seek to revoke a private utility's operating franchise so as to take over operations. Internationally, there has been far greater controversy; whole industries have been nationalized in the name of economic security and well-being.
>
> From an economic standpoint, is it better to regulate a private sector monopolist or ensure that all such firms are directly owned and operated by the government? In theory, a well-run government organization should do just as well as a private firm. In practice, however, this is as likely an outcome as having a "benevolent" dictator. The history of government-run firms is littered with inefficiency. While there may be no direct profit motive for such government-run entities, there are often strong incentives for those entities to engage in other behavior that reduces economic well-being, including bloated payrolls that raise overall supply costs, nepotism, and outright corruption. These inefficiencies almost always far exceed the real or perceived inefficiencies of regulated, privately held firms. The solution to inefficient regulation is not to have direct government control, but rather to improve regulation so that economic efficiency is increased.

2.5   Profit Maximization Under Monopoly

To investigate the goals and methods of economic regulation, when a fully competitive market cannot be supported, it is useful to review how an unfettered monopolist will behave and what the economic impacts of that behavior will be. This will also help illustrate the challenges faced by regulators who seek to mimic the competitive market outcomes.

Consider Figure 2-4, which shows the production decision process of a monopolist. The key factor to remember is that a monopolist is a *price setter*, rather than a price taker like the competitive firms in the left-hand side of Figure 2-1. Unlike a competitive firm, which sees the market price as an exogenous factor, the monopolist has to account for the fact that its output decision will affect the market price. That is, to sell another unit, the monopolist must lower its price on all units sold. As a result, the monopolist will set the quantity of

---

[14]   Dennis W. Carlton and Jeffrey M. Perloff, *Modern Industrial Organization*, 2d. ed. (New York: Harper Collins, 1994), 113.

output and the price where marginal revenue, MR, (i.e., the incremental revenue received from selling an additional unit, accounting for the decrease in price of all units sold) it receives from each additional unit it sells just equals the marginal cost of producing that unit.[15] This is shown in Figure 2-4. MR lies below the industry demand curve, D, because each additional unit the monopolist produces and sells results in a lower market price for all units sold, not just the marginal unit.

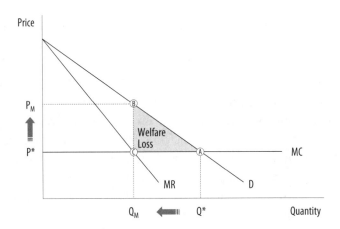

Figure 2-4: The Monopolist's Output Decision

Suppose the marginal cost (MC) of producing each unit is constant. The competitive outcome would be to produce quantity Q* with a resulting market price of P* (Point A). The monopolist, however, will restrict output to Q_M, where MR = MC, and set a higher price equal to P_M (Point B). One of the consequences of this output restriction will be to reduce the overall value of the market. Consumer surplus is reduced because consumers are forced to pay a higher price for fewer units of output. As a result, the monopolist transfers some of the consumer's surplus to profits for itself. However, because the monopolist also restricts output below the competitive ideal, there is a *welfare loss* to society, equal to the shaded triangle *ABC*. The reason economists call this shaded area a "welfare loss" is that consumers are willing to pay more for an additional $Q^* - Q_M$ units than it costs the monopolist to produce those units, which in a perfectly competitive market would, in fact, be produced.

---

[15] We are assuming the monopolist cannot *price discriminate*. Price discrimination is defined as selling at different prices to different consumers. If, say, McDonald's could price discriminate and discern how hungry a customer was, it might try to sell Big Macs at a higher price the hungrier the customer.

2.6 The Contestability of Markets

Traditionally, economists and regulators have assessed the competitiveness of markets using a structural approach—and more specifically, using what is called the "structure-conduct-performance" paradigm.[16] Under this approach, market *structure* (i.e., the number of active buyers and sellers and the relative concentration of activity among those buyers and sellers) is expected to have a strong impact on the *conduct* of individual market participants (i.e., their individual pricing behavior) and ultimately their *performance* (i.e., their profitability). This approach recognizes that market participants' conduct and performance can also affect market structure, e.g., by using profits to invest in activities that ultimately create barriers to entry to potential new entrants, or by setting prices and output at levels that will discourage new entry or hasten market exit by existing competitors.

In order to assess the competitiveness of a particular market, the traditional structural approach typically focuses on measuring individual firms' market shares or overall market concentration.[17] Economic theory predicts that as concentration increases, prices are likely to increasingly rise above a competitive level. Thus, for example, if a proposed utility merger were to increase concentration in an already highly concentrated market, economists and regulators would be expected to oppose the merger unless adequate mitigation was put in place to prevent the transaction from increasing prices in the future. A high level of market concentration is also expected to increase the ability and incentives of a dominant market participant to engage in various forms of anticompetitive behavior, such as creating artificial barriers to entry in order to protect its dominant market position.

A more recent development regarding the ability of firms to charge prices above the competitive level is the theory of *contestable markets*.[18] In contrast to the traditional structural focus on market concentration, the theory of contestable markets first analyzes barriers to entry. While the traditional structural approach to analyzing market power often draws inferences about barriers to entry from the observed market structure, the contestable markets approach examines such barriers to entry directly. Once the presence or absence of barriers to entry is established, predictions can be made about the behavior and performance of market participants (both buyers and sellers) that are largely independent of market

---

[16] For a thorough discussion of the structure-conduct-performance approach, see, Frederick Scherer, *Industrial Market Structure and Economic Performance*, 3rd. ed. (Boston: Houghton Mifflin, 1990).

[17] We discuss measures of market concentration, as well as other tests used by regulators to assess market competitiveness, in Chapter 9.

[18] For a detailed discussion of the conditions necessary for contestability, see William J. Baumol, John C. Panzar, and Robert D. Willig, *Contestable Markets and the Theory of Industry Structure* (New York: Harcourt Brace Jovanovich, 1982).

structure.[19] As we will discuss in Chapter 9, the contestability of a market is an important consideration when evaluating the competitiveness of specific energy markets and deciding whether to regulate market prices.

A market is said to be *perfectly contestable* when firms are capable of entering the market at no cost. In such a case, there are no barriers to entry precluding firms from entering a market, and there are no barriers to exit preventing firms from leaving the market. In a perfectly contestable market, even a monopolist cannot set the price above the competitive market price. Otherwise, other firms could instantly enter the market and reduce the market price. Because the notion of perfectly contestable markets is based on somewhat heroic assumptions regarding the ease of market entry and exit, perfectly contestable markets are a theoretical construct similar to perfect competition. In practice, all markets are characterized by the degree to which they are contestable. For example, residential garbage collection is usually considered a fairly contestable market. The most economically efficient situation is for a single firm to collect all of the garbage in a neighborhood. But, if that firm was to try and charge above-market prices, other firms could easily enter the market, putting downward pressure on prices.

2.7 The Regulator's Pricing Challenge

If the industry is characterized by natural monopoly, such as that for a local distribution company, regulators face a challenge in setting an appropriate price, as shown in Figure 2-5. Recall that the natural monopolist has a declining average cost curve, meaning that the marginal cost of producing each additional unit of output is less than the average cost (at least in the relevant range of production). If the regulator sets the price at the purely competitive solution, $P^* = MC$, then the monopolist has a problem: its total sales revenues ($P^* \times Q^*$) will be less than its total production cost by an amount equal to the shaded rectangle, and the monopolist will eventually go out of business.

---

[19] While an analysis of concentration measures is frequently a central issue in merger analysis, as discussed above, it should be noted that the Department of Justice (DOJ), Federal Trade Commission (FTC), and Federal Energy Regulatory Commission (FERC) also examine barriers to entry in such proceedings. For example, the DOJ/FTC Horizontal Merger Guidelines (and FERC Order No. 592) call for an assessment of whether entry would be "timely, likely, and sufficient" to counteract the effects of a merger. A contestable markets approach, however, places a considerably greater emphasis on the analysis of barriers to entry rather than concentration. If a contestable markets approach were used to assess market power issues in other contexts, such as in market design or market-based rate applications, an analysis of barriers to entry would play a more central role in these other proceedings as well.

Fundamentals of Energy Regulation

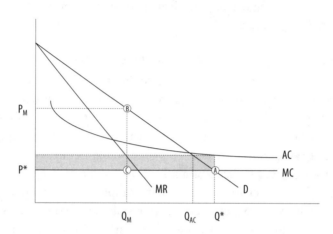

Figure 2-5: The Regulatory Challenge

The economic challenge faced by regulators, therefore, is to obtain the benefits of a competitive market outcome, while keeping the monopolist in business. In other words, the economic regulator would like output to equal Q* and price to equal P*, while allowing the monopolist to earn enough to recover its costs.

One solution would be for the regulator to set price equal to average cost, as shown in Figure 2-6.

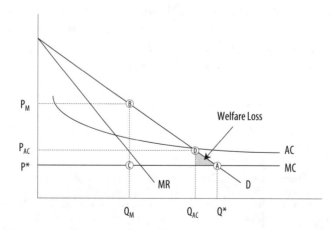

Figure 2-6: One Regulatory Solution: Average Cost Pricing

If the regulator sets the price to P_{AC}, the total quantity demanded will decrease to Q_{AC}. The monopolist will recover its costs, but there will still be a welfare loss to society, as shown by the small shaded area, because the value of the market is less than it would be in a purely competitive market. This problem has a more economically efficient solution, which we will discuss in Chapter 7, and that is to adopt marginal cost pricing coupled with a fixed charge, or through the use of *multipart tariffs*. These tariffs can provide sufficient revenues for the firm, while allowing prices to reflect true marginal costs.

When setting prices, regulators can be confronted with several other complicating factors. First, regulators must often address *intergenerational equity* concerns. Electric and natural gas utilities are capital-intensive industries with long-lived assets like pipelines and generating plants. It would be unfair to recover from today's customers all of the costs of constructing (for instance) a new coal-fired power plant with an expected life of 40 years, since the plant is expected to provide benefits to future customers as well. At the same time, current customers should probably contribute some amount toward recovering construction costs, as well as toward variable operating costs associated with the electricity the plant generates. Since there is no unique method for allocating costs over time to ensure either efficient or equitable treatment of current and future customers, regulators must use their judgment to allocate costs. One common approach is to base recovery on two factors: the duration of the financing for the assets (i.e., how long is the "mortgage" payment?), and the time span over which the asset will be depreciated.[20]

A second issue regulators must often confront in setting prices is that the regulated firm must not only recover its direct costs (e.g., the cost of fuel, employee salaries, debt service, etc.), but it must also be allowed to earn a return on its capital investment. Otherwise, investors and banks will be unwilling to provide the firm with the necessary capital to build plants and buy equipment. Thus, the rate of return must be high enough to compensate investors for the risk they take in providing the firm with capital.[21]

Price Setting if Average Costs are Increasing

It is often argued that the downward-sloping average cost curves shown in Figures 2-5 and 2-6 do not exist anymore, at least in the electric industry. One reason is that new, large baseload generating resources are more costly to build and operate than existing resources. A second reason is that new modular technologies have led to a much smaller minimum efficient scale (i.e., where average cost is minimized). This can affect how regulators set

---

[20] Although depreciation is a somewhat arcane topic, it can have a surprisingly large impact on the price charged both current and future customers. We discuss depreciation methods in Chapter 5.

[21] We address how to establish the regulated firm's rate of return and its capital structure in Chapter 5.

prices in several ways. First, rather than addressing a revenue shortfall if price is set to marginal cost, as shown in Figure 2-6 (again, because revenues collected will not cover the monopolist's total costs), the monopolist may be allowed to overcollect revenues. The reason is that the monopolist's average cost curve generally includes a "normal" return on its investment—"normal" in the sense that it is commensurate with the business and financial risks faced by the firm. In Figure 2-7, the efficient price and output level is shown as Point A, where demand intersects marginal cost.

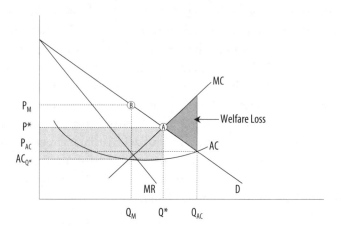

Figure 2-7: Pricing When Average Costs Are Increasing

If the regulator sets the price to P*, the monopolist will earn "excess" profits equal to the lightly shaded rectangle. If the regulator sets the price to the monopolist's average cost (P_{AC}), however, the monopolist will produce too much output (Q_{AC}), resulting in a welfare loss to society equal to the cross-hatched triangle in Figure 2-7. Solving this problem requires using either fixed charges, multipart tariffs, or a combination of both.

2.8 Other Complicating Factors

Even accounting for under- or overcollection of revenues, the regulatory solution to natural monopoly seems straightforward. So, why has regulation been so complex and controversial, especially in the electric industry? We discuss some specific controversies in later chapters. In this section we focus on some of the basic issues that complicate *efficient* economic regulation.

Consider again the economic regulator's goal: *to mimic a competitive market outcome when the underlying market is not competitive.* The first problem faced by regulators is actually measuring costs. While it is easy to draw marginal and average cost curves, determining a firm's actual cost structure is not so simple a task. This is why, as we discuss in Chapter 3, detailed revenue requirement studies are the basis for <u>all</u> forms of price regulation.

Pricing becomes particularly complex when firms produce multiple goods and services using common equipment and facilities. In that case, regulators must grapple with allocating joint costs among different goods and services, and among different customers.

As an example, when an electric generator runs, it produces electric energy and capacity. These are two different goods. Electric energy powers appliances and the like, while capacity ensures that the transmission and distribution systems run reliably (by having sufficient generation to meet the instantaneous demand for electricity), thus ensuring that the entire system does not collapse.[22] When the generating plant is operating, how much of the marginal cost should be allocated to energy and how much to capacity? As Kahn notes:

> When ... products are truly joint, in that they can be economically produced only in fixed proportions, neither of them has a genuine, separate incremental cost function ... The economic product is the composite unit; the only economically definable cost of production, marginal or average, and "price" or "marginal revenue" are those of the composite unit.[23]

Another complexity arises if some of the goods and services produced by the regulated firm are sold in a competitive market and others are not. This is becoming more common as a result of industry restructuring and utility mergers. For example, a number of electric utilities today have both regulated local distribution subsidiaries providing electricity to consumers and unregulated generation subsidiaries selling electricity in highly competitive wholesale markets. If those subsidiaries share common costs, for example, accounting services at the parent company, regulators can face a daunting task: They must allocate those common costs in a manner that does not provide the unregulated generating subsidiary with an unfair competitive advantage, while also setting rates for the regulated local distribution utility in a way that maximizes economic efficiency.

---

[22] For an excellent introduction to how electric systems work for nonengineers, see Frank Graves, *A Primer on Electric Power Flow for Economists and Utility Planners*, Report No. TR-104604, (Palo Alto, CA: Electric Power Research Institute, 1995).

[23] Kahn, *supra* note 1, vol. I, at 79. The "classic" economic example of a joint product is meat and leather produced by a steer.

From the regulator's perspective, therefore, the exact shape and location of the firm's average cost curve will be uncertain. Moreover, depending on whether the regulator establishes prices based on the firm's overall *cost of service* (COS) or based on some form of *incentive regulation*, the regulated firm may have an incentive to disguise its true costs. Consider, for example, the case shown in Figure 2-8.

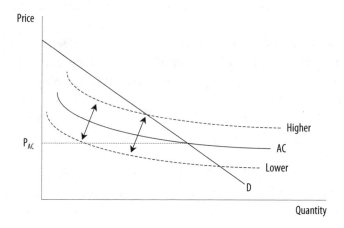

Figure 2-8: Regulation When AC Is Uncertain

In Figure 2-8, the firm's actual average cost curve may be either higher or lower than advertised. Under strict COS regulation, if the firm's actual costs are lower than what regulators believe, then the firm will be allowed to charge "too much," and consumers will be worse off. If, however, the firm's costs are higher than what regulators believe, then the regulated price may be too low; the firm will be unable to recover its costs and provide a sufficient return to investors.

Still another complication can arise when regulators enact policies that affect the regulated firm's overall cost structure. Natural gas, and, especially, electric utilities, have often been viewed as convenient tax collectors and policy vehicles. A common example of this is the provision of low-income rates to increase the affordability of electricity. While well-meaning, developing a separate rate structure for low-income customers is economically inefficient. It is more efficient to provide low-income customers with direct cash contributions that can be used to pay down their electric bills, rather than to have utilities design special rates that distort consumption decisions. Moreover, if low-income customers are provided with special, discounted prices, the residual costs to serve those customers must be recovered from other customers. Not surprisingly, this can create disputes in utility rate cases over which groups of customers should bear those additional costs.

As a second example, in the last few years a number of states, including those that have restructured their electric industries and those that have not, have imposed renewable portfolio standards (RPS) on their local electric utilities. Under an RPS, a utility can be required to obtain a minimum percentage of its total generation resources from renewables, even if those resources are more expensive than traditional fossil-fuel resources. In some cases, these utilities can "buy" so-called "green tags," which are the renewable equivalent of tradable emissions allowances created under the 1990 Clean Air Act Amendments. Figure 2-9 demonstrates the effect on a firm's cost structure from such public policy requirements. Regulatory policies can increase the firm's overall average and marginal costs, reducing sales and increasing the market-clearing price. Strictly speaking, this leads to a lower overall market value, as both consumer's and producer's surpluses are reduced from the perspective of society.

Figure 2-9: Effect of Regulatory Policies on a Firm's Cost Structure

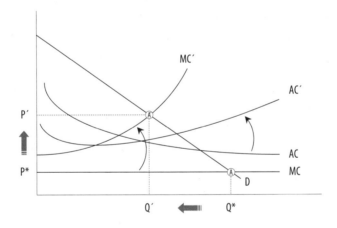

However, advocates of such regulatory intervention often point to the need to address "externalities" created by energy use. Economists define externalities as costs and benefits that are not directly accounted for in a firm's decisions. Air pollution emitted by coal-fired power plants, and contamination of groundwater supplies in areas where natural gas wells are drilled, are common examples of externalities. Because conflicts between energy and environmental regulation continue to fester, in Chapter 11 we will address the issue of whether energy regulators are best placed to address these externalities.

Still another complication arises, especially in electric markets, because of the *public good* nature of electric reliability. Since public goods are not supplied efficiently by markets, regulatory intervention is required to ensure sufficient supply. Because electricity cannot be stored cost-effectively, changes in demand must be met with instantaneous changes in generation supply. Coordinating those changes requires a complex balancing act to ensure that individual generators' actions do not disrupt an entire regional transmission system, or that a downed power line does not lead to cascading outages, as occurred throughout much of the Northeast in August 2003.

2.9 How Deregulation Can Lead to More Regulation

Both the electric and natural gas industries have been substantially deregulated. For example, wellhead natural gas prices were completely deregulated by the early 1990s, and wholesale natural gas markets are well established, with actively traded futures and forward markets. The structure of the natural gas industry was also changed as a result of a series of orders issued by FERC, most notably Order 636, which decoupled pipeline ownership from wellhead suppliers and local distribution companies.

The electric industry presents a far more complex picture. The goal of competitive wholesale electric markets was established in 1992 as part of the Energy Policy Act, when Congress created a new type of entity called an "Exempt Wholesale Generator" (EWG). The idea was to develop a vibrant market of wholesale generators independent from traditional, vertically integrated electric utilities. In 1994, California became the first state to restructure its utility industry and introduce retail competition for electricity. That restructuring effort, which paved the way for many other states to restructure their electric industries as well, led to horrific complications. Not only did California's utility regulators and politicians fail to anticipate and adjust for some of those complications (such as how to create equitable access, adjust to the state's transmission grid, and develop an efficient price system), they created a framework that precluded consumer exposure to market prices—one of the fundamental tenets of a competitive market.

Regulators have also had to grapple with ensuring that all customers are supplied with electricity under so-called "provider of last resort" (POLR) contracts. And, in large measure, state regulators have yet to determine rules for how an electric distribution company, the "poles and wire service" to ultimate customers, should be regulated. While vertically integrated utilities were said to have an *obligation to serve* under the *regulatory compact*, a divested distribution company has an *obligation to connect* under retail competition. What the obligation to connect means in terms of regulation is not clear, since there are generally no reliability standards that local distribution utilities must meet.[24]

Restructuring, in both industries, has created more regulation, because restructuring required the creation of new entities. Natural gas pipelines and electric transmission facilities must be regulated, because they are what economists term "bottleneck" or "essential" facilities. In other words, to move natural gas or electricity from point A to point B, one must use a specific facility. Electric transmission markets continue to evolve. These markets, which must be carefully integrated to ensure a reliable transmission network and to prevent widespread blackouts, have to provide sufficient incentives for investors to build new facilities and for generators to connect to them. As we will discuss in Chapter 12, this continues to be a complex and contentious issue.

Moreover, as wholesale generating markets evolve, it is still necessary for regulators to ensure that individual generators do not possess market power and that transmission system owners do not discriminate against independent wholesale suppliers that require access to those transmission systems to sell to their customers. We will discuss this type of regulation, which falls under FERC's "market-based rate" application process, in Chapter 9.

Another issue that continues to confront regulators is infrastructure development. The processes for siting new generation facilities and for relicensing existing hydroelectric and nuclear facilities are complex and expensive. Not only must developers and owners navigate through a host of often-conflicting regulations, they must deal with typical "not-in-my-backyard" objections and, in some cases, political grandstanding. With the advent of deregulated markets, a more Machiavellian interaction can also come into play, as competitors may have significant economic incentives to block development of facilities that increase competition and reduce prices.

---

[24] In 2006, FERC issued a Notice of Proposed Rulemaking (NOPR) on reliability standards for transmission companies. See *Mandatory Reliability Standards for the Bulk-Power System,* Docket No. RM06-16-000. On March 16, 2007, FERC finalized 83 standards in this docket.

2.10 Chapter Summary

Fundamentally, economic regulation is about ensuring efficient outcomes that mimic a competitive market outcome when the underlying markets are not competitive. As we discuss in the rest of this book, the regulatory complexities we encounter all boil down to that. If a firm is a natural monopoly, or if a market is not workably competitive, a key goal of economic regulation is to prevent market power abuse either by restructuring the market to make it competitive or by regulating firms' behavior. In an ideal world, this is straightforward to accomplish. Regulators can set a firm's prices in such a way as to mimic the competitive market, while ensuring the firm remains financially viable. Regulators can also create new markets and new participants where none have existed.

Alas, reality often intrudes. Measuring firms' costs is not an exact science, especially measuring concepts such as a firm's cost of capital or the physical and economic lifetimes of its capital assets. Firms may have an incentive to inflate their true costs, and regulators may have incentives to lower them. Regulators can also have multiple objectives that extend beyond economic efficiency. Fairness and equity, for example, can lead to far different regulatory outcomes than what strict economic efficiency would lead to. And, regulators, like most of us, can have their own "agendas" and seek to establish specific policies. Additionally, regulatory jurisdictions can overlap and conflict. Energy regulators and environmental regulators, for example, often have vastly different goals. Not only can the firms they regulate be caught in the middle, but such conflicts can also exacerbate inefficiency and uncertainty.

In the next chapter, we begin to explore the process by which regulated prices are established, and we look first at revenue requirements. We show why determining a firm's revenue requirement forms the basis of all types of regulation, including traditional cost-of-service regulation and more recent incentive-based approaches.

CHAPTER 3
THE ROLE OF THE REVENUE REQUIREMENT

3.1 Introduction

No firm can operate as a charity and withstand the rigors of the marketplace. To survive, any firm must take in sufficient revenues from customers to pay its bills and provide its investors with a reasonable expectation of profit, while fending off competitors. Regulated firms are no exception. They face the same constraints, with the exception that, typically, their competitors are limited either by economics or by statute.[1]

A basic concept underlying all forms of economic regulation is that a regulated firm must have the *opportunity* to recover its costs. Privately held firms must be able to obtain a "reasonable" return on *prudent* investments, two loaded words that have been, and continue to be, key areas of regulatory disputes. Without the opportunity to recover all of its costs and earn a reasonable return, no regulated private company can attract the capital necessary to operate. And if an investment is not prudent, it is not likely to be made.

Regulatory regimes in all countries and all political jurisdictions, at least those that wish to have well-functioning electric and natural gas industries, rely on this cost recovery plus investment return concept, which underlies all of the different forms of rate regulation we will encounter. Depending on the jurisdiction, the concept is called variously: *allowed revenues, value added of the regulated activity* (such as distribution or transport), *permissible revenues, rate base, regulated revenues, tariff base,* or *total revenue*. We use the term *revenue requirement*.[2]

Two primary components make up the revenue requirement: *operating costs* and *capital costs*. Operating costs include such diverse categories as administrative and general costs (rent, employee salaries, etc.), fuel costs (e.g., for generating electricity and operating natural gas

---

[1] Even for a pure monopolist, at some price there will always be a "competitive" alternative.
[2] The literature in regulatory economics has referred to the same concept widely. *See, e.g.*, Charles F. Phillips, *The Regulation of Public Utilities* (Arlington, VA: Public Utilities Reports, Inc., 1993), 176.

pipeline compressors), depreciation expenses, and taxes. Capital costs are primarily a return on the undepreciated value of capital assets (power plants, transmission lines, pipelines, etc.) and a return on *working capital*.[3]

3.2 Meeting the Regulatory Challenge

In Chapter 1, we noted that the U.S. electric and natural gas industries were at first unregulated. They eventually were regulated because of industry consolidation and, in the United States, competitive abuses prior to passage of PUHCA. But the other driving force for regulation by government agencies was a determination that electric and natural gas utilities (as well as some other industries) provided services that were either (1) determined to be "affected with the public interest," (2) considered to be natural monopolies, or (3) both.

Electric and natural gas utilities are required to follow a set of basic standards and practices, which together constitute *Good Utility Practice*. FERC defines *Good Utility Practice* for regulated electric utilities as follows:

> Any of the practices, methods and acts engaged in or approved by a significant portion of the electric utility industry during the relevant time period, or any of the practices, methods and acts which, in the exercise of *reasonable* judgment in light of the facts known *at the time the decision was made,* could have been expected to accomplish the desired result at a reasonable cost consistent with good business practices, reliability, safety and expedition. Good Utility Practice is not intended to be limited to the optimum practice, method, or act to the exclusion of all others, but rather to be acceptable practices, methods, or acts generally accepted in the region.[4]

Good Utility Practice covers a wide range of actions, from billion-dollar investments in new transmission and generating facilities, to maintenance that ensures trees are not constantly flopping onto high-voltage power lines. We will discuss these actions in detail and examine how regulators determine whether utilities are in compliance with *Good Utility Practice*.

---

[3] In some jurisdictions, the return is calculated on equity plus the costs of debt financing. Working capital refers to the day-to-day capital needed to keep the firm operating, and is generally based on the time when a firm pays its bills and the time when it receives payments from its customers. We define working capital in Section 3.5, *infra*.

[4] FERC, Pro Forma Open Access Transmission Tariff (OATT), Appendix B (emph. added), 72 Fed. Reg. 12,266–12,531 (March 15, 2007) (to be codified at 18 C.F.R. pts. 35 and 37).

Note also that FERC's definition specifies *reasonable judgment* based on the information the utility possesses at the time of its actions. Thus, *Good Utility Practice* implies neither perfection nor clairvoyance.

When a utility's actions do not conform to *Good Utility Practice*, the firm's actions may not be in the public interest, and regulatory disputes are unavoidable. Since the vast majority of these disputes ultimately affect regulated prices (i.e., *tariffs* or *rates*), a clear set of principles must be followed in order to determine what can or cannot be included in those prices. These principles underlie all revenue requirement estimates and the methodologies used to develop them.

3.3   Key Regulatory Principles

Ideally, *Good Utility Practice* incorporates three regulatory principles that determine whether utilities will be allowed to recover their costs and earn a return on their capital investments. These principles combine regulatory "carrots and sticks" to encourage utilities to make disciplined economic operating and investment decisions. In determining the revenue requirement, costs and investments are examined as to whether they are (1) "prudent," (2) "used and useful," and (3) "known and measurable."[5]

Allowed expenses, whether capital or operating, must satisfy these principles to be part of a firm's revenue requirement. Those that do are called *above-the-line* expenses, and they can be included in the firm's revenue requirement. Those that fail to satisfy any of the three principles are called *below-the-line* expenses, and they cannot be included in the revenue requirement. In essence, below-the-line expenses cannot be charged to ratepayers. Of course, the regulated firm that wishes to lard its executives with luxurious cars and lavish offices is still free to do so. However, the associated expenses should be borne by the company's shareholders alone.

---

[5] Some regulators include the "just and reasonable" standard as a fourth principle. However, the just and reasonable standard really applies to rates and tariffs, not costs.

Prudence and Prudent Management

Under *Good Utility Practice,* a regulated firm's operating and investment decisions are typically considered prudent unless proven otherwise.[6] In other words, utility management is given the benefit of the doubt, and management's decisions are presumed reasonable unless the facts show otherwise. For example, the regulator would need to establish that providing luxurious cars and lavish offices to the regulated firm's executives was not a necessary part of providing electric service. Moreover, the prudence of managerial decisions must be judged on their reasonableness at the time those decisions were made and based on information then available. Prudence is not meant as an exercise in hindsight regulation. In essence, a prudent decision is one that a reasonable person could have made in good faith, given the information and decision tools available at the time of the decision.

In the early 1960s, several economists identified the possibility that regulated utilities would engage in imprudent behavior by *gold-plating* investments.[7] Gold-plating occurs when a utility spends excessively on equipment to provide services that could be provided more efficiently or that are not necessary. Gold-plating leads to artificial increases in regulated rates.[8]

Used and Useful

A second regulatory principle states that an asset should be "used and useful" in order to be included in the rate base for calculating regulated tariffs. The only criterion that is tested as "used and useful" is whether the assets are used in providing services and are useful to the ratepayers. For example, suppose a nuclear plant investment was prudent at the time construction began, but that construction was never completed because of cost overruns. As a result, the unfinished plant would not be used and useful, since it would not be generating any electricity.

---

[6] For example, U.S. Supreme Court Justice Brandeis referred to the prudence of investments as follows: "Every investment may be assumed to have been made in the exercise of reasonable judgment, unless the contrary is shown," *Missouri ex rel. Southwestern Bell Tel. Co. v. Mo. PSC,* 262 U.S. 276 (1923).

[7] *See* Harvey Averch and Leland Johnson, "Behavior of the Firm under Regulatory Constraint," *American Economic Review,* December 1962, 1052–1069. *See also,* Stanislaw Wellisz, "Regulation of Natural Gas Pipeline Companies: An Economic Analysis," *Journal of Political Economy,* February 1963, 30–43. These authors argued that utilities had an incentive to increase capital costs so as to maximize the return on their investments.

[8] Although less common, even expenditures to improve safety can be considered gold-plating if the safety levels exceed minimum requirements established by the government.

In the 1980s, the used and useful principle was expanded by some regulators, and controversially so, to include an economic component. For example, Phillips notes a 1986 case before the Massachusetts Department of Public Utilities.[9] In that case, the regulator found that the electric utility's investment in new generating capacity would be used and useful only if the net cost of that capacity was less than alternative investments. As we discuss in Chapter 5, the problem with an economic used and useful principle is that it replaces a reasoned judgment standard, as defined under *Good Utility Practice*.[10]

Known and Measurable

To be included in a regulated firm's revenue requirement, costs must be *known and measurable*. That is, the regulated firm must justify with documentation, facts, and methodology those costs it wishes ratepayers to reimburse. Typically, a regulated firm is required to prove that all of the costs it is requesting to recover are legitimate expenditures. For example, the firm should be able to describe the details of the duties and obligations for the services provided by its employees. Essentially, all of the costs the regulated firm wishes to recover from captive ratepayers must be realistic. Moreover, the firm should provide enough information to show that those costs are a necessary part of its operations.

The Regulatory Compact and the "Just and Reasonable" Principle

There is also a long-standing, but unwritten, rule that governs cost recovery and lies at the heart of establishing *regulated* prices. This rule is known as the *regulatory compact*. Under the regulatory compact, the regulator grants the company a protected monopoly, essentially a franchise, for the sale and distribution of electricity or natural gas to customers in its defined service territory. In return, the company commits to supply the full quantities demanded by those customers at a price calculated to cover all operating costs plus a "reasonable" return on the capital invested in the enterprise.[11] The first half of this "compact" protects the company from would-be competitors and secures for the public the substantial

---

[9] *Re Western Mass. Elec. Co.*, 80 PUR4th 479, at 520 (Mass. D.P.U. 1986).

[10] For a much more detailed discussion, see Jonathan Lesser, "The Economic Used and Useful Test: Implications for a Restructured Electric Industry," *Energy Law Journal* 23, no. 2 (2002): 349–81.

[11] In other cases where rates are regulated, such as a wholesale generator that is not allowed to sell power at market rates because of market power concerns or an interstate natural gas pipeline owner that is considered a bottleneck facility, there is no regulatory compact per se, since there is no obligation to serve.

economies of scale available in the large-scale production of electricity.[12] The second half of the "compact" counteracts the injurious tendency of monopolists to raise prices above the level that would prevail in a competitive market.

Because the regulatory compact is nowhere written down, you may get different answers as to whether it, in fact, exists, depending on whom you ask. Not so with the *just and reasonable* standard, which can trace its origins to the *just price* doctrine of medieval times and to the Takings Clause of the Fifth Amendment of the U.S. Constitution.[13] Where the just and reasonable standard comes into play arises from the concerns raised by Alfred Kahn. The regulatory compact is a tacit agreement between regulators and the regulated, but it does not give regulated firms *carte blanche* to recover any and all costs. Regulated firms are not guaranteed recovery of the costs associated with lavish offices, "gold-plated" plants, and multimillion-dollar salaries for all.[14] The costs must be just and reasonable.[15]

Together, the regulatory compact and the just and reasonable standard provide the crucial foundation for rate regulation. Both underlie the estimation of a regulated firm's costs, the allocation of those costs among different customers, the allowed return on the firm's capital investments, and the prices that regulators set for different classes of customers. Moreover, as we discuss in Chapter 9, the just and reasonable standard also underlies assessments of a firm's market power and the reasonableness of allowing a firm to compete unfettered in different markets.

3.4 Why Revenue Requirements Underlie All Regulatory Structures

At the beginning of this chapter, we noted that the revenue requirement underlies all regulatory structures, even if the methodologies used to calculate revenue requirements and the regulatory regimes within which firms operate differ substantially. Despite their differences,

---

[12] The company is not necessarily protected against unregulated competitors. For example, if you decide your natural gas furnace is too expensive to operate, you can always install an oil-fired one and tell the natural gas company you no longer want its services.

[13] *See, e.g.*, Charles F. Phillips, *The Regulation of Public Utilities*, 3d ed. (Arlington, VA: Public Utilities Reports, 1993), 89–93.

[14] A detailed discussion of the "A-J-W" effect can be found in Alfred Kahn, *The Economics of Regulation: Principles and Institutions*, vol. II (New York: Wiley, 1970), 49–59. The actual extent of the A-J-W effect has been debated for many years.

[15] The *just and reasonable* standard has also been adopted in other countries. For example, many Latin American countries that privatized their electric and natural gas industries included a *just and reasonable* standard in the initial privatization legislation. *See, e.g.*, Article 40 of Law Nº 24,065, "The Electricity Law," (January 16, 1992), Argentina.

all of the methodologies are based on providing an opportunity (but not an assurance) for the regulated firm to recover its costs and earn a *just and reasonable* return on capital investments.

As we discuss in the next few chapters, a number of factors need to be taken into account when calculating the revenue requirement for a regulated firm. These factors include the choice of *test year*, whether the revenue requirement is based on a historic or future review of costs, the regulatory standards used that govern the myriad calculations, and how the revenue requirement is ultimately set for the firm.

Regulators in some countries, such as Peru, do not use historical test year information. Instead, they base the revenue requirement on what an "efficient" company would spend to provide an equivalent level of service. In other countries, such as Portugal, either econometric calculations using peer companies (either domestic or from other countries) or direct benchmarking with peer companies provide the basis for revenue requirement calculations.

The Test Year

The *test year* serves several purposes. First, because standard regulatory practice requires that all costs be known and measurable, there must be a basis for auditing the firm's costs. In the United States, the most common approach is to review the firm's accounts over the most recent 12-month period for which complete cost data are available.[16] Assuming these audited costs are found to be known and measurable, the test year is used to forecast future costs and, hence, the revenue requirement, by adjusting and adding as necessary to account for inflation, known future expenditures, and so forth. Of course, this approach assumes that the past is an accurate predictor of the future. As energy markets have become more volatile, however, that assumption has become less tenable, and many regulated firms have adopted "alternative regulation" approaches that provide automatic adjustments to rates.[17]

In some cases, regulators will use a future test year as the basis for estimating a firm's costs and revenue requirements and setting regulated rates. Future test years sometimes comprise a mix of actual and projected data (called a *partial test year*) or a test year that is completely based on forecast data. A future test year approach is useful when a firm's historic costs are

---

[16] In some cases, firms will estimate their average costs over a 13-month test year. This is done to help smooth out cost anomalies.

[17] For example, many natural gas LDCs have "fuel adjustment clauses" that provide an automatic adjustment to customer rates whenever natural gas prices change, and some electric utilities have "power cost adjustment clauses" to address volatility in wholesale power market prices and changes in the prices of fossil fuels used by the utility's generating units.

not likely to be a good predictor of its future costs. Or, the firm may be growing rapidly, and the additional costs to serve new customers are much different than in the past, so that a simple projection of past costs will not be accurate.[18]

Finally, test year data are generally adjusted to reflect "normal" operating conditions. For example, in 2005, Hurricanes Katrina and Rita caused extensive damage to natural gas gathering and electric distribution facilities along the U.S. Gulf Coast. Damage to collection facilities caused a significant spike in natural gas prices, which, in turn, greatly increased the cost of gas for many natural gas LDCs. Similarly, several electric distribution utilities were faced with tremendous repair costs and one, Entergy New Orleans, was forced into bankruptcy. Data for the year 2005 would not be a good basis for a test year, because 2005 had many nonrecurrent costs.

Vetting Costs

We have already discussed how the revenue requirement is based on costs that are prudent, used and useful, and known and measurable. However, since all three concepts involve a measure of interpretation, the vigor with which the different costs that make up the revenue requirement are vetted can vary substantially among regulators. In particular, although most regulatory agencies outside the United States follow the same general practice, they often apply different levels of rigor towards what is and is not known and measurable. As a result, costs that are considered to be known and measurable by one regulator may be viewed as speculative by another.

Regardless of how vigorously regulators vet known and measurable costs, most combine historical and forecast data to determine revenue requirements. The observed differences among regulators in different jurisdictions reflect the level of subjectivity that has been adopted for different regulated industries, as well as the breadth of industries that are subject to rate regulation. The more heavily a country's regulators rely on forecasts, benchmarking, or simulations to calculate the revenue requirement, the more subjective the ultimate estimates.

---

[18] In other countries, regulators either use a similar historic test year standard or estimate the revenue requirement for each year of the regulatory period based on an initial base (historical) or benchmark year.

Cost Definitions

Although it would seem that "costs are costs," it turns out that tallying up a regulated firm's costs for the purpose of setting rates requires that we define "cost" more carefully. For purposes of rate regulation, there are three general cost distinctions that must be agreed on, lest regulators and regulated firms end up with wildly different cost tallies. These are *private vs. social costs, original vs. replacement costs,* and, perhaps most importantly, *short-run vs. long-run costs.*

Private vs. Social Costs

In most cases, regulators, like the rest of us, deal with *private costs.* Private costs are the costs that would come to mind for a typical manufacturing firm, such as raw materials and production costs, operations and maintenance expenses, carrying costs, and so forth. In Chapter 2, we discussed differences between marginal and average costs and their relevance to price in both competitive and monopolistic markets. Implicit in that discussion, however, was the idea that all of the costs were private, in other words, directly incurred by firms themselves.

Social costs are different—they are imposed by individuals or firms on others. Typical economic examples are the social costs of traffic congestion and pollution.[19] Consider, for example, traffic congestion. Individuals who drive take up space on the highway. As long as there is excess highway capacity, say, late at night, then individual drivers will not slow anyone else down. But approaching rush hour, as the highway becomes more crowded, drivers begin to slow each other down. The resulting traffic congestion is a type of social cost: Driver A imposes costs (in the form of greater travel time) on all other drivers, but Driver A does not bear the full cost of his actions. This is what economists call an external cost, or an *externality.*[20]

Historically, in setting rates, regulators dealt only with firms' private costs. In the earliest days of electric and natural gas regulation, social costs were not even recognized, much less accounted for. It was not until the late 1980s, when state energy regulators became keenly interested in addressing (especially) the environmental costs of electric generation and use, that they began considering ways to *internalize* external environmental costs into regulated rates.

---

[19] In Chapter 11, we will discuss the cost impacts of environmental regulations on the energy industry.

[20] Readers who are economists may wish to chastise us for the imprecision of our definition of external costs. While we recognize this imprecision, our definition captures the essence of the private vs. social cost dichotomy. Moreover, a treatise on externalities is far beyond the scope of this book.

Perhaps not surprisingly, many of those regulators made a hash of accounting for environmental costs for two reasons: social costs are difficult to estimate, and they may already be internalized through other regulations.[21] For example, without any pollution controls, a coal-fired power plant emits tons of smoke and soot, which impose costs on those downwind of the plant. If environmental regulators require the plant's owners to install emissions control equipment, the amount of pollution emitted by the plant will decline.[22] Presumably, the utility that owns the plant will ask its regulator to be compensated by ratepayers for the costs of the required control equipment. Assuming the energy regulator agrees, the social cost of pollution will have been transformed into a private cost that will be added to the utility's COS. Even with the pollution controls, however, the plant will still emit some pollution. Thus, there will continue to be a social cost. However, assuming the emissions controls are properly set such that the marginal cost of additional pollution just equals the marginal benefit of further reductions, no further internalization of the remaining social costs is needed. Regulators should, therefore, base the utility's COS on this new level of private costs.

Original vs. Replacement Costs

The second area of divergence in cost definitions is critical, because it affects how a regulated firm's allowed return on investment is calculated. This is another area that appears at first glance to be straightforward. For example, suppose a natural gas pipeline company invested $100 million 20 years ago to build a new pipeline for its system. That $100 million represents the *original cost* of the pipeline investment. Under the regulatory compact, the pipeline company is allowed to earn a fair rate of return on that $100 million investment. Suppose that the pipeline has an expected life of 40 years and half of the original investment, $50 million, has been depreciated. If the appropriate rate of return was 10%, the pipeline should earn $5 million (10% × $50 million) on the undepreciated portion of its investment.

The twist occurs if we ask "How much would it cost to build the exact same pipeline today?" In other words, what is the *replacement cost* of the pipeline today, and should that be the basis for calculating a return on the pipeline company's investment? Several difficulties with this concept should spring to mind. First, is it even relevant to discuss the cost of reproducing the exact same asset using the same technology that existed when it was first built? You own a five-year old computer, which now sits in your basement gathering dust. It is probably not something you would want to reproduce today, because it is technologically obsolete

---

[21] For a discussion, see Daniel Dodds and Jonathan Lesser, "Can Utility Commissions Improve on Environmental Regulations?" *Land Economics* 70 (February 1994): 63–76.

[22] This is referred to as "internalizing" an *externality*. We discuss externalities in Chapter 11.

and has no market value. This leads to a second complication: even if the investment were reproduced, the technology used to build it is almost certainly different. This makes calculating true replacement cost difficult, at best.[23] When regulators decide which costs are most relevant for setting rates, they must often confront the incongruities between original and replacement costs, as we discuss in Chapter 5. However, whereas in unregulated markets original cost is almost always irrelevant, in regulated markets it is often the most equitable cost definition to adopt when determining "just and reasonable" rates.

Short-run vs. Long-run Costs

For purposes of establishing a regulated firm's COS, the most important distinction is between short-run and long-run costs. Not only are these costs treated differently from an accounting perspective—the former are *expensed* while the latter are *capitalized*—but short- and long-run costs also can be an important factor in establishing regulated rates. Finally, there is the time dimension again, as regulators must determine how to allocate costs between the regulated firm's current and future customers.

As we have discussed above, regulated utilities tend to invest in long-lived capital assets, such as new generating plants, transmission lines, and pipe. Utilities also incur costs every day, such as the cost of fuel, wages and salaries for employees, and so forth. In establishing a regulated firm's COS, the inclusion of all of the firm's (reasonable) short-run costs is straightforward. Long-run costs are more difficult, since regulators have to decide what proportion of those costs should be recovered from today's ratepayers and what proportion should be recovered from future ratepayers.

In economic terms, short-run costs are those incurred assuming capacity is fixed. If there is a spike in electric demand today because of a heat wave, or if one is expected tomorrow, generating plant owners will respond by ramping up production from their units, including peaking units that can be on-line providing electricity within (say) 30 minutes. What cannot be done is to build new generating plants in the next 24 hours. Therefore, overall production capacity is fixed. That is the short run.

---

[23] In a famous case, *Smyth v. Ames*, 169 U.S. 466 (1898), the U.S. Supreme Court defined a third value called "fair value" that lies somewhere between original and replacement cost. Unfortunately, setting rates based on "fair value" ultimately became circular because the "fair value" of a regulated firm's assets depended on the rates the firm was allowed to charge. The Court reasoned its way out almost half a century later, in *Federal Power Commission v. Hope Natural Gas*, 320 U.S. 591 (1944). Yet, several U.S. states continue to base regulated utility rates on "fair value." For a detailed discussion, see Phillips, *supra* note 2, Chapter 8.

In the long run, production capacity can be changed. New generating plants can be built, new natural gas pipelines constructed, and so forth. Unfortunately, there is no specific cut-off point or formula to differentiate between the two kinds of costs, and so we cannot categorize costs as short-run or long-run with perfect certainty. As a result, regulators must apply judgment in differentiating between short- and long-run costs.

A more difficult issue is how to incorporate long-run costs into the firm's current COS. For example, suppose a utility invests $500 million to build a new generating plant that has an expected operating life of 40 years. Intuitively, allocating the entire $500 million to the company's COS today does not make sense. Not only would it be unfair to current ratepayers, who would have to pay the entire amount while future ratepayers paid nothing, it would result in wild swings in overall rates. Suppose the utility issued 20-year bonds to pay for the plant. Should the costs be recovered over 20 years (the life of the bonds) or 40 years (the expected life of the plant)? It turns out that the answer is a combination of the two. The utility will recover depreciation expenses based on the expected life of the plant and earn a return on its investment that will incorporate both a return on equity and required interest payments the firm must make on the bonds it issues.[24]

Calculating the Revenue Requirement

Once the test year has been chosen and the appropriate costs have been vetted, the revenue requirement for the *rate year* can be calculated. Typically, the rate year is the first year that new rates will be applied. For example, an electric utility may request that its rates be changed on January 1 of the following year based on the costs incurred during its most recent fiscal year. However, some regulators outside the United States combine the expected costs (capital and operating) for an entire multiyear regulatory period to calculate the revenue requirement. This creates additional complications because of the *time value of money*. Most, but not all, regulators incorporate the time value of money in order to *levelize* the regulated firm's revenue requirement.[25, 26]

---

[24] In Chapter 5, we discuss how depreciation costs and a regulated firm's overall weighted cost of capital are determined.

[25] *Levelization* is used to create a constant stream of revenues, either in real, inflation-adjusted terms or in nominal terms. For example, a typical 30-year home mortgage payment is *nominally levelized*. As inflation increases, the real cost of the mortgage payment decreases.

[26] For example, Mexico's Comisión Reguladora de Energía (CRE) has, in past decisions, determined average maximum tariffs for natural gas transport and distribution pipelines simply by dividing the year's estimated revenue requirement by either the sum of each year's estimated pipeline capacity or volumes. *See*, for example, CRE Resolution 138/97 (September 19, 1997) for natural gas distribution and CRE Resolution 089/99 (June 2, 1999) for natural gas transportation.

3.5 Revenue Requirement Components

We have already discussed how a regulated firm's revenue requirement is the sum of its allowed operating expenses and allowed capital expenses. *Operating expenses* refer to all of the ongoing costs to provide uninterrupted services or products, including operation and maintenance (O&M) costs, administration and general (A&G) expenses, depreciation, and all taxes. *Capital expenses* include a *return* on the firm's undepreciated capital investment, called the *rate base*, plus an allowance for *working capital*, which is the amount of money a firm needs to have on hand every day to pay its bills.

The *rate of return* represents the *weighted average cost of capital* (WACC) and is based on the firm's *capital structure* (i.e., the relative proportions of the firm's debt and equity). Income taxes are normally included in this calculation to adjust for the opportunity cost of capital and to ensure that sufficient revenues are collected to pay for those anticipated income taxes.[27] The rate of return is multiplied by the rate base to determine the firm's total return on capital. This ensures that the firm can consistently recoup its capital costs (which benefits investors) while it maintains a high credit rating (which benefits ratepayers).

The revenue requirement can be expressed in mathematical form as:

$$RR = O\&M + A\&G + T + D + (WACC \times RB) \qquad (3\text{-}1)$$

where:

RR is the revenue requirement;

O&M is operation and maintenance expenses;

A&G is administration and general expenses;

T is taxes;

D is depreciation;

WACC is the weighted average cost of capital; and

RB is the rate base that is equal to the gross value of assets minus accumulated depreciation plus working capital.

---

[27] This is known as *grossing up* for taxes. We present an example of this in Chapter 5. An emerging regulatory issue is how to treat deferred taxes and tax offsets. Specifically, should a firm be allowed to recover from ratepayers taxes that the firm might never pay? The answer should be "no."

Treatment of O&M and A&G Costs

In general, O&M and A&G costs are treated as *above-the-line* expenses. However, for purposes of setting rates, some of these costs may be treated as *deferred* or *accrued* costs. Moreover, because known and measurable costs are ultimately allocated among different groups of ratepayers, regulators must grapple with *joint* and *common* costs.

Deferred and Accrued Costs

Deferred costs are those that have been paid for by the company but which have yet to be included for ratemaking purposes, usually by recording a *regulatory asset* or *deferred debit* on the company's books.[28] A typical example is the cost of decommissioning a nuclear power plant. The regulated firm pays into an account each year to fund eventual decommissioning. While deferred costs are not directly included in the revenue requirement, they can earn a return and be amortized.

Accrued costs are very nearly the opposite of deferred costs. Accrued costs refer to items that have not been paid for by the firm but which the firm has recovered in its rates. For example, suppose a firm's wage cycle ends on the 15th of the month, and employees are paid at the end of the month. Employees will not be paid for the period from the 16th through the end of the month until the next wage cycle. However, their salaries will accrue over that time period. Regulated rates need to reflect that. As a result, accrued costs must be carefully estimated over the entire test year.

Direct and Indirect Costs

Identifying *direct* and *indirect* costs is particularly important in the rate-setting process. After regulators determine all of the costs to be included in the revenue requirement, they must allocate those costs to different *rate classes* (e.g., residential, commercial, industrial, etc.) as a precursor to designing tariffs.[29,30] Regulators must sort costs into different bins to ensure they are allocated fairly. This can be a troublesome exercise, depending on the nature of the costs to be sorted.

---

[28] For additional discussion on accounting methods for regulated utilities, see, James E. Suelflow, *Public Utility Accounting: Theory and Practice*, (Lansing, MI: Michigan State University, Institute of Public Utilities, 1973). *See also,* Leonard S. Goodman, *The Process of Ratemaking* (Vienna, VA: Public Utilities Reports, 1998).

[29] We address how different rate classes are themselves established in Chapter 7.

[30] For example, FERC sets firm transportation rates for interstate natural gas pipelines using a "straight-fixed-variable" rule. Clearly, FERC must be able to identify both fixed and variable types of costs accurately.

Direct costs are straightforward to sort. These are costs that can be directly attributed to a specific service, and so they are easily apportioned. For example, the cost of maintaining electric meters will be assigned to the metering function of a utility. *Indirect costs*, on the other hand, are troublesome because they cannot easily be attributed to a single service. For example, the salary of a corporate accountant at a vertically integrated electric utility cannot be allocated to a single activity (generation, transmission, distribution, metering, marketing, etc.), because the accountant's duties extend to all of those activities. To make things even more troublesome, there are two different types of indirect costs: *joint costs* and *common costs*.

Joint Costs

The National Association of Regulatory Utility Commissioners (NARUC) defines a *joint cost* as one that "occur[s] when the provision of one service is an automatic by-product of the production of another service."[31] Although economists typically use the example of a steer jointly producing meat and hide, that example is not especially germane for a book on energy regulation. A better example is the cost of producing natural gas, propane, butane, and other gases from a gas well. All of those gases can be produced from the same gas well and, in fact, are typically extracted simultaneously. As a result, it makes little sense to ask which portion of the drilling costs were the result of the propane produced, which portion were the result of the butane produced, and so forth. For true joint products, where the only possible manner of production results in a fixed ratio of the different products (e.g., one cow = one meat + one hide), there is, in fact, no unique way of allocating costs to the separate products. Because of that, a number of different methodologies have been developed to allocate joint costs. We explore these in Chapter 6.

Common Costs

As with joint costs, *common costs* are associated with producing multiple products. The difference is that common costs refer to products that cannot be produced simultaneously. For example, a petroleum refinery can produce different proportions of gasoline, diesel, heating oil, etc. from each barrel of crude oil. The cost of maintaining the refinery represents a common cost across all of the refined products, but it is not a joint cost. The reason is that, unlike the cow from which one always derives the same quantities of meat and hide, there is an inherent trade-off between the amounts of each product refined per barrel of crude: produce more gasoline and the amount of diesel that can be produced must fall, and so forth. Identifying common costs is straightforward; allocating them can be difficult.

---

[31] NARUC, *Electric Utility Cost Allocation Manual* (1992), 15.

Recurrent and One-time Costs

Recurrent costs are costs that occur repeatedly in the course of providing the regulated firm's services, for example, annual insurance premiums to cover plant and equipment expenses. Recurrent costs are added to the revenue requirement as operating expenses. Recurrent costs are neither depreciated nor included as part of the rate base. The firm cannot expect to earn a return on those costs, only reimbursement for them.

One-time costs include unexpected outlays, such as the costs of recovering from a hurricane or buying new accounting software. Unexpected costs obviously cannot be applied every year, but, unlike recurrent costs, they may be capitalized and depreciated, or amortized accordingly, depending on the circumstances. If capitalized, these one-time costs, which have been added to the rate base, provide a return for the firm's investors.

One reason for spreading one-time costs out over time is to provide rate stability for customers. For example, a utility that was confronted with massive cleanup and repair costs as a result of a natural disaster, such as Entergy New Orleans was after Hurricane Katrina in 2005, could not reasonably charge customers the entire cleanup cost immediately without rates rising so much as to be unaffordable. Moreover, it makes intuitive sense to recover costs over the economic lifetime of an asset.

Historical and Future Costs

Most revenue requirement studies are based on historic costs that were incurred to provide regulated services or products during a certain period of time. This may seem like the best way to estimate future costs, but it is not. Sole reliance on historical costs can result in prices that are either too low or too high for the new regulatory period. Prices change over time, but not always *proportionately*. For example, fuel costs may be expected to decrease, whereas the costs to insure the firm's employees may increase.

The known and measurable standard allows the utility to use *expected* future costs in the rate year to calculate regulated prices and tariffs. Different regulators use expected future costs to different extents. Some regulators may allow only a few items in the cost of service to be adjusted (e.g., future labor costs arising under a union contract). Other regulators will allow forecasts of almost all of a regulated firm's costs to be used, as is the case in some *long-run incremental cost* studies.

Depreciation

As we discussed previously, operating expenses include an allowance for depreciation costs.[32] Depreciation costs are usually collected to account for the effects of capital equipment that wears out over time or otherwise reaches the end of its economic lifespan.

There are a number of definitions of depreciation, depending on the context. From an engineer's perspective, depreciation relates to the actual physical condition of a property. Thus, the engineer would consider a 50-year-old natural gas pipeline that is rusting away and leaking progressively more natural gas to be a fully depreciated asset, because it could be unsafe to operate and require heroic amounts of maintenance. An economist's perspective of depreciation is rather different. For an economist, depreciation is based on the change in the *value* of the services a property provides over time. From an economist's perspective, a 20-year-old computer system that is used to send out customer bills is probably functionally obsolete, especially if nobody can reprogram it. Finally, from an accountant's perspective, depreciation is simply a cost of doing business that must be included on the firm's books.

The accountant's perspective is the most relevant for establishing a regulated firm's overall revenue requirement. Under the accountant's perspective, depreciation implies a systematic allocation of plant and equipment costs, e.g., for generators, transmission and distribution facilities, etc., collectively, *utility plant*, that are expensed at a rate consistent with that utility plant's useful life. This allows the regulated firm to fully recover the cost of its capital investment and earn a return on the net, undepreciated portion of utility plant, called *net asset base*.

Taxes

The revenue requirement also includes a number of taxes (property taxes, payroll taxes, gross receipt taxes, value-added taxes (VAT), franchise taxes, income taxes, etc.) that are limited only by the imagination of governments. To calculate the revenue requirement, taxes are included with the other components in the following ways:

- Property taxes, payroll taxes, franchise taxes, and other taxes are included in the O&M and A&G components.

---

[32] We discuss depreciation methods in detail in Chapter 5.

- Gross receipt taxes, VAT levies, sales taxes, and other taxes collected on top of actual tariff prices are typically not included in the revenue requirement, but instead are charged separately to customers. In these cases, the regulated firm acts as a convenient tax collection agent for the government authority that ultimately receives the monies collected.

- Income taxes are *grossed up* in the rate of return.

Numerous factors can affect the overall amount of taxes included in the revenue requirement such that the level of taxes will differ from the amounts paid to the relevant tax authority. The two most common are:

1. *Tax normalization.* In certain countries, firms can use an *accelerated depreciation* scheme to estimate their income tax payments. However, if the regulator requires regulated firms to use straight-line depreciation, which is typical, there will be a difference between taxes the firm actually pays and the amount for taxes collected through rates. These tax "savings" are temporary because the situation will ultimately reverse; depreciation deductions will be lower than the depreciation expense in the revenue requirement. Tax normalization is the ratemaking process under which these differences are accounted for.

2. *Interest synchronization.* In some cases, the regulator may annualize the interest expense to be included in the rate case of the regulated firm and ignore the actual interest payments the firm uses to calculate its taxes.[33] Through the computation, the regulatory agency is either making sure that the interest used in the tariff calculation matches the total amount of interest that is taken as a deduction by the firm, or that the firm is using the amount of interest that corresponds with the approved capital structure.

Return on Capital Assets

When an investor makes his funds available to a firm, he is forgoing the option of using those funds for some other purpose (either current consumption or another investment). He is also putting his funds at some risk. Together, these conditions define the investor's *opportunity cost*. In exchange, the investor will expect to earn a return on his funds that is commensurate with that opportunity cost. Thus, if the regulated firm is to compensate its investors adequately, it must be allowed, as a component of its cost of service, to earn a *fair rate of return* on its capital investment.

Generally, a firm's cost of debt is easily determined because it is based on the firm's overall creditworthiness as perceived by financial ratings agencies (e.g., Standard & Poor's, Moody's, Fitch, etc.). However, setting an appropriate *return on equity* (ROE) is more prob-

---

[33] This presumes interest payments are tax-deductible, which is not universally true.

lematic because ROE cannot be measured directly. As a consequence, a number of methods, none infallible, have been developed to estimate ROE. We discuss these methods in Chapter 5. The regulated firm's overall return on its capital assets is typically calculated by multiplying its allowed rate of return (i.e., its WACC) by the rate base (i.e., net asset base plus working capital).

Net Asset Base

The *net asset base* is the nondepreciated value of the assets that are used in providing utility services to ratepayers. It equals the value of the assets minus accumulated depreciation. However, to make things more complex, there are three ways to measure the value of the assets for a regulated firm: (1) *original cost*, (2) *replacement* or *reproduction cost*,[34] and (3) *value of service*. As we previously discussed, original cost is simply what the firm paid for the asset initially. Replacement and reproduction costs are different estimates of what it would cost to build the asset today; the difficulty here is that it may either be impractical (e.g., why reproduce obsolete technology?) or impossible (e.g., the facility could never be built as is because of environmental regulations) to do so. Value of service is based either on a prior period of time (such as the end or average value in the historic test year) or on the projected value of the assets for a future regulatory period. In either case, regulators typically include only those assets that are prudent and used and useful. In general, plant not in service and, in some cases, construction work in progress, are not included in the rate base.

Working Capital

Working capital represents cash that a firm requires for its day-to-day operations, such as operating expenses, rent, and some taxes. Firms may also require working capital to meet capital expenditures, such as quarterly dividend payments to shareholders and bond interest payments. Working capital represents the amount of money a firm needs to "bridge the gap between the time that expenditures are required to provide service and the time collections are received for that service."[35] Working capital focuses exclusively on actual cash expenses. Noncash expenses, such as depreciation and deferred income taxes, are not included.

There are two general approaches to estimating a *working capital allowance*. The first, and most accurate, is to perform a "lead-lag" study. A lead-lag study measures the difference between the average number of days when revenues are received (the revenue *lag*) and the number of days before the firm must pay its expenses (the expense *lead*). For example,

---

[34] Replacement and reproduction costs are two different concepts, as we will subsequently explain.
[35] *Re Columbus Southern Power Co.*, 133 PUR4th 525, 550 (Ohio P.U.C. 1992).

suppose a firm pays its expenses on average 30 days after incurring them, while it receives revenues from customers on average 45 days after sending out bills. In that instance, there is a net 15-day lag between when expenses must be paid and when revenues are received. In such a case, the firm's investors are providing additional capital, above and beyond the rate base, and the working capital allowance will be based on the net cost to the firm's investors to supply those funds.

The second approach to estimation of a working capital allowance is to use a formula estimate, which is essentially a rule-of-thumb estimate. For example, some state regulatory commissions in the United States set a firm's working capital allowance equal to the average monthly O&M expenses. The FERC formula is based on a 45-day or one-eighth formula, taking annual O&M expenses and dividing by eight (365 days per year divided by eight is approximately 45 days). Regulators in Mexico and Bolivia also use one-eighth of annual O&M expenses in their working capital calculations.

Not all firms will require a working capital allowance. In some cases, firms will have a net lead, meaning that they receive funds on average prior to paying expenses. In other cases, the lead and lag times will be the same. This is why the second approach is best avoided.

3.6 Other Issues

There are a number of other issues that may need to be considered when calculating a regulated firm's revenue requirement, depending on the regulatory approach used. These are: (1) the industry that the firm is part of, (2) exogenous impacts, and (3) the prevention of cross-subsidies between regulated and competitive subsidiaries.

Company vs. Industry

In some countries, regulators estimate a revenue requirement for an entire regulated industry rather than for the individual firms operating within that industry. If implemented correctly, this approach rewards the most efficient firms in the industry and penalizes the least efficient. The reason is that the average revenue requirement for the industry should be above the level of the most efficient firm and below the level of the least efficient firm.

However, in practice, incentive problems can be created when regulators establish benchmarks for the firms in an industry and then use those benchmarks to disallow costs incurred by the least efficient firms. Regulators often fail to understand that the operations of two regulated firms, even within the same industry, are not directly comparable. As a result, disallowing costs on the basis of such direct comparisons can penalize an entire industry.[36]

Exogenous Impacts

As we discussed previously, firms sometimes incur one-time costs. In some cases, such as the costs to recover from a hurricane, the events leading up to the costs are unforeseeable. Regulators deal with these situations differently. Some regulators will conduct *extraordinary rate reviews* if the cost impact is expected to be permanent. Other regulators will calculate the cost impact and include it on the firm's books as a *regulatory asset* to be recouped in future rate reviews. Finally, in some specific cases, regulators will address the cost impact through preestablished formulae.

Ring-Fencing

When a regulated firm provides several products or services, some that are regulated and some that are not, it is important to ensure that the nonregulated costs are not tagged with the regulated costs. Doing so will not only unfairly increase the regulated prices the firm's customers pay, but it can nobble the firm's unregulated competitors, who are forced to set their competitive market prices without benefit of cross-subsidies. The approach used to prevent cross-subsidies between regulated and competitive subsidiaries is called *ring-fencing*. As its name implies, ring-fencing is designed to allocate costs fairly. There are a number of ways ring-fencing works in practice. Most involve establishing clear guidelines for firm behavior, coupled with strict accounting overview.

---

[36] For example, in Puerto Rico, the milk processing industry historically has been regulated. The regulator, ORIL, estimates the overall industry return. There are two companies providing milk-processing services. While one company (Company A) is a stand-alone entity where all activities are performed within the regulated firm, the other company has some activities being handled by its holding company. Specifically, most IT services are provided for Company B by the holding company and are charged to the milk-processing firm as part of a management fee. Management fees are included in the account "Third Party Services." Therefore, given that "Third Party Services" for Company B is much larger than that for Company A, ORIL reduces Company B's level of the account to match that of Company A and does not increase other expenses to account for the IT services not included. *See* Luis E. Cintron & Co. (2005): "Independent Auditor's Report," prepared for ORIL, Puerto Rico. This practice (and others) penalizes both companies, because the revenue requirement that is used by the regulator to calculate regulated margins is lower than that observed in the industry. The practices by the regulator remain disputed.

Regulatory Accounting

Regulatory accounting procedures are used in almost all regulated markets.[37] The most important reason to set up specific regulatory accounting systems is to establish and monitor the linkage between costs and revenues. However, regulatory accounting can only <u>facilitate</u> these linkages. The regulatory pricing structure, in fact, determines whether those linkages can be established in practice.

Regulatory accounting procedures are used to different extents by different countries. In places without well-defined regulatory accounting procedures but with certain guidelines, all parties typically say they conform to general regulatory reporting guidelines. Unfortunately, variations in corporate structures, operating practices, and accounting, as well as a lack of specificity in reporting guidelines, ensure that costs are not accounted for consistently. Even in the case of a single company, changes in structure, internal cost definitions, and accounting practices can affect the costs that are used to set regulated prices.

Detailed regulatory accounting procedures provide an opportunity to create greater specificity in cost definitions and greater consistency between companies over time. Ideally, regulatory accounting procedures also provide transparency between costs incurred and the revenues that are required to compensate for those costs. These procedures provide regulators with information on current pricing mechanisms, and they also provide information about potential price impacts that would be caused by changes to the current system. Regulatory accounting procedures can also reveal cases where cost differences by industry result from differences in how reporting guidelines are interpreted, thus providing the opportunity to further enhance uniformity among reporting firms.

> **Best International Practice in Regulatory Accounting**
>
> Of all countries, the United States has the longest experience with regulatory accounting procedures used to calculate regulated prices. At the federal level, FERC regulates companies that provide interstate services, such as long-haul natural gas pipelines. Each year, electric utilities, natural gas pipelines, and liquid (e.g., petroleum and refined product) pipelines are required to provide detailed cost information. Electric utilities are required to submit FERC Form 1 ("Annual Report of Major Electric Utilities"), natural gas pipelines are required to submit FERC Form 2 ("Major Natural Gas Pipeline Annual Report"), and interstate liquid pipelines are required to file FERC Form 6 ("Annual Report of Oil Pipeline Companies").

---

[37] The only exception is under some forms of yardstick competition, in which regulators use data from other markets to set prices for a regulated company.

> While the information submitted by electric utilities and natural gas pipelines is used for tariff calculation purposes, oil pipelines are different. FERC has not revised the maximum volumetric tariffs for these pipelines since the 1980s. The tariff is adjusted each year based on a formula that uses the Producer Price Index (PPI). Moreover, the liquids transportation service has become so competitive that, in many cases, FERC has simply stopped regulating those pipelines and allows them to set their tariffs based on market conditions.[38]
>
> At the individual state level, water, natural gas, and electric utilities all must use the *Uniform System of Accounts* developed by FERC and/or the National Association of Regulatory Utility Commissioners (NARUC). While regulatory accounting has been around for almost seven decades, the rules and accounts are updated on occasion. The natural gas and electric accounts were last updated in 1976. Water utility accounts were updated in 1996.

Revenue Requirements and Regulatory Risk

One major concern for a regulated firm's investors, in addition to the firm's overall financial performance, is how the firm's regulators behave. Firms whose regulators have well-established procedures to determine revenue requirements, and that implement those procedures fairly and uniformly, will be perceived by investors as having lower financial risk compared to those whose regulators are mercurial. While an investor might not like a regulator's decision, it is far easier to respond to decisions that are based on clear guidelines than it is to respond to decisions based on whims or political expediency. The latter tend to cause greater regulatory uncertainty, which investors loathe.

3.7 Chapter Summary

In this chapter, we have seen how determining a regulated firm's revenue requirement underlies many different regulatory approaches. We also provided a quick tour of the key components that make up the revenue requirement and, ultimately, establish the regulated prices firms charge their customers. In the five chapters that follow, we delve into all of these issues in more detail. We will build the revenue requirement component by component and provide a description of how these components are addressed. After we have established the components, we will discuss how those costs are allocated among different customers and how the rates those customers ultimately pay are determined. Finally, we will discuss how costs and rates are updated over time.

---

[38] Liquids pipelines face competition from barges, railways, and overland trucking.

CHAPTER 4
ALTERNATIVE REGULATORY STRUCTURES

4.1 Introduction

As we discussed in Chapter 1, government regulation of the electric industry began in earnest during the 1930s in the United States. In the ensuing decades, regulation has evolved as a body of case law to better define foundational concepts such as the *regulatory compact* and the *just and reasonable* standard. Outside the United States, the history of utility regulation is much shorter, because direct government ownership of public utilities was prevalent until the latter part of the twentieth century.

The traditional U.S. regulatory approach merged the *revenue requirement* standard with a COS concept (in which regulated prices are based on historical costs plus known and measurable changes and a return on capital investment).[1] Beginning in the early 1980s, however, the complexity of regulation increased as new regulatory regimes developed. Privatization was one of the main reasons for this increase in regulatory complexity.[2] Privatization, which was initiated by Great Britain in the early 1980s, created numerous private utilities out of previously state-owned companies. Rather than simply adopt the same COS standard so prevalent in the United States at the time, many of these newly minted regimes were designed to align utility performance and profitability. The goal was to realize economic efficiencies that were not obtained, at least not without much gnashing of teeth, under traditional COS regulation.

As a result of these privatization efforts, a number of different regulatory regimes were created.[3] In general, these regimes fall into three structures: (1) COS regulation, (2) *performance-based regulation* (PBR),[4] and (3) *yardstick competition*.[5]

---

[1] In Great Britain, economists refer to COS regulation as *rate-of-return* regulation.

[2] We analyze this trend in more detail in Chapter 13.

[3] Although regulatory regimes can share many similarities, no two are identical. The unique characteristics of firms and the environments in which they operate mean that the same regulatory methods will generally lead to different outcomes.

[4] Performance-based regulation goes by a number of names, including *incentive regulation* and *RPI-X regulation*.

[5] Although yardstick competition is similar to *benchmarking*, in fact, many regulators use *benchmarking studies* to assess the reasonableness of the regulated firm's costs under all three regulatory structures. We discuss this in Section 4.7 *infra*.

Fundamentals of Energy Regulation

In the remainder of this chapter, we first identify the common aspects of these three regulatory structures. Next, we discuss why outcomes can differ, sometimes significantly, between firms, even when the same regulatory regime is applied. Finally, we describe each regulatory structure and identify each structure's similarities and differences with respect to the other two.

4.2 Common Aspects of Regulatory Structures

Many, although not all, policymakers who have developed regulatory structures have busied themselves with developing incentives to help regulated firms improve their operating efficiency and profitability, while lowering regulated prices. Although a number of variations of the three types of structures mentioned in the previous section have been developed, all of these regulatory structures have some aspects in common.

All regulatory frameworks share the same structure to determine regulated prices. In general, a simple set of rules determines regulated prices,[6] as shown in Figure 4-1.

Figure 4-1: Three Sets of Rules to Determine Regulated Rates

---

[6] In general, we will refer to prices or rates when we describe the process of regulating prices.

The first set of rules deals with how costs are transformed into a revenue requirement. The calculations can be carried out by the regulated firm as needed, when requested by the regulator, or on a set time schedule (e.g., every five years under price cap regulation). The calculations include estimations of: a fair rate of return (based on the opportunity cost of capital), the firm's asset base, depreciation costs, operating expenses, and taxes.

For price regulation to be effective and fair, the rules and procedures for calculating the revenue requirement also must be clear. Poorly defined rules, or rules that change frequently and unpredictably, waste resources and set the stage for administrative and judicial conflicts between regulators and firms.

The second set of rules encompasses a service and pricing model that transforms the calculated revenue requirement into a set of tariffs and regulated prices.[7] Although different regulatory structures may use different models and cost elements, they all ultimately convert calculated revenue requirements into a set of tariffs. The structure of tariffs embodies all of the elements that are considered desirable in a regulated pricing regime, including fairness, efficiency, stability, and transparency. Thus, the tariff structure contains, among other things, the economic signals that are intended to encourage efficient levels of consumption—within the constraint represented by the need for the projected tariffs to collect the revenue requirement at the time those tariffs are designed.

The third set of rules specifies the methods used to change tariffs from one year to the next, for a predetermined length of time. For example, a price cap formula typically includes adjustments for inflation (the *RPI factor*), productivity (the *X factor*), and changes to costs (such as income tax rates) beyond the regulated company's control (the *Z factor*).[8] Each adjustment is intended to promote increased efficiency by not automatically passing through all cost increases.[9] At the end of the specified price cap formula periods (e.g., five years), the entire process (i.e., revenue requirement calculation, pricing model calculations, and price cap formula specification) is repeated all over again, so as to ensure the pricing formula is consistent with both the firm's current makeup and broader economic conditions that may have changed.

---

[7] Again, because U.S. and international terminology differs, we define *tariff* to mean an entire price schedule that may encompass multiple rates (e.g., the tariff for residential customers provides for the first 500 kWh at a rate of 10¢ per kWh, the next 500 kWh at a rate of 8¢ per kWh, and so forth).

[8] In some jurisdictions, this adjustment for exogenous costs is called a *Y factor*.

[9] Another approach that is often used is based on a revenue-sharing concept between a regulated firm's shareholders and its ratepayers. We discuss revenue sharing in Section 4.5 *infra*.

4.3 Cost Differences and Operating Environments

One of the basic tenets of economics is that firms have unique cost structures. As a result, the costs to provide the same commodities or services will differ among firms. The uniqueness of firms' cost structures results not only from differences in input prices, but also from differences in management talent, operating environments encompassing general macroeconomic conditions (economic growth, tax rates, etc,), geography, and legal systems. For example, the fuel boffins at Utility A may always be spot-on with their natural gas purchases, yet the utility could still have higher rates than Utility B because the latter operates in a state with lower taxes. Utility A is more economically efficient than Utility B, even though the rates it ultimately charges are higher.

When regulators base the rates they allow a regulated firm to charge on benchmarks of other firms' costs—which is the basic thrust of yardstick competition—they create a potential regulatory hazard for both the firm's investors and its customers. The central problem when comparing regulatory regimes across different jurisdictions is, therefore, how to account for the diverse variables that explain real differences in operating and capital costs. For example, electric utilities operating in hurricane-prone regions typically have higher local distribution costs than utilities in other regions, because hurricanes are fond of blowing down utility poles.

In any particular regulatory regime, all of the factors that affect costs, but which are beyond the control of the regulated firm, should be taken into account when evaluating the reasonableness of known and measurable costs, the prudence of investment plans, depreciation, the allowed rate of return on investment capital, and so forth. These factors, which describe a firm's *operating environment*, include the firm's physical location and surrounding geography, the legal and tax regime in which the firm operates, competitiveness of input markets, and even socioeconomic factors. A regulator's failure to account for the costs faced by a regulated firm (and the factors affecting those costs) can impose additional, unnecessary financial risks on the regulated firm. The eventual result will be higher costs, reduced service quality and reliability, or both. This benefits neither investors nor ratepayers. In short, regulators will violate the *just and reasonable* standard.

4.4 Cost of Service

Previously, we discussed how the revenue requirement concept overlays all regulatory structures. We now turn to the most common regulatory structure of all—one based on a regulated firm's COS. To distinguish between a firm's COS and cost-of-service regulation, we use the acronym COSR for the latter.[10] COSR is used widely in the United States and in a number of other countries to establish regulated prices and tariffs. A COS study will include an estimate of the regulated firm's costs. This estimate is based on prudent costs incurred during the test year, plus known and measurable changes, plus a return on the firm's net (undepreciated) asset base.[11] Of course, a firm's COS is a necessary component of COSR. However, calculating the COS is also a necessary component of other regulatory frameworks.[12]

The rate of return is typically calculated as the weighted average cost of capital (WACC) and is based on the cost of debt, a "fair" return on equity (ROE), and the firm's capital structure. Because ROE cannot be observed directly, it is one of the most contentious parameters in COSR.

A common misconception is that COSR allows the regulated firm to request a general tariff review whenever its costs are not aligned with its rates. However, any regulated firm assumes the risk that its costs can change rapidly, and, as a result, the rates it is allowed to charge will diverge from its costs.[13] In some cases, regulated firms are granted automatic cost adjustment mechanisms to reduce the divergence between costs and rates, for example, to accommodate changing fuel costs.

---

[10] In his seminal book, Bonbright refers to "the cost of service" and "the cost standard" interchangeably. *See*, James C. Bonbright, *Principles of Public Utility Rates*, 2d ed. (Arlington, VA: Public Utilities Reports, 1988). To make things even more confusing, European regulators refer to COSR as *rate-of-return regulation*. Regardless of the form of regulation that befalls it, every regulated firm has a cost of service.

[11] Not all countries use an original historical "cost less depreciation" definition of the asset base or include inflation as does the United States. For example, Bolivia calculates a return on electric generating assets based on current cost accounting. *See* Decreto Supremo Nº 08438 (the "Electricity Code"), July 31, 1968 (although Law Nº 1604, December 21, 1994, outlined a reformed electricity sector, a few clauses from the Electricity Code still apply to an electric generator in the La Paz region, COBEE).

[12] Not only is the COS the most common basis to establish overall revenue requirements, it is also a fundamental component for newer, performance-based regulation (PBR) approaches. In Chapter 6 we examine different types of costs and illustrate how a typical COS model—usually a computer spreadsheet—is constructed, focusing especially on the most contentious and problematic aspect of COS: allocating regulated costs among different customer groups. Another issue is the cost allocation complexities, and opportunities for mischief, when a firm has both regulated and unregulated business lines.

[13] This is sometimes called *regulatory lag*.

In a typical regulated rate case, whether for a natural gas pipeline, electric transmission company, or natural gas or electric local distribution company (LDC), the process of establishing regulated rates and tariffs requires that regulators determine the firm's cost of doing business. That cost will include normal business operating costs such as employee wages, fuel costs, operations and maintenance expenditures, working capital (the money a firm needs to have on hand to fund day-to-day expenditures), and taxes. The cost of doing business will also include a fair return on the firm's undepreciated capital investment, which is called the *rate base*, including interest payments on short- and long-term debt and a return on equity capital.[14] Once the regulated firm's costs have been measured, they are allocated among the firm's different customers, e.g, residential, commercial, industrial, and so forth. Finally, after the costs are allocated to the different groups, rate structures can be established for each customer group. Those rates can use a variety of pricing principles, such as those we introduced in Chapter 2 and will discuss in more detail in Chapter 6.

Determining a regulated firm's COS would seem straightforward: just add up the firm's total operating costs, throw in an allowed return on capital investment, and, voilà, one has a COS study. As with most aspects of economic regulation, however, things are not quite so simple. There are different cost concepts, each of which can lead to different estimates of a firm's overall COS.[15] Yet, regulators cannot establish a firm's COS without first agreeing on what types of costs should be incorporated. Whereas the regulated firm's executives may all enjoy being chauffeured around in Mercedes limousines, regulators may determine that the reasonable decision is to allow the firm to recover only enough money for its executives to drive themselves around in Chevrolets.[16] Finally, because of the long-lived nature of many regulated investments (including natural gas pipelines and electric generating plants), and in order to abide by the established regulatory maxim that rates must be "fair, just, and reasonable," regulators must also determine a time frame over which a regulated firm's costs will be recovered. In establishing such rates, regulators must not only allocate costs among different groups of today's ratepayers, but they also must allocate costs between current and future ratepayers so as to address *intergenerational equity*.[17]

---

[14] In some countries, the debt component is calculated based on the average rate for companies with the same credit rating plus country risk because there could be financial transactions with related companies in other countries.

[15] A related issue is whether one adopts a "top-down" or "bottom-up" approach to costs for different regulated customer groups. Specifically, most regulators determine a firm's overall COS and then allocate it between the firm's different customer groups, rather than determining the COS for each customer group and then adding up those costs to determine the firm's overall COS.

[16] Recurrent costs that are known and measurable are referred to as *above-the-line* costs, while other costs are *below-the-line*. Similarly, revenues earned by the regulated firm are distinguished between above- and below-the-line categories.

[17] As we discuss in Chapter 5, there are also costs that may be incurred today, but whose recovery is nevertheless "deferred." For example, a utility may be able to defer a fraction of its income tax payments until a later date. The appropriate accounting for cost deferrals and how they enter into COS can be a tricky financial issue, best left to accounting professionals and not economists like us.

Finally, COS estimates can be problematic because costs themselves can change frequently. As domestic and international electric and natural gas markets have become more volatile, for example, regulated local distribution companies (LDCs) have faced greater variability in their overall costs of providing energy. Yet, maintaining rate stability has traditionally been an established regulatory goal. Achieving and maintaining rate stability, while ensuring that firms can pay their bills in a timely fashion and consumers receive the appropriate price signals, is no easy task.

4.5 Performance-Based Regulation

Performance-based regulation (PBR)—alternatively called *incentive regulation*, *price-cap regulation,* or *RPI-X* regulation—has gained popularity over the last 20 years as an alternative to COSR. PBR was developed to address a major flaw of COSR, namely, that it provides no incentive to regulated firms to increase operating efficiency. In contrast, PBR emphasizes rules for setting prices over time and provides the opportunity for a regulated firm to increase its rate of return by reducing its operating costs.

Moreover, PBR can reduce problems caused by *regulatory lag*, which refers to the period between the time that changes in actual costs occur and the time that those changes are reflected in a firm's revenue requirement and COS. Regulatory lag is an especially common lamentation under COSR, because rate cases are typically drawn-out affairs over many months. If a firm's costs are rising, but it cannot recover those higher costs under its current rate and tariff structure, its financial condition can deteriorate.

Under PBR, rather than having a set rate of return determine the prices the regulated firm charges, the firm faces a set price.[18] As a result, the more success the firm has in reducing its costs through improved operating efficiency and innovation, the higher its return.[19] PBR also incorporates projected productivity increases into pricing rules to induce outcomes that would be expected in fully competitive markets.

Although the most common form of PBR uses price caps, some regulators use a *revenue-cap* approach. As the name implies, revenue caps limit growth in revenue per customer, rather than limiting growth in price per unit of output. Companies are allowed to set their

---

[18] This is usually referred to as *decoupling* prices and costs.

[19] In order to avoid cost reductions achieved solely by reducing the level of service, such as reducing the number of customer service staff who handle billing inquiries, by not trimming trees, and so forth, PBR typically incorporates well-defined service quality standards.

own prices subject to an overall maximum revenue per customer. The touted advantage of this approach is that it encourages energy conservation by eliminating the regulated firm's incentive to maximize sales.[20]

PBR has become more widespread in the United States and, especially, internationally. The increasing prevalence of PBR stems from the widely held view that the approach is a less costly form of regulation and that it produces more efficient results, because it encourages a regulated company to reduce costs and exceed the average pace of industry productivity gains.

PBR is usually implemented with a formal rate review process that occurs periodically, but with an extended period between reviews, typically three to five years. Between formal reviews, the formula-based pricing mechanism accounts for changes in costs that are beyond the control of the regulated company. By reducing the number of formal reviews compared to a COSR approach, PBR also reduces the direct costs of regulation, for both the regulated firm and its regulator. The formula-based pricing mechanism, in turn, reduces the indirect costs of regulatory lag. Since the structure of a PBR mechanism changes the regulated firm's overall risk/reward trade-offs, it is often necessary to change the base return on equity for the regulated firm from what it otherwise might be under COS regulation. Typically, PBR mechanisms begin with a baseline return on equity to account for the firm's ability to improve its profitability. However, depending on the specific type of PBR mechanism, the firm's baseline return on equity actually may need to be increased.[21] This is especially true in light of another common component of PBR structures: *shared-savings* mechanisms.

Determining appropriate adjustment factors, especially the X factor (which is designed to capture expected improvements in the overall productivity in the industry) can be problematic.[22] The reason is that defining, to say nothing of measuring, "productivity" remains elusive. This likely explains why there are wide variations in the ways regulators determine adjustment factors—from what are, essentially, arbitrary pronouncements, to using sophisticated empirical methods, such as *total factor productivity* (TFP) estimates.[23]

---

[20] Revenue caps may also be prone to "gaming" by creating new customers. For example, a typical industrial firm may have hundreds of meters on site. Under a revenue-cap approach, the regulated firm could convert each meter into a new "customer."

[21] For a discussion, see Jonathan Lesser, "ROE: The Gorilla is Still at the Door," *Public Utilities Fortnightly* 145 (July 2004): 19–23.

[22] We discuss productivity measurement issues in Chapter 8.

[23] For an application, see Jeffrey Bernstein, "X-Factor Updating and Total Factor Productivity Growth: The Case of Peruvian Telecommunications, 1996–2003," *Journal of Regulatory Economics* 30, no.3 (2006): 316–42.

Shared-Savings Mechanisms and Off-Ramps

Ironically, one concern raised by PBR mechanisms is that the regulated firm's performance will change radically, perhaps because of exogenous events, benefiting either shareholders or ratepayers, but not both. Although this "zero-sum" approach to regulation is naïve, newly minted PBR mechanisms may be approached warily by firms and their regulators. Regulators may be concerned that firms will "game" the rules or somehow increase their operating efficiency far more than regulators think possible. Firms, on the other hand, may be concerned that if they do improve their operating efficiency, regulators will simply raise the bar, rather than allow investors to enjoy greater returns. Moreover, firms may also be concerned about *asymmetric regulation*—a sort of "lose/lose" proposition in which, if the firm does well, its profits are reduced, but if it fares poorly, investors must absorb all of the losses.[24] Sharing mechanisms and off-ramps can help allay these fears.

Sharing mechanisms can be based on either revenues or earnings. Earnings-sharing mechanisms (ESMs) are established rules for sharing earnings between companies and customers. Typically, ESMs reduce investors' downside risk by truncating the level below which the firm's earnings can fall, based on agreed-upon adjustment formulas. (ESMs also affect upside earnings potential.) Revenue-sharing mechanisms (RSMs) work in the same way, except they focus on the firm's revenues, rather than earnings.

> **Green Mountain Power Corporation's Alternative Regulation Plan**
>
> In 2006, Green Mountain Power Corporation, an investor-owned electric utility in Vermont, submitted an alternative regulation plan to the Vermont Public Service Board. The GMP plan contained a number of features, including an automatic rate adjustment mechanism to reflect changes in power supply costs, an earnings-sharing mechanism, and an automatic adjustor on the company's ROE. Specifically, under the company's plan, changes to power costs would be adjusted quarterly, but would be capped so that rates would never increase by more than one cent per kilowatt-hour per year. Additionally, the adjustor contains a *deadband* of ±$1.6 million annually. If costs go up or down within the deadband, there are no adjustments to rates. So, if the company reduced its costs by $1 million in a year, the savings would be reflected as increased earnings for shareholders.

---

[24] Asymmetric regulation is a form of *risk truncation*, in which the "tails" of an overall distribution of returns are cut off. With regulatory asymmetry, the top "tail" is chopped, while the lower is not, or at least not as much. *See, e.g.,* "Productivity Commission Inquiry Report, Review of the Gas Access Regime," Report No. 31 (June 11, 2004), Appendix B.

> Two mechanisms affect the company's ROE. The first is an automatic adjustment to the company's "base" ROE. This adjustment is set to 50% of the change in yields on 10-year U.S. Treasury bonds over a defined time period. For example, suppose GMP's base ROE equals 10%, and the interest rate on Treasury bonds is 5% today. If the rate on those bonds increases by 1% (i.e., 100 *basis points)* to 6%, then the company's base ROE would increase by one-half of that change, or 0.5% (50 basis points). So, the company's ROE would be automatically adjusted to 10.5%.
>
> The earnings-sharing adjustor works as follows: The company calculates its actual ROE compared with the base value. The earnings deadband is 0.75% (75 basis points). So, assume again that the baseline ROE is 10%. If the company's actual ROE falls between 9.25% and 10.75%, there is no rate adjustment. If the company's ROE goes above 10.75%, its customers receive 100% of the benefits. So, if the company's ROE is 12% in a given year, rates would be adjusted downwards the following year to return the excess earnings to customers. On the downside, if the company's actual ROE falls below the 75-basis-point deadband, then the shortfall is shared equally among customers and investors.

Finally, PBR mechanisms often contain "off-ramps" that allow both firms and regulators to modify, and in some cases end, the PBR process when certain threshold conditions occur. For example, suppose the firm's return on equity is capped at 12% under an ESM. If inflation becomes rampant, a 12% cap on ROE may not provide a sufficient real (after-inflation) return on equity to allow the firm to raise capital. Off-ramps are the equivalent of major surgery. Their design and use, especially the underlying conditions that trigger them, must be thought through carefully. Otherwise, they can either introduce too much regulatory risk to the firm or fail to provide the firm with sufficient incentives to improve its performance.

Drawbacks of PBR Mechanisms

While PBR offers a number of advantages in both theory and practice, it is not a panacea for overcoming regulatory difficulties. One argument in favor of PBR is often overstated. The gist of this argument is that PBR reduces the amount of information a regulator needs from a company and lessens problems that arise from the company having better information than the regulator (called *information asymmetry*). There clearly are benefits to formula-based price (or revenue) regulations, but setting initial values and parameters, and evaluating and making changes to the process over time, are still significant challenges that are often subject to political meddling. The need for good information is not lessened, though it might be argued that the relevant information is needed less frequently.

There may also be practical limits to savings from fewer regulatory reviews. If there are extended periods between formal proceedings, regulated companies and regulators alike are less likely to retain the boffins most familiar with all of the intricacies of performing rate reviews. Having to retrain staff each time a formal review is undertaken may increase the costs associated with each review and negate previous cost savings.

Another difficulty can arise from how broadly the group of regulatory stakeholders is defined. PBR offers clear benefits to consumers and regulators and may well be better for shareholders as well. Employees, however, may not fare so well. Often, the most immediate way to increase productive efficiency is to reduce the amount of labor required per unit of output, typically resulting in job losses. (This is one reason for incorporating service quality standards.) The experience in Great Britain, where PBR was largely pioneered, was successful in terms of increasing productive efficiency in the natural gas and electric industries. However, employees shouldered a significant part of the burden through job cuts.

4.6 Yardstick Competition

Despite sharing similar characteristics, *yardstick competition* is distinct from PBR. Yardstick competition has been proposed as a way of regulating utilities where there is *asymmetric information*, i.e., where firms know more about the industry than their regulators.[25] Unlike PBR, under yardstick competition, firms compete against one another. The profitability of any individual firm, therefore, depends on how it performs relative to all of the other firms in its industry, much as students who are "graded on a curve."

The rationale of yardstick competition is that prices and, hence, profits, are based on the average costs of all firms in the industry. Firms whose costs are below the industry average will be more profitable; those whose costs are above average will be less so. In the long term, firms try to beat the average cost "yardstick" by increasing their operating efficiency and lowering their costs; this also benefits customers. Typically, yardstick competition uses some of the same factors to adjust tariffs during the regulatory period, just as under PBR.

Three main problems have been identified with yardstick competition: collusion, commitment, and comparability. Collusion can arise because firms can learn how the comparison method works and then collude to provide information that will benefit all of them in the next tariff review. The smaller the group of firms that comprises "the industry," the easier it will be to collude. Commitment problems arise because, in theory, the worst-performing

---

[25] Andrei Schleifer, "A Theory of Yardstick Competition," *Rand Journal of Economics* 16, no. 3 (1985): 319–27.

firms should go bankrupt. If regulators, or as is more likely, politicians, intervene to prevent bankruptcy, the entire rationale for yardstick competition disappears.[26] Finally, with respect to comparability, yardstick competition applications often fail to account for the inherently unique characteristics in the firms considered. For example, in 2005 the Portuguese regulator considered a yardstick competition model for Electricidade do Portugal (EdP) by breaking up the company into regional units with diverse geographic and economic characteristics. Not only were there too few companies to establish an accurate sample, the comparisons were, in essence, made against the firm itself. Ultimately, although yardstick competition seems an attractive approach in theory, especially to some economists, practical problems make its implementation almost impossible.[27]

4.7 Comparing Different Regulatory Regimes to Set Tariffs

Many regulators using either PBR or yardstick competition regimes have been increasingly relying on empirical regression models to compare costs between different utilities across many regions, and even countries. These comparisons then determine firms' revenue requirements and tariffs. While this has an intuitive appeal—after all, why not "raise the bar" by benchmarking individual firms against a broader group worldwide—this approach has a number of potential pitfalls that must be carefully addressed. Otherwise, the results will be unreasonable, harming customers and investors.

As we noted earlier, all firms have unique aspects. As the group of firms used becomes more widespread and diverse, the number of attributes, especially exogenous ones, also tends to grow. But if number-crunching models fail to account for these attributes adequately, then the results will be skewed. The difficulty is that, as the pool of firms is broadened, it becomes tougher to develop easily measurable attributes that apply to all firms.

If all of the diverse aspects of different operating environments affecting the selected companies are not directly comparable, or if they are not considered in the modeling work, the results will be biased. So, what appears to be a difference in operating efficiency between

---

[26] Economists call this *moral hazard*. If a firm knows that, no matter how inefficient, it will be "bailed out" by regulators or politicians, it will have no incentive to operate efficiently.

[27] For example, Richard Green and Martín Rodríguez Pardina, "Resetting Price Controls for Privatized Utilities. A Manual for Regulators," *EDI Development Studies*, 1999, 64–67. Although the authors explain how some heterogeneity across companies can be accounted for, their results cannot separate the effects of other characteristics from differences in efficiency.

a utility in Chile and one in China may not be a difference at all. Or, worse, an estimate concluding that the Chilean firm is falling down relative to China could be the exact opposite of what is true.

There are five main differences that are typically observed in international operating environments. They are:[28]

- **Location.** Differences with respect to weather and climate can lead to far different approaches to vegetation management and related operating costs. For example, tree-trimming expenses for a distribution company in the Arizona desert probably will not be the same as for a company on the Pacific Coast.

- **Legal and Tax Systems.** Legal and tax systems affect costs of companies operating in different regions. Even mundane items such as municipal fees can affect companies differently and can also affect their perceived efficiency. For example, a transmission line project that passes through multiple counties may have to contend with those counties charging different siting fees; some counties may set fees based on the project's cost, while others may set fees based on kilometers or miles of line installed.

- **Private vs. Public Ownership.** Private and government ownership clearly affect a firm's costs. State-owned companies may have cost structures that are radically different than those of private firms, because of administration constraints, tax collections, and job guarantees imposed by government owners. For example, Mexico's state-owned petroleum company, Pemex, is required to pay massive levies to the Mexican government and must set aside large amounts of money to fund a very generous employee pension plan.

- **Socioeconomic Factors.** Companies that operate in urban or rural areas, or in different countries, can face hugely different costs. A rural electric company will have a higher distribution cost per customer than one serving a large city. A company whose customers are poor may have to deal with higher amounts of uncollectibles.[29]

- **Integration of the Inputs Markets.** The remoteness of some regions or countries can make integration into integrated national markets for key inputs, such as fuel, impossible. For example, the State of Hawaii has some of the highest electric rates in the United States, because the cost of shipping fuel to the island system is much higher than, say, the cost of shipping fuel to Midwest generating plants.

---

[28] These differences not only occur across countries but also in companies within the same country.

[29] For example, in some Latin American countries, poor people create financial and safety problems by illegally hooking up to the electric system network. However, it is often difficult or impossible to disconnect these individuals. In some cases, populist politicians prevent disconnections. In other cases, the weakness of the judiciary system can mean that disconnection orders by judges, if they can even be obtained, are not enforced by the police.

All of these factors mean that investment and operating costs are not directly comparable across different areas, regions, and countries. Thus, regulators who want to compare companies efficiently and equitably need to accurately account for all of these sorts of exogenous factors. This is a difficult empirical exercise, at best.

Finally, comparisons of key regulatory inputs, such as estimates of allowed ROE, can create problems when compared across jurisdictions if key differences are not addressed. For example, if Latin American regulators set a firm's ROE based on comparisons of allowed ROE values in other countries, they need to account for differences in business and financial risks, including forecast inflation rates, so-called *country risk* premiums, tax rates, and so forth.[30]

4.8 Chapter Summary

The most important point to take away from this chapter is that the revenue requirement underlies and is an integral component of all three regulatory structures we reviewed. Of these three structures, the most obvious link to revenue requirements is COS regulation. One of the benefits of COS regulation is its straightforwardness. Because it has the fewest arbitrary policy variables, such as adjustments for industry productivity, COS regulation is, in some ways, easier to implement than either PBR or yardstick competition. Alas, that relative simplicity is also the Achilles' heel of COS regulation: the absence of incentives for firms to improve their economic performance and profitability.

PBR mechanisms can correct this defect in COS regulation. Properly structured, PBR mechanisms can align the interests of both customers and investors. Still, undertaking PBR requires periodic assessments of the regulated firm's costs, including an estimate of the initial cost of capital and return on equity. Although sharing mechanisms and off-ramps can reduce risks for both regulators and firms, especially when a new PBR mechanism is put into place, they must be designed carefully so as to preserve the very performance incentives on which PBR is based.

Finally, yardstick competition, while attractive in theory, has a sorry record in practice. The unique factors faced by different firms in an industry are extremely difficult to capture accurately in empirical models. As a result, firms can end up suffering because of factors beyond their control. When that occurs, investors flee, ultimately to the detriment of customers.

---

[30] One potential solution is to evaluate rates of change in efficiency between firms, rather than absolute differences in efficiency.

CHAPTER 5
COST MEASUREMENT

5.1 Introduction

The process of establishing regulated prices, which are also called *rates* or *tariffs*, is the *sine qua non* of economic regulation. As we discussed in Chapter 2, if regulators are to achieve economically efficient outcomes based on a firm's fixed and variable costs, they must be able to measure and assign those costs accurately. In theory, the goal of cost estimation and subsequent cost allocation under regulation is to mimic the results of a competitive market. In such markets, goods and services are produced at the lowest cost (called *productive* or *x-efficiency*) and are priced so that consumers reap the greatest value from them (called *allocative efficiency*).[1] In this chapter, we discuss how the major cost components we first identified in Chapter 3 are measured, and we examine the controversies surrounding that measurement.[2]

5.2 Why Regulators Measure Costs

No method that sets a regulated firm's prices can progress without first measuring operating and capital costs. Equally as important, cost measurement is the only way for a firm's investors to measure their returns. In Chapter 4 we described the three sets of rules used to determine an overall structure of regulated prices (see Figure 4-1).

The price *structure*, however, contains more than just prices themselves. To see this, consider Figure 5-1. Whereas a regulated firm's tariff structure always includes prices and service terms, the overall services regime typically includes other provisions, such as policies on the

---

[1] Additionally, regulation is often concerned with meeting equity goals, such as "universal service." For example, a utility's rural residential customers are generally not charged more for electric service than its urban customers, even though the fixed costs per rural customer tend to be higher. In the U.S., this cost allocation is consistent with the goals established by Congress in the Rural Electrification Act of 1936, which sought to make electricity available to all. Of course, it would be naïve to ignore the pervasive influence of politics on some regulatory outcomes. Just how pervasive this influence is depends on whom you ask.

[2] Although some may find this chapter daunting in both its length and some of its more technical aspects, we have relegated more technical material to text boxes and an appendix. Readers who wish to skip these materials can do so and still understand the concepts covered.

disconnection of nonpaying customers, the negotiation of rates with individual customers to encourage economic development, and other special services, such as access to a firm's transmission and distribution network.

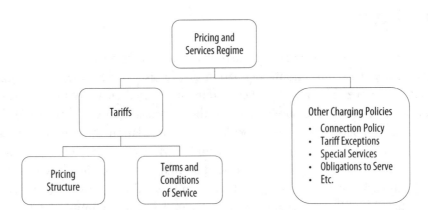

Figure 5-1: The Framework for Developing Regulated Services and Prices

Any good regulatory model must be able to transform costs into just and reasonable prices, while offering investors a return commensurate with the financial risks they bear. End results, however, are not enough. A good model ought to clearly specify <u>how</u> costs are transformed into a set of tariffs and prices. That sort of clarity benefits everyone—customers, investors, and regulators. Firms and investors are protected against capricious regulatory changes, while customers benefit not only from lower financing costs, but also from a measure of fairness that assures consumers that the rates they pay are truly just and reasonable. Cost measurement thus provides a foundation for the entire regulatory process.[3]

Well-designed methodologies typically transform costs into regulated prices using a five-step process:[4]

1. **Set the revenue requirement** (discussed in Chapter 3).

2. **Functionalize costs.** Regulated companies typically provide many services. Ensuring that those costs are allocated properly across those services requires assigning them to the correct bins.

---

[3] As we discussed before in Chapter 3, a consistent and sensible system of accounts is also needed to calculate cost-based tariffs.

[4] Not all pricing methodologies follow this five-step procedure. In Chapter 7 we discuss what those other methodologies are and why they do not follow this procedure.

3. **Classify costs.** Functionalized costs still are classified into fixed and variable components and specific customer costs. This allows regulators to establish different price components, including ready-to-serve (per customer) and volumetric (per-kWh or per-Btu) charges.

4. **Allocate costs.** The now functionalized and classified costs are allocated among predetermined customer classes.

5. **Set rates and tariffs.** Using specific *billing determinants*, regulated prices are calculated for each customer class.

Figure 5-2 summarizes this five-step procedure.

Figure 5-2: The Five-Step Procedure to Calculate Regulated Prices

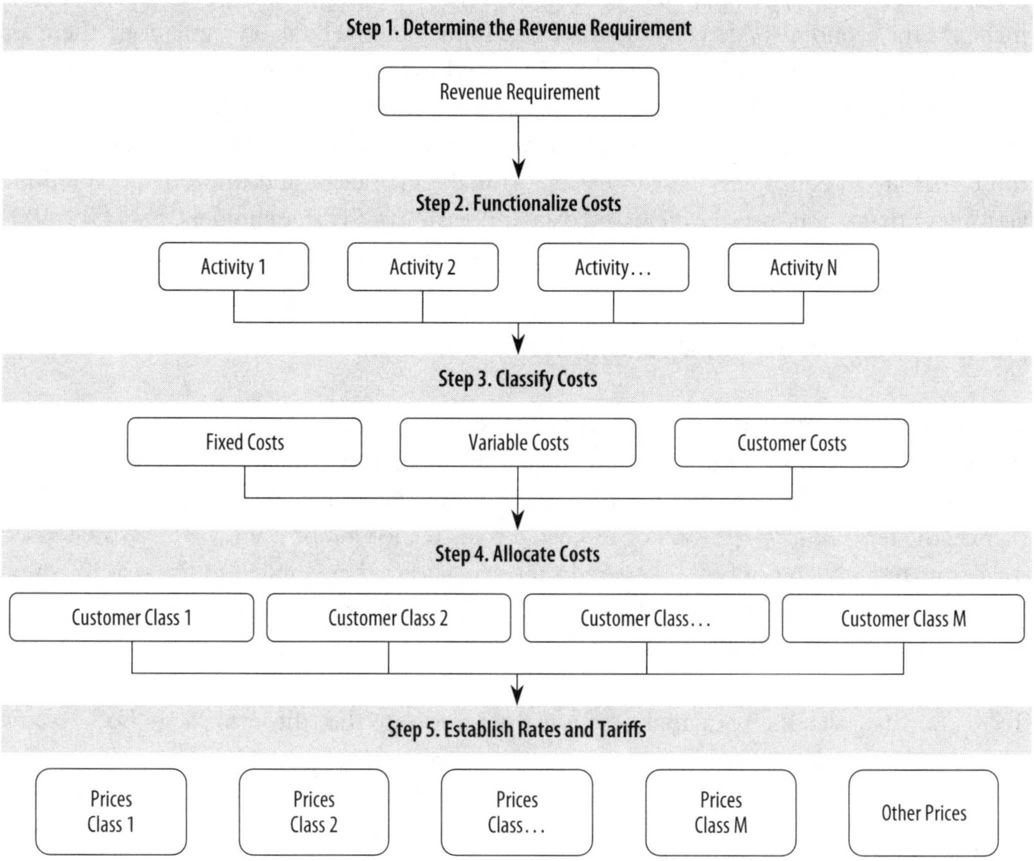

```
Step 1. Determine the Revenue Requirement
            Revenue Requirement
                    ↓
Step 2. Functionalize Costs
   Activity 1    Activity 2    Activity...    Activity N
                    ↓
Step 3. Classify Costs
   Fixed Costs    Variable Costs    Customer Costs
                    ↓
Step 4. Allocate Costs
   Customer Class 1   Customer Class 2   Customer Class...   Customer Class M
                    ↓
Step 5. Establish Rates and Tariffs
   Prices      Prices      Prices       Prices        Other Prices
   Class 1     Class 2     Class...     Class M
```

Although Figure 5-2 appears to be a set of independent and sequential steps, in practice these steps are somewhat interdependent. For example, determining the allowed costs that make up the revenue requirement (Step 1) often depends on identifying the relevant services the firm provides (Step 2). Moreover, regulators will sometimes need to allocate costs and revenues to any unregulated services an otherwise regulated firm provides (Step 4) to determine the revenue requirement (Step 1). Otherwise, regulated customers may pay too much, and competing providers of those unregulated services may be placed at a competitive disadvantage.

In the remainder of this chapter, as well as the next three, we will follow the five steps shown in Figure 5-2. The rest of this chapter deals with Step 1—setting the revenue requirement.

Recall from Chapter 3 that a firm's revenue requirement underlies all regulatory regimes. It equals the sum total of the regulated firm's operating expenses, tax payments, an allowance for depreciation, and, perhaps most controversial, a *fair rate of return* on its capital investment. As the economist Alfred Kahn discussed in his seminal book on regulation,[5] there are a number of reasons regulators must be concerned with estimating these costs accurately. Most importantly, regulators want to decrease the risk that a firm will (1) conceal profits by exaggerating its costs, (2) recover excessive depreciation charges, (3) incur costs beyond those that are in consumers' best interests, (4) make inefficient and imprudent capital investments that unnecessarily increase costs and earnings for shareholders, and (5) misallocate costs between regulated and unregulated activities or affiliates.

Practical Aspects of the Known and Measurable Principle

In Chapter 3, we introduced the concepts of the *test year*, the *rate year*, and the *known and measurable* standard. To summarize, a regulated firm's total costs are usually (but not always) calculated over a 12-month period called the *test year*, which may be based on historic costs (hence, the term *historic test year*) or projected costs (called a *future test year*). In some cases, regulators require a bit of both. Generally, those costs are then applied to the year in which new rates will take effect, called the *rate year*, although those costs can also be used to establish a multiyear rate path.

To recover its costs, the regulated firm must demonstrate that those costs are both *known and measurable* and *prudent*. Some costs, such as wages and salaries or fuel for maintenance trucks, are driven by competitive market forces that the firm has little or no control over. Other costs, such as corporate taxes, are set by federal, state, and local governments. Still

---

[5] Alfred Kahn, *The Economics of Regulation: Principles and Institutions*, vol. I, (New York: Wiley, 1970), 27–28.

other costs, such as advertising and investments in new plant and equipment, are determined by the firm itself. Finally, some costs, including annual depreciation, the allowed rate of return on rate base, and payments on customer deposits, are set by regulators.

The *known and measurable* standard means that, regardless of whether the regulated firm has control over a particular cost or not, to be included as part of the firm's revenue requirement, costs must have a realistic basis. For example, suppose a firm's COS study includes an additional $10 million in costs of wages and salaries in the rate year. To be accepted as known and measurable, that salary increase must have a realistic basis. Justifying an increase by telling regulators, "We think we will hire 30 or 40 new employees next year," will likely not meet the known and measurable standard. We say "likely" because there is no single definition of "known and measurable," and different regulators apply the standard with different levels of rigor.

Regulated firms earn a return on their rate base. That return is called the firm's *cost of capital*. Under long-established legal precedents that we discuss in Section 5.5, a regulated firm must be allowed to earn a fair rate of return on its capital investment, as long as those investments are *prudent* and *used and useful*. Of course, what is "fair" cannot be measured directly, and for this reason establishing a regulated rate of return for regulated firms can be, and often is, controversial. Moreover, as wholesale energy markets have become more volatile, both as a result of market forces, and even "volatile" regulation, establishing a fair rate of return has become more complex. Finally, determining whether a firm's investments are prudent and used and useful has, in the past, been another source of regulatory and legal controversy, which we discuss in Section 5.4.

A regulated firm does not earn any return on its operating costs, because those costs are treated as current expenses. In other words, a firm is entitled to a return of its prudently incurred operating costs, not a return on them. This rate treatment also applies to electric companies that purchase generation from other firms. In the United States, such purchased power agreements (PPAs) have become far more important as the electric industry has restructured. However, as we will discuss, PPAs also raise interesting and controversial issues as to the risks regulated utilities bear when they enter into such contracts. This is because financial institutions treat such contracts as debt instruments, much as if the utility issued bonds. This so-called *debt-equivalency* issue raises difficult questions with regard to the overall COS, because what may be a lower-cost purchased source of generation may raise a utility's overall cost of capital.[6]

---

6   A discussion of debt-equivalency is, alas, beyond the scope of this book.

The Role of Regulatory Accounting

An accurate set of accounting books is the principal tool that individuals and interested institutions rely on to understand regulated firms' operating results, financial position, and cash flows of a business enterprise.[7] For example, accurate accounting data are required for a firm's management to coordinate both day-to-day operations and to plan for the future. Similarly, suppliers and creditors are interested in determining whether a firm has the financial capacity to pay for the services and supplies it purchases and for the money it borrows. And, investors need accurate accounting data to evaluate financial risks and growth prospects so they can determine whether to buy, sell, or hold a firm's securities.

For regulators, a good accounting system is just as crucial. Regulators must be able to determine whether a regulated firm's costs are just and reasonable, to say nothing of known and measurable. The cost accounting system for a regulated firm should include detailed data and information reflecting operating and maintenance expenses, depreciation accruals, and income and property taxes. Moreover, regulators need accurate data on a firm's capital investments, which establish its rate base and the return earned on that rate base. Without that data, regulators cannot establish a firm's overall revenue requirement, apportion costs between classes of customers efficiently and equitably, or, ultimately, set rates.

Regulatory accounting is a formal, standardized approach to maintaining firms' books that regulators use for rate-making purposes. The same accounting records are used for statutory and tax accounts, but for three different purposes: to determine whether the company is profitable, to compute taxes owed to the government, and to provide information to the regulators. This is shown in Figure 5-3.

Figure 5-3: The Three Sets of Books

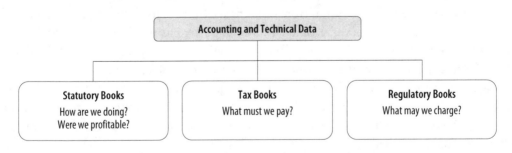

---

[7] Although there are well-known cases, such as Enron, in which individuals have used "creative" accounting to mislead investors and regulators, our focus here is on the role of honest and accurate accounting.

In the United States, the need for accurate data led to the design of accounting systems called the *Uniform System of Accounts,* which are used by all public utilities. Several institutions govern how accounting data are collected and reported. For example, the Financial Accounting Standards Board (FASB) periodically issues "Statements" about certain accounting principles. FASB's *Statement of Financial Accounting Concepts No. 2* specifies that accounting data must be *relevant* and *reliable.* FASB defines relevance as information that can make a difference in a decision. To be relevant, accounting data must also be *timely.* A report on the value of a utility's call options for purchasing electricity, for example, will not be especially useful if the report is provided after all of the options have expired. Thus, for accounting data to be timely, it must be able to affect the decision-making process.

The *reliability* of accounting data arises from the "faithfulness with which it represents what it purports to represent" and an "assurance for the user, which comes through verification, that it has that representational quality."[8] Reliable accounting information must be complete, unbiased, and independently verifiable. Of course, verifiability does not guarantee that an accounting method used is appropriate. Your accountant may be able to replicate how you cheated on your income tax return, but that does not make it appropriate for you to have done so.

Another institution that weighs in on U.S. accounting standards is the Securities and Exchange Commission (SEC). Its "Final Data Quality Assurance Guidelines" provide guidance to assess whether accounting data and information are verifiable, reasonable, and probable, and therefore known and measurable, based on *objectivity* and *reproducibility.*[9] Objectivity means that accounting information is presented in a clear, complete, and unbiased manner, and that the substance of that information is accurate, reliable, and unbiased. Reproducibility means that "influential" information is capable of being substantially reproduced, subject to an acceptable degree of imprecision. Creating numbers out of thin air, therefore, does not meet the reproducibility requirement.

Finally, the American Institute of Certified Public Accountants (AICPA) weighs in with guidance on the "reasonableness" of accounting estimates. This can be particularly important for regulated firms whose forthcoming rate-year revenue requirements depend on estimates of future costs. According to the AICPA, for an estimate to be reasonable, an auditor should be able to (1) identify the data sources used by management in forming assumptions, and (2) assess whether the data and factors are relevant, reliable, and sufficient for their intended purpose. The auditor should also determine whether the assumptions of manage-

---

[8] Financial Accounting Standards Board, *Statement of Financial Accounting Concepts No. 2,* May 1980, 28.

[9] Securities and Exchange Commission, "Final Data Quality Assurance Guidelines," www.sec.gov/about/dataqualityguide.htm (accessed May 18, 2007).

ment are consistent among themselves and with supporting data, and the auditors should be able to test and verify the calculations used by management to convert assumptions and key factors into accounting estimates.

Presuming the regulated firm's books are accurate, the data are used to calculate each component of the firm's revenue requirement. In the remainder of this chapter, we turn to how those calculations are actually performed.

5.3 Estimating and Regulating Operating Costs

We begin our analysis of costs and the revenue requirement with the procedures used to estimate and regulate operating costs, which include wages and salaries, insurance, fuel, rent, maintenance, depreciation, taxes, postage for mailing out bills, and so forth. Some of these costs are influenced by the firm itself; wage and salary costs, for example, depend on how many employees the firm hires. Other costs are driven by market conditions: the local electric distribution utility cannot influence the price of diesel fuel used by its repair trucks, nor can it influence the postage rates that must be paid when sending out customer bills.[10]

Even those costs that are driven by competitive market forces are regulated for several reasons. First, regulators want to ensure that ratepayers are not required to pay for unnecessary or excessive operating costs. Second, even where the regulated firm appears to have no control whatsoever over costs, such as a vertically integrated electric utility that must purchase natural gas for use in its gas-fired generating plants, regulators may want to determine whether the utility has managed those costs prudently, such as by hedging fuel costs in a volatile market.[11]

When it comes to determinations of the *prudence* of those costs, however, the utility is given the benefit of the doubt. In other words, the utility's management is assumed to operate in "good faith" and under a presumption of prudence. Therefore, cost imprudence must be proven affirmatively, rather than the other way around.[12] So, for example, the salaries and benefits the utility pays its employees are assumed to reflect local market conditions, unless shown otherwise.

---

[10] The utility can reduce its billing frequency, of course, but that can raise other issues, such as exacerbating the need for working capital.

[11] Regulators will also want to determine whether the gas-fired generating plant itself, a capital cost, was prudent.

[12] This is equivalent to "innocent until proven guilty."

Operating costs determined by competitive market conditions are usually not subject to extensive regulatory scrutiny, especially if they are truly outside the firm's control. Things become more complicated, however, when arguments ensue as to the extent that such costs really are outside the firm's control.[13] For example, the regulated firm may argue that it cannot influence the cost of health insurance for its employees, because insurance premiums are determined by competitive forces, national trends, and so forth. While this might be true, it might also be the case that the utility pays 100% of its employees' health care premiums, whereas most other firms pay only 80%. In that case, regulators could argue that paying 100% of employees' health insurance premiums is not prudent and disallow the other 20%, thus excluding that fraction from the firm's overall revenue requirement. The regulator's disallowance decision will depend on whether applying a typical standard is reasonable or whether there are specific reasons for the difference, such as a union contract.

> **Actual vs. Budgeted Costs**
>
> Typically, regulators review historic operating costs and the reasonableness of the firm's projections. Not surprisingly, these projections of operating costs can lead to disputes. For example, suppose a regulated firm's current budget for employee wages and salaries equals $40 million. The firm projects this amount to increase next year by the general rate of inflation, which the firm estimates at 5%, leading to an anticipated budget of $42 million. It all sounds perfectly reasonable. However, suppose the firm, while having budgeted $40 million for 500 employees, actually spent only $36 million. What amount should regulators allow in rates? The answer harks back to the known and measurable standard. Since *known and measurable* costs for wages and salaries are $36 million, it would be reasonable to apply an inflation adjustment to that figure, rather than the budget figure of $40 million, unless the firm could demonstrate why its wage and salary expenses would, in fact, increase by $6 million between the test year and the rate year.

Alternative Methods to Estimate Operating Costs

Whereas in the United States regulators rely primarily on historical accounting costs as the basis for estimating and adjusting operating costs, in other countries a more relaxed *known and measurable* standard has led to different approaches to estimating operating costs. For example, Mexico's energy regulator uses multiyear cost trends to forecast future operating costs for regulated natural gas pipelines.

---

[13] Whereas the types of costs that can be included in the cost of service are generally agreed on in the U.S, in other countries with much less regulatory history, heated debates over appropriate costs continue. In Bolivia, for example, there was an intense dispute concerning how much insurance should be purchased by a generating company (regulated under COS) and how much of the resulting insurance premium should be paid by ratepayers. The regulator decided that, although the company could insure generating assets for their market value, ratepayers are required to pay only a fraction of the premium corresponding to the assets' book value.

Other countries use what is called a *model company* approach to estimate operating costs. Similar to yardstick competition, the model company approach estimates a regulated firm's operating costs based on what it would cost an efficient company to provide existing levels of service over time. For a regulated firm, this approach introduces a plenitude of uncertainty. The many unique attributes of firms, which we discussed in Chapter 4, mean that defining a hypothetical standard for efficiency is almost impossible.

Depending on the country where this method is implemented, operating costs are estimated using either a *top-down* approach (in which existing costs are adjusted to implement potential efficiencies) or a *bottom-up* approach (in which a hypothetical organization and its costs are built up for the "efficient" company).[14]

Finally, regulators in several other countries have experimented with sophisticated empirical methods that compare the costs of regulated companies to those of their peers, and then adjust a regulated firm's costs accordingly. The specific techniques include Data Envelope Analysis (DEA), Stochastic Frontier Analysis (SFA), Ordinary Least Squares (OLS), and Corrected OLS (COLS). Although using sophisticated models may make economists' hearts flutter, these empirical techniques have typically resulted in significant reductions to regulated firms' allowed operating costs and called into question the reasonableness of these techniques, despite their outward sophistication.

Model Company

While the top-down model company approach resembles a "relaxed" version of a COS study as performed in the United States, the bottom-up approach is an almost purely theoretical engineering exercise.

As with a typical COS study, the top-down approach starts with a test year. The regulator and the regulated company discuss which cost efficiencies can be achieved by the company and over what time frame. Those efficiencies are then reflected in the overall COS forecast for the regulatory period. The cost efficiencies are based on direct measures that a regulated firm can implement within that regulatory period, such as reducing natural gas pipeline leaks through improved repair programs, or staffing more crews to reduce commercial losses from illegal hook-ups in the electric distribution system.

---

[14] For example, Guatemala has applied the former approach and Peru the latter to their respective electric distribution companies.

The bottom-up approach is far different and far more problematic. The bottom-up approach essentially creates a theoretical company from scratch. It includes the number and types of employees the company will have, the quality of service the company should provide, the operating and maintenance procedures that should be used, and so forth. The approach also creates earnings and revenue penalties that should be applied to encourage regulated companies to achieve the theoretical levels of operating perfection. Although the approach sounds thoroughly objective and fair, practical realities typically intrude. As a result, some model company results resemble nothing so much as a horse designed by committee. Chilean regulators, for example, estimate the model company's costs by taking a weighted average of the costs estimated by consultants hired by the regulator and consultants hired by the regulated company. (For reasons not fully understood, the cost estimates made by the regulators' consultants are always lower than those made by the companies' consultants.)

The most significant problem with the model company approach is that, rather than providing incentives for regulated companies themselves to identify the best opportunities for improving efficiency, the approach directs regulated companies to impose specific efficiencies, often ignoring key company-specific attributes. In essence, the model company approach is similar to the *command-and-control* approach to environmental regulation, and is, ironically, just as inefficient.[15] Worse, in some cases regulators have considered imposing further requirements, such as an X factor productivity adjustment, in addition to model company results. This is clearly wrong, because the efficiency gains that would be required by imposing an X factor are already incorporated into the model company design.

Data Envelope Analysis

Data Envelope Analysis (DEA) uses linear programming techniques to determine an efficient frontier, or "envelope," that describes different levels of costs and output levels. Once the envelope is determined, a DEA score (or "efficiency" score) is calculated for the company under consideration. A company on the frontier receives a score of 100. A company within the frontier receives a score below 100. This is shown in Figure 5-4.

---

[15] We discuss command-and-control environmental regulation and its impact on company costs in Chapter 11.

Fundamentals of Energy Regulation

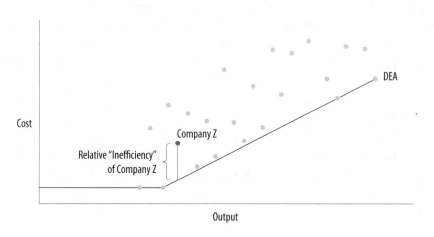

Figure 5-4: Data Envelope Analysis

Rather than relying purely on theoretical constructs like the model company approach, however, DEA calculates a cost frontier based on a sample of similar firms. In the figure, the envelope is estimated based on the total sales (kilowatt-hours) and costs per kilowatt-hour sold of 26 companies, A through Z. Regulators would fit an envelope curve based on the cost structures of these firms and then examine the relative position of the company under review (Company Z in the figure). The vertical distance from the envelope curve equals the relative inefficiency of Company Z; the larger the vertical distance, the more inefficient Company Z is judged to be.

The main problem with DEA is too-small sample sizes used to estimate the envelope itself. The number of firms available in any one country to perform this analysis will always be limited. Moreover, as we discussed in Chapter 4, there are many attributes that underlie a firm's cost structure, including its location, the legal system in which it operates, the tax structure, ownership, and broad economic conditions. As a result, explaining operational differences between firms in any meaningful way requires using numerous firms in any empirical study.[16] This prevents DEA from being used effectively. Additionally, any meaningful DEA study must consider the interdependence of operating and capital costs. Yet, typically, DEA studies focus only on operating costs. When that happens, the envelope that is estimated will be biased. For example, suppose a company performs more preventive maintenance than its peers in order to reduce capital expenditures on equipment replacement. If a DEA study focuses only on O&M expenses, that company will appear relatively inefficient compared to its peers, even though it may, in fact, be the most efficient firm of

---

[16] This is technically a "degrees of freedom" issue. Too many variables and too few firms lead to meaningless analysis.

all. Moreover, if DEA imposes an efficiency standard on the frontier shown in Figure 5-4, it should also adjust the firm's investment return to reflect better-than-average efficiency. In other words, it is inconsistent for regulators to impose an efficiency standard for a regulated firm based on absolute efficiency, while only providing a return to investors based on the operating efficiency of the "average" firm.[17]

Ordinary Least Squares and Corrected OLS

OLS and COLS are two other econometric (i.e., regression model) approaches used to estimate a firm's costs in the same way that a DEA estimates an efficient cost frontier.[18] The difference, however, is that OLS and COLS do not estimate relative efficiency levels like DEA. Instead, these two methods attempt to estimate a firm's operating costs based on factors such as the number of customers, customers' total electric consumption, miles of transmission lines the firm must maintain, and so forth.

For example, in a 2006 study, the Panamanian electric regulator estimated a series of regressions based on data from U.S. electric companies to obtain cost coefficients. The regulator then applied those coefficients to each of Panama's electric distribution companies to estimate their operating costs and revenue requirement. Administrative costs were estimated as a function of each company's peak demand and the number of clients served, and they used the formula that the regression analysis showed was most accurate in explaining administrative costs for U.S. electric companies.[19]

COLS keeps the same slope as that calculated by OLS, but it modifies the intercept term to ensure that no company has costs below the fitted COLS line. In other words, COLS is a regression technique where the supposedly most "efficient" company defines the efficient operating cost level. Thus, COLS attempts to merge the results of a DEA study with an OLS estimate of a firm's costs as shown in Figure 5-5.

---

[17] This is another example of an *asymmetric return*.

[18] A basic regression model works by positing a relationship between variables. Consumer demand of electricity, for example, depends on the price of electricity, the price of fuel inputs, weather, and so forth. Since no model is perfect, all regression models have error terms, which can be thought of as bins for all of the random factors that can affect a model's results. OLS regressions assume these error terms average out to zero and have the overall look of a bell-shaped curve (or, technically, independently distributed with a normal distribution). If that assumption turns out to be wrong, the regression model may be biased. For an introduction to OLS regression models directed to lawyers and policymakers, see Alan Sykes, "An Introduction to Regression Analysis," Working Paper 020, John M. Olin Program in Law and Economics (University of Chicago), October 1993.

[19] Autoridad Nacional de los Servicios Públicos (ANSP), Resolution AN No. 435-ELEC, Appendix A, (December 1, 2006).

Figure 5-5: OLS and COLS

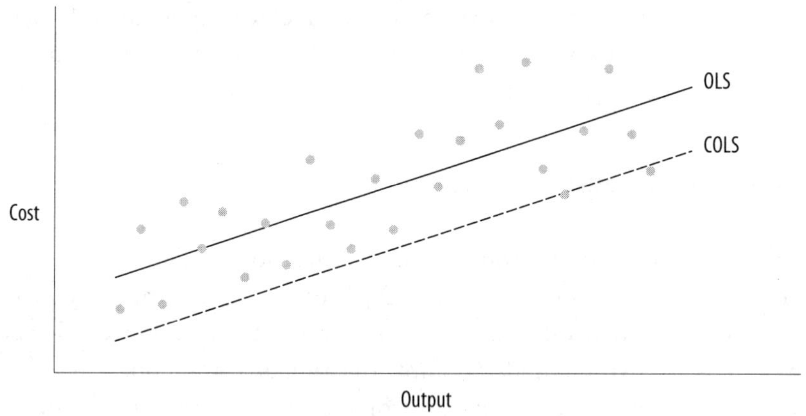

Cost (y-axis) vs *Output* (x-axis), with scatter points, an OLS line and a dashed COLS line below it.

While the COLS approach sounds appealing, the assumptions that underlie its use typically do not hold, meaning the resulting cost estimates have little relevance.[20] As a result, OLS and COLS equations are easily misspecified and typically fail to capture the many different characteristics of companies.

Stochastic Frontier Analysis

Stochastic Frontier Analysis (SFA) is yet another empirical technique to estimate an *efficiency frontier*. SFA breaks the regression error term into two components: one that captures all the (random) exogenous factors beyond the control of the regulated firm, and another that is always positive and measures the inefficiency of the regulated firm. The problems raised by this approach are exactly the same as those occurring under OLS and COLS: too few samples of companies to develop reasonable results and a priori specifications of how firms are inefficient. Figure 5-6 shows the result of estimating SFA with the same data used for Figures 5-4 and 5-5.

---

[20] If the original OLS estimates are wrong, then so too will be any COLS adjustments. Moreover, both models assume that all of the data used to develop the cost estimates are measured accurately. However, because accounting cost data are not always correct, the resulting regression estimates can be worthless.

Figure 5-6: Stochastic Frontier Analysis

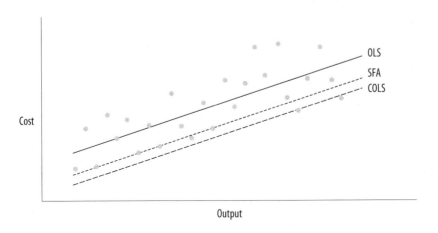

Moreover, SFA practitioners must specify just what those two components of the error term look like, and the assumptions they make can greatly affect the estimation results.[21] Ultimately, the amount of data torturing required to develop the "right" model specification and error term distributions defeats the entire purpose of an SFA exercise.

Depreciation Costs[22]

A major component of operating costs is *depreciation*.[23] Depreciation costs are estimated and collected from customers to account for the effects of wear and tear on capital equipment or to account for equipment that otherwise reaches the end of its economic lifetime. Coupled with the arcane methods used to estimate depreciation rates, estimation of prudent depreciation costs can be contentious.

As we discussed in Chapter 3, there are three broad definitions of depreciation depending on the context in which they are considered: (1) the actual physical condition of a property, including operational safety, required maintenance, technical obsolescence, and ability to provide the services for which it is designed; (2) the change in value of the services a

---

[21] For example, error terms may be *heteroskedastic*, which means their size is not purely random, but, instead, that they are related to operating costs.

[22] A useful reference for understanding how depreciation costs are calculated for public utilities is *Introduction to Depreciation and Net Salvage of Public Utility Plant and Equipment*, which was published jointly by the Edison Electric Institute and the American Gas Association in May 2003 (EEI/AGA 2003).

[23] In some countries, actual depreciation is not considered directly in the revenue requirement. Instead, an annuity on the rate base is calculated including the return on capital and an amortization allowance that replaces actual depreciation.

property provides over time; and (3) simply a cost of doing business. Under the third definition, which is most relevant for rate regulation, depreciation implies a systematic allocation of plant and equipment costs, e.g., for generators, pipelines, poles and wires, trucks, etc., (called *utility plant*) that are recovered over time, consistent with their *useful lives*. This is done so the regulated firm can recover the cost of its capital investment.[24]

How useful lives are estimated is one source of controversy. An engineer will base useful life on whether equipment can operate safely, if at all. An economist will want to know whether the equipment has any value. An accountant will want to ensure that the costs associated with the equipment, whether to keep it running or to bulldoze it to the ground, are tracked accurately. Loathe as economists and engineers may be willing to admit, in establishing the operating cost component of cost of service, it is the accountant's perspective that is most important, even though the physical condition of an asset and its economic lifetime are also factors that affect depreciation costs.

Recall from Chapter 3 that a regulated firm's *rate base* (RB) equals the depreciated value of utility plant and equipment. This is just *original cost* (i.e., what the firm paid at the time it was purchased) less the aggregate (called *accrued*) depreciation. Thus, we can write

$$RB = OC - BR \qquad (5\text{-}1)$$

where OC is original cost and BR equals total accrued depreciation (called *book reserve*). For example, if an asset's original cost was $100 and the firm has depreciated $20 of the asset, then the book reserve is $20 and the rate base is $80.

Over time, as the firm's existing plant and equipment age, the depreciated value of that equipment decreases, just like the depreciated value of a car decreases over time. As the firm's rate base decreases, it earns fewer total dollars in return on its capital investment.

If the firm's aggregate depreciation expense were not included in its rates, then eventually, when all of that plant and equipment were fully depreciated, the utility would earn no return. Moreover, if the number of years over which plant and equipment were depreciated exactly matched the physical depreciation of the plant and equipment, then the firm would not have the necessary capital to replace that plant and equipment. Ideally, therefore, accruing an annual depreciation expense and recovering that expense in rates provides a regulated firm with the funds necessary to replace plant and equipment at the end of their useful lives.

---

[24] This is different than earning a return on that capital investment.

Typically, depreciation expenses for regulated electric and natural gas entities are estimated and recovered using the *straight-line* method. The total undepreciated amount of an investment (less *net salvage*) is recovered over an estimate of its lifetime in equal increments.[25] So, if the undepreciated value of an investment is $10 million, and we expect it to last another 10 years, then the annual depreciation amount (ignoring net salvage values) will be $10 million ÷ 10 years = $1 million per year. Typically, the most contentious issue for depreciation estimates is how those lifetimes are calculated, i.e., whether they are based on the expected life from the time an asset is first installed or on the asset's expected remaining life.

Estimating Average Life

One of two types of lifetime estimates is usually constructed to determine depreciation costs. These types are *average service life* (ASL) and *average remaining life* (ARL). ASL refers to the number of years an asset is expected to physically function from the time it is installed.[26] A large hydroelectric dam, for example, may have an ASL of over 100 years, while a typical natural gas pipeline compressor may have an ASL of only 15 years. ARL refers to the estimated remaining life of an asset, given its current age and condition. A natural gas pipeline that is 30 years old, for example, may have an ARL of 30 years, while a local electric utility's wood distribution poles, with an average age of 30 years, may have an ARL of only 10 years.

For the benefit of economists, a third factor, called *economic life*, can also enter into some average life estimates. To understand economic life, suppose a company must decide whether to construct a new natural gas pipeline. To make a decision, management will consider a number of factors. These include the likely revenues the company will earn transporting natural gas. Those revenues will depend, in large part, on how full the company can keep the pipeline, and that will be influenced by the number of competing pipelines and the total quantity of natural gas available to transport. If the available supply of natural gas decreases over time, eventually the pipeline will not be able to cover its operating costs, much less its capital costs, and will shut down. The time when the pipeline would be expected to shut down determines its economic life.[27]

---

[25] *Net salvage* is defined as *gross salvage* (what an asset can be sold for when scrapped), less the cost of actually scrapping the asset. So, if the market value for a natural gas pipeline's old cast iron pipe is $100,000 (the gross salvage value), and it costs the pipeline $50,000 to scrap the pipe, the net salvage value will equal $50,000.

[26] The exception to this is when an asset's *economic life* is expected to be less than its physical life. This is discussed below.

[27] Some argue that physical shutdown does not determine economic life or death. Rather, they argue that simple unprofitability does. The problem with this argument, at least in our view, is that profitability has different definitions and is affected by operating decisions, including setting rates.

Estimating economic lives is fraught with uncertainty. Again, consider the natural gas pipeline example. The supply of natural gas available for transport will be determined by many factors, including the demand and price of natural gas, the amount of natural gas that can be extracted from existing wells, technological improvements in drilling new wells, the availability of liquefied natural gas, and so forth. Much uncertainty surrounds each of those factors individually, and there is significant interaction among them as well. Moreover, while regulators typically cap the rates that can be charged by a pipeline, there is nothing to prevent the pipeline owner from offering lower rates and thereby increasing the demand for its services.

Depreciation Mechanics

Because depreciation methods are arcane, the mechanics of actually calculating depreciation can be tedious. Tedious or not, however, it is important to understand the basics of how depreciation rates are calculated, since depreciation rates can have a significant impact on regulated rates.

Typically, depreciation rates are first calculated in percentage terms and are then converted into absolute dollar terms for estimating the impacts on operating costs and rate base. There are two general ways of calculating depreciation rates: the *whole-life* technique, which is based on ASL, and the *remaining-life* technique, which is based on ARL.

The whole-life technique calculates the annual depreciation rate, D%, as:

$$D\% = \frac{100\% - (NS \div O)}{ASL} \tag{5-2}$$

where:

O = original cost;

NS = net salvage cost (equals gross salvage less removal costs); and

ASL = average service life.

Translated into English, the annual percentage depreciation rate is based on the original cost of the asset, less the percentage of that original cost estimated to be net salvage, divided by the asset's expected service life. So, suppose an asset costs $100,000 when installed. Its gross salvage is expected to be $50,000, but the cost of removal is expected to be $40,000. The asset is expected to be in service for 10 years from the time it is installed. Then,

$$D\% = \frac{100\% - \left[\left(\$50{,}000 - \$40{,}000\right) \div \$100{,}000\right]}{10} = \frac{90\%}{10} = 9\% \text{ per year}$$

The disadvantage of calculating depreciation using the whole-life technique is that, as the asset ages and its physical condition deteriorates, its average remaining life may not correspond closely to the calculated depreciation rate. For example, you might have computed an annual depreciation rate of 10% for your car based on an ASL of 10 years. However, after several years of too-fast driving on bad roads, your car's remaining life may be much shorter. If you do not adjust the depreciation rate for this fact, your car will wear out long before it is fully depreciated. For this reason, depreciation rates are usually calculated on a going-forward basis based on the average remaining lifetimes of the firm's assets.

Under the straight-line, remaining-life approach, the annual percentage depreciation rate, D%, is calculated as follows:

$$D\% = \frac{100\% - (BR \div O) - (NS \div O)}{ARL} \tag{5-3}$$

where:

O = original cost;

BR = book reserve, i.e., the amount of depreciation that has already been accounted for by the firm;

NS = net salvage cost, i.e., the cost of removing equipment, less the revenues obtained from selling it off as scrap; and

ARL = average remaining life.

Therefore, the depreciation rate under the straight-line, remaining-life approach for the first year is calculated as follows:

$$D\% = \frac{100\% - (0 \div \$100{,}000) - \left[\left(\$50{,}000 - \$40{,}000\right) \div \$100{,}000\right]}{10} = \frac{90\%}{10} = 9\% \text{ per year}$$

The calculation for the second year is:

$$D\% = \frac{100\% - (\$9{,}000 \div \$100{,}000) - \left[\left(\$50{,}000 - \$40{,}000\right) \div \$100{,}000\right]}{9} = \frac{81\%}{9} = 9\% \text{ per year}$$

and so forth.

In other words, the depreciation rate equals the net undepreciated value, accounting for *net salvage* costs (i.e., the value of salvaged equipment less the cost of removal), divided by the expected years of remaining life.

Estimating net salvage costs is another potentially contentious issue. In depreciation studies, care must be taken when estimating net salvage. It is tempting to base future salvage costs on past experience. However, historic salvage costs may have little to do with salvage costs at the end of an asset's useful life. Again, a natural gas pipeline provides a good example. It is not uncommon for portions of a pipeline to be replaced, for example, when relocating a pipeline to avoid a new highway. In that case, the portion of the pipeline that is to be relocated is dug up and installed elsewhere. However, when a pipeline is permanently retired, it may be plugged and left in the ground. If so, the salvage costs associated with past relocation and replacement are unlikely to be the same as the salvage costs that will be incurred at retirement. For this reason, many regulators require firms to perform detailed salvage studies that provide accurate estimates of the salvage costs associated with retirement.

Actuarial Methods

To estimate ARL, depreciation studies typically rely on what are called *actuarial methods*.[28] Actuarial methods are based on analysis of past, recorded experience to project future events. In the context of a depreciation study, past experience about the lives of different types of equipment is used to project remaining life, much as an insurance company's actuaries will predict your lifespan based on your current age and your health. The fundamental premise of the actuarial method is that the past is an accurate predictor of the future. A secondary premise is that the experience of a large number of assets (or individuals, in the case of a life insurance actuary) will tend to "average out" random individual deviations.

The actuarial method is most useful when there is a long history of plant additions and retirements. That history allows regulators to determine how equipment has "aged" in the past and, presuming that past is prologue, how it will continue to age in the future. In situations where there are few, or no, actual observed equipment retirements, actuarial methods cannot reliably be used. In those cases, regulators can either use simulation models that "fit" plant balance data to known retirement patterns (such as Iowa Curves),[29] or they can rely

---

[28] For a discussion of other methods used to estimate depreciation, see EEI/AGA 2003, *supra* note 22. For the benefit of interested readers, the appendix to this chapter provides several sample calculations of depreciation *survivor curves*, which are used to determine average lives. In the early twentieth century, researchers at Iowa State University developed a set of 18 different survivor curves to explain the rates at which numerous types of equipment fail over time. These survivor curves, known as the *Iowa Curves*, are used today by almost all U.S. regulators to determine depreciation costs. An example of an Iowa Curve is shown in the appendix to this chapter.

[29] The *simulated plant record* method, for example, attempts to duplicate year-by-year plant account balances using a series of simulated balances developed based on the assumption that each year's actual additions were subsequently retired in accordance with the pattern demonstrated by the particular Iowa Curve used. The Iowa Curve that results in a set of simulated plant balances most closely matching actual year-to-year plant balances is used to determine ASL or ARL and, hence, depreciation rates.

on experience at other utilities gathered from survey data. For example, if natural gas pipe typically has been found to have a 60-year ASL in other rate cases, regulators might assume that such equipment will have that same 60-year ASL in a case at hand.

Depreciation and the Trade-Off Between Current and Future Ratepayers

One of the curiosities about the effects of depreciation on regulated rates results from the basic revenue requirement equation. Recall that the revenue requirement is the sum of operating costs plus the return earned on the depreciated value of the firm's undepreciated rate base. As current-year depreciation increases, total current-year operating expenses increase, and the return on investment decreases. Regardless of the depreciation period, aggregate depreciation is always equal to the total investment, I. The effect of a higher annual depreciation rate, therefore, is to "front-load" the firm's total revenue requirements.[30]

Figure 5-7, for example, compares two cases in which a firm's capital investment is depreciated: over 10 years and over 20 years. The initial capital investment is $200,000. Nondepreciation-related operating costs are assumed to equal $10,000 per year and to increase at the rate of inflation. As can be seen, the 10-year depreciation schedule results in a larger revenue requirement for the first 10 years, which is followed by a large drop. Under the 20-year depreciation schedule, rates are lower for the first 10 years than under the 10-year depreciation schedule. The effect of the lower 20-year depreciation rate, therefore, is to shift the overall burden of costs from current to future ratepayers by shifting cost recovery further into the future. This trade-off between current and future ratepayers is one of the fundamental aspects of establishing just and reasonable rates.

---

[30] Depreciation rates also have tax implications. For a discussion, see Alfred Kahn, *supra* note 5, at 32–34.

Fundamentals of Energy Regulation

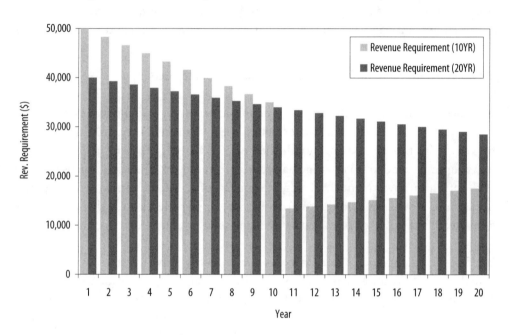

Figure 5-7: Effect of Depreciation Rate on Revenue Requirement

An interesting question in selecting depreciation rates, therefore, is whether a firm should prefer shorter or longer depreciation schedules. The *net present value* (NPV) of overall depreciation costs and the firm's revenue requirement remain the same, regardless of the depreciation schedule. However, different depreciation rates lead to different present values for the firm's *return on investment*, in other words, overall earnings. Specifically, the firm's total earnings are lower under the shorter, 10-year depreciation schedule than under the longer, 20-year schedule by almost 40%; thus, for this example, by choosing a shorter depreciation schedule, the firm sacrifices about 40% of its investment income in exchange for recovering 10% greater revenues. However, many firms seek to maximize depreciation rates in their rate filings, while consumer advocacy groups often seek to minimize depreciation. A higher depreciation rate translates into less income tax paid in the earlier years and a higher cash flow up front, even though the earnings levels are lower (the amount of depreciation is added to net income when calculating the free cash flow available). Additional reasons may stem from both uncertainty regarding future regulatory treatment of the firm's capital assets and high discount rates that encourage "bird in the hand" decisions.

5.4 Estimating and Regulating the Rate Base

We have seen how revenue requirements are based on a regulated firm's operating expenses, including depreciation expenses associated with its capital investments and a return on the undepreciated remainder, which forms the rate base. In this section, we address how regulators evaluate the elements of a firm's rate base and determine the return earned on that rate base. Specifically, how do regulators determine whether a firm has made wise capital investments, which the firm's ratepayers will be expected to pay for under the regulatory compact?

From a historic standpoint, the legal battles over rate base have been extremely important, because they have established a number of precedents for answering a critical question: how do regulators measure the "value" of regulated investments to determine whether the costs of those investments are "just and reasonable"? This question, in turn, underlies the basis for determining whether investments are prudent, which is the ultimate determinant of whether a regulated firm receives compensation for its investments.

Defining Value

Value seems like a straightforward concept. Indeed, for an unregulated firm, the value of its investments is whatever the market says those investments are worth. Not so for a regulated firm, where the value of investments is determined by the regulators themselves. Further complicating the problem is that regulators have used, and continue to use, different concepts of value. Nevertheless, in establishing a regulated firm's rate base and, hence, the overall dollar return on its capital investment, only a few issues are of critical importance in defining and estimating value.

The value of a capital investment, such as a natural gas pipeline, can be broken down into two parts. First, value can be thought of as what it actually cost to build or purchase the investment, plus the cost of subsequent capital additions. So, if a pipeline originally cost $100 million to build in 1970, its *actual* or *original cost value* is $100 million. Second, if the firm adds new equipment over time and replaces some of the associated pipeline equipment, then the *book value* will be the cost of all of the equipment, including the subsequent equipment additions, less accrued depreciation.

Value can also be defined based on *replacement* or *reproduction cost*. These are two quite different concepts. Reproduction cost is the cost of rebuilding existing plant with substantially identical new plant. Replacement cost is the cost of replacing the present output of services using a plant of modern configuration.[31]

Which value measure makes more economic sense? The choice depends on competing factors: efficiency, objectivity, consistency with legal precedent, ability to assure investors of the safety of their capital and thus attract more of it, ease of understanding, and consistency with underlying bookkeeping and tax practices. For unregulated firms, replacement cost is the better measure, because a competitive market bases the value of an asset not on what it cost to build, but on the expected net present value of the cash flows that will arise from the asset's use. The economic value of an asset has nothing to do with its original cost, as anyone who has an antiquated personal computer collecting dust can attest.

With a regulated firm, however, original cost makes more economic sense when you consider the context in which those costs are used. First, and most importantly, under the regulatory compact, firms are exchanging an ability to collect their costs, including a fair return on investment, for the provision of service to all customers. The fact that the original cost of the assets may be significantly different than the current market value of the assets is immaterial.[32]

Second, determining replacement cost requires determining what the replacement will be and how it will be replaced. For example, suppose you own a 20-year-old personal computer, for which you paid $3,000. What is its replacement cost? It is probably impossible to replace it with an equivalent computer, because the processor, disk drives, etc., are utterly obsolete. The equivalent amount of computing power is probably less than that in the disposable calculator the bank gives you for opening a checking account. The "how" of replacement cost reflects the impossibility of reproducing the conditions that existed when the plant was constructed. A 40-year-old, coal-fired power plant not only has different technology than a modern plant, but the construction techniques and equipment used to build modern plants today are entirely different. The cost of borrowing may also be much different today than it was 40 years ago, and so forth.

---

[31] Another value, known as *fair value*, was an arbitrary estimate between original cost and replacement cost. Regulators began using "fair value" in the 1890s, and the U.S. Supreme Court developed what came to be known as the "Fair Value" Doctrine in a decision it issued in *Smyth v. Ames*, 169 U.S. 466 (1898). As we will discuss in the next section on prudent investment, the Court later abandoned the Fair Value Doctrine, first in favor of replacement costs and then on an "end-results" basis that remains in effect to this day.

[32] FERC uses original cost as the basis for regulated asset valuation. Most state utility regulators do too, although there are a few states, such as Indiana, where either fair value or replacement cost is used.

Nevertheless, despite the appeal of using original cost, the actual choice of cost concept used for ratemaking purposes depends on several issues: how depreciation is treated, how inflation is accounted for, and whether the assets (some of which may be very old) are efficient, given the current nature of the services provided.[33]

In general, the "original book cost" (or net investment) standard for utility capital valuation measures rate base by adding up the original book cost of all capital assets and then subtracting all of the accumulated depreciation, regardless of how that depreciation has been recorded in the firm's account books. The terminology surrounding the concept is a bit varied, with the terms "historical cost," "prudent investment," and "new investment" all being used somewhat interchangeably in various jurisdictions to refer generally to the same concept. Because the value of assets so defined equals their relatively unambiguous book value (or the value as measured on the balance sheet of the company in question), original cost is relatively uncontentious and, hence, is an attractive measure to use in rate determinations.

> **FERC Trended Original Cost (TOC) Valuation**
>
> In 1985, FERC adopted a one-time alternative valuation method known as *Trended Original Cost* (TOC) to estimate rate base for oil pipelines.[34] In the case of the initial rate base for oil pipelines, oil pipeline owners wanted the value set to the most recent replacement value, but shippers using those pipelines wanted value set to original cost less depreciation. FERC compromised between these two different points of view and developed the TOC methodology. Under TOC, FERC allowed oil pipelines, just that one time, to restate book value from original cost less depreciation (net book value) to a weighted average between net book value and reproduction cost net of depreciation.[35] The weight assigned to the reproduction cost value equals the percentage of equity to total capitalization. For example, suppose the original cost of the pipeline is $10 million, reproduction cost is $40 million, accrued depreciation is $5 million, and a firm has a capital structure consisting of 60% equity and 40% debt. Then, under TOC, the pipeline's rate base value will equal (0.4) × ($10 million − $5 million) + (0.60) × ($40 million − $5 million) = $23 million.

Two factors affect how the original cost of a firm's capital stock is translated into a component of the revenue requirement: (1) the appropriate cost of capital to apply to the rate base in order to derive the "return" portion of the revenue requirement, and (2) the impact of inflation. Section 5.5 addresses estimating an appropriate cost of capital. The impact of inflation can be addressed either by adjusting the value of the capital stock or, equivalently, adjusting the rate of return.

---

[33] The original cost does not determine the efficiency of the assets or their current economic value.

[34] *Re Williams Pipe Line Company,* Docket Nos. OR79-1-000 and 022 (Phase I), Opinion No. 154-B, 31 FERC ¶61,377 (1985).

[35] *Id.,* at ¶61,839.

The Prudent Investment Standard

One issue common to all three definitions of value is that regulators may have to decide whether the firm spent too much on its investment. For example, if regulators thought the firm could have built the $100 million pipeline for just $75 million, then the $25 million difference between what the firm spent and what regulators think <u>should</u> have been spent can be deemed imprudent and excluded (called a *disallowance*) from the firm's revenue requirement. Having to decide what is and is not prudent, however, leads to use of the original cost concept, which forms the basis for the *prudent investment* standard.

Prudent costs are original costs less any costs deemed fraudulent, unnecessary, or unwise. At the heart of the prudent investment standard, therefore, is an important role for economic analysis: choosing the "best" from among different, and competing, investment alternatives.

The development of a prudent investment standard culminated in 1944 when the U.S. Supreme Court issued its decision in *Hope Natural Gas*.[36] In *Hope*, the Court reaffirmed an "end results" focus and explicitly recognized the riskiness of investments made in public utilities, such that "return to the equity owner should be commensurate with return on investments having corresponding risks."[37] What this means in practice is that investors can expect to earn the cost of capital, which is defined as the expected rate of return in capital markets on investments having similar business and financial risks. *Hope* also changed the regulatory focus from determining the fair value of the rate base to determining a fair rate of return.[38]

Although the *Hope* decision typically is invoked in regulatory decisions concerning fair rates of return, the decision also established a foundation for regulatory "adjustments." The U.S. Supreme Court determined that when a requested rate was claimed to be outside a just and reasonable boundary, the end results were again what mattered. Thus, under *Hope*, allowing a regulated firm to incorporate all of its prudently incurred costs into the rates it charged could result in rates that were not "just and reasonable." This "end results" re-

---

[36] *Federal Power Comm'n v. Hope Natural Gas Co.*, 320 U.S. 591 (1944).

[37] *Id.*, at 605.

[38] The problem with fair value is its "circularity." The traditional way to measure the value of any enterprise is to calculate the present discounted value of the net earnings stream that flows from it. For any regulated firm, one can always perform such a valuation—as long as that valuation does not form the basis for setting the rates from which the regulated firm ultimately derives its earnings. The reason is that when future prices depend on a ratemaking formula that references the value of the firm's capital stock, one has created a circular process. One cannot determine value based on prices that are, voilà, determined based on value in the first place. The 1944 U.S. Supreme Court decision in *Hope Natural Gas* broke this circularity by affirming that *cost*, not *value* would provide the basis for the utility rate base and tariffs,

quirement proved critical in subsequent *used and useful* determinations, ironically, because decades later, a number of utilities faced financial ruin owing to the costs of nuclear power plants whose construction they had embarked on.

Used and Useful

Used and usefulness is not the same as prudence. An imprudent investment can still be used and useful, whereas a prudent one may not be. If regulators decide that the $100 million pipeline should have only cost $25 million, the investment is imprudent. But if the pipeline transports natural gas, it is physically used and useful. Similarly, the firm might have spent $75 million on construction but failed to obtain the necessary permits to operate the pipeline. In that case, the expenditure would be prudent, but the pipeline would not be used and useful. Thus, prudence is based on fundamental economic principles, whereas used and usefulness has, for the most part, been a physical concept.

The origins of the "used and useful" concept can actually be traced back to the fair value doctrine initially established by the U.S. Supreme Court in *Smyth v. Ames*.[39] Rather than investment costs, the Court decided to focus on the measures of value that could be used to determine whether the rates established were confiscatory. As we mentioned in Chapter 3, Justice Brandeis's dissenting opinion in *Southwestern Bell* proposed the concept of "prudent investment" as an alternative to fair value determination,[40] and this idea linked specifically to the concept of "usefulness." In doing so, he introduced more economic relevance to the determination of "fairness," stating that:

> Historical cost, on the other hand, is the amount, which normally should have been paid for all the property, which is <u>usefully</u> devoted to the public service. It is, in effect, what is termed the prudent investment… What is now termed the prudent investment is, in essence, the same thing as that which the court has always sought to protect in using the term present value.[41]

---

[39] *Smyth v. Ames*, 169 U.S. 466 (1898).

[40] *Missouri ex rel. Southwestern Bell Tel. Co. v. Missouri Pub. Serv. Comm'n* (Brandeis, J. dissenting) 262 U.S. 276 (1923).

[41] *Id.*, at 309 fn. omitted, (emph. added). *See also*, Charles F. Phillips, *The Regulation of Public Utilities*, 3d ed. (Arlington, VA: Public Utilities Reports, 1993), 325–26.

Put another way, Justice Brandeis developed a more economically efficient means to achieve distributional equity between investors and ratepayers using an obvious standard: does the plant in question provide captive ratepayers with actual physical benefits?[42]

The Nuclear Plant Legacy and Economic Used and Usefulness

Used and usefulness rose to prominence in the utility regulatory framework because of the legacy of unfinished and over-budget nuclear power plants, both of which threatened customers with large rate shocks. While there were a number of controversial plants—including Washington Public Power Supply System (WPPSS) plants, Public Service of New Hampshire's Seabrook facility, and Long Island Lighting's Shoreham plant—two cases, *Jersey Central* and *Duquesne Light*, stand out because they were used to justify a concept of *economic used and usefulness*.[43]

In the late 1960s, Jersey Central Power & Light (JCP&L) began development of a nuclear power plant in Forked River, New Jersey. By 1982, after having committed $397 million to the still-uncompleted project, JCP&L abandoned the project and sought recovery of that investment. JCP&L sought to recover the cost of the investment by amortizing it over a 15-year period. JCP&L requested that the unamortized portions be included in rate base, with a rate of return sufficient to cover the carrying charges on the debt and the preferred stock portions of that unamortized investment, but JCP&L did not request a return to common equity.[44] FERC responded by summarily denying inclusion of the unamortized $397 million in rate base, stating that "consistent with Commission precedent...unamortized investment in cancelled plants must be excluded from rate base."[45] JCP&L persisted, stating that its financial health had been severely impaired and that the Commission had violated the U.S. Supreme Court guidelines set out in *Hope*. Thus, JCP&L argued, the Commission had imposed an illegal regulatory taking, contrary to the Fifth and Fourteenth Amendments of the U.S. Constitution.

At about the same time JCP&L embarked on the construction of its Forked River nuclear plant, Duquesne Light Company joined four other utilities in a venture to construct seven nuclear power plants. By 1980, after the second Arab oil embargo and the accident at Three Mile Island, four of the plants were canceled. In 1982, the Pennsylvania Public Utility Commission (PUC) nevertheless permitted the utilities to amortize the costs they had incurred on these four plants in rates. Soon thereafter, the Pennsylvania legislature enacted a law precluding construction costs of facilities from being included in rate base if those facilities were not "used and useful." Using this legislation as a basis, a consumer group sued Duquesne and the PUC. The PUC argued that the law permitted the utilities to recoup their investment in the abandoned plants, but it did not permit them to earn a return on that investment.

---

[42] See, for example, *Denver Union Stockyard Co. v. United States*, 304 U.S. 470 (1938), in which the Court found that some of the expenses used for a livestock show and property were not pertinent (useful) towards operation of the stockyard, and thus would not be included in the stockyard's rates.

[43] *Jersey Central Power & Light v. FERC*, 810 F.2d. 1168 (D.C. Cir. 1987); *Duquesne Light Co. v. Barasch*, 488 U.S. 299 (1989). This section is adapted from Jonathan Lesser, "The Economic Used and Useful Test: Its Evolution and Implications for a Restructured Electric Industry," 23 *Energy Law Journal* 2 (2002): 349–81.

[44] 810 F.2d. 1168, 1171.

[45] *Re Jersey Central Power & Light Co.*, 19 FERC ¶ 61,208, 61,403 (1982), (fn. omitted). The Commission cited as precedent its decision in a case that involved a previously abandoned nuclear power plant that had been owned by New England Power Company (NEPCO), relying on an "end results" approach.

The Pennsylvania Supreme Court, however, reversed the PUC. The court concluded that the legislation prohibited collection of both the return of and the return on the investment. On appeal, the U.S. Supreme Court affirmed. The Court concluded that disallowing "recovery of capital investments that are not 'used and useful in service to the public'" did not constitute a "taking" under the Fifth and Fourteenth Amendments of the U.S. Constitution.[46] While this was consistent with the findings of the court of appeals in *Jersey Central*, in *Duquesne* the U.S. Supreme Court opened the door to the long-discarded fair value regulation of *Smyth v. Ames*.

The court of appeals' decision implied that a switch from a prudent investment standard, under which investors received a return of (but not on) unused and unuseful investments, to a used and useful test, under which neither a return of nor return on unused and unuseful investments was received, did not constitute a regulatory taking. The court suggested this would be a return to the pre-*Hope* fair value standard and would "mimic the operation of the competitive market."[47] However, the court's reasoning would apply only if risk and return were truly symmetric. In many instances, however, this is not the case, reflecting a fundamental economic misunderstanding of a fair rate of return.[48]

The *Jersey Central* and *Duquesne* decisions led to a distinct economic used and useful test in the mid-1980s. The concept was proposed by consumer advocates, primarily in conjunction with prudence reviews of nuclear power plants like Forked River. Even though the cost overruns were addressed in prudence cases, in several of these cases consumer advocates took positions that the plants should have been cancelled rather than completed and that even a portion of the prudently incurred costs should be disallowed on the grounds that the investment had turned out to be uneconomic.

This reasoning allowed the economic used and useful test to supplement or, indeed, trump the traditional prudence standard. A specific cost incurred could be excluded from a utility's cost of service, whether or not prudently incurred, if it turned out to be anything other than the least-cost option based on developments in the "market" occurring well after the acquisition was made. Under the economic used and useful test, therefore, a prudent and "used," but subsequently uneconomic ("unuseful") investment may be disallowed.

From a regulatory standpoint, however, the economic used and useful test clearly does not offer any "symmetry" whatsoever in the allocation of risk between ratepayers and investors. The test is also at odds with long-term planning requirements still required of many electric utilities, especially with the collapse (whether temporary or not) of restructuring efforts. Lastly, applications of economic used and useful tests in conjunction with long-term resource planning obligations can result in economic "double jeopardy" that may, in principle, guarantee regulatory disallowances of utility generation supply costs. Such an outcome hardly seems what the U.S. Supreme Court hoped its decision in *Hope* would achieve.

---

[46] 488 U.S. 299, *supra* note 43, at 300, 307–16.

[47] *Id.*, at 309.

[48] For a detailed discussion of the *Duquesne* decision, see Lawrence Kolbe and William Tye, "The Duquesne Opinion: How Much 'Hope' is There for Investors in Regulated Firms?" *Yale J. Reg.* 8 (1990), at 113. Kolbe and Tye focus on the economic implications of the Court's findings, notably the asymmetry of regulated returns and the crucial differences between expected and allowed rates of return.

International Rate Base Issues

Internationally, one can find real-world examples of each of the three methods to value assets. However, because there is much less regulatory history elsewhere than there is in the United States, many countries have approached setting the initial value of the rate base and adjustments to that initial value using diverse, and often problematic, methods. This is especially true in countries that privatized their government-run energy industries. Almost none of these countries adopted the original cost approach commonly used in the United States to set initial rate base values. Moreover, some countries do not update rate base values based on net book value (i.e., original cost, plus new additions, less depreciation), which we previously argued is the most economically rational method to value a firm's regulated assets.

Setting the Initial Value of Assets

Many countries that did not adopt the original cost approach to establish the initial value of rate base (especially countries in which government firms were privatized) have found themselves mired in regulatory and legal disputes. The reason is that there is a general "rule of thumb" for privatization efforts: The value of the assets that make up the rate base and that are to be included in the revenue requirement should be known by prospective bidders before privatization takes place. Not surprisingly, the fact that bidders have little idea how the assets on which they are supposed to bid will be valued by the regulator places rather a damper on bidders' enthusiasm. Not only do such auctions tend to have fewer bidders, but the bidders that do participate will tend to discount the estimated market value of the assets more heavily to account for the additional regulatory risk.

There are several approaches that can be used to establish initial asset values. Arguably the best approach is to use either a reproduction or a replacement cost valuation.[49] The reason for this is that adopting existing book values of state-owned companies may have little to do with the true market value of the assets. Not only have some countries' financial accounts been what might charitably be called "opaque," but in some cases those accounting values have also been larded with extraneous assets.

In many privatizations, governments have hired consultants to provide either minimum bidding values or "indicative" values of assets in total, such as an entire electric distribution or natural gas pipeline company, rather than by valuing individual assets. Typically, these minimum and indicative values have been estimated using discounted cash flow (DCF) models. Of course, DCF estimates depend on the discount rates used. However, in privati-

---

[49] For example, Petróleos Mexicanos valued all of its natural gas transportation assets at reproduction cost, and that value was considered as the initial value of the assets when it obtained its natural gas transportation permit in Mexico.

zations, this leads to a conundrum: The value of an asset depends on the anticipated revenue stream that will be forthcoming, but the revenue stream depends on the value of the assets. The only way around this problem is to adopt a different initial asset value.

Another common international practice has been to adopt the price paid at the time of privatization as the regulatory book value.[50] This also creates another conundrum, since if prospective bidders know in advance that the price they pay will equal the "book" value of the assets, they will have an incentive to overbid. The reason is that a higher bid will be compensated by a larger overall return, up until the point when a bid amount is capped either by the bidder's credit limit or when the bidder's cost of borrowing exceeds the anticipated regulated rate of return or the maximum affordable rate for customers in the future.[51] Since too high a price paid for privatized assets will result in higher regulated rates, both customers and the economy will suffer.

The best practice is to establish a clear regulatory structure before privatization so that bidders understand how the assets they acquire will be regulated and how the returns they earn on those assets will be set. Then, the assets can be revalued individually prior to privatization. The resulting values should be the new "original cost," which will be subsequently modified by future additions and retirements and, in some countries, by inflation.

Alternative Updating Mechanisms

In Section 5.3 we explained some of the alternative mechanisms used to determine operating expenses. It turns out that some countries use those same mechanisms to determine some or all of the capital expenses (either the value of the existing assets or the value of the expected investments). The same caveats that applied to operating expenses also apply to capital expenses.

A number of countries use replacement cost estimates to value capital assets at each tariff review.[52] Although there are many ways that replacement value can be estimated, several of the most commonly used approaches merit further discussion.

New Zealand, for example, values assets at each tariff review using what is called *Optimized Derived Value* (ODV). This is similar to an optimized depreciated replacement cost (ODRC) value in that it is based on "efficient" assets that would be built by a new entrant. However,

---

[50] This practice was adopted by some regulators in Argentina after privatization.

[51] Another practical problem is that bids may include the anticipated value of unregulated activities.

[52] In some countries, the replacement value used for regulatory purposes is either referred to as Depreciated Optimized Replacement Cost (DORC) or as Optimized Depreciated Replacement Cost (ODRC).

ODV goes one step further in that the estimated value of the assets is always the lower of ODRC and economic value (where economic value is the net present value of the net revenue stream from a competing service or product in a competitive market).

Latin American countries that use a *model company* approach value capital assets at replacement value during each tariff review and call it *New Replacement Value* (NRV, or VNR in Spanish). Each country uses a slightly different variation of a typical engineering approach to determine what assets are needed to "efficiently" provide the expected level of service.[53]

The general problem with using replacement cost methods for updating asset values is that these methods will often send the wrong economic signals for long-term investment. For example, during a tariff review, the value of assets based on contemporaneous prices may differ significantly from the original acquisition cost of those assets. Moreover, technological improvements will likely be incorporated into the valuation estimates to capture improved efficiency. For example, a firm that had invested in new technology a few years before a tariff review and whose assets are still not amortized could discover that the regulator now bases the value of those assets on a different, lower-cost technology, thus deeming the original investment not economical.[54]

5.5 Estimating the Regulated Rate of Return

Under the regulatory compact, a regulated firm agrees that the prices it charges will be set by regulators, and regulators agree that the prices they set will allow the firm to recoup its operating costs plus a reasonable profit. For a regulated firm, "reasonable profit" is defined as the rate of return sufficient to attract the capital the firm needs to continue to meet its obligations.

The capital attraction (or "opportunity cost") standard is key in determining the fair rate of return for regulated firms. When investors make their funds available to a firm, regulated or not, they are forgoing the option of using those funds for some other purpose (either current consumption or another investment). They are also putting their funds at some risk. In return for forgoing current consumption and incurring risk, those investors will expect

---

[53] While most countries value all of the assets, and such valuing requires significant effort and expense, Guatemala adopted in 2003 a sampling approach based on what is called *cluster analysis*. Under cluster analysis, assets are sorted into similar bins, called "clusters," based on their characteristics. Then a small sample of assets in each cluster is valued in detail and those estimates are used to set the value of all of the capital assets.

[54] Note the resemblance of this approach to an economic used-and-useful valuation. A Latin American regulator who has used the NRV method for three consecutive tariff reviews agreed with one of the authors that the methodology was flawed. However, since the method is enshrined in law, the regulator must continue to apply the methodology.

to earn a return on their funds. If the firm is to compensate its investors adequately for their forgone current consumption and for the financial risk they incur, the regulated firm must be allowed to earn a *fair rate of return* on its investment.

There are two main components to any firm's overall cost of capital: the cost of debt and the cost of equity. The cost of debt generally can be directly measured as a weighted average of the firm's outstanding debt (bond) issues and its coupon rates (i.e., the stated interest rate). A bond with a 10% coupon rate pays 10% of the bond's face value each year in interest.[55] The cost of equity, however, cannot be directly measured. As a consequence, determining an appropriate return on equity and an overall fair allowed rate of return for a regulated firm is one of the oldest issues in rate regulation. As far back as 1909, in *Consolidated Gas*,[56] the U.S. Supreme Court directly discussed the relationship between risk and return, reasoning that a fair rate of return encompassed a return on invested capital and a return for risk. But perhaps the most explicit statement by the U.S. Supreme Court is contained in *Hope*:

> [T]he return to the equity owner should be commensurate with <u>other enterprises having corresponding risks</u>. That return, moreover, should be sufficient to assure confidence in the financial integrity of the enterprise, so as to maintain its credit and attract capital.[57]

Just what "corresponding risks" really means has been debated for years. But for most regulated firms, the allowed rate of return can be thought of as a long-term "set point" that generally remains fixed for a number of years, since most utilities prefer not to file rate cases every year. Sometimes a regulatory commission will require a firm to wait a certain number of years between filings. In other situations, a firm will be loathe to file for an adjustment in its allowed rate of return, fearing regulators will open up a "Pandora's Box" of other issues, such as whether the firm's other costs are reasonable.[58]

The allowed rate of return is based on two factors: capital structure (i.e., the relative fractions of debt and equity) and the cost of equity capital. In some cases, regulators accept the utility's actual capital structure at the time of its rate case filing and simply adjust the allowed cost of equity. In other cases, regulators adopt a "hypothetical" capital structure that reflects what they believe is more appropriate for the firm given market conditions.

---

[55] A more precise measure of value for bonds that are publicly traded is the yield to maturity (YTM). The YTM is calculated based on the bond's trading price relative to its face (par) value and its coupon rate.

[56] *Wilcox v. Consolidated Gas Co.*, 212 U.S. 19 (1909).

[57] 320 U.S. 591, 603, *supra* note 36 (emphasis added).

[58] Typically, regulators do not allow "single-issue" ratemaking.

For example, historically, electric and natural gas utilities were considered relatively "low-risk" enterprises whose activities would be judged within the context of the regulatory compact. In such an environment, utility investors could accept higher overall debt levels (compared with unregulated firms) because utilities faced little competition. Earnings were relatively stable, as were dividend payments, and "widows and orphans" could sleep well at night secure in the knowledge that, whatever the ups and downs of the market might be, their utility would provide financial stability.

The Cost of Capital Defined

The cost of capital is defined as the expected return investors require, based on the risks those investors perceive in investing in a firm. For any firm, regulated or not, publicly held or privately held, *the cost of capital represents the opportunity cost of attracting and retaining capital in an efficient and competitive capital market.* In an efficient capital market, investors can diversify risk. Indeed, modern investment theory is based on the concept of portfolio risk, because the risk stemming from any individual asset can be reduced by holding a diverse portfolio of investments.

Not all risk can be diversified away, which is why investment risk is characterized as *diversifiable* and *nondiversifiable*. Whereas diversifiable risk reflects those risks that can be reduced (or eliminated) by holding a diverse portfolio of assets, nondiversifiable risk reflects the overall risk of the entire market. For example, one can buy a so-called "index" fund that contains the same proportions of all the S&P 500 stocks that make up the S&P market index. Because it would be highly unlikely for all 500 stocks to either increase or decrease in value simultaneously, owning this index fund would reduce the unique risks associated with each individual stock. But returns from this index fund would still vary, because the index fund cannot itself be diversified, hence the terms *nondiversifiable risk, systematic risk,* and *portfolio risk*. The overall risk of an investment will increase as this nondiversifiable risk of investment increases. Investors require higher expected returns to compensate for increasing portfolio risk.

The *weighted average cost of capital* (WACC) is based on the relative percentages of total equity, E, and debt, D, (i.e., stocks and bonds, respectively) and the costs of each. Thus,

$$\text{WACC} = \lambda R_D + (1 - \lambda) R_E \qquad (5\text{-}4)$$

where:

λ = ratio of debt to total capitalization, i.e., $D \div (D + E)$;
R_D = the average cost of debt; and
R_E = the cost of equity.

In practice, equation (5-4) can be modified to separate out the amounts of common and preferred equity. Moreover, the cost of debt is generally estimated as a weighted average of a firm's outstanding bonds. In estimating a firm's WACC, the difficulty lies in estimating its cost of common equity.[59] Therefore, estimating a regulated company's rate of return on common equity rests on determining the company's overall financial and business risk, especially those risks that cannot be diversified.

It is also common to separate an individual firm's risk into *business risk* and *financial risk*. Business risk increases as uncertainty surrounding a company's future net operating income (i.e., earnings before interest and taxes) increases. Financial risk depends on the extent of a company's leverage (i.e., investment capital financed with debt). The greater the leverage, the greater the financial risk. The cost of debt and the cost of common equity both increase as financial risk increases, although change in their costs also depends on overall financial risk.[60] The cost of debt increases, because as leverage increases so does the likelihood that earnings volatility will preclude repayment of that debt. The cost of common equity increases as financial risk increases, because debt has a senior claim on a company's earnings. Thus, increased debt financing shifts additional earnings uncertainty onto equity holders.

Although debt financing provides a tax shield, the tax advantages of additional debt financing can be offset by the increased cost of debt, the increased likelihood of financial distress, and the uncertainty of the value of the tax shield itself. For this reason, one cannot simply conclude that continuously increasing the overall level of debt financing benefits customers. Indeed, at some point, increased debt financing may materially harm customers, as well as investors.

The Efficient Markets Hypothesis

Underlying all of the methodologies used to estimate a regulated firm's rate of return is a fundamental hypothesis that capital markets are, in fact, efficient. If they are not, in other words, if capital markets are not competitive or are somehow "rigged" in favor of some investors over others, then none of the underlying estimation methodologies used will be valid. There are at least two requirements for an efficient capital market—or indeed, any efficient market: *allocative efficiency* and *exchange efficiency*.

---

[59] Preferred equity is more "bond-like," and thus its cost is easier to determine than common equity.

[60] This subject was first investigated in a seminal paper by Franco Modigliani and Merton Miller, "The Cost of Capital, Corporation Finance, and the Theory of Investment," *American Economic Review* 48, no. 3 (June 1958): 261–97. The authors showed that in a world without taxes, the cost of capital was invariant to capital structure. However, with taxes, risky debt, and costs associated with bankruptcy, things change, and greater leverage eventually leads to higher costs of both debt and equity. For further discussion, see Thomas E. Copeland and J. Fred Weston, *Financial Theory and Corporate Policy*, 2nd ed. (New York: Addison-Wesley, 1988), chaps. 12–13.

Allocative efficiency embodies the distribution of goods and services to their highest values. In the context of capital markets, there are both borrowers and lenders. Borrowing and lending decisions are a function of individual preferences. Collectively, individuals' borrowing and lending decisions determine an overall market interest rate. In essence, borrowers and lenders allocate their funds based on their individual time preferences. Impatient individuals are borrowers, while "rainy day" savers are lenders. Those collective allocations determine a market price of money, which is the prevailing market interest rate. Exchange efficiency refers to the ability of borrowers and lenders to transfer funds between one another at the lowest possible cost. In the context of capital markets, this implies high liquidity and minimal transaction costs.

Professor Eugene Fama defined three types of efficient capital markets: weak, semi-strong, and strong.[61]

> *Weak form.* All past market prices are completely reflected in current prices. No investor can earn excess returns by developing trading rules based on past price information.
>
> *Semi-strong form.* No investor can earn excess returns from any publicly available information, such as corporate Annual Reports, 10-K forms, *Wall Street Journal* columns, etc.
>
> *Strong form.* No investor can earn excess returns using any information, whether public or not.

Collectively, these three definitions have been termed the *Efficient Markets Hypothesis* (EMH). Although there are academic debates over which form of the EMH, if any, is relevant, it seems clear that the strong form of the EMH is overly restrictive. Insider trading occurs, even though illegal, which renders the strong form invalid. There is more debate over the relevance of the weak and semi-strong forms, but for purposes of estimating the rate of return for regulated firms, the semi-strong form of the EMH is usually regarded as relevant because it provides the conceptual basis for focusing on expectations about <u>future</u> performance, rather than on past performance.

---

[61] Eugene F. Fama, *Foundations of Finance*, (New York: Basic Books, 1976), chapter 5. *See also,* Thomas E. Copeland and J. Fred Weston, *Financial Theory and Corporate Policy,* 3d ed. (New York: Addison-Wesley, 1988), chapter 9.

Estimation Methodologies

Because the cost of debt is more easily observed, methodologies used to estimate regulated firms' overall cost of capital focus on estimating the cost of common equity. However, since the cost of equity cannot simply be "looked up" the way you might look up a phone number, the appropriate cost of common equity is estimated using fundamental economic and financial principles. In doing so, it is important to recognize that estimating a cost of common equity that is "commensurate with other enterprises having corresponding risks," as discussed in *Hope*, will always be an inexact process requiring judgment.

A number of methodologies have been developed for estimating the return on equity. The three most common are the Discounted Cash Flow Model (DCF), the Capital Asset Pricing Model (CAPM), and the Risk Premium Model (RPM). Of these three, the DCF method, which was first used in the United States in the mid-1960s, has become the most common approach used by U.S. regulators for both natural gas and electric companies, although many regulators look at the results from multiple methods.[62]

Selecting Comparable Firms

Since the foundation of cost of equity estimation is to provide regulated firms with an opportunity to earn returns that correspond (are comparable) to other firms having similar business and financial risks, the first step in estimating the cost of equity is to select a proxy group of comparable firms. This requires a trade-off between the degree of comparability (since no two firms are exactly alike) and the size of the comparable group (more firms in the group mean less weight will be given to any individual firm).[63]

In general, proxy group firms must be: (1) publicly traded (otherwise, it is difficult to obtain any financial data about them), (2) from the same or a similar industry (the cost of equity for a grocer likely has little relevance for a natural gas pipeline company), (3) similar in size (because different sized firms will have different financial risks), and (4) pay dividends (if one uses the DCF approach). They must also have similar bond ratings, and they must not be merging with, or acquiring, another firm. (The comparability of the merged entity may be very different than the unmerged one.)

---

[62] The DCF approach is much less relied upon in international applications, especially in countries that lack sufficiently liquid stock markets.

[63] This is the same as a basic issue in statistics: determining what is the smallest, statistically valid sample that can be used to make inferences about a population. The decreasing availability of proxy firms, especially "pure-play" natural gas pipelines, has become a significant regulatory issue because of mergers and the increasing frequency of firms that have been acquired by private investors. FERC discusses this issue in regard to natural gas pipeline companies in *Kern River Gas Transmission Company*, 117 FERC ¶ 61, 077 (Opinion No. 486), October 2006.

The DCF Model[64]

The DCF model assumes that a firm's stock price today equals the expected value of all future cash flows associated with that stock, including all future dividend payments and appreciation in the stock's price.[65] This is why the DCF model is also known as the "Dividend Growth Model," since the cash flows from a stock held forever will all be future dividend payments. The "perpetual" DCF model is the most commonly used form of the DCF models. It assumes that dividends are paid in discrete time periods (annually, quarterly, etc.) and will continue to be paid in the same manner forever. If we assume that the stock is held forever, then there will be no revenue received in the future from the sale of the stock, and the stock price today will solely reflect the stream of expected dividend payments. And, if we further assume that the dividend payments will grow at a constant rate over time, the cost of equity for a regulated firm can be shown to equal the stock's current dividend yield plus the expected long-term growth in earnings over time, i.e.,[66]

$$k = D_0(1+g) \div P_0 + g \qquad (5\text{-}5)$$

where:

D_0 = the current stock dividend;

P_0 = the current stock price; and

g = the forecast dividend growth rate.[67]

In practice, because the daily price of a firm's stock can be quite volatile, and because that volatility can reflect other factors not related to any changes in a firm's overall risk, the stock price used in equation (5-5) is often based on an average of past closing prices. While this technically violates the tenets of the EMH, it is sensible for practical reasons, notably that a regulated return on equity is typically set for a relatively long period under COS regulation. If the firm's long-term earnings and its overall financial viability depend on the stock

---

[64] For a thorough discussion of the DCF Model, see Roger A. Morin, *New Regulatory Finance*, (Vienna, VA: Public Utilities Reports, 2006), chaps. 8–11.

[65] The theory underlying the DCF model holds for any stock. However, historically, the use of the DCF method to estimate utilities' cost of equity was ideally suited because utilities paid steady dividends.

[66] The derivation of this formula can be found in many financial textbooks. For the mathematically inclined, deriving equation (5-5) is a good way to understand it.

[67] The appropriate growth rate to use is often controversial. In our view, the appropriate growth rate is one based on a forecast of long-term growth in earnings, since a firm's earnings ultimately determine its ability to pay dividends. Moreover, the tenets of the EMH mean that investors will care about expected returns in the future, not historic growth rates. And, while historic growth rates may provide information to investors in forming their expectations of future growth rates, one cannot simply assume that past growth rates will continue perpetually into the future.

price on a single day, then the rate-setting process will be highly time-dependent. That, in itself, can impose additional financial risk, as well as raise fairness issues for both investors and ratepayers.

Another issue that is sometimes disputed is the appropriate growth rate to use in equation (5-5). We favor the use of earnings growth rates, rather than forecast dividend growth rates. The reason for this is that growth in dividend payments ultimately <u>must</u> depend on growth in earnings per share. While some companies pay dividends even when earnings fall, this is obviously not sustainable. There are also issues concerning short-term and long-term growth rates. A firm that is growing rapidly cannot do so forever. Otherwise, one would have firms that were larger than the entire economy. To address this issue, several "multi-stage" DCF models can be used. These include developing average growth rates that reflect a short-term component (usually five years) and a long-term component, such as forecast growth in the underlying economy, as measured by gross domestic product (GDP).

There are a number of different versions of the DCF model shown in equation (5-5). These are based on different frequencies of dividend payments, differences between short-term and long-term earnings growth rates, and even "nonconstant" growth rate models.[68] All of these different versions, however, are based on the same underlying theory, namely, that the price of stock today reflects all expected future cash flows. As an example, FERC traditionally has used an approach that reflects one-half the annual growth rate in the expression for D_1, since companies tend to increase their quarterly dividends at different times of the year.

The Capital Asset Pricing Model

The Capital Asset Pricing Model (CAPM) is based on the relationship between portfolio risk and return. The model states that the expected return on any security (typically, a stock) is directly proportional to its risk relative to the market portfolio. The CAPM shows that investors need not concern themselves with the unique risks of individual securities, because those risks can be eliminated with diversification. Thus, investors do not require a higher expected return to cover a security's unique risk. As a result, the expected return investors require can be estimated as the risk-free rate of return, plus a risk premium based on (1) the overall expected return of the market less the risk-free rate, and (2) the volatility of the return on the individual security <u>relative</u> to the overall return in the market. Mathematically, the CAPM can be written as:

---

[68] Morin, *supra* note 64, contains a detailed discussion of alternative DCF models, as well as other models used to estimate the rate of return for regulated firms.

$$E(R) = R_f + \beta \left[E(R_m) - R_f \right] \tag{5-6}$$

where:

$E(R)$ = expected return on the security;

$E(R_m)$ = expected return on the market portfolio;

R_f = risk-free rate of return; and

β = "Beta," which measures the volatility between market return and the return on the individual security.

Equation (5-6) states that, in equilibrium, every security is priced so it lies along a straight line called the *security-market line*. Along this line, the required risk premium for any security equals the quantity of risk (measured by β),[69] times the price of risk (measured as the slope of the security-market line). $E(R)$ equals the cost of equity to the firm, since it represents the return expected by investors given the firm's level of nondiversifiable risk relative to the market as a whole. The CAPM is known as a "one-factor" model because expected return is a linear function of the equity risk premium. No other explanatory factors are included to determine expected returns.[70, 71]

Beta measures the volatility of an individual security relative to the overall market portfolio, which theoretically includes all securities. For example, if the beta of a stock equals 1.0, then the stock has the same amount of nondiversifiable risk as the overall market, and it will exhibit volatility to the same degree as the market. If the market return increased by 1%, we would expect the individual security's return to jump the same amount. Securities with beta

---

[69] In many international applications, a *country risk premium* is added to the estimate to account for the overall risk in a country's financial markets.

[70] The *Arbitrage Pricing Model* (APM) is probably the best-known *multifactor* model. In fact, the simplest form of the APM is the CAPM. Some analysts have suggested using the APM rather than the CAPM for estimating return on equity. The difficulty comes in determining which factors are most appropriate to include and how to obtain the necessary data. Another well-known multifactor model is called the Fama-French 3-factor model, developed by Prof. Eugene F. Fama and Prof. Kenneth R. French. Their model includes the effects of small capitalization firms and firms with low market-to-book price ratios (so-called "value" stocks). For more detail, see Eugene F. Fama and Kenneth R. French, "Multifactor Explanations of Asset Pricing Anomalies," *Journal of Finance* 51, no. 1 (1996): 55–84.

[71] In some countries, such as Australia and New Zealand, the CAPM needs to be modified to account for the effects of an *imputation tax* credit. Under an imputation tax system, investors who receive corporate dividends also receive a tax credit for corporate taxes that the firm has paid. This is done to address double taxation of earnings (first at the corporate level and then at the individual level.) An imputation tax system affects the estimated rate of return since, whereas returns typically consist of capital gains and dividends, under an imputation system, an imputation tax credit must be added. The combined value of a dividend and its associated tax credit is sometimes called the "grossed up dividend." Similarly, the total return to shareholders (capital gains plus grossed up dividends) is called the "grossed up return." Typically, the factor that accounts for the imputation tax credit is referred to as "theta." For additional discussion, see, for example, Robert Officer, *The Cost of Capital of a Company Under an Imputation Tax System*, (Victoria, Australia: Parkville, 1991); C. Graham Peirson, R. G. Bird, R. Brown and P. Howard, *Business Finance*, 6th ed., (Sydney: McGraw-Hill, 1995).

values greater than 1.0 will tend to amplify movements in market returns. Securities with betas less than 1.0 will tend to dampen movements in market returns. A security with a beta of 0.5, for example, would tend to rise only half as much as the market when the market rises, and it would fall by half as much when the market falls.

The A-B-Cs of Betas

There are actually three different types of betas that are used in rate of return applications with the CAPM. The observed beta values are known as *levered* betas. A firm's observed beta reflects its underlying nondiversifiable business and financial risk. Financial risk is reflected by a firm's capital structure, specifically the extent to which the firm relies on debt. The greater the proportion of debt-to-equity capital, the more highly *levered* is the firm. So, suppose you select a proxy group of firms that will be used to estimate the rate of return for a firm under rate review. However, the firm under review is not publicly traded. (Hence, you cannot calculate its beta.) You need to ensure that the rate of return value calculated from the proxy group firms will provide a return that is comparable, given the business and financial risk of the firm under rate review.

To get around this problem, the equity betas of the proxy group firms are unlevered to remove the financial risk component. The resulting beta values are called *asset betas*. Next, these asset betas are *relevered*, based on the capital structure of the firm under review. The unlevered beta is calculated using the following equation:

$$\beta_L = \beta_U \left[1 + (1-t) \frac{D}{E} \right]$$

where β_L = the levered beta (the same beta as shown in equation 5-6), β_U = the unlevered beta, t = the marginal tax rate, and D/E = the debt-to-equity ratio.[72] For example, suppose the average (observed) levered beta for the proxy group firms is 0.70, the average debt-to-equity ratio (often referred to as "gearing" in international applications) is 40%:60% (i.e., 40% debt and 60% equity), and the corporate tax rate is 40%. Then, we have

$$0.70 = \beta_U \left[1 + (1-40\%) \frac{40\%}{60\%} \right]$$

Solving for β_U, we obtain $\beta_U = 0.50$. Next, suppose the firm under rate review has an actual capital structure of 60%:40%. (In other words, the firm under review is more heavily levered than the proxy group.) We then relever β_U using that new capital structure. Thus,

$$\beta_L = 0.50 \left[1 + (1-40\%) \frac{60\%}{40\%} \right] = 0.95$$

Finally, we reapply the CAPM using this relevered beta, using the appropriate risk-free and market risk premium rates to derive the cost of equity for the firm under rate review.

---

[72] This is known as the *Hamada* formula. *See* Robert S. Hamada, "The Effect of the Firm's Capital Structure on the Systematic Risk of Common Stocks," *Journal of Finance* 25 (May 1972): 435–52. This formula assumes that the beta of debt equals zero. That is, there is no correlation between the volatility of the return on a firm's debt and returns in the market. This assumption is commonly applied in the electric and natural gas industries.

Of the many assumptions of the CAPM, the choice of the appropriate risk-free rate of return is often the most debated. For U.S. applications, some analysts suggest that the interest rate on a short-term Treasury bill is the best measure because it has negligible interest rate risk and, thus, will not be "biased" through the incorporation of an interest rate premium that compensates for this risk.[73] Others point out that yields on three-month T-bills tend to be far more volatile than long-term Treasury bonds, because the former are influenced by short-term factors, such as Federal Reserve Open Market Committee (FOMC) actions.[74] Ultimately, of course, there is no "perfect" choice of a prospective risk-free rate, simply because none of the different rates are truly "risk-free." But because we are concerned here with the value of (presumably) long-lived corporate assets, a long-term Treasury bond rate is the most appropriate choice.

The Risk Premium Model

The Risk Premium Model (RPM) is based on the fact that, from an investor's perspective, common equity capital is riskier than debt, because debt has a senior claim over a firm's assets. As a result, potential investors in a company require a premium on top of the cost of debt issued by that company to induce them to provide equity capital. This equity risk premium is <u>not</u> the same as the equity risk premium used in the CAPM, which equals the difference between the expected future market return and the risk-free rate.

The RPM shares similarities with the CAPM in that many times both use "beta" values to determine the appropriate equity risk premiums. However, whereas the CAPM addresses *systematic* (i.e., nondiversifiable) market risk, the RPM directly incorporates both systematic and *unsystematic* (diversifiable) risk. Unsystematic risk is reflected in the RPM by the use of prospective company-specific (or class-specific) long-term bond yields. As a result, the two methodologies are quite distinct.

Choosing from a Range of Estimates

Applying the models to the firms that make up the proxy group will yield a range of estimates. Sometimes, this range may be narrow; other times it may be quite large. For example, suppose a DCF analysis of a group of 10 proxy firms yields a range of estimates

---

[73] Interest rate risk refers to the potential for a long-term interest rate that is locked in (e.g., by purchasing a Treasury bond) to deviate from the market interest rate.

[74] *See, e.g.,* Eugene F. Brigham and Louis C. Gapenski, *Financial Management: Theory and Practice,* 6th ed. (Chicago: Dryden Press, 1991), 308.

between 8.0% and 15%, or 700 *basis points*.[75] Regulators, however, ultimately must select a single number to apply to the regulated firm. This raises the question of what is the most appropriate value in the range.[76]

Selecting an appropriate value is ultimately based on judgment. While an obvious candidate is the average (mean) value, if the number of firms in the proxy group is small and the distribution of estimates skewed, then a single estimate might be given too much weight. Using the median value of the range is one way of overcoming this difficulty, but it may be inappropriate if the business and financial risk profile of the firm under review is not the same as the "average" proxy group firm. For example, suppose the firm under review is in violation of its *bond covenants* because it has failed to meet specific *interest coverage ratios*.[77] In that case, the firm might require a higher ROE value to boost its earnings to meet the terms of its bond covenants and, thus, avoid a financial crisis if bondholders called the bonds due.

> **Estimating the Rate of Return in Developing Countries**
>
> Many developing countries do not have well-established and highly liquid financial markets like the NYSE and the London Stock Exchange (LSE), which are deeply traded. As a result, estimating regulated rates of return in these countries can be more challenging, not only in terms of developing reasonable estimates, but also, in some cases, in terms of simply obtaining the necessary data.
>
> To address these complexities, several approaches are typically used. The most common approach is to estimate the rate of return based on a proxy group of firms from a country with a well-established financial market and then add a specific *country-risk premium* to the results. A number of methods to estimate country-risk premiums have been developed, including (1) examining the relative credit rankings of a nation's currency awarded by ratings agencies like Standard & Poor's or Moody's, (2) evaluating default spreads (i.e., the difference between the country's "risk-free" bond rate and the U.S. Treasury bond rate), and (3) measuring the relative market volatility between the country's equity market (presuming it has one) and the U.S. market. Which methods are the most accurate remains controversial.[78]

---

[75] A basis point equals 1/100 of 1%.

[76] In 2006, as part of its desire to encourage new transmission system infrastructure, FERC issued new guidelines on the appropriate choice of ROE within a range of estimates. *See Re Promoting Transmission Investment Through Pricing Reform*, Order No. 679, 116 FERC ¶ 61,057, July 2006, Order No. 679-A, 117 FERC ¶ 61,345.

[77] An interest coverage ratio is a measure of how well a firm can cover its debt obligations. It equals a firm's earnings before interest and taxes (EBIT) divided by total interest payments.

[78] *See, e.g.*, Campbell Harvey, "12 Ways to Calculate the International Cost of Capital," National Bureau of Economic Research, unpublished paper, December 2005.

> Another approach, which is sometimes used when the rate of return is estimated using the CAPM, is to "adjust" the beta values for regulatory risk. In a 1996 paper, Mayer, Alexander, and Weeds, researchers at the World Bank and Oxford Economic Research Associates, evaluated the effects of regulatory regimes on regulatory risk.[79] Their study analyzed how regulatory regimes affect shareholder risk for regulated utilities in Canada, Europe, and Latin America, as well as the U.K. and the United States. Specifically, their study estimated betas of more than 100 infrastructure firms and estimated the differences in betas of firms under price-cap and rate-of-return regulation regimes. These regimes were characterized as "high-powered," "intermediate," or "low-powered" based on the existing regulatory structure. Traditional COS regulation was classified as a "low-powered" regime, while pure price-cap regulation was classified as "high-powered." Mixed regulatory regimes, common in Europe, were classified as "intermediate." The authors determined that price-cap regulation creates more risk for businesses, increases earnings volatility, and raises regulated firms' cost of capital. As a result, otherwise equivalent firms had higher betas under price-cap regulation than under rate-of-return regulation, with implicit beta adjustment factors between 0.20 and 0.60. The reasonableness of this beta adjustment factor is also disputed. Nevertheless, a number of energy regulators in Latin America have used it.
>
> Finally, in some countries the cost of debt can be related to transactions with affiliated companies in other countries. In these cases, therefore, in order to provide the appropriate economic incentives, regulators use a notional cost of debt equal to the average or median percentage of a credit rating agency for utilities with a similar credit rating as the company whose prices are regulated plus country risk.

Book vs. Market Capitalization

Another issue that affects determinations of the appropriate return on equity for a regulated firm is whether one should base it on *book value* capitalization or *market value* capitalization. Book value capitalization reflects the book value of a firm's equity. A company's book value equals the total depreciated value of its assets less the total value of its liabilities. In essence, book value is the net value of a firm that would remain if the firm were shut down. So, if the depreciated value of a firm's assets, including plant and equipment, money in the bank, buildings and land, etc., equals $100 million, and its outstanding debt is $50 million, then the firm's book value is $50 million. If the firm had issued 10 million shares of stock, the book value would equal $5 per share.

One problem is that the book value of a firm's assets may bear little relationship to its market value. For example, suppose the Empire State Building in New York City has been fully depreciated by its owner. In that case, its book value is zero. One can imagine, however, that the market value of the Empire State Building is much greater than zero.

---

[79] Ian Alexander, Colin Mayer, and Helen Weeds, "Regulatory Structure and Risk: An International Comparison," World Bank Policy Research Working Paper No. 1698, December 1996.

As discussed previously, a firm's financial risk will depend on its leverage, which is determined by the firm's debt-to-equity ratio; the more leveraged the firm, the greater the financial risk to equity holders, whose claims on the firm's assets are subsidiary to those who own the firm's debt. Recall from equation (5-4) that a firm's WACC is based on that debt-equity ratio, i.e.,

$$\text{WACC} = \lambda R_D + (1-\lambda) R_E \tag{5-4}$$

where λ = the ratio of total debt to total capitalization. We can rewrite this equation to specifically reflect the firm's debt, D, and equity capital, E, noting that total capitalization, C, equals D + E. Thus, we have

$$\text{WACC} = \frac{D}{C} R_D + \frac{E}{C} R_E \tag{5-7}$$

While it is possible to determine the market value of a firm's debt, the most common approach is to assume the market value of debt equals its cost. For example, suppose you took out a 5.0% mortgage and that interest rates today are higher. If the remaining balance on your mortgage is $100,000, we assume its value is also $100,000, regardless of the interest rate. That is not strictly correct.

Suppose inflation was running at 6% per year. Then, the real, inflation-adjusted interest rate you would be paying would be negative 1.0%. In effect, the bank will be paying you for the loan you took out, and you probably will not be in a hurry to pay off your mortgage. The bank, on the other hand, desperately wants you to pay that mortgage off, so it can loan that $100,000 at current, higher market rates. So, the bank might offer you a deal: instead of paying $100,000, it will let you pay off your entire mortgage for only $90,000. From the bank's perspective, the value of the bond debt it holds (your mortgage) is lower than the book value, and so it will be willing to sell the bond (in this case back to you) for less than the book value. This explains the observed inverse relationship between interest rates and bond prices.

Because it is often difficult to estimate the market value of an individual firm's debt, especially if it is not widely traded, the value of D in equation (5-7) is usually assumed to equal the book value of debt. The market value of publicly traded equity, on the other hand, is readily determined. Hence, we have the dilemma as to whether the value of equity, E, in equation (5-7) should reflect book or market value when determining the appropriate return on equity, R_E. Traditionally, regulators have used only book values, but a good case can be made for using market value, because the variability of equity returns relative to the market (in essence, a stock's beta) depends on the market value of equity and not the book value. As such, it makes more economic sense to use market values, ideally for both debt and equity, than to use book values.

5.6 Deferred Costs and Regulatory Assets[80]

Not all prudently incurred regulated costs are flowed through to customer rates immediately. For example, when a firm invests in a capital asset, such as a new generating facility or a pipeline, it finances those costs over time, just like a home mortgage. Similarly, it depreciates the value of that asset over time, though not necessarily over the same time period as the asset is financed. Because the costs of capital assets are recovered over many years, the costs can be thought of as being deferred. As we discussed in Chapter 3, a *deferred cost* is one that the firm has paid for but which has not been included in its rates.[81]

Regulatory assets are a specific type of deferred cost. A regulatory asset is a deferred cost that is included in rate base, where it earns a rate of return. Firms carry regulatory assets on their balance sheets rather like promissory notes; there is an expectation that the costs will be repaid over time by ratepayers, with interest. However, the fact that a firm defers some fraction of its costs does not mean that the firm's customers are liable for repaying those costs, much less for earning a rate of return on those deferred costs. For that to occur, regulators must determine the deferred costs to be prudent.

The specific rules for what costs can be deferred, and when, vary, but all deferred costs must conform to Generally Accepted Accounting Principles (GAAP).[82] Most regulators do not allow firms to defer costs without prior approval. And, for a deferred cost to be considered a regulatory asset, the firm must have a reasonable expectation that the costs will, in fact, be repaid. This can be problematic, especially if a firm's balance sheet becomes weighted down with a high proportion of regulatory assets.

Just like a bank that has too many outstanding loans relative to cash on hand, a regulated utility whose deferred cost balance grows with abandon begins to face higher financial risks. Those risks, in turn, will tend to reduce the firm's credit rating, and this leads to a higher weighted average cost of capital. A deferred cost is really just another form of debt, and all debt carries with it a risk of default. Even regulatory assets carry a default risk, since regulators generally are not bound by the decisions of their predecessors.

---

[80] For a more detailed discussion, see Leonard S. Goodman, *The Process of Ratemaking*, Volume 1, (Vienna, VA: Public Utilities Reports, 1998), 321–29.

[81] In some cases, costs are collected in advance from ratepayers, but the firm can defer payment. The most common example is deferred income taxes.

[82] For a complete discussion, see David Wirick and John Gibbons, "Generally Accepted Accounting Principles for Regulated Utilities: Evolution and Impacts," National Regulatory Research Institute, NRRI 95-07, 1994.

5.7 Chapter Summary

This chapter has focused on accurately measuring a regulated firm's costs, since those are crucial components for determining regulated rates, regardless of the specific pricing policies regulators adopt. Estimating operating costs and an appropriate return on the regulated firm's capital investments presents challenges, since several major cost components—depreciation and a comparable rate of return—cannot be directly observed.

As we discuss in the next chapter, once a firm's overall costs have been estimated, and before regulated rates can be established, those costs must be allocated among different customer groups. This requires several steps. First, there must be a logical approach for establishing different groups. For example, are all residential customers to be treated alike? Should we distinguish between "small" and "large" commercial customers? Should commercial customers be distinguished from industrial customers? What criteria should be used to make such determinations? Second, once we establish different customer groups, we have to develop a methodology for allocating costs, especially joint and common costs. Third, once costs are allocated, rates must be set so that the firm can recover its costs while regulators attempt to mimic a competitive market outcome. These three steps present their own set of challenges, as we shall soon see.

APPENDIX: Depreciation Mechanics

Consider the sample data in Table A.5-1, in which 100 units of equipment are installed at time zero. Over the next 10 years, we observe that some of the equipment fails and is retired. By the end of the tenth year, all of the equipment has been retired.

Table A.5-1: Surviving Equipment Over Time—Original Group Method

Interval No.	Age Interval	Retirements in Interval	Average Survivors During Interval	Percentage Surviving
	(1)	(2)	(3)	(4)
1	0.0–0.5	0	100	100
2	0.5–1.5	0	100	100
3	1.5–2.5	4	96	96
4	2.5–3.5	8	88	88
5	3.5–4.5	18	70	70
6	4.5–5.5	24	46	46
7	5.5–6.5	18	28	28
8	6.5–7.5	13	15	15
9	7.5–8.5	9	6	6
10	8.5–9.5	6	0	0

No. of Units Installed Initially: 100

To determine the ASL for this equipment, we determine the average age of the surviving units in column (3) over the entire 10-year period, recognizing that in the first year after installation, the average age equals one-half year.[83] Thus, we have

$$\frac{[\frac{1}{2}(100) + 100 + 96 + \ldots + 6 + 0]}{100} = \frac{499}{100} = 4.99 \text{ years} \qquad (A.5\text{-}1)$$

Now suppose we want to determine ARL at the beginning of interval 5. To do that, we modify equation (A.5-1) to account only for intervals 5–10.

$$\frac{[70 + 46 + 28 + 15 + 6 + 0]}{70} = \frac{165}{70} = 2.36 \text{ years} \qquad (A.5\text{-}2)$$

---

[83] This is called a "half-year" convention.

Figure A.5-1 plots the "percentage surviving" data in column (4) of Table A.5-1. The solid line is called a *survivor curve*. It turns out that ASL is just the area under the entire survivor curve, while ARL is the area under the curve from a given year onwards.[84]

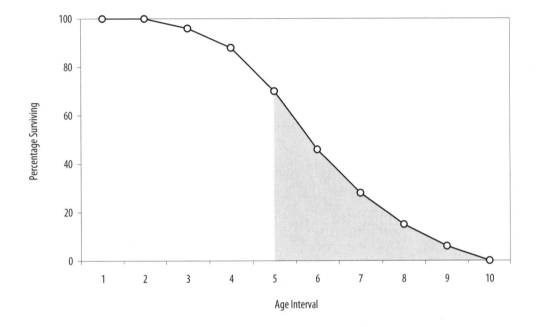

Figure A.5-1: Percentage Equipment Surviving Over Time

While calculating ASL and ARL is straightforward in this example, in practice, of course, the firm will not have the data to draw the entire survivor curve—otherwise there would not be any equipment left to depreciate. Instead, what would be seen is a partial, or "stub" survivor curve, as shown in Figure A.5-2. Using the "stub" data and knowledge about the future, the goal is to fit an appropriate survivor curve and then determine ARL.

---

[84] For readers who understand or remember calculus, ASL equals the integral under the entire curve. ASL is the expected value of the function, and for any function, f(x), its expected value = $\int_0^\infty xf(x)dx$. For equipment that is T years old, its ARL is just the integral under the curve from year T forward, i.e., $\int_T^\infty xf(x)dx$.

Figure A.5-2: Stub Survivor Curve

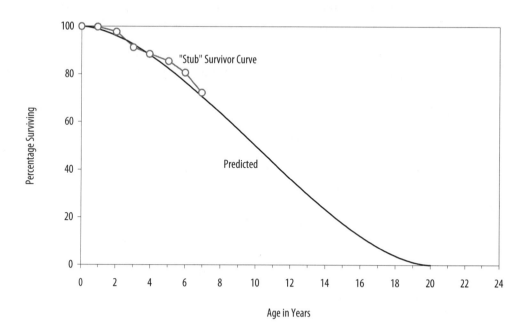

Table A.5-1 and Figure A.5-1 provide examples of what is called the *Original Group* method, which assumes that all equipment is a single *vintage* and has been installed in the same year.[85] For example, an electric utility may install wood poles every year as its service territory grows and as existing poles are replaced because of damage from cars or wind. Therefore, if we were estimating depreciation rates for an electric utility with multiple vintages of poles, the Original Group method could only be applied to the portion of the company's poles that was installed in a given year. As a result, the Original Group method has limited application. Because of this limitation, the *Annual Rate* method is most often used.

The general approach under the Annual Rate method is the same as under the Original Group method, except that different plant vintages are addressed simultaneously in developing survivor curves. While this complicates the analysis, the underlying approach—determining a stub survivor curve and fitting it to an appropriate overall survivor curve—remains the same.

---

[85] Technically, a single vintage need not be equipment installed in a single year. It can refer to whatever time period defines a single "interval." Typically, however, "vintage" is synonymous with year.

With the Annual Rate method, annual additions and retirements are tracked separately. Each year is considered a different "vintage" of equipment. Essentially, under the Annual Rate method, different vintages of equipment are grouped by age, as are retirements. In this way, the surviving equipment at the beginning of each interval (called *exposures*) and retirements occurring during each interval are tracked jointly. This allows us to estimate a survivor curve, which is then used to determine ARLs and depreciation rates.

Table A.5-2 provides an example of plant additions and retirements grouped by vintage. For example, in 1999, the table shows that $98,220 worth of plant was installed. A small portion, $1,860 of what was installed, was retired later that year, leaving a net plant balance of $96,360 at year's end. In 2000, an additional $112,500 of plant was installed, but there were no retirements. In 2001, $194,910 of plant was installed. And, in that same year, $5,400 worth of 1999 vintage plant (2 years old) was retired, $3,060 worth of year 2000 vintage plant (1 year old) was retired, and $1,230 of 2001 vintage plant (0 years old) was retired. Table A.5-3 summarizes these data in a more convenient format for estimating survivor curves and calculating overall depreciation rates.

Table A.5-2: Summary of Plant Account Activity by Year

	Year of Plant Activity	Dollar Value of Plant Installed	Plant Retirements Dollar Value of Retired Plant	Year Installed	Age at Retirement	Balance of Plant at End of Year
		[1]	[2]			[3]
a	1999	$98,220	$1,860	1999	0	$96,360
b	2000	$112,500	$0	–		$208,860
c	2001	$194,910	$5,400	1999	2	
			3,060	2000	1	
			1,230	2001	0	
		Subtotal 2001	$9,690			$394,080
d	2002	$398,520	$9,360	2000	2	
			5,540	2001	1	
			2,610	2002	0	
		Subtotal 2002	$17,510			$775,090
e	2003	$268,470	$1,800	1999	4	
			2,610	2000	3	
			14,130	2001	2	
			18,630	2002	1	
		Subtotal 2003	$37,170			$1,006,390
f	2004	$975,210	$3,240	1999	5	
			5,910	2000	4	
			52,200	2001	3	
			14,610	2002	2	
		Subtotal 2004	$75,960			$1,905,640
g	2005	$854,760	$6,270	1999	6	
			5,820	2000	5	
			6,210	2001	4	
			7,110	2002	3	
			20,520	2003	2	
			25,200	2004	1	
			2,340	2005	0	
		Subtotal 2005	$73,470			$2,686,930
h	2006	$592,950	$8,340	1999	7	
			10,200	2000	6	
			9,220	2001	5	
			14,220	2002	4	
			12,480	2003	3	
			38,430	2004	2	
			23,910	2005	1	
		Subtotal 2006	$116,800			$3,163,080

Chapter 5: Cost Measurement

In Table A.5-3, Column [1] shows the total plant investment in each year. Columns [2]–[9] show the total amount of plant, of a given vintage, at the beginning of each age interval and the amount of plant retired that was installed in the year listed.[86] For example, reading across the top row, of the $98,220 of 1999 vintage plant installed, we see that $1,860 was retired in the first (half) year, leaving $96,360 (Column [3]), none was retired the following year, $5,400 was retired the year after that, and so forth. At the beginning of 2006, the last year of the study, $79,650 of 1999 vintage equipment remains, and $8,340 of that is retired by the end of that year.

Table A.5-3: Annual Exposures and Retirements

	Additions	\multicolumn{8}{c}{Age Intervals: Plant Net of Retirement by Vintage}
		0.0–0.5	0.5–1.5	1.5–2.5	2.5–3.5	3.5–4.5	4.5–5.5	5.5–6.5	6.5–7.5
Year	[1]	[2]	[3]	[4]	[5]	[6]	[7]	[8]	[9]
1999	$98,220	$98,220	$96,360	$96,360	$90,960	$90,960	$89,160	$85,920	$79,650
		($1,860)	$0	($5,400)	$0	($1,800)	($3,240)	($6,270)	($8,340)
2000	$112,500	$112,500	$112,500	$109,440	$100,080	$97,470	$97,470	$91,650	
		$0	($3,060)	($9,360)	($2,610)	$0	($5,820)	($10,200)	
2001	$194,910	$194,910	$193,680	$188,140	$174,010	$168,100	$161,890		
		($1,230)	($5,540)	($14,130)	($5,910)	($6,210)	($9,220)		
2002	$398,520	$398,520	$395,910	$377,280	$325,080	$317,970			
		($2,610)	($18,630)	($52,200)	($7,110)	($14,220)			
2003	$268,470	$268,470	$268,470	$253,860	$233,340				
		$0	($14,610)	($20,520)	($12,480)				
2004	$975,210	$975,210	$975,210	$950,010					
		$0	($25,200)	($38,430)					
2005	$854,760	$854,760	$852,420						
		($2,340)	($23,910)						
2006	$592,950	$592,950							
		$0							
A. Total Exposures:		$3,495,540	$2,894,550	$1,975,090	$923,470	$674,500	$348,520	$177,570	$79,650
B. Total Retirements:		($8,040)	($90,950)	($140,040)	($28,110)	($22,230)	($18,280)	($16,470)	($8,340)

After 4 years, $90,960 of the $98,220 plant installed in 1999 remains.

In 2001, $5,400 of 1999 vintage (1.5–2.5 years old) equipment was retired.

The triangular shape of these entries occurs because, in the present (2006), the oldest vintage of 2006 equipment is 0.0–0.5 years, of 2005 equipment 0.5–1.5 years, and so forth.

---

[86] In the example, the *vintage* of the plant refers to the year it was installed. The age of the plant is based on the year in which a given vintage is retired. So, 1999 vintage plant retired in the year 2005 will be in the 5.5–6.5 year age interval.

At the bottom of Table A.5-3, two lines are shown: Total Exposures and Total Retirements. Total Exposures equals the sum of all plant of a given age that has not been retired. So, it adds up all remaining plant of a specific age at the beginning of each age interval. Total Retirements equals the sum of all retirements of that age that occur during that age interval.

Using the Total Exposures and Total Retirements data, we can construct an Observed Life table, as shown in Table A.5-4.

Table A.5-4: Observed Life Table

Age Interval	Exposures in Interval [1]	Retirements in Interval [2]	Ret. Ratio in Interval [3]	1 - Ret. Ratio in Interval [4]	Survivor Curve [5]
0.0–0.5	$3,495,540	($8,040)	0.23%	99.77%	100.00%
0.5–1.5	$2,894,550	($90,950)	3.14%	96.86%	99.77%
1.5–2.5	$1,975,090	($140,040)	7.09%	92.91%	96.64%
2.5–3.5	$923,470	($28,110)	3.04%	96.96%	89.78%
3.5–4.5	$674,500	($22,230)	3.30%	96.70%	87.05%
4.5–5.5	$348,520	($18,280)	5.25%	94.75%	84.18%
5.5–6.5	$177,570	($16,470)	9.28%	90.72%	79.77%
6.5–7.5	$79,650	($8,340)	10.47%	89.53%	72.37%

Notes:
[1] From Table A.5-3 (Row A)
[2] From Table A.5-3 (Row B)
[3] Equals [2] ÷ [1]
[4] Equals 1.0 – [3]
[5] In Interval 0, equals 100% by definition. Else, equals $[4]_{t-1} \times [5]_{t-1}$

Columns [1] and [2] just repeat the Total Exposures and Total Retirements data from Table A.5-3. Column [3] shows the Retirement Ratio, which equals the percentage of equipment of a given age that is retired. So, Table A.5-4 shows that the *retirement ratio* for plant between 0.5 and 1.5 years of age equals 3.14%. Column [4] is the *survivor ratio* for that age of equipment, equal to one minus the retirement ratio. Finally, Column [5] is the survivor curve, which is the percentage surviving at the beginning of each age interval times the survivor ratio for that age group. By definition, the initial survivor curve starts at 100%, since all equipment initially installed must exist for some amount of time before it is retired. For example, at the beginning of the second age interval, 0.5–1.5 years, the survivor curve percentage is the surviving percentage at the beginning of the previous interval times the percentage that survived that previous interval. Thus, the 0.5–1.5 year survivor percentage equals 100.0% × 99.77% = 99.77%. The 1.5–2.5 year survivor percentage equals 99.77% × 96.86% = 96.64%, and so forth. By graphing the survivor percentages in Column [5] of Table A.5-4, we create the stub survivor curve shown in Figure A.5-3.

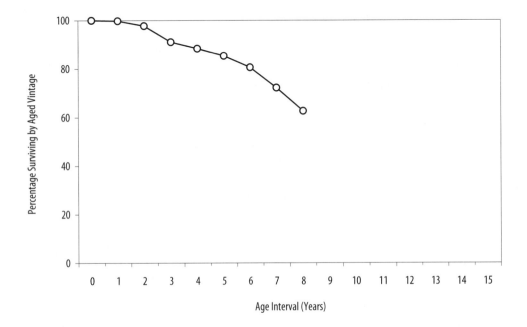

Figure A.5-3: Derived Stub Survivor Curve

The calculations made in Table A.5-4 are geared toward fitting the "stub" survivor curve data to an established survivor curve. The reason is that, by fitting these data to a known survivor curve with a well-defined shape, we can estimate the expected ASL and expected ARL for the account under study, and we can ultimately determine the appropriate "just and reasonable" depreciation rates for that account. That is where previously established survivor curves enter the picture. If we are going to use an established survivor curve to estimate ASL and ARL, it will be important to determine which curve best fits the observed retirement data. It is as important, however, to determine whether future retirements will continue to follow the observed pattern of past retirements. Since the latter is judgmental, determining the "right" rate of depreciation as part of a regulated firm's COS can be difficult and controversial, especially where actual depreciation experience is limited.

Empirical Estimates of Survivor Curves: the Iowa Curves

The most commonly used survivor curves for depreciation analysis are the so-called *Iowa Curves*, which were developed in the early part of the twentieth century.[87] These curves were developed at Iowa State University based on data collected for 53 different types of industrial property, from electric lamps to locomotives. Subsequently, the 53 types of property were collected into 18 different types of generalized survivor curves. The 18 curves were based on three general properties related to whether the greatest rate of retirements was likely to occur prior to the property reaching its average age (called "L" curves because they are asymmetrical to the left of the mean), after the property reached its average age (called "R" curves because they are asymmetrical to the right of the mean), or at the time the property reaches its average age (called "S" curves because they are symmetrical about the mean). There are six different types of "L" curves, seven types of "S" curves, and five types of "R" curves. For example, a "10-S0" Iowa Curve means that it is a Symmetrical curve with a 10-year ASL. The "0" designation refers to the shape within the class of symmetrical curves.

Figure A.5-4 presents an example of an "L3" Iowa survivor curve and its various components. For this type of curve, the greatest rate of retirements (the *mode* of the "Retirement Frequency Curve") lies to the left of the average life (and, hence, retirement age) shown as the dashed vertical line at 100% of average life.

This particular survivor curve extends to 240% of the average life, meaning that the longest lifetime of a piece of equipment in this class would have a lifespan 2.4 times the average lifespan. The probable life curve is derived from the survivor curve. It provides an answer to the question, "What is the remaining life expectancy of equipment with an average of X years today?"

---

[87] Robley Winfrey and Edwin Kurtz, "Life Characteristics of Physical Property," *Iowa Engineering Exp. Sta. Bul.* 103 (1921); Robley Winfrey, "Statistical Analyses of Industrial Property Retirements," Bulletin 125, Engineering Research Institute (formerly Iowa Engineering Experiment Station), Iowa State University, 1935.

Figure A.5-4: Iowa "L3" Survivor Curve and its Derivative Curves

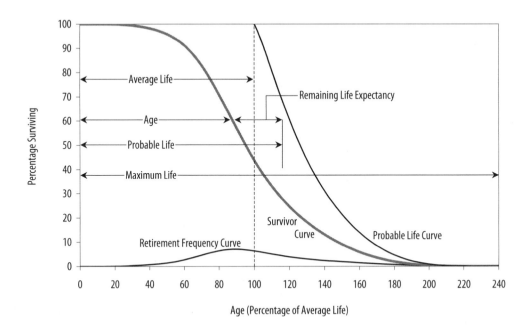

By using what are called *aged data*, such as the data presented in Table A.5-3, one can determine the best-fitting survivor curve, typically by using a *least-squares* approach to fitting the stub survivor curve data.[88] Of course, if there are very little historic retirement data, no statistical curve fitting procedure will be accurate. In those cases, or in cases in which future retirements are not expected to follow the observed historical pattern, a depreciation analyst must use judgment, based on the retirement experience at other companies, industry studies, or specific conditions for the equipment being studied. This is one more reason why depreciation studies can be controversial.

---

[88] "Least-squares" is the most common curve fitting technique and is based on minimizing the sum of squared residuals. For an introduction to least-squares analysis, see David Freedman, Robert Pisani, and Roger Purves, *Statistics*, 3d ed. (New York: W.W. Norton, 1998).

CHAPTER 6
COST ALLOCATION

6.1 Introduction

In the previous chapter, we introduced the five-step procedure to calculate regulated prices. We then examined in detail Step 1: how to calculate the revenue requirement, including estimation of a regulated firm's operating costs, depreciation, rate base, and rate of return. In this chapter, we turn to the next three steps. Together, these three steps determine how the revenue requirement is eventually allocated into different customer bins (e.g., residential, commercial, industrial). Only then can the fifth and final step—determining the rates that customers will be charged—be completed.

Typically, a cost-of-service (COS) model is just an electronic spreadsheet in which all of a regulated firm's costs are entered. To create this model, the firm's costs are accounted for in three steps.[1] First, all of the firm's (*known and measurable*) costs are distributed into major functional categories, such as production, transmission, distribution, retailing, and other unregulated activities. This is called cost *functionalization*. Functionalized costs are often broken down further into subfunctions. For example, production for a vertically integrated utility will likely be broken down by generating type: fossil, hydroelectric, renewable, and so forth. Similarly, transmission and distribution costs may be broken down into overhead and underground categories, or by voltage level.

Second, the now functionalized costs are further classified into specific categories: (1) costs that can be assigned directly to the regulated firm's customers (e.g., the costs of sending out bills and processing payments), (2) variable costs that depend on how much electricity or natural gas the firm sells (e.g., expenditures on fuel), and (3) fixed costs that are incurred regardless of sales (e.g., interest payments on debt instruments, fixed operation and maintenance costs, etc.). This second step is, not surprisingly, called cost *classification*. For example, functionalized production costs associated with electric generation are usually classified into *demand* (fixed) and *energy* (variable) categories, while meters that record consumers' electricity use are classified as customer costs.

---

[1] For a detailed explanation of cost accounting, especially methods of allocating joint costs, see, National Association of Regulatory Utility Commissioners (NARUC), *Electric Utility Cost Allocation Manual* (Washington, DC: NARUC, 1992).

Third, the classified costs are allocated among all of the regulated firm's customer groups. In a regulated rate proceeding, this last step is often the most controversial of the three. The reason is that there are no uniformly correct ways of allocating *joint* and *common* costs.[2] It is not uncommon, for example, to see different customer groups all making exactly the same argument before regulators, namely, that some portion of their costs should be allocated to the other groups. Since allocating costs among customers is a zero-sum game, such squabbles can become rather heated.

The next three sections of this chapter deal with each one of these three steps.

6.2 Cost Functionalization

Cost functionalization, which is Step 2 in our tariff-making procedure, is shown in Figure 6-1. When costs are functionalized, it means they are separated based on the major functions for which they were incurred, such as production, transmission, and distribution.

In the United States, FERC established a *Uniform System of Accounts* for this purpose. By establishing these accounts, regulators are able to more easily review how costs are functionalized and, ultimately, allocated among different customers. For example, in the United States, typical cost functionalization categories for regulated electric utilities include production, transmission, distribution, customer service and facilities, and administrative costs.[3]

Cost functionalization is important for several reasons. First, it can help avoid inefficient and inequitable cross-subsidies between regulated and nonregulated services. By ensuring that costs are allocated properly and by eliminating so-called "spillovers," customers pay only those costs directly associated with the regulated product or service provided to them, and sellers of unregulated products can compete fairly.[4] Second, even in the absence of unregulated activities, cost functionalization is critical to efficient rates. Without functionalizing costs correctly, the ultimate rates charged to different customer groups will not be economically efficient. Some customers will pay too much; others will pay too little.

---

[2] Recall the definitions of joint and common costs from Chapter 3. Joint costs are those that occur when the provision of one service is automatically simultaneous with production of another. Common costs refer to products that cannot be produced simultaneously, in other words, where producing more of one product means producing less of another.

[3] NARUC, *Electric Utility Cost Allocation Manual, supra* note 1, at 19–20.

[4] In many countries, this represents the main rationale for *ring-fencing*: to completely separate regulated and unregulated activities.

Figure 6-1: Cost Functionalization

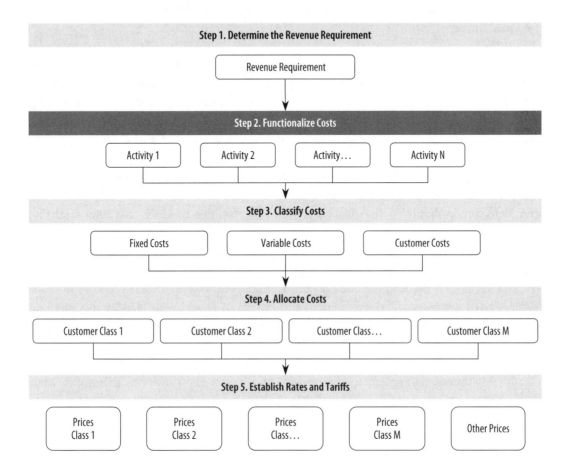

For a regulated company with multiple activities, each activity's costs are functionalized individually. Since the majority of a regulated firm's costs are easily allocable to the different functions identified, functionalization is usually straightforward. For example, the costs of building and maintaining a 500-kV electric transmission line are easily assigned to "transmission" categories.

The more challenging issue is functionalizing nonallocable costs, notably overhead, or "administrative and general" (A&G) costs. These include accounting costs, office costs such as rent, and so forth. Functionalizing these nonallocable costs requires additional analysis to identify the corresponding activities.

Two well-known methods used in the United States to functionalize nonallocable costs are the *Kansas-Nebraska* method and the *Massachusetts* method. (These methods have also been used in some other countries.)

The Kansas-Nebraska method allocates each cost account to either labor or plant. This choice depends on the main purpose or nature of each cost account. The advantage of the Kansas-Nebraska method is that it standardizes cost functionalization, thus providing both consistency and predictability. Typically, when the Kansas-Nebraska method is used, the majority of accounts are categorized as labor. For example, if the method is applied to A&G costs, it might be determined that 60% of A&G costs should be allocated to labor, and the remaining 40% allocated to plant. Once this step is accomplished, the labor and plant costs can then be assigned to specific functional activities. For example, once it has been determined that 60% of A&G costs are to be classified as labor, that total might be distributed as 30% generation, 15% transmission, 40% distribution, 10% retailing, and 5% to other unregulated activities, based on the directly allocated costs to each activity.

The Massachusetts method expands on the Kansas-Nebraska method by taking into account derived revenues as a third factor in addition to labor and plant. Under this method, each of the three factors is given equal weight. Under the Massachusetts method, the percentages of total labor payroll, operating revenue, and gross plant applicable to each function are calculated. For each function, the average of the three percentages is computed. Finally, this average is applied to the nonallocable expenses in order to determine what share of the A&G expense should be allocated to each function.[5]

Table 6-1 provides a simplified version of functional and classified costs. Each row represents a different cost function; each column, a different cost classification.

Table 6-1: Typical Accounts for an Electric Utility

Function	Classification		
Production	Capital costs	Fuel costs	O&M costs
Transmission	Rights-of-way	Capital costs	Payments to grid operators
Distribution	Tree trimming	Electric poles	Meters
Administrative & General (A&G)	Office lease	Health care	Employee salaries
Accounting	Billing system	Postage	Collection agency fees

---

[5] Internationally, in countries where both methods have been considered to functionalize costs, the Massachusetts method has generally not been selected. The reason is that some of the prices of products and activities have not been cost-based historically, because they were either subsidized or competitively provided. In either case, using the Massachusetts model would lead to volatile allocation results because of the revenue component.

In the United States, the actual cost classification categories are based on the *Uniform System of Accounts* developed by FERC, which developed separate account classifications to be used by electric and natural gas companies.[6] These accounts are broken down into balance sheet (i.e., debt and equity), plant (capital assets), and operation and maintenance expenses. For example, Table 6-2 shows a sample of the FERC natural gas plant distribution plant accounts.

Table 6-2: Sample Natural Gas Distribution System Plant and Expense Accounts

Distribution Plant		Distribution Expenses—Operation	
374	Land and land rights.	871	Distribution load dispatching.
375	Structures and improvements.	872	Compressor station labor and expenses.
376	Mains.	873	Compressor station fuel and power (Major only).
377	Compressor station equipment.	874	Mains and services expenses.
378	Measuring and regulating station equipment—General.	875	Measuring and regulating station expenses—General.
379	Measuring and regulating station equipment—City gate check stations.	876	Measuring and regulating station expenses—Industrial.
380	Services.	877	Measuring and regulating station expenses—City gate check stations.
381	Meters.	878	Meter and house regulator expenses.
382	Meter installations.	879	Customer installations expenses.
383	House regulators.	880	Other expenses.
384	House regulatory installations.	881	Rents.
385	Industrial measuring and regulating station equipment.		
386	Other property on customers' premises.		
387	Other equipment.		

Source: FERC

6.3 Cost Classification

Cost classification just means identifying costs as either fixed, variable, or customer-based, as shown in Figure 6-2. Variable costs are dependent on the amount of a regulated firm's output or sales, while fixed costs are incurred regardless of output. Customer costs are directly incurred by customers and can be categorized by customer types.

---

[6] Complete copies of these accounts can be found at http://www.ferc.gov.

Fundamentals of Energy Regulation

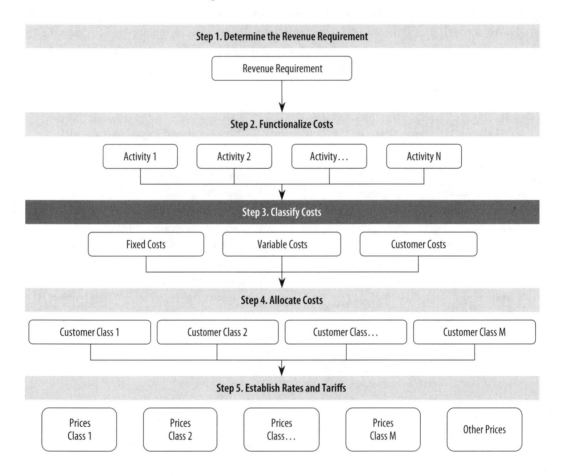

Figure 6-2: Cost Classification

By distinguishing between these three types of costs in determining regulated rates, cost classification can better match rates to costs. The optimum method of classifying costs not only matches each account to its appropriate cost category in the accounting system but also includes an allocation mechanism to deal with accounts comprising a mix of both fixed and variable costs. Of course, good regulatory accounting design will avoid accounts having such a mix, but in some countries, account designs were established before tariff methodologies were developed, and, thus, an allocation mechanism is required.

There are other methods for classifying costs, including the Atlantic-Seaboard method and the modified Seaboard method. These methods classify costs based on fixed ratios of percentages (e.g., 50:50, 75:25, etc.). These, too, are used in the United States, although there is little supporting rationale for their use. Instead, such use is the result of negotiations among parties to regulatory litigation.

Not all countries classify costs into fixed, variable, and customer categories. In some countries, especially where price formulas have already been agreed to, once the revenue requirement is functionalized, costs may be classified into numerous categories related to subactivities (e.g., low-voltage O&M, medium-voltage O&M, marketing, etc.), because different subactivities enter into different formulas. For example, some Latin American countries separate out marketing costs that are directly charged to certain types of customers.

6.4 Cost Allocation

Cost allocation—the process of matching the different types of classified costs to different groups of customers—represents the fourth, and arguably most difficult, step in setting regulated prices. Questions regarding how to determine appropriate cost allocation factors have been debated for decades. As the U.S. Supreme Court recognized in 1919 in *Groesbeck*, "it is much easier to reject [cost allocation] formulas presented as being misleading than to find one apparently adequate."[7] Moreover, cost allocation factors that may be appropriate at one time for one case may not necessarily be appropriate in later cases.

The courts have recognized that the regulatory agencies must constantly confront not only economic efficiency, but also questions of fairness in what they do. Thus, as a matter of law, "considerations of fairness, not mere mathematics, govern the allocation of costs."[8] Utilities often price their services with only a small degree of cost analysis. The result is less an assignment of cost in accordance with cost causation than an allocation of joint costs through more or less arbitrary factors.[9] Electric utility costs, for example, may be assigned according to peak responsibility or time-of-day factors, but the relatively low levels of usage that may be swept into some of these cost schedules can bear little, if any, causal relation to any particular costs.[10]

---

[7] *Groesbeck v. Duluth, S.S. & A.Ry*, 250 U.S. 607, 614–16 (1919).

[8] *Colorado Interstate Gas Co. v. F.P.C.*, 324 U.S. 581, 591 (1945).

[9] As we discuss in the next chapter, for interconnected electric utility systems, transmission costs are *rolled in* and assigned systemwide by the FERC, rather than assigned to the particular classes that benefit from them.

[10] For further discussion, see Leonard S. Goodman, *The Process of Ratemaking*, vol. I (Vienna, VA: Public Utilities Reports, 1998), 380–82.

One fundamental regulatory principle is to allocate costs to those who cause them.[11] Yet, allocating costs among different customer groups is almost always a contentious part of a COS analysis. There are several reasons for this. The most important is that, whereas it is generally straightforward to allocate variable energy costs (such as fuel costs) among different customers, allocating joint costs (such as the costs associated with meeting peak energy demand) is more difficult. As we discussed in Section 3.5 of Chapter 3, there is no unique way to allocate joint costs. Thus, determining who is causing what costs is not always straightforward. Moreover, there is always an incentive to "prove" that someone else is the cost causer. Thus, large industrial customers may try to justify allocating proportionately more costs to residential customers based on the latter group's highly volatile energy demand over time, relative to industrial customers' steadier demand.[12]

A second controversy can arise when costs are allocated based on another fundamental economic principle: avoiding cross-subsidies. In practice, however, it can be difficult to estimate cross-subsidies. Moreover, even if cross-subsidies are identified, other rate-setting principles that stress equity between customers, notably "just and reasonable" requirements, can conflict with economic goals. For example, urban consumers typically subsidize rural ones. Otherwise, the low population density of rural customers would mean they would pay exorbitant rates to cover the fixed costs of providing service.[13]

Still another cost allocation controversy (albeit a derivative one) can arise when avoiding cross-subsidies clashes with another cost allocation principle: allocating costs to those customers who benefit from the expenditures. At first glance, these two principles appear to converge to the same idea: if there is no cross-subsidy, costs cannot *not* be allocated to those who benefit. This proposition is not as incontrovertible as it seems, however, because the definition of "benefit" can be, and often is, vague and elastic. For example, if an industrial customer of an electric utility has a substation built on its property for the sole purpose of serving its load, then aligning costs and benefits would seem to be straightforward: the industrial customer pays all of the substation costs. However, it is not unknown for large

---

[11] From a purely economic standpoint, there are cases where it does not matter how costs are allocated. This is a consequence of the *Coase Theorem*, which we discuss in Chapter 11, in regard to environmental regulation.

[12] The ratio of average to peak energy demand over time is called *load factor*. As we discuss below, load factor is a common measure with which cost allocation is performed. However, determining the appropriate time period over which to measure load factor (by month, by year, etc.) is not always easy.

[13] Prior to the Rural Electrification Act of 1936 in the U.S., individuals living in rural areas rarely had electricity. The goal of that Act, which created the Rural Electrification Administration, was to create universal access to electric service.

industrial customers to argue that a utility's other customers all receive indirect economic benefits from the industrial customer's presence, most notably jobs, and, as a result, those customers should bear some cost responsibility as well.[14]

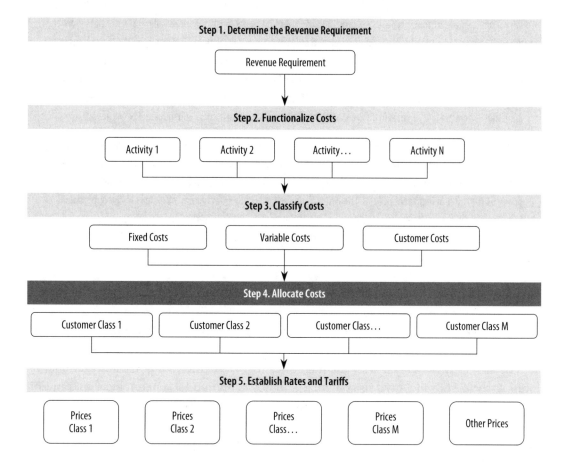

Figure 6-3: Cost Allocation

---

[14] Sometimes large customers may even issue veiled economic threats that, unless they receive cost consideration, they may move out of the utility's service territory. In Chapter 7, we will discuss similar issues in the discussion of rate setting and economic development rates.

> **Class Acts**
>
> There is also another complication when allocating fixed costs among different customer groups: defining those groups, called *rate classes,* in the first place.
>
> According to NARUC, rate classes are determined "according to certain characteristics which are common to all members of the class."[15] Although there are innumerable attributes regulators can conceivably choose from, the factors that historically have been used are customer type, usage type, and consumption characteristics. For example, customer classes are traditionally separated into residential, commercial, and industrial categories. However, subgroups of those three customer groups are often created as needed, such as distinguishing between "large" and "small" industrial customers, depending on the nature of the services provided.[16] Although defining "large" and "small" is clearly subjective, these subgroup definitions are less problematic than the differences in the ways regulators determine which customers are commercial and which are industrial. (There are few vagaries in differentiating between residential customers and industrial or commercial ones.)
>
> One reason is that differences in classifying customers as either commercial or industrial can create problems resulting from multijurisdictional comparisons. For example, suppose industrial customers in State A have higher average electric rates than industrial customers in State B. This does not necessarily mean that State B's industrial customers are faring poorly as the result of inefficient utilities. The cost differences may result entirely from differences in customer classification. If that is the case, policymakers who decide to "do something" to address observed rate differences can end up adopting policies that misallocate costs and reduce economic efficiency.

Cost Allocation Methodologies

Allocating variable costs is generally straightforward because such allocations are based on volumetric measures. By definition, variable costs vary with respect to output or sales, and so they are easily associated with the quantities that cause the variations. For example, allocating the cost of fuel used to operate a compressor station for a natural gas distribution system can be based on an individual customer's natural gas use.

Allocating fixed costs is quite another story. Since many types of fixed costs are joint or common, there is no unique method for their allocation. As a result, numerous methodologies have been developed to allocate fixed costs between different customer groups.[17] And, not surprisingly, these methodologies, which are especially prevalent for electric companies, can be controversial.

---

[15] NARUC, Staff Subcommittee on Gas, *Gas Distribution Rate Design Manual* (Washington, DC: NARUC, 1989), 16.
[16] *Id.*
[17] *See,* NARUC, *Electric Utility Cost Allocation Manual, supra* note 1.

Although, from an economic perspective, costs should be allocated to those who cause them, this is a particularly difficult principle to follow when dealing with joint and common costs. Determining what share of each joint or common cost should be allocated to which service, activity, or product—and eventually customer—is more art than science. Regardless of the methodology used, however, it is critical to follow a predetermined set of cost categories applicable across the industry, such as the aforementioned Uniform System of Accounts developed by the FERC to ensure consistency and efficiency.

In cases where allocating fixed costs poses a challenge, it may be possible to use allocation factors that reflect cost causation. For example, Pemex allocates common fixed costs based on wages and benefits paid to employees to its regulated subsidiaries in Mexico.

Allocating Fixed Costs

Allocating fixed electric costs can be particularly problematic. The reason is that determining the responsibility for those costs on an annualized basis is difficult. For example, on a hot day, the demand for air conditioning increases. Residential, commercial, and industrial customers all turn on air conditioners. As a result, the local electric utility may have to operate one of its peaking units. Even though the peaking unit may only be used once or twice a year, it will still need to be maintained over the entire year, it will need to have an available fuel supply, and it must have operators who can quickly start the plant and run it safely.

How to allocate those costs, however, depends on a number of factors, all of which ultimately stem from establishing cost causation. Would the peaking unit have been needed but for all of those residential customers using their air conditioning? Or perhaps it was all of the commercial office buildings and their air conditioning use that was the deciding factor. Moreover, even if one can accurately point a finger of responsibility at the appropriate customer group, that responsibility may change each time the peaking unit is used.

Even deciding how to allocate the variable operating costs associated with the peaking unit, including fuel costs, may not be straightforward. For example, if we could establish that the peaking unit would not have run but for residential customers' air conditioning load, should those customers be responsible for 100% of the peaking unit's operating costs? These complexities have given rise to the development of many methods that can be used to allocate production, distribution, and transmission costs.

Examples of Cost Allocation Methodologies

Some costs are straightforward to allocate. For example, the costs to produce a customer bill are the same regardless of the level of consumption, and so billing costs are typically allocated to each customer group based on the number of customers in each group. Similarly, allocating the total cost of coal purchased for a coal-fired power plant is likely to be based on the relative consumption of electricity by each customer group.

Table 6-3 shows customer and energy allocation factors for a natural gas LDC. For example, Column [2] shows the customer allocation factors. These factors are derived by dividing the average number of per-class customers in the test year by the average number of all customers. Similarly, the consumption (energy) allocation factors shown in Column [4] are derived by dividing total natural gas consumption by class shown in Column [3] by the aggregate total consumption. As the table shows, the customer and consumption allocation factors are quite different. For example, whereas the industrial class customer allocation factor is just over 1%, the industrial consumption allocation factor is almost 50%. This is so because industrial consumption is almost as great as residential and commercial consumption combined.

**Table 6-3: Natural Gas Distribution Company—
Estimation of Customer and Energy Allocators (2006 Test Year)**

Customer Class	Avg. No. of Customers	Customer Allocation Factor	Total Consumption (106 cubic feet)	Consumption Allocation Factor	Consumption per Customer (103 cubic feet)
	[1]	[2]	[3]	[4]	[5]
Residential	40,000	94.11%	3,600,000	39.56%	90
Commercial	2,000	4.71%	1,000,000	10.99%	500
Industrial	500	1.18%	4,500,000	49.45%	9,000
Total	42,500	100.00%	9,100,000	100.00%	

Energy and customer allocators are generally straightforward because they are easily measured and they preserve the goal of aligning costs and benefits. If residential customers account for 40% of total natural gas purchase costs, it makes intuitive sense to allocate 40% of the natural gas cost to them.

Demand allocators, however, are more problematic. The reason is that natural gas and electric distribution systems are geared towards meeting peak demands. Thus, natural gas distribution pipe must be sized so that enough natural gas can flow through to meet customers' demand on the coldest days, when heating needs are highest. Similarly, local electric utilities must own or contract for enough generating reserves to meet peak demand and to ensure a reliable electric system. While both electric and natural gas utilities present cost allocation challenges, allocating production, transmission, and distribution costs for an electric system is arguably the most complex undertaking of all, perhaps a testament to the many different methods that have been developed and used by regulators and analysts to allocate those costs.

Again, the fundamental difficulty in establishing demand allocation factors is that we are trying to allocate joint (or common) costs, and there is no uniquely correct way to do so. As a result of the lack of unique, or even intuitive, allocation approaches, regulators have developed a number of alternative approaches. Most of these examine the relationship between individual group peak demand at the time of, or *coincident* with, system peak demand.

Consider, for example, Table 6-4. The top of this table shows annual and *coincident peak* loads (i.e., the load of each customer group at the time when the entire utility system reaches its peak demand) for an electric distribution utility for each of three customer classes—residential, commercial, and industrial.[18] For each customer class, Column [1] shows the maximum annual coincident peak load, while Columns [2]–[5] show the seasonal coincident peaks. Column [6] shows average annual demand and, finally, Column [7] is the annual system load factor for the class.[19]

The highest system peak load for the test year, 21,500 MW, occurs in the summer. However, while residential peak load is also highest at this time, 7,700 MW, commercial and industrial loads do not peak in summer. Instead, these sectors peak in the winter, as shown in Column [3].

The bottom half of Table 6-4 shows a variety of allocation factors: (1) those based on peak loads over the entire year and each quarter [Columns 1 to 5], (2) those based on an average of the four quarterly *coincident peaks* [Column 6], and (3) those based on *reciprocal load factor* [Column 7].[20, 21] As the table shows, the percentage of costs that is allocated to each customer group varies greatly depending on the methodology used. Industrial customers,

---

[18] The "Total System" load shown in Column [1], 21, 890 MW, is greater than the annual coincident system peak load because the Column [1] values occur at different times of the year.

[19] Average annual demand equals total annual consumption (MWh) ÷ 8,760 hours. System load factor equals average annual demand divided by annual peak coincident demand.

[20] A reciprocal load factor approach uses the share of the inverse of the load factor on the sum of the inverses of each customer class load factor.

[21] Another approach is the average-excess demand method, which allocates a portion of the capacity costs to each customer based on each customer's average load, and the rest is allocated using the noncoincident peak method.

for example, would be assigned almost 44% of demand-related costs using the "4-CP" method (based on the average of the four quarterly coincident peak loads for each customer group), but only 26% of costs using the reciprocal load factor. Not for nothing do most round-the-clock industrial customers argue that their high load factors mean they should be assigned the least amount of peak demand-related costs. Residential customers, however, would be strongly inclined to argue that regulators use the 4-CP method to allocate demand-related costs.

Table 6-4: Electric Distribution Company—Estimation of Demand Allocators (2006 Test Year)

Customer Class	Annual Maximum Class Peak (MW)	Summer Coincident Peak (MW)	Winter Coincident Peak (MW)	Spring Coincident Peak (MW)	Fall Coincident Peak (MW)	Average Annual Demand (MW)	Average Annual Load Factor (%)
	[1]	[2]	[3]	[4]	[5]	[6]	[7]
Residential	7,700	7,700	6,410	5,400	5,505	3,752	48.73
Commercial	5,380	5,100	5,380	4,350	4,100	3,360	62.45
Industrial	8,810	8,700	8,810	8,350	8,295	6,831	77.54
Total System	21,890	21,500	20,600	18,100	17,900	13,943	–

			Alternative Allocation Factors				
Customer Class	Annual Noncoincident	Summer	Winter	Spring	Fall	4-CP	Reciprocal Load Factor
	[1]	[2]	[3]	[4]	[5]	[6]	[7]
Residential	35.2%	35.8%	31.1%	29.8%	30.8%	31.9%	41.5%
Commercial	24.6%	23.7%	26.1%	24.1%	22.9%	24.2%	32.4%
Industrial	40.2%	40.5%	42.8%	46.1%	46.3%	43.9%	26.1%
Total System	100.0%	100.0%	100.0%	100.0%	100.0%	100.0%	100.0%

In fact, there are many methods that have been developed to allocate different functionalized types of joint and common electric and natural gas utility costs.[22] Each method has its own logical appeal and, depending on the results, its own advocates. Since cost allocation ultimately is a zero-sum game, however, regulators inevitably face difficult choices, as well as strong opposition from customer groups who believe they have been allocated more than their "fair share" of costs.

---

[22] The NARUC *Electric Utility Cost Allocation Manual* contains numerous other examples of cost allocators and their derivation, *supra* note 1.

6.5 Chapter Summary

As the previous chapter showed, the five-step procedure to develop appropriate regulated rates and tariffs requires a complex set of procedures to estimate the *known and measurable* costs that establish a regulated firm's revenue requirement. In this chapter, we turned our attention to Steps Two through Four of the rate-setting process. Once the overall revenue requirement has been established, the costs associated with that revenue requirement are *functionalized* among the different regulated activities. This ensures that regulated activities paid for by a firm's ratepayers do not subsidize unregulated activities that benefit shareholders. The latter is called *ring-fencing*.

Step 3 takes the now functionalized costs attributable to regulated operations and classifies them as either fixed, variable, or customer costs. These cost categories can then be used to set the rates for regulated services based on ratepayers' usage of such services. Finally, Step 4 allocates the now classified costs among the different customer classes. Because there are so many diverse ways to allocate costs, and because cost allocation is a zero-sum game, cost allocation can often be contentious.

Having presented the first four steps, we are now ready to investigate the fifth and final step in calculating regulated prices: determining the actual rates and tariffs charged to customers. That is the subject of the next chapter.

CHAPTER 7
RATE-SETTING PRINCIPLES AND PROCEDURES

7.1 Introduction

We come now to the fifth and final step in the process of determining regulated rates. As shown in Figure 7-1, the process began with estimating the revenue requirement. Next, the costs making up the revenue requirement were functionalized. Then the functionalized costs were classified as either fixed, variable, or customer costs and were allocated among different customer groups. The final step is determining prices, which at its most basic level consists of dividing the allocated costs by the appropriate consumption measures. For example, suppose Utility A's residential customers have been allocated $10 million in costs. If total residential consumption during the test year is expected to be 100 million kWh, then regulators could simply set a flat rate equal to $10 million ÷ 100 million kWh, or 10¢ per kWh.

In practice, however, regulators typically design tariffs that are more complex. For example, suppose that of the $10 million allocated to residential customers, $1 million was allocated to customer charges, such as meter reading, sending out bills, and so forth. Suppose there are a total of 10,000 customers. Then, an alternative tariff design would levy a $100 per customer charge per year (or $8.33 per month) plus 9¢ for each kWh consumed (= $9 million ÷ 100 million kWh).[1] This alternative tariff design would also recover $10 million, assuming that residential consumers still consume 100 million kWh at the lower price.[2]

In fact, there are innumerable ways to set regulated rates. Not only do regulators use different rate-setting and tariff design methods, they also have different social and economic goals. Moreover, the complexity of tariff design results from the oft-competing objectives of tariff designers. At the most basic level, for example, conflicts can arise between regulatory principles of economic efficiency and of aligning costs to causation, versus principles of equity and fairness. At the more technical level, the ways in which regulators design tariffs and rates have an effect on total consumption. Thus, when designing tariffs, it is important

---

[1] The $8.33 per month is obtained by dividing $1,000,000 by 10,000 customers (= $100 per year) divided by 12 months.
[2] We discuss this issue in the next section on *billing determinants*.

to accurately estimate the factors that affect consumption. Those factors include the number of customers in each rate class and consumption per customer. How these factors are estimated is the subject of the next section.

Figure 7-1: Determining Prices

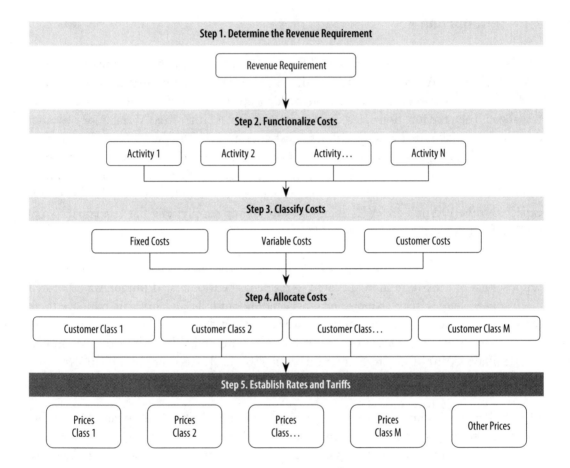

7.2 Billing Determinants

Billing determinants are simply the units on which prices are actually levied (e.g., therms, kilowatts of demand, kilowatt-hours, and so forth). They typically are estimated based on overall energy consumption and peak energy demand. The types of billing determinants needed for rate and tariff setting also depend, in part, on the types of cost allocators used to divvy up costs between the different rate classes. For example, if all costs were allocated on the basis of aggregate energy consumption, it would make little economic sense to set tariffs that were based on peak energy demand.

In establishing billing determinants, the first step is developing an accurate forecast of consumption. Although billing determinants are sometimes based on so-called *naïve forecasts* (in which current consumption is used to establish billing determinants), most regulators require more sophisticated forecasts that account for anticipated changes in the number of customers as well as macroeconomic conditions that affect consumption. Still more sophisticated approaches address the impacts of anticipated changes in regulated energy prices themselves. For example, a vertically integrated utility forecasting changes in electric demand would wish to simultaneously consider the relative change in consumption and the anticipated changes in prices.[3] This, not surprisingly, raises the issue of how, if we are to forecast changes in consumption and demand so as to determine new prices, can we use the anticipated change in prices as an input? The answer is that economists use what are called *simultaneous equations* methods to equilibrate both impacts.[4]

Another key component in setting billing determinants is *weather normalization*. Most customers' energy consumption is affected by weather conditions that affect the demand for heating and cooling, lighting, and so forth. For example, the demand for natural gas varies substantially from day to day, especially among residential and small commercial-industrial customers, who use natural gas almost exclusively for space heating. As a result, demand tends to be much higher in the winter than during other seasons, with the highest demand on the coldest days. Given year-to-year variability in weather, basing billing determinants on historic consumption levels without correcting for weather conditions will almost certainly lead to pricing errors.

---

[3] Economists measure changes in consumption arising from changes in prices using *price elasticity* of demand. Price elasticity is defined as the percentage change in consumption arising from a percentage change in price. For example, if a 10% increase in the price of electricity reduces consumption by 5%, the price elasticity of demand will equal (-5%) ÷ (10%) = -0.5.

[4] Although there are many sophisticated techniques to forecast demand that account for price responses, many demand forecasts used for regulatory purposes do not consider those responses. Instead, these types of forecasts rely on "bottom-up" engineering approaches that estimate total demand based on assumptions about specific types of end-use equipment and process use (e.g., lighting, heating, cooling, etc.).

Estimation Methods

Regulators rely on numerous methods and procedures to estimate billing determinants. This is not surprising, since the types of billing determinants used to set rates and tariffs depend on the specific cost allocation and pricing methodologies regulators rely on.[5] Moreover, once the types of billing determinants to be used are selected, regulators must choose whether to base billing determinants on historical test year data or on forecast billing determinants for the rate year.

As we discuss in more detail in Section 7.3, rate and tariff structures can take numerous forms. The reason for this is the design characteristics of natural gas and electric distribution. Electric distribution systems are designed to serve peak loads, because electricity cannot, as yet, be stored cheaply. Natural gas distribution systems are also sized to account for peak demand, although natural gas is often stored centrally to smooth out peak capacity needs where pipeline capacity is constrained.[6]

Because electric and natural gas systems are designed to meet peak consumer demand, regulated rates and tariffs almost always incorporate multiple consumption measures and take on different structures that consumers rarely see elsewhere. Most consumers, for example, would be taken aback if the grocer charged higher prices for bread at mealtimes than during the rest of the day. In fact, politicians often pass laws against "price gouging"—such as boosting prices for ice and water after a natural disaster—to prevent such behavior.[7] Thus, distribution and transmission utilities typically charge consumers based on total consumption (e.g., kWh of electricity, therms, Btus, or Mcf of natural gas) and on the maximum rate of consumption (e.g., kilowatts in a given hour, natural gas usage per day).[8]

For electric utilities, both consumption and peak demand will change constantly in response to changes in the number of consumers, weather conditions, the mix of local business and industry, and so forth. Natural gas consumption and demand are a bit more complex and depend on whether the focus is on local distribution to retail consumers or pipeline transport for wholesale (and a few large retail) consumers. Local natural gas distribution firms typically deal with the same consumption and peak demand issues as electric distribution

---

[5] There are so many different combinations of allocation and pricing methods that an exhaustive analysis of them is beyond the scope of this chapter. The rest of the chapter provides a discussion of the general concepts used in tariff-making procedures.

[6] Natural gas is stored in either liquid form (i.e., LNG) or underground in old oil and gas wells, salt caverns, or even abandoned mines.

[7] Antigouging laws, however, are often hopelessly vague for competitively priced goods.

[8] The maximum rate of electric consumption is called *peak demand*. The maximum rate of natural gas consumption is typically a daily measure of *capacity*.

firms. Both consumption and peak demand are constantly changing. For natural gas pipelines, however, demand is more commonly measured as capacity subscribed by individual shipping customers.[9]

To make matters still more complex, different types of peak demand are calculated by utilities to estimate rates and tariffs. Specifically, utilities consider both *coincident peak* (i.e., the highest usage of the facilities at any point during the year) and *noncoincident peak* (i.e., the sum of the peak demands of each individual customer or customer group).[10] Moreover, tariffs can be based not only on annual coincident and noncoincident peaks, but also on seasonal or monthly peaks. For example, an electric utility whose system peaks every summer because of residential air conditioner loads, and every winter because of commercial heating loads, may examine winter and summer coincident peaks when allocating costs.

Finally, utilities also estimate *load factors* for rate and tariff setting. A load factor is just average usage divided by peak usage. So, if Megacorp's annual average electric consumption is 10 MW, but its peak demand in summer is 25 MW, its load factor equals 10 ÷ 25 = 40%. Naturally, there are different load factors, too: *system load factor*, which is the average of the entire utility divided by the coincidental peak load; *sector load factor*, which is average usage of a certain group of customers divided by their coincidental demand; and *customer load factor*, such as in our Megacorp example.

While usage information is easily collected, demand information is more difficult to gather because it requires measuring consumption every hour or day. However, most common consumption meters do not have the capacity to provide time-of-use data, especially for residential customers.[11] To get around this problem, especially for residential customers, electric utilities or regulators typically hire independent firms to conduct *peak demand studies* that sample consumption patterns of a small, but statistically valid, group of customers

---

[9] In Chapter 1, we briefly described how FERC deregulated the natural gas industry by separating production, transport, and distribution functions in the U.S. Wholesale natural gas customers typically purchase *firm capacity* on a pipeline that guarantees them access to a certain percentage of a pipeline's total capacity. (This is also called *contract carriage*, as opposed to oil pipelines, which offer service on a first-come, first-served basis, known as *common carriage*.) To prevent market manipulation, shippers that do not use all of their firm capacity could offer it to other customers. This is called *capacity release*.

[10] Since the peak demand of each customer can be observed at different times of the year, the noncoincident peak is always larger than the coincident peak. There are other methods that are also used that combine one of these two methods. For example, the "Average and Excess Demand" formula assigns the capacity expected at a load factor of 100% based on the average load, and the excess over that capacity (maximum load minus average load) is assigned to customers based on their noncoincident peak.

[11] This is changing as metering technology advances and costs decrease.

over a period of 12 to 18 months. The data collected are then evaluated to understand demand patterns, and the results are used to estimate billing determinants to be employed in the tariff calculation.[12]

Natural gas distribution utilities face measurement issues that are different from those of electric utilities. Peak natural gas demand is directly correlated with cold weather; storage allows utilities to reduce ("shave") their peak pipeline transportation requirements. Distribution utilities and regulators determine how much natural gas to store each year based on historical usage and weather data. The amount of storage, in turn, affects retail tariffs. In the case of natural gas transportation, for example, a typical peak measure that is taken into account is the sum of the highest accumulated three days of consumption per client.

Forecasting

There are as many ways to forecast demand and usage as there are economists and engineers. Covering all of these methods is far beyond our scope. Thus, in this section we focus only on the conceptual aspects of forecasting billing determinants.[13]

Forecasting Energy Consumption

Forecasting usage is easier than forecasting peak demand. For example, to forecast residential electric demand, one gathers a sufficiently long *time series* of data and fits a demand curve to that data. The demand curve takes into account the price of electricity charged, the prices of other competing fuels (e.g., natural gas, oil, propane, etc.), the number of residential customers, some measure of personal income, weather variables, and whatever other factors are required to torture the data to obtain a sufficiently accurate result. Forecasting commercial and industrial consumption proceeds in the same manner, except that business-specific factors (e.g., floor space, production output, etc.), rather than personal income, are typically used.

---

[12] These studies are not always current. For example, whereas Latin American countries typically perform these studies about two years before a new tariff is approved, the State of Vermont still uses a statewide study performed in the 1980s.

[13] For an introduction to forecasting methods, see, e.g., Patricia E. Gaynor and Rickey C. Kirkpatrick, *Introduction to Time-Series Modeling and Forecasting in Business and Economics*, (New York: McGraw-Hill, 1994), and Glenn D. Westley, *New Directions in Econometric Modeling of Energy Demand. With Applications to Latin America*, (Washington, DC: Inter-American Development Bank, 1992).

For residential customers, demand estimation is best done on a per capita basis; it is easier to estimate energy use for a typical residential customer than for the entire residential sector. Of course, this requires that the total number of potential customers for the rate period be estimated. This will be a function of predicted population growth, housing construction, rural/urban mix, trends towards urbanization, and so forth.

As we mentioned earlier, some regulators do not use econometric approaches to forecast demand and calculate billing determinants; they use a bottom-up engineering approach. These estimates calculate usage for specific types of equipment (e.g., lighting, cooking, process heat, etc.) based on observed utilization, alternative fuels, and potential sector growth for a given price path. The forecasts are then constructed based on assumptions about how customers switch equipment over time (based on estimated equipment lifetimes), the price of fuel used by the equipment, mandated efficiency standards, and so forth.

> **Common Problems Observed in Demand Forecasting**
>
> The most common problems we have observed (not an exhaustive list) when forecasting demand include the following:
>
> - Lack of official government forecasts or even records of macroeconomic data, such as inflation, GDP, employment, and population
> - Too much data aggregation that prevents more detailed forecasts from being estimated
> - Lack of reliable data (such as geographically disaggregated data), or small sample problems
> - Limited range of variation in the data (for example, a government establishing a price freeze or fixing prices in real terms and adjusting only for inflation)
> - Time series variables that move in concert with one another (this creates an econometric problem called *multicollinearity*)
> - Obsolete survey data

Forecasting Peak Demand

As we noted, estimating and forecasting peak demand is more difficult than estimating and forecasting aggregate consumption. There are a few reasons for this. First, peak demand is, by definition, an "outlier" of sorts, resulting from extreme events—staggeringly hot and humid weather, bitter cold, and the like. While it is straightforward to forecast trends in "averages," forecasters tend to be less adept at predicting extreme events, because, by their nature, extreme events are relatively rare. For example, whereas we could probably accurately forecast the average height of professional basketball players worldwide for the next decade, forecasting the number of players that will be over seven feet tall is more of a challenge.

The physical characteristics of a distribution or transmission system can also constrain peak demand forecasts. For example, a ski area's demand may be constrained today because the local electric distribution system cannot support more load without serious erosion of reliability. If the distribution system were expanded, the ski area might choose to expand, further increasing its peak requirements. However, if new distribution capacity were added just to meet the needs of the ski area, rates would also increase, and this likely would reduce the ski area's peak demand. This dilemma can be solved using a system of *simultaneous equations* that integrate demand and pricing models.

To further complicate estimates, some jurisdictions classify the investment impacts of additional demand and additional customers into two categories: horizontal and vertical growth. New customers for which a utility must expand its network beyond the existing configuration are classified as *horizontal growth*. New customers whose growth can be incorporated within the existing network are classified as *vertical growth*. The distinction raises regulatory issues because of two conflicting regulatory goals: the *obligation to serve* (since local distribution utilities are granted service monopolies on the condition they provide service to everyone in their service territory) and the requirement that rates be *fair, just and reasonable*. Although individual residential customers are rarely singled out as contributing to horizontal growth, individual large commercial and industrial customers often are. As a result, regulators, politicians, and these sorts of customers often enter into a complex, musical chairs-like dance of cost allocation, with all parties seeking to allocate costs to someone else's constituents.

Estimating Maximum Peak Capacity and Peak Demand

Maximum peak capacity is a very important estimation for a natural gas distribution company. The distribution system is designed with a capacity that can satisfy that theoretical peak, and the company contracts to guarantee that natural gas availability. Peak demand is the maximum demand in an hour, generally on one of the coldest days of the year.

Maximum Peak Capacity

The maximum capacity of a natural gas distribution network can always be transformed into a probabilistic number. In other words, a certain maximum capacity corresponds with the possibility of a curtailment every X years.

A probabilistic method is performed following these steps:

- Obtain daily data on consumption and temperature for a certain period

- Calculate an econometric relationship between consumption and temperature (which is always negative—the higher the temperature, the lower the natural gas demand)

- Obtain daily data on average temperature for a long period of time

- Study the data on temperature to obtain a statistical distribution

- Use the statistical fit of demand and temperature and temperature distribution to simulate a large number of winters

- Use the results of the simulation to calculate the probability of demand exceeding a certain level

One of the keys in obtaining robust results is to consider cold snaps, when very low temperatures persist for two or more consecutive days. For example, Figure 7-2 shows the temperature distribution in winter for a two-day cold snap in a North American city for a period of four years.

Figure 7-2: Observed Temperature Distribution

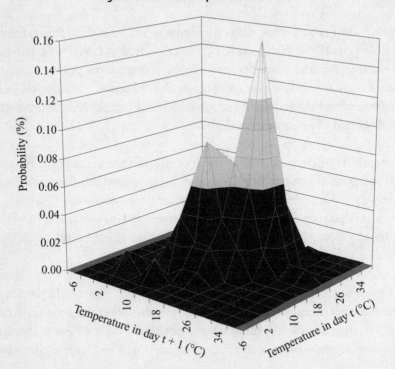

Peak Demand

Using the same simulations, load factors for each year and each sector can be estimated. Then, an average load factor per sector can be calculated based on forecast usage, which allows peak demand per sector to be determined.

Weather Normalization Methods

Weather normalization is a critical component of billing determinant estimates. Moreover, weather normalization plays an important role in other regulatory implications, such as determining the need to hold natural gas in storage to meet peak-day demand. Although a complete discussion of weather normalization methods is beyond the scope of this book, we review the basics in this section.

Most weather normalization begins with the *degree-day* concept, which can be applied for both heating and cooling purposes. A *heating degree day* (HDD) equals the difference between the average temperature for the day and a reference average temperature. In the United States, the reference average temperature is typically 68°F. For example, if the high and low today are 40°F and 20°F, respectively, for an average temperature of 30°F, then the HDD for today equals 68°F − 30°F = 38. When the average temperature is above the reference temperature, HDD equals 0.

Since energy demand is also affected by the demand for air conditioning, the concept of *cooling degree days* (CDD) is also used. CDD is calculated in exactly the same manner as HDD: it is equal to the difference between the day's average temperature and a reference temperature, and it is zero if that average is below the reference.[14] In addition to HDD and CDD measures, energy demand can be affected by humidity, cumulative temperatures over the past few days, and even hours of daylight.

Typically, economists weather normalize energy consumption using linear regression techniques. Total energy consumption or peak demand is estimated as a function of a number of variables: energy price, number of customers, and weather conditions. Once the regression is fit (one presumes accurately), demand is estimated based on actual and "normal" weather conditions. The difference between those estimated values is subtracted from the observed demand to derive weather-normalized demand.

One peculiarity of the estimation process is defining "normal" weather. In the United States, "normal" weather has generally been defined as the average over the previous 30 years. Why normal should be defined as a 30-year average is not clear. Nor are 30-year averages the best naïve predictors of future weather conditions. For example, if we believe climate conditions

---

[14] A natural question that can arise is whether the reference temperature to measure HDD and CDD must be the same. Although one's intuition would expect the answer to be "yes," in fact, the reference temperatures used can be different. The reason for this is that there is often a temperature "deadband" in which consumers have neither heating nor cooling demand.

in a particular area are changing, whether the result of global climate change or metropolitan "heat island" effects, using a shorter time frame to calculate "normal" conditions may result in more accurate predictions and normalized weather demand estimates.

7.3 Tariff Design

To understand tariff design, we first return to one of the fundamental goals of regulation: to mimic the outcome of a competitive market. In a competitive market, price should equal marginal cost, and the amount of output produced should provide the greatest overall level of benefit to society. To the extent that regulated energy firms are natural monopolies, we discussed in Chapter 2 how those firms would restrict their output and charge higher than competitive prices. Thus, regulators step in to prevent such an undesirable outcome.

However, we also noted that in the presence of declining average costs, requiring the firm to charge a price (P*) equal to marginal cost (MC) such that the amount of services provided is Q* (as shown in Figure 7-3) would not allow the firm to recover its total costs, which is Q* times AC*. Instead, a loss would result, equal to the shaded rectangular area in Figure 7-3. The regulator could set the price equal to average cost (P_{AC}), but doing so would result in a welfare loss to society equal to the small shaded triangle. That welfare loss occurs because consumers are willing to pay more for the good than what it costs the firm to produce it.

Figure 7-3: The Pricing Dilemma

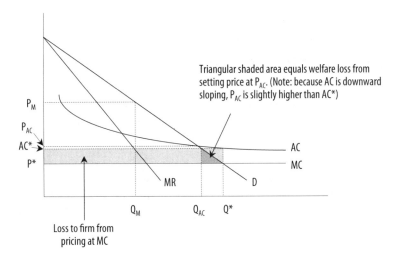

From a purely economic standpoint, this is what tariff design boils down to: is there a way to structure tariffs to induce firms to produce the "correct" level of output and sell that output at the "correct" price?

Of course, the real world is not as simple as the theoretical ones economists are fond of creating. Tariff design is often complicated by numerous "messy" factors, including (1) policy objectives for fairness between customer groups today, (2) current and future customers, (3) accounting for environmental costs of energy consumption, and (4) differences between short- and long-run marginal costs. Phillips summarized these multiple policy goals as follows:[15]

- Ensure "just and reasonable" rates
- Prevent excessive (monopoly) profits
- Prevent unreasonable (inequitable) price discrimination among customers and places
- Provide regulated firms with "adequate" earnings
- Provide service to the most customers possible
- Promote "economic development" and employment

Regulators will not necessarily weigh these goals equally, nor will different regulators necessarily weigh them identically. Moreover, as we have discussed in previous chapters, there is much "wiggle room" in some of these goals. The entire concept of "just and reasonable" rates, for example, cannot be tested by formula alone, nor can "adequate" earnings, or even promoting economic development and employment.

7.4 Alternative Design Structures

Under traditional ratemaking principles, that is, excluding incentive rate designs such as performance-based regulation, there are at least eight broad types of tariff design. These include:

1. One-part tariffs
2. Two-part tariffs
3. Multiblock tariffs
4. Incentive rate structures
5. Entry-exit tariffs
6. Interruptible rates
7. Time-of-use rates
8. Seasonal rates

---

[15] Charles F. Phillips, *The Regulation of Public Utilities*, 3d ed., (Arlington, VA: Public Utilities Reports, 1993), 172–73.

Each of these tariff structures has advantages and disadvantages. A *one-part tariff*, for example, is simply a single volumetric charge based on consumption. For any customer group, one would simply divide the allocated cost to that group by an aggregate consumption billing determinant to derive a price per unit that would recover the firm's costs and provide it with an adequate return. However, if you examine Figure 7-3, you can see that there is no single price that can be charged without incurring some form of welfare loss (either the firm losing money or consumers purchasing too little).[16]

One way of getting around this problem is through a *two-part tariff*. A two-part tariff combines a fixed charge (sometimes called a "ready-to-serve" charge) with a volumetric charge. Ideally, a two-part tariff will set the fixed and variable price components to reflect the true breakdown between the regulated firm's fixed and variable costs. For example, FERC uses this approach to set interstate natural gas pipeline rates.[17]

Under a two-part tariff, for example, the variable cost component would be set such that P* is equal to MC, as shown in Figure 7-4. Total consumption would equal Q* units, and the regulated firm would need to collect an amount equal to the shaded area [(P_{AC} minus P*) times Q*] to cover its fixed costs. In the simplest case, the regulator could then set a fixed charge equal to that amount divided by the expected number of customers in the rate year.

Figure 7-4: Two-Part Tariff Pricing

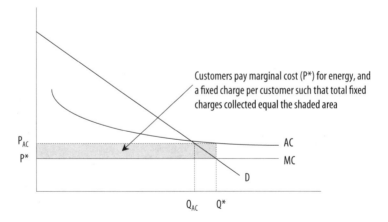

---

[16] The same conclusion holds if average costs are increasing. This can be seen by examining Figure 2-7.

[17] FERC's approach is called the *straight fixed variable* (SFV) method.

> **Interstate Natural Gas Transportation Tariffs in the United States**
>
> The most straightforward way of allocating the cost of service for a natural gas pipeline is to assign all fixed costs, including the fixed component of common costs, to the fixed part of the tariff and to allocate the variable component to the variable part. This is the method currently followed by FERC in the "Straight Fixed Variable" (SFV) pricing rule used for interstate transportation services.
>
> An alternative is to assign a part of fixed costs to the volumetric or usage component of the tariff. The latter was used by FERC under the "Modified Fixed Variable" (MFV) rate in which a portion of the fixed costs, namely, the rate of return and taxes, was allocated to the usage component. The latter method is also used by most public utility commissions for pricing local distribution company (LDC) services. The typical LDC tariff for residential customers has a monthly charge that incorporates fixed customer costs and some of the other fixed costs, as well as a natural gas usage component that incorporates all other costs, including costs of natural gas commodity and upstream capacity and storage, and local distribution.

Block tariffs, on the other hand, distribute the price among blocks of consumption. Under a block tariff structure, prices can be set efficiently without resorting to a fixed charge.[18] For example, Figure 7-5 illustrates a three-part *declining block* price structure. The price of the first Q_1 units of consumption is set to P_1, the next Q_2 minus Q_1 units have a price equal to P_2, and all remaining consumption (to a total of Q_3 units) is priced at marginal cost ($P_3 = MC$).

Figure 7-5: Block Rate Design

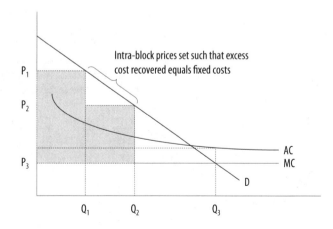

---

[18] Fixed charges and block tariff designs are also usually combined.

Since the last Q_3 minus Q_2 units are priced at the firm's marginal cost, these sales do not recover any of the firm's fixed costs. Thus, prices P_1 and P_2 are set so that the shaded areas shown in Figure 7-5 recover those fixed costs (equal to the shaded rectangle in Figure 7-4).

Increasing block price structures can also be designed. Common reasons for designing increasing block rates include subsidies for low-income consumers (e.g., *lifeline rates*, discussed in Section 7.6), increasing marginal cost structures, and social policy designed to reduce energy consumption because of real or perceived *external costs* associated with consumption, such as pollution.[19] For example, in Figure 7-6, we assume increasing marginal costs.

Figure 7-6: Block Rate Design Under Increasing Marginal Costs

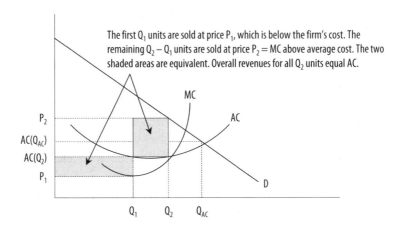

In Figure 7-6, the economically efficient solution is total consumption of Q_2 units. If the firm charges a uniform price, P_2 per unit, however, it will earn too much, since at the level of Q_2 the price is higher than average cost. However, charging a uniform price equal to average cost $[P = AC(Q_{AC})]$ will result in too much consumption of Q_{AC} units. The solution is to charge a price P_1 for the first Q_1 units and P_2 for the remaining Q_2 minus Q_1 units. The loss the firm realizes on the first Q_1 units (since P_1 is less than the average cost) will be exactly offset by the excess above the average cost the firm recovers for the remaining units.

---

[19] We discuss external costs in Chapter 11.

Incentive rate structures can be designed in a multitude of ways. Typically, incentive rates are paired with special economic development rates that provide lower-cost energy in exchange for a firm creating new jobs. The difficulty with incentive rates is that it is easy to go from incentive to cross-subsidy, something regulators, to say nothing of other customers who are providing the subsidy, generally wish to avoid.

Other rate structures abound. For example, rates for European natural gas pipeline companies are based on an *entry-exit* scheme. Shippers who transport natural gas from one zone to another pay a pipeline entry fee and a pipeline exit fee, plus commodity (usage) charges. Thus, an entry-exit regime is similar to a multipart tariff with fixed charges (entry and exit fees) and variable charges (commodity usage fees).

Many distribution utility and pipeline companies offer *interruptible rates* to customers who do not require firm service, offering lower prices in exchange for an ability to curtail or interrupt service to those customers. In exchange for receiving a lower rate, an interruptible customer agrees to allow service to be curtailed under certain conditions, usually periods when there is high demand. The specific conditions for service interruption can be quite varied, specifying the maximum number and duration of interruptions each billing period, restricting interruptions to certain times of the year, and so forth.

Designing interruptible rates can become rather contentious depending on how the firm's fixed costs are allocated among customers. For example, suppose part of an electric distribution utility's service territory has a distribution system that has not kept pace with increased demand and is increasingly overloaded. The utility designs an interruptible rate for large industrial customers in the area; this allows the utility to reduce those customers' demand so that overloading the distribution circuits can be avoided. What percentage of fixed costs, especially those allocated on the basis of peak demands, should those customers bear, if any? As with most allocation questions involving fixed costs, there is no correct answer.

There is one frequent argument raised by firm customers who are allocated additional fixed costs that would otherwise be allocated to interruptible customers: if interruptible customers are rarely interrupted, particularly under conditions of excess capacity, then they essentially are receiving "firm" service while paying much less than other firm customers. Hence, the argument goes, price discrimination is occurring, but without having any basis in differing costs. This argument is rather weak for several reasons.

First, customers who agree to interruptible rates face a probability of service interruption, not a guarantee of interruption.[20] Second, if actual interruption were a requirement for an interruptible rate, a natural question to ask would be: how many interruptions are required? Any answer would lack foundation from both a standpoint of economic efficiency and equity. Finally, many interruptible customers, especially those who are on interruptible natural gas tariffs, will have alternatives to taking regulated service. For example, some large industrial firms may generate their own electricity, especially if they can sell excess to their local electric utility (in the United States this occurs under the guise of PURPA).[21] Natural gas customers may be able to connect directly to interstate pipelines or use alternative fuels, such as fuel oil. In such situations, these customers will have more price elastic demand than typical firm customers. As such, increasing the rates they pay may cause them to leave the system, thus saddling remaining customers with additional costs.

Finally, *seasonal rates* and *time-of-use* rates incorporate the *time dependence of consumption*. For example, many electric utilities experience peak demands during the middle of the workday and during the summer months, when cooling loads are largest. Seasonal rates and time-of-use rates can, in theory at least, better equate marginal cost and prices throughout the year, thus encouraging more efficient consumption. However, there are several drawbacks to both rate mechanisms. First, many customers do not like their overall rates to increase in peak seasons, wrongly perceiving that the regulated firm is somehow taking advantage of them. Second, time-of-use rates can only be implemented if customers have more sophisticated meters that measure consumption in each hour. While such meters are commonly used for large commercial and industrial customers, historically the cost of these meters has exceeded the estimated efficiency gains from installing them for all customers. Third, both seasonal and time-of-use rates can conflict with regulatory goals of rate stability, especially for residential and small commercial customers.

---

[20] We are not aware of situations where retail electric distribution customers, at least in the U.S., have been <u>forced</u> to accept an interruptible rate tariff; such a situation would violate a local electric utility's obligation to serve. The situation is different for natural gas pipeline and local distribution customers, who may wish to connect to a system when there is simply no capacity available.

[21] It is also becoming more common in the U.S. for state energy regulators to encourage *net metering* by smaller commercial and residential customers. Under net metering, customers generate electricity on-site and can sell excess generation back to the local distribution utility at their tariff rate. While politically popular, this is both economically inefficient and inequitable (because of not taking advantage of economies of scale, among many other reasons).

7.5 Tariff-Setting Methods

Once the revenue requirement and the billing determinants have been estimated, many methods can be used to design retail rates and tariffs. Although some economists advocate specific methods over others and debate among themselves endlessly, the reality is that specific circumstances, goals of regulators and regulated companies, policy objectives, and even legal restrictions all must be considered when determining what tariff methods make the most sense. The methods used to set rates and tariffs are, after all, a means to an end: setting rates that are fair, just, and equitable (and, we hope, efficient). Since all of the methods are flexible, the assumptions used when calculating tariffs are what condition the final results, regardless of the methods used. In the remainder of this section, we discuss the most widely known methods for tariff making: *incremental cost* and *embedded cost* methods. Before we do so, however, we discuss two important aspects of rate and tariff setting that are frequently ignored: *tariff levelization* and *revenue checks*.

Tariff Levelization and Revenue Checks

Tariff levelization addresses the time value of money associated with a multiyear tariff schedule. At the beginning of a new, multiyear rate-setting period, the initial tariffs (or average revenue in a revenue cap or yield) will be based on an average of revenue requirements and volumes predicted over the period. Since the revenue formula includes predicted costs and revenues for multiple components, the differences between the nominal values and the discounted present values of these components may be large.

If regulators do not adjust for these differences (i.e., if they fail to incorporate the *time value of money*), they will create a downwards bias in allowed revenues. That bias can be eliminated by levelizing the tariffs—a simple procedure where both future revenues and billing determinant units are discounted to the present to calculate regulated rates.[22]

Revenue checks simply ensure that the estimated rates and tariffs will provide regulated companies with the opportunity to collect their revenue requirements. After rates and tariffs have been calculated, a revenue check should be performed to make sure the calculated tariffs will allow the utility an opportunity to collect its revenue requirement. A revenue check tests the accuracy of the final regulated prices by estimating the revenues the pro-

---

[22] For example, the energy regulator in Mexico failed to adjust for the time value of money when it set the rates for natural gas pipelines based solely on forecast nominal revenues over the five-year period 1999–2004. *See* PGPB Permit G/061/TRA/99, Appendix 6 given by CRE on June 2, 1999.

posed prices would generate. Those revenues are then compared to the revenue requirement for the regulated company. If prices have been calculated correctly, then the revenues generated should closely (if not exactly) match the revenue requirement.

Although a revenue check seems like an obvious part of the regulator's rate-setting checklist, not all regulators perform it. For example, in one case, the transport regulator in Peru used a discounted cash flow model to estimate regulated prices but had a different idea than the regulated companies as to what *discount rate* should be used to perform the present value calculations. As a consequence, the revenues allowed from the prices determined by the regulator failed to cover the regulated companies' revenue requirements in a revenue check.[23]

Embedded and Marginal Cost Methods

Economists, who are wont to ensure prices are as efficient as possible, frequently hold up the standard model of market competition as the basis for efficient pricing. We did so ourselves in Figure 2-1, which shows how, in a competitive market equilibrium, the market price will equal the marginal cost of production. In setting efficient rates for regulated firms, the same goal applies in principle. However, when designing rates and tariffs, setting prices based on the regulated firm's costs to provide service will rarely result in collecting the same revenues as setting prices based on regulated customers' value of obtaining that service.

Embedded Cost Approaches

Historically, regulators based rate and tariff structures on "costs" as defined in strict engineering and accounting terms. As we first discussed in Chapter 3, COS regulation is based on adding up the prudent and known-and-measurable costs incurred by a firm to establish the firm's revenue requirement. Those cost estimates were based on actual monies spent (or *embedded*) for plant and operating expenses, and they were then allocated to different customers using principles of cost causation.

Since many assets, such as natural gas pipelines and generating plants, are sized based on forecast peak demand, individual contributions to peak demand became the most common factor for allocating the capital costs of those facilities. Far easier is allocating variable costs, such as fuel burned in a generating plant, since those costs can be allocated based on cus-

---

[23] The problem was that the regulator discounted future cash flow and did not include the interest payments for the capital structure assumed in the weighted average cost of capital, underestimating the required price to reach the allowed return. *See* Organismo Supervisor de la Inversión en Infraestructura de Transporte de Servicio Público (OSITRAN), Resolution Nº 010-2004-CD-OSITRAN (March 31, 2004), Peru.

tomer usage. Finally, costs that vary with the number of customers but not with consumption are typically allocated by customer. And so, cost allocation generally evolved into three cost classifications: demand, energy, and customer.

Thus, embedded cost studies rely on accounting costs on the company's books for the test year as the basis for setting rates and tariffs. If the test year is based on historic costs, the accuracy of the firm's costs can be audited and verified, either when the firm files for a change in rates or at the end of the projected rate period.

Marginal Cost Approaches

Marginal cost approaches are based on the principles of competitive markets, specifically that the amount consumers are willing to pay for the last (marginal) unit of a good or service is the (marginal) cost of producing that unit.[24] When goods and services are priced accordingly, they will be allocated among consumers efficiently, hence the term *allocative efficiency*. The regulator wishing to achieve this same sort of allocative efficiency takes the firm's observed demand as a given and sets rates equal to the firm's marginal cost at that level of output. For example, determining a regulated electric utility's marginal cost requires detailed studies that estimate the change in generation, transmission, and distribution costs that are a result of providing an additional increment of service over time (see box).[25]

> **Conducting a Marginal Cost Study for an Integrated Electric Utility**
>
> Most electric utility marginal cost studies begin with the utility's planning documents. For example, before the U.S. electric industry was restructured, many state energy regulators required electric utilities to prepare detailed *integrated resource plans* (IRPs) that spelled out what investments the utility would make over the next 10 to 20 years.[26] Less frequently, utilities would include planned additions to transmission and distribution facilities, such as new high-voltage lines, substations, and so forth.
>
> Estimating the marginal cost of additional generation requires information about the specific costs of both existing and new generating resources, including forced outage rates (how often plants are not available when needed), operating and maintenance costs, dual fuel capabilities, and existing plant retirement schedules. It also requires information on the capital and operating costs of planned generating facility units, market prices for short- and long-term energy purchases and sales, as well as associated transmission charges. However, marginal cost studies must also estimate the cost

---

[24] Marginal cost studies are also called *incremental cost* studies.

[25] Some firms conduct *decremental cost* studies. These studies examine the change in costs from decreasing (or *decrementing*) the amount of service provided. In theory, the results of an incremental or decremental analysis should be quite close.

[26] Recently, a number of U.S. states have begun efforts to reregulate their electric industries. In doing so, some regulators and politicians are promoting "integrated portfolio management." Although the name sounds fancy and technical, it is simply a rehash of IRP.

> to transmit and distribute additional power to retail customers. Those estimates require detailed engineering power flow models that are used to develop system expansion plans. All in all, preparing an accurate marginal cost study is not for the fainthearted.

Once marginal costs have been calculated, revenue checks can show whether the implied prices will lead to over- or underrecovery of the regulated firm's costs.[27] Odds are the calculated prices will not match revenue requirements. In that case, regulators apply one or more *revenue reconciliation* methods. The best known of these is called the *Ramsey Pricing* or *Inverse Elasticity* method. Under Ramsey Pricing, the difference between the revenue requirement and the revenues estimated based on calculated marginal costs (the *revenue differential*) is allocated to the different customer classes based on the inverse of the price elasticity of demand. What this means in practice is that the least price-sensitive consumers (typically residential ones) end up with rates that deviate the most from marginal cost.

Another method that is sometimes used is called the *Equal Proportion of Marginal Cost* (EPMC). This method increases marginal costs in proportion to the revenue differential. For example, if the revenue differential is 50% of the revenue requirement, then all marginal costs are increased by exactly 50%.[28] However, unlike Ramsey Pricing, the additional costs are allocated to each customer class proportionally without regard to price sensitivity.

The fundamental problem with the marginal cost approach for ratemaking purposes, in addition to the analysis required, is that charging all customers the marginal price will result in the firm collecting its revenue requirement, which is based on embedded costs, only by chance. Thus, rates somehow must be reconciled to the allowed revenue requirement. Once rates and prices diverge from marginal cost, there is no way to know whether the ultimate outcome is allocatively efficient.

Which Approach Is Better?

The fundamental difference between the embedded and marginal cost approaches lies in how each defines "cost." Embedded cost studies rely on accounting costs on the company's books for the test year as the basis for setting rates and tariffs. In contrast, marginal cost studies estimate the incremental costs of the firm providing an additional unit of production. However, once "cost" is determined, the procedures for allocating those costs among different services, jurisdictions, and customers are largely the same. Ultimately, debates over

---

[27] For example, when entry-exit tariffs were estimated for a natural gas company in Great Britain, some of the marginal costs obtained in the first step of the procedure were negative.

[28] In marginal cost studies for energy utilities, these percentages are often quite large because most of the costs are fixed.

marginal cost studies typically center around developing the cost estimates themselves, and debates over embedded cost studies focus on how costs taken directly from a regulated firm's account books should be divided among customers.

Advocates of marginal cost pricing believe that efficient resource allocation cannot be had without it. Embedded cost pricing supporters believe that the greater precision, verifiability, and general simplicity of embedded cost methods outweigh hoped-for efficiency benefits of imperfect approximations to marginal cost pricing. Both approaches have their merits. In our view, which approach is "best" hinges on several factors, including the quality and accuracy of available accounting data, the ability to accurately estimate marginal costs (especially in the face of significant uncertainty as to future costs), and the policy objectives of regulators themselves.

Alternative Approaches

As if the debate over embedded and marginal cost approaches were not sufficient, regulators outside the United States use still other methods. We analyze the Discounted Cash Flow (DCF) approach, the model company approach, and benchmarking methods.

The DCF approach obtains a set of rates using financial concepts. Essentially, regulators develop a financial model to estimate the regulated firm's *free cash flow* (i.e., the remaining cash a firm has after the expenditures required to maintain or expand its asset base). The prices input into this model are then modified to achieve a targeted rate of return. In practice, such financial models tend to be poorly designed with numerous and often wholly subjective assumptions. In addition to the revenue check problem discussed in this section, regulators sometimes add restrictions that increase the volatility of the estimates.[29] Alternatively, some regulators set too many parameters using the DCF approach, essentially wresting cost control from regulated firms.[30]

---

[29] For example, the natural gas regulator in Argentina included a K factor in the price adjustment formula, using a financial model based on a 35-year forecast. However, the companies' concessions were for only an additional 30 years. As a consequence, the last five years of the regulator's forecast covered a period during which the companies would have no control. See Ente Nacional Regulador del Gas (ENARGAS), Resolution ENARGAS N° 469 (June 30, 1997), Argentina.

[30] In Chapter 8, we discuss how British regulators used the same model to determine initial prices and parameters of the price adjustment formula, setting up a system in which any combination of initial prices and adjustment parameters could be chosen to equal the DCF estimate.

We first referred to the model company approach in Chapter 5. As we discussed, it is primarily an engineering approach that attempts to estimate the costs for a hypothetical "efficient" company providing the same level of service as the firm under review.[31] Once those theoretical costs are estimated, they become the regulated firm's actual allowed revenue requirement and are allocated into different categories to obtain a set of tariffs.[32]

> **Bad Company**
>
> Peru's regulator uses the model company approach to set tariffs for electric and natural gas firms. In using the approach, the regulator adds a unique twist. After the regulator calculates tariffs, it runs a financial model to estimate the expected investment returns of the regulated firms. If the returns are within a band determined by the country's electricity law, the calculated tariffs are accepted and finalized. However, those estimated returns are calculated using a flawed model. Specifically, the regulator adjusts the value of each firm's capital assets for potential efficiencies or current input prices. (This is somewhat similar to "fair value" regulation, which essentially was abandoned in the U.S. many years ago.) Thus, imagine an electric utility that expanded its transmission and distribution network into a new neighborhood three years ago. Today, the utility's costs are reviewed. If asset prices are lower today than three years ago, the company will not recoup its investment costs. If prices have risen, but the company is deemed to be less than efficient, again it will not recoup its investment costs.

With regard to benchmarking tariffs, we can be blunt: Setting tariffs based on comparisons of rates in other jurisdictions is not only unfair, it is dishonest and violates all of the principles we discussed in Section 4.7 of Chapter 4. Comparisons across companies should only be performed for the sole purpose of benchmarking industry practices and never for setting rates.

Industry Practices

We turn next to a review of several key tariff practices. Tariff practices in the natural gas industry are primarily variations of two-part tariffs. However, the components of those tariffs and the ways those components are determined vary extensively by country. The electric industry, on the other hand, displays an almost limitless variety of regulatory regimes and tariff pricing methods. Traditionally, one of the most important tariff approaches has been the *peaker method*, which determines how the fixed costs of generating units are allocated and priced. However, as the electric industry continues to deregulate wholesale generating markets, the traditional peaker method, while still common, is gradually being supplanted

---

[31] Many types of professionals are involved in the calculation since there are engineering, economic, financial, accounting, and statistical aspects in the calculation.

[32] See Section 5.3 of Chapter 5 for a more detailed explanation.

by complex transmission system pricing structures designed to guarantee "equal access" to scarce transmission facilities and provide sufficient generating capacity so that the lights stay on.

Pipeline Tariff Methods

As we discussed in Section 7.4, a two-part tariff consists of a fixed component and a variable, usage-based component. In designing two-part tariffs, the basic issue is how to allocate costs between the two. That, in turn, depends on whether access to pipeline capacity is based on a *contract carriage* or an *entry-exit* regime.[33]

In the United States, Canada, and most of Latin America, pipelines offer *open access* transportation services (meaning transport is available to anyone) on contract carriage terms. Most pipeline shippers purchase service on a firm basis (reserving or "leasing" a specific amount of capacity for a set period of time). Pipelines also tend to offer an *a la carte* menu of other services, such as interruptible transport and backhaul (i.e., transport in a reverse direction), but most of their revenues are collected through fixed capacity charges.

Under contract carriage, a pipeline assigns a contract amount of capacity (commonly called *maximum daily quantity*—MDQ—or "contract demand") that will be made available to the shipper on any given day. A customer pays for this capacity whether it uses the service or not, hence the term *take-or-pay*. This is a *capacity right*, and it represents the advance sale of a service that will be provided by the pipeline in accordance with the terms and conditions of a service contract.

Typically, capacity rights are assigned, or *subscribed*, based on long-term contracts, many of which are signed when a pipeline is first constructed, although they are often resold in the open market.[34] The capacity rights, as such, are "sold" with the original agreement between transporters and customers/shippers to construct the pipeline transportation facilities. Indeed, the length of capacity rights coincides generally with the life of the transportation contracts used to provide the service.

---

[33] There is a third regime, called *common carriage*, in which capacity is available on a first-come, first-served basis. Under common carriage, which in the U.S. is used for pipelines that ship petroleum products, one-part tariffs are used, based on revenue requirements divided by shipping volume.

[34] Initial capacity rights typically are assigned through an *open season*, which provides potential customers an opportunity to enter into nonbinding commitments for a fraction of planned capacity. Moreover, there are secondary markets in which capacity is traded. Thus, shippers who want additional capacity can purchase existing firm capacity rights from other shippers. In a competitive market, the prices at which this capacity trades should approximate the marginal cost of pipeline expansion. Thus, owning firm capacity rights carries with it an opportunity cost equal to the marginal cost of expansion.

Contract carriage is similar to renting commercial office space. Capacity (like floor space) is purchased under a long-term contract (a lease). The landlord sets the lease price at a level that pays for the construction and maintenance of the office space. The lease is a contract that gives the tenant specified rights over how to use or sell that capacity (sublet) to others. On contract carriage natural gas transportation systems, the cost of building, operating, and maintaining the system is usually assessed on the proportional shares of contract capacity rights held by shippers. Those shippers have the right to use their capacity or sell it on a temporary (*interruptible*) or permanent basis to others as they see fit, with one key limitation: shippers cannot withhold unused capacity from the market so as to raise prices in downstream markets.

There are two main methods to allocate fixed and variable pipeline costs: *zone-gate* and *Mcf-mile*. Under the zone-gate methodology, costs are first allocated by geographic zone. Then, the costs in each zone are allocated based on zone-specific billing determinants. One of the complexities of the zone-gate method is that allocating costs across different zones can be arbitrary. To get around this problem, the zone-gate method has, in many locations, been supplanted by the Mcf-mile approach, which is more straightforward and far easier to implement.

The Mcf-mile method has been used in the United States and elsewhere for nearly 50 years to calculate "distance-weighted" allocation factors.[35] It applies the systemwide average unit cost on a mileage basis, assigning the same cost of transporting an Mcf of natural gas per mile, regardless of where the transportation occurs. The greatest simplifying assumption is that it makes no attempt to separate out and identify specific cost categories (i.e., operating expenses, return, taxes, etc.) with specific zones, as the zone-gate method does.

Mcf-mile Mechanics

Calculating tariffs using the Mcf-mile method requires three steps:

1. Multiply peak and annual quantities for each delivery point by the mileage from each delivery point to each receipt point to obtain total peak and annual Mcf-miles in each zone.

2. Divide the total fixed pipeline costs by total peak Mcf-miles to obtain the average cost per peak Mcf-miles. Perform the same calculation for all variable costs and annual Mcf-miles to determine the average cost per annual Mcf-mile.

3. Multiply the unit cost per peak (annual) Mcf-mile by the number of peak (annual) Mcf-miles in each zone to obtain the fixed (variable) distanced costs allocated to each zone. Alternatively, multiply the unit price per Mcf-mile by the average haul to the particular zone to obtain the price per Mcf for distanced costs in that zone.

---

[35] The initial set of tariffs after privatization in Argentina and Bolivia and the current tariff model used by PGPB in Mexico were developed with the Mcf-mile method.

Pipeline pricing in Europe has taken a different path. Most European countries base natural gas pipeline tariffs on an *entry-exit regime*. Under this regime, shippers contract to inject natural gas into one zone (entry) and to take it out of another (exit). Although the tariff structure differs from that of a contract carriage system, the tariff principles are quite similar; they combine fixed (entry and exit) fees and variable charges (commodity charges) with contracts providing entry to or exit from specific zones. The main difference between entry-exit and either zone-gate or Mcf-mile methods is the regionalization of pipeline networks into zones and tariffs that are not distance-based.

Although the entry-exit method has worked well, European efforts to liberalize the natural gas market in much the same way that the United States liberalized its natural gas market in the 1980s and 1990s have required each country to unbundle services and allow *Third Party Access* (TPA, equivalent to open access). This has set off a debate (similar to the marginal cost vs. embedded cost debate we discussed earlier) as how best to estimate entry-exit costs.

Like their U.S. counterparts, many European economists believe that the marginal cost method is best. On a pipeline system, marginal costs are estimated by using complex flow models that examine the costs of all possible flows. One complication is that certain flows can reduce total costs, implying negative marginal costs,[36] which can make for increasing tariff design. The other alternative is to use an embedded cost approach, allocating both fixed and variable costs and entry and exit revenues.[37]

Peaker Methods

In many restructured markets, generators receive both energy and capacity payments, apart from other revenues from the *ancillary services* generators provide.[38] Whereas energy revenues are simply revenues from the sale of electricity on a volumetric, per kWh basis, capacity revenues are meant to compensate generators for the fixed costs of providing *capacity* to the system. The purpose is to ensure enough investment in new generating plants and to maintain long-term system reliability.[39]

---

[36] We referred to negative marginal costs in note 27, *supra*. The actual calculations assume a baseline network and include pipeline expansions to support additional demand over time. The present value of the cost differences between that baseline case and the expanded network case equals the incremental marginal cost.

[37] For example, the Italian regulator calculates a bottom-up estimate of the cost of each possible flow and uses those costs to estimate entry-exit charges. *See*, L'Autorità per l'Energia Elettrica e il Gas, Deliberazione n. 166/05 (July 29, 2005).

[38] In the U.S., providing separate capacity payments to generators is a hotly debated topic. We discuss this issue in the context of markets for *reliability* in Chapter 12.

[39] For example, most developing countries need capacity payments to attract additional private investment in new generating capacity to satisfy increasing demand.

Although different regulators measure and pay for capacity differently, the same basic concept applies to all capacity payments: they are designed to compensate investors for the fixed investment and operation costs associated with a peaking unit. The reason is that, at the optimal level of installed capacity, the cost of adding another kW of peaking capacity should be the same as the expected cost of having to curtail a kW of load.[40]

To determine the capacity payments, regulators must first choose an "efficient" peaking plant that the market would build, usually a simple-cycle gas turbine.[41] Next, they calculate the total fixed investment cost for the plant, including the cost of the turbine itself, permitting, land, interconnection equipment, and so forth. Then, using an assumed cost of capital (sometimes calculated using the methods we discussed in Chapter 5), the total fixed investment cost is levelized over the plant's expected lifetime. Finally, a fixed operation and maintenance (O&M) cost may be added to the annual fixed cost.

Regulators differ significantly in how they actually pay generators for supplying capacity. In some countries, such as Peru, generation owners receive fixed monthly payments for "iron on the ground" independent of whether their plants operate or not.[42] In other countries, such as Argentina, generators are paid only when they sell energy.[43]

Electric Transmission Tariffs

Like natural gas pipelines, electric transmission is characterized by large fixed costs and small variable ones. But unlike natural gas pipelines, along which the flow of gas molecules can be physically tracked, electrons are more recalcitrant; they respond to the laws of physics, rather than the contractual wishes of lawyers and economists.[44] As a result, developing well-functioning transmission tariffs has been a technical and policy challenge.

---

[40] The expected cost of load curtailment equals the probability of curtailment times the value consumers place on not having their power interrupted.

[41] In Bolivia, for example, this is defined as the unit with the minimum total cost (fixed and variable) of serving a limited number of peak-demand hours. See Superintendencia de Electricidad (SSDE), Resolution SSDE N° 040/2007 (February 8, 2007), Bolivia.

[42] Owners of generating plants that are physically incapable of operating are typically not paid. Instead, payments are based on some measure of availability *when demanded*. In the U.S., for example, a common measure of this availability is called *equivalent forced outage rate demand* (EFORd). An explanation of how EFORd is calculated can be found in the New York ISO Installed Capacity Manual, Appendix J, www.nyiso.com.

[43] The way that generation owners are compensated will ultimately affect the portfolio of generation resources available, since investors will prefer the types of generation most likely to capture capacity payments.

[44] Chapter 12 contains a short introduction to how electric power systems work.

Regulators have used a plethora of methods to price electric transmission. None we are aware of has provided appropriate economic signals to encourage long-term investment. For example, Argentina used to impose a transmission usage charge that was determined every five years based on a locational pricing model. To satisfy advocates of marginal cost pricing, the usage charge reflects transmission losses,[45] a connection charge based on the cost to connect to the system, and a capacity charge based on access to each 100 km of transmission line.[46] Great Britain, on the other hand, uses a two-part tariff with a connection charge and a usage ("Use of System") charge. The latter is estimated based on marginal cost pricing methods using an engineering model that estimates the incremental costs of increased generation demand at every location.[47] The connection charge itself is based on a capital component, which includes depreciation and a return on investment, as well as a noncapital component based on O&M costs.[48]

> **The Evolution of Transmission Pricing in the U.S.**
>
> In the United States, regional and state power pools had crafted a variety of tariffs for transmitting electricity within, through, and around them. In general, these tariff structures discouraged transmission (called "wheeling") that reduced transmission owners' ability to sell their own electricity at wholesale.
>
> In the early 1990s, however, both the process of developing transmission tariffs and their structure underwent extensive change. When Congress passed the Energy Policy Act of 1992, one of the goals was to enhance wholesale competition, which previously had been limited to *qualifying facilities* authorized under PURPA. The Energy Policy Act authorized a new type of independently owned and operated wholesale generating facility, called an *exempt wholesale generator* (EWG), and set in motion an extensive chain of events, including broad restructuring of the electric industry.
>
> Many of these new competitive generators, however efficient and innovative they were, encountered a crippling problem: they could not gain reasonable access to the high-voltage transmission networks that were owned by vertically integrated utilities.[49] Therefore, in 1995, FERC issued a Notice of Proposed Rulemaking (NOPR) to address transmission access issues and require regional transmission owners to develop transmission tariffs with uniform structures. In 1996, FERC issued

---

[45] Congestion charges were not part of the revenues of the transmission company in Argentina.

[46] The other charges are needed since pure marginal costs typically fall short of collecting the transmission company revenue requirement. *See* Ente Nacional Regulador de la Electricidad (ENRE), Resolution ENRE Nº 1619/1998 (November 13, 1998), Argentina.

[47] National Grid, *The Statement of the Use of System Charging Methodology*, Issue 2, Revision 1, Effective from April 1, 2006.

[48] National Grid, *The Statement of the Connection Charge Methodology*, Issue 2, Revision 1, Effective from April 1, 2006.

[49] Transmission networks are one example of *bottleneck facilities*, which we discuss in Chapter 9.

its final rule on transmission access, better known as Order 888, which required each public utility that owns, operates, or controls facilities used for transmission in interstate commerce to offer unbundled transmission service pursuant to a standard (or *pro forma*) Open Access Transmission Tariff (OATT).[50]

The OATT is a single, open-access tariff offering both *network service* and *point-to-point* contract-based service. *Network service* allows users to reserve space on the transmission network for a certain period of time without specifying where power is to be received (injected) or delivered. It is as if you agree to lease a jet for a certain number of hours over the year without specifying where you wish to fly. Both types of service are based on revenue requirement calculations.[51]

Point-to-point service is the equivalent of booking a nonstop, direct flight. Additionally, transmission service can be provided on either a firm or non-firm basis, in much the same way that natural gas pipeline transportation can be provided on a firm or interruptible basis.

The complexity of regional transmission tariffs is a consequence of the myriad services required to transmit power. The OATT, for example, includes the following services:[52]

- **Schedule 1: Scheduling, System Control and Dispatch Service.** This service is required to schedule the movement of power through, out of, within, or into a Control Area.

- **Schedule 2: Reactive Supply and Voltage Control from Generation Sources Service.** In order to maintain transmission voltages on the Transmission Provider's transmission facilities within acceptable limits, generation facilities under the control of the control area operator are operated to produce (or absorb) reactive power. Thus, Reactive Supply and Voltage Control from Generation Sources Service must be provided for each transaction on the Transmission Provider's transmission facilities.

---

[50] Docket No. RM95-8-000, *Promoting Wholesale Competition Through Open Access Non-Discriminatory Transmission Services by Public Utilities*, 75 FERC ¶ 61,080 (Order No. 888), April 24, 1996. At the same time, FERC also issued Order No. 889, which imposed Standards of Conduct on vertically integrated electric utilities to prevent those utilities' unregulated merchant generating subsidiaries from obtaining preferential access to transmission information. This was called the Open Access Same-Time Information System (OASIS). *See, Open Access Same-Time Information System (formerly Real-Time Information Networks) and Standards of Conduct*, Final Rule, 75 FERC ¶ 61,078 (Order No. 889), April 24, 1996. In the years since Orders 888 and 889 were issued, FERC has continued to modify them. An excellent history of these reforms to date can be found in Docket Nos. RM05-25-000 and RM05-17-000, *Preventing Undue Discrimination and Preference in Transmission Service* (OATT Reform), Notice of Proposed Rulemaking (NOPR), May 19, 2006. On March 15, 2007, FERC issued an order in this consolidated docket (Order No. 890), effective May 14, 2007.

[51] A complicating factor in developing transmission tariffs for interconnected transmission systems is how to "roll in" transmission assets that were built and paid for by individual utilities. To address this, individual utility investments are rolled in to overall transmission network rates over a fixed time period. For example, the New England transmission independent system operator, ISO-NE, rolls in rates over a 10-year period under a settlement agreement dating from the early 1990s.

[52] FERC, OATT Reform NOPR, Appendix B, Pro-Forma Open Access Transmission Tariff, www.ferc.gov/industries/electric/indus-act/oatt-reform/nopr/pro-forma.pdf (accessed February 19, 2007).

> ■ **Schedule 3: Regulation and Frequency Response Service.** Regulation and Frequency Response Service is necessary to provide for the continuous balancing of resources (generation and interchange) with load and for maintaining scheduled Interconnection frequency at sixty cycles per second (60 Hz). Regulation and Frequency Response Service is accomplished by committing on-line generation whose output is raised or lowered (predominantly through the use of automatic generating control equipment) as necessary to follow the moment-by-moment changes in load.
>
> ■ **Schedule 4: Energy Imbalance Service.** Energy Imbalance Service is provided when a difference occurs between the scheduled and the actual delivery of energy to a load located within a Control Area over a single hour.
>
> ■ **Schedule 5: Operating Reserve—Spinning Reserve Service.** Spinning Reserve Service is needed to serve load immediately in the event of a system contingency. Spinning Reserve Service may be provided by generating units that are on-line and loaded at less than maximum output.
>
> ■ **Schedule 6: Operating Reserve—Supplemental Reserve Service.** Supplemental Reserve Service is needed to serve load in the event of a system contingency; however, it is not available immediately to serve load but rather within a short period of time.
>
> ■ **Schedule 7: Long-Term Firm and Short-Term Firm Point-To-Point Transmission Service.**
>
> ■ **Schedule 8: Non-Firm Point-To-Point Transmission Service.**
>
> ■ **Schedule 9: Generator Imbalance Service.** Generator Imbalance Service is provided when a difference occurs between the output of a generator located in the Transmission Provider's Control Area and a delivery schedule from that generator to (1) another Control Area or (2) a load within the Transmission Provider's Control Area over a single hour.
>
> The OATT applies only to the series of regional transmission organizations (RTOs). It has nothing to do with local transmission service, which must also be addressed by state regulators in rate proceedings.

7.6 Pricing and Social Policy

One of the most vexing issues confronting regulators is melding traditional rate-setting principles with social policy goals. One of the best known examples is whether a multipart tariff design should be increasing or decreasing. As we discussed in Section 7.4, determining which, if either, design is economically efficient depends on the marginal cost of consumption and production.

In the "golden age" of electricity in the United States, for example, utility tariffs often used decreasing block tariff designs both to reflect economies of scale (an economic efficiency factor) and simply to encourage additional electric consumption (a marketing factor).[53] By

---

[53] For example, in the 1960s, a number of U.S. electric utilities marketed all-electric "Gold Medallion" homes.

the 1980s, however, encouraging electric consumption had become an anathema to many energy regulators and policymakers. Instead, energy conservation had become the key policy goal, and many regulators adopted increasing block tariffs to discourage electric use. In other cases, regulators adopted various forms of time-of-use tariffs to discourage consumption and, in theory, send more accurate price signals to retail customers.

From the standpoint of economic efficiency, tariff designs that more accurately reflect the true marginal cost of energy use are welcome. In times of peak energy demand, it makes sense for customers to face price signals that accurately reflect marginal costs. However, from a general policy perspective, in some cases tariff design has had less to do with economic efficiency and more to do with promoting social policies. In the United States, regulators have often created special tariffs for low-income and elderly customers, usually called *lifeline rates*, to improve energy affordability.[54] The rationale for lifeline rates,[55] which have been developed for both electricity and natural gas, is that both are necessities of life and, because of this, should be provided at rates that are "affordable," even if such rates are below the utility's embedded (average) or marginal costs.[56]

Setting aside social policy concerns for the moment, from a purely economic perspective, lifeline rates make no sense. By their very definition, lifeline rates subsidize one or more groups of consumers, while other consumers make up the difference. Subsidies, however, are inefficient, because they distort consumption decisions. Moreover, providing subsidies to some violates an important tenet of cost allocation we discussed in the previous chapter: aligning costs and benefits.

Clearly, energy affordability is an issue for some customers, and no one is suggesting that low-income and elderly consumers "freeze in the dark." There have been numerous alternatives proposed, including voluntary contributions from customers solicited by utilities to help pay the bills of low-income customers and programs that offer free energy conservation assistance, including energy audits, free home weatherization, and so forth, and finally direct government transfers, such as tax credits, that provide consumers with additional income without distorting price signals.[57]

---

[54] For a more detailed legal discussion and case citations, see Charles F. Phillips, *supra* note 15, at 450–52.

[55] These subsidies are also common in other countries. Many countries in Latin America have adopted so-called "social tariffs" where the first kWh of consumption (for example, 75 kWh per month in Mexico) is subsidized or customers consuming less than a certain monthly threshold (for example, 300 kWh in Guatemala and 700 kWh in the Dominican Republic) are provided electricity at below cost.

[56] Another form of subsidy provided to residential customers is the prohibition against service disconnections, typically in winter. Such prohibitions increase collections losses, which must be paid by other customers.

[57] For a discussion of some assistance programs, see Howard Spinner, "Choosing an Efficient Energy Assistance Program," *Public Utilities Fortnightly* 126 (December 1990), 27–31.

7.7 Electric Restructuring and Default Service

Up to now, this chapter has focused on how regulated rates and tariffs are set using traditional procedures. However, another important pricing exercise has taken place in many jurisdictions that have restructured their electric industries: how to price "default" service physically provided by the local electric distribution company.[58]

When electric restructuring and deregulation were initially begun, it was envisioned that all customers would eventually choose their electric suppliers the way they now choose their mobile telephone provider. However, many policymakers and regulators recognized that, at least for an interim period, some form of default service was necessary, especially for residential and small commercial customers. Policymakers were concerned that consumers might sign up with retail electric providers who would fail to meet their service obligations. Policymakers and regulators were also concerned that some retail providers might refuse to provide service to certain customers, such as those who used little electricity or who were perceived as less likely to pay their bills. And, finally, they were concerned that, as with choosing a mobile telephone provider, some customers would simply be unwilling or unable to choose a different electric supplier.

To address these concerns, countries and states that restructured their electric industries created several different types of "default" service provisions, each having different price attributes and each encompassing social and political, as well as economic, objectives. A few states in the United States, such as Texas, created a type of default service called *price-to-beat* (PTB), whose goal—and pricing—was designed to encourage customers to switch to alternative providers by preventing local utilities from "undercutting" competitive prices. More common are states that, within the smoke-filled rooms of political negotiation, created *standard offer service* (SOS), sometimes called *provider of last resort* (POLR) service,[59] which encompassed multiyear retail price caps in exchange for regulated utilities being allowed to recover "stranded" generating costs.[60] A third type of default service, which was tendered more to larger commercial and industrial customers with time-of-use metering, is, in fact, referred to as "default service." Under this type of service, customers typically pay the hourly wholesale spot market price for their electricity.

---

[58] As we discuss in Chapter 12, electric systems obey the laws of physics, rather than contracts. Moreover, unlike salmon, it is impossible to physically "tag" electrons and identify from whence they came. Nor, apart from physical disconnection from the distribution grid, can electrons be prevented from flowing to certain customers.

[59] In Europe, this is called *Supplier of Last Resort* (SOLR).

[60] Stranded generation costs are defined as the difference between book value and market value. During the heyday of restructuring efforts in the late 1990s and early 2000s, stranded costs associated with nuclear power plants, which ironically became some of the most valuable generating resources as fossil fuel prices increased significantly between 2002 and 2006, were the focus of much heated debate.

The same principles apply in the international experience. Figure 7-7 presents a summary of the POLR experience across countries. The first column indicates which countries specifically refer to the POLR obligation (all except Argentina and Mexico). The second and third columns (Retail Competition) show which countries have implemented retail competition for industrial or for commercial and residential customers. Columns four and five (Who is Covered?) show which groups of customers are offered POLR service. Finally, the last column shows in which countries LDCs continue to have an obligation to supply commercial and residential customers.

Figure 7-7: Selected International POLR Experience

	POLR Definition	Retail Competition		Who is Covered?		LDCs with Obligations to Supply (C&R)
		Industrial	C&R	Industrial	C&R	
Argentina		X				X
Australia	X	X	X		X	
Mexico		X				X
UK	X	X	X	X (small)	X	
US	X	X	X		X	

C&R: Commercial and residential customers
Source: Authors' research.

Electric Restructuring and the "Price-to-Beat" in Texas

As part of its electric restructuring plan, Texas regulators introduced a "price-to-beat" (PTB) system. Unlike many other state restructuring plans that included multiyear price caps, price-to-beat imposed a *price floor*. Specifically, under PTB, the local electric utility (known as the *incumbent provider*) is not allowed to offer competitively priced electricity to customers who can choose their electric suppliers below an administratively determined price. In Texas, that price was tied to the price of natural gas. Thus, when natural gas prices rose sharply in late 2005 through 2006, PTB rates went up significantly as well.

The intended regulatory purpose of PTB was to foster market competition by preventing incumbent utilities, known in Texas as Affiliated Retail Electric Providers (AREPs), from undercutting competitive retail providers and to encourage retail customers to switch to competitive providers of electricity. (Just as was the case when long-distance telephone service was deregulated in the U.S. and many customers wanted to stay with "Ma Bell," many customers do not want to switch to other retail electricity providers.) Although the idea sounds plausible, in practice the benefits of PTB to retail customers are few. The reason is that if a market has one large firm and many small ones, the large (or *dominant*) firm provides a price "umbrella," under which all other firms can set their prices. For example, if the PTB is 10¢ per kWh, all of the small competing firms know that they can charge up to that price without losing sales to the dominant firm. Not surprisingly, competitive prices offered by competing electric suppliers have been just below the PTB. Whereas artificially high prices benefit competitors, they do not benefit retail consumers, and they do not foster true market competition. Moreover, not all customers have access to competitive suppliers. In those cases, customers have been unwillingly forced into accepting artificially high electric prices.

Still another problem with PTB has been its one-way adjustment. Although natural gas prices fell from their historic high values in the 2005–2006 period, AREPs are not required to lower their default service prices if natural gas prices decrease, as they did by the end of 2006.

One solution that has been proposed (but, as we write this in early 2007, was never implemented) to address the adverse economic consequences of PTB is *competitive procurement,* which is used in several other states that have restructured their electric industries, including Maryland and New Jersey. In these two states, the right to provide default service to customers is auctioned off in small "slices" of load, called *tranches,* and there are limits on how much load any one supplier can provide. Typically, auctions are set up annually, and tranches with different durations (e.g., one year, two years, etc.) are auctioned. The auctions that have been held have all been highly competitive, although they are obviously not immune from the effects of higher fossil fuel prices.

7.8 Chapter Summary

As we noted at the beginning of this chapter, there are innumerable ways to structure rates and tariffs. Although tariffs based on energy use are usually straightforward, the same cannot be said for tariffs designed to recoup fixed costs. However tariffs are set, they require a set of billing determinants, that are estimated based on forecasts of overall energy consumption and peak energy demand.

The complexity of tariff design arises from the oft-competing objectives of their designers. Conflicts can arise between regulatory principles of economic efficiency and those aligning costs to causation, versus principles of equity and fairness. Tariff design has also been influenced by other social policies, such as ensuring affordable rates for low-income consumers and providing default service for customers in markets that are undergoing restructuring.

Perhaps the most complex issue facing energy regulators today is designing electric transmission system tariffs. The sheer engineering complexity of high-voltage transmission systems, the need to coordinate the operation of hundreds of generating plants, and the design of economic incentives to encourage competitive pricing and new private investment continue to be daunting tasks.

CHAPTER 8
RATE AND TARIFF ADJUSTMENT MECHANISMS

8.1 Introduction

In the previous three chapters, we described all of the components necessary to develop regulated rates and tariffs: estimating the revenue requirement; functionalizing, classifying and allocating costs; and designing tariffs. In Chapter 4, we expanded our discussion of tariffs by introducing the concept of tariff adjustment mechanisms used under "alternative" regulation, especially performance-based regulation (PBR) regimes. We explained that these mechanisms specify the methods used to <u>change</u> tariffs from one year to the next, for a predetermined length of time. In Chapter 4, we also discussed how those regimes typically include adjustments for inflation (the *RPI factor*), productivity (the *X factor*), and changes to costs (such as income tax rates) beyond the regulated company's control (the *Z factor*), and we pointed out how each adjustment is intended to promote increased efficiency by <u>not</u> automatically passing through all cost increases.

Later in this chapter, we examine tariff adjustment mechanisms in more detail, describing how they are estimated, and we note the pitfalls that surround those estimates. We begin, however, with a discussion of simple pass-through mechanisms, which are increasingly used under COS regulation. Pass-through mechanisms differ from tariff adjustment mechanisms because they are more limited in scope. Rather than adjusting for changes in all of a regulated firm's costs, such as with an inflation adjustor, pass-through mechanisms typically focus on fuel and power costs alone.

8.2 Pass-Through Mechanisms

As we first discussed briefly in Chapter 3, one issue that can vex both regulators and regulated firms is *regulatory lag*. Given the time needed to gather and analyze all of the data on a firm's costs and investment decisions—to say nothing of the often extended legal jockeying—traditional rate cases can drag on for many months. Coupled with increasing electric and fuel price volatility, price swings have become larger and more frequent. Given that volatility, if rates remain constant between formal rate cases, the result can be large discrepancies between rates and actual costs. When prices are increasing, this can mean that a regulated firm's established revenue requirement is too low, and this may force the firm to borrow more money and jeopardize its credit rating. If prices are falling, it can mean the firm is collecting too much revenue based on too high prices; this can reduce economic efficiency and dampen economic well-being.

One of the ways to reduce the effects of regulatory lag, therefore, has been to employ automatic price adjustment mechanisms (especially fuel adjustment clauses) to more easily align costs and rates. Although these mechanisms can be part of performance-based regulation (PBR) regimes, such as we described in Chapter 4, many have become integral under traditional COS regulation. (Indeed, the concept that regulated prices can move between rate cases is one of the most novel features of rate regulation.) More recently, price adjustment mechanisms have become common in restructured electric markets where local distribution utilities are required to offer *provider of last resort* (POLR) service, especially to residential customers who either cannot or will not select an alternative retail electric provider.

By creating an automatic adjustment for changes in input costs, regulated firms (and regulators themselves) can avoid litigation expenses, and they can avoid prohibitions against so-called *single-issue ratemaking*, which may prevent regulators from focusing solely on one aspect of a cost change. In other words, a firm that formally requests rate relief solely because its fuel costs have risen nevertheless must open its accounts for a complete and time-consuming review. Moreover, when rates are allowed to adjust automatically over time, corresponding efficiency incentives, such as those we discuss in Section 8.4, are better able to influence regulated firms' operations.[1]

Typically, pass-through mechanisms are based on a well-defined index of input prices. For example, a natural gas distribution company's rates might include a quarterly adjustment based on the wholesale price of natural gas trading at Henry Hub (a large oil and natural gas price reference point in Louisiana) or an average of forward prices on the New York Mercantile Exchange (NYMEX). A vertically integrated electric utility might have a fuel adjustment mechanism based on the price of coal burned at its generating stations, while a restructured electric distribution company could have an adjustment tied to changes in wholesale spot market prices within a power pool.

The mechanisms themselves often balance several conflicting goals. As we discussed in Chapter 2, one of the most important goals of regulation is to mimic the pricing that would prevail in a fully competitive market. Pass-through mechanisms make this goal easier to achieve, because prices can adjust more quickly. Another goal of regulation, however, is price stability. When retail rates change constantly, it can be more difficult for firms to operate

---

[1] Allowing rates to reflect input price changes also improves *allocative efficiency* (i.e., ensuring that goods and services are consumed efficiently), which we first discussed in Chapter 2.

efficiently, using the lowest cost mix of inputs. Still another goal is to ensure firms have an incentive to manage their costs. Allowing firms to pass along every price increase without having ever considered prudent hedging measures removes that efficiency incentive.

Because of these conflicting goals, pass-through mechanisms sometimes include time lags that can provide an incentive for firms to increase their efficiency. For example, suppose an electric distribution utility's retail rate tariff includes an adjustment based on the average spot market price for the last quarter, and that this average price is 10% higher than the previous quarter. Rather than allowing the utility to impose the 10% increase immediately, regulators may limit the adjustment to one-half the total increase each quarter.

8.3   Inflation Adjustments

Inflation adjustments are a principal element of most automatic adjustment plans. Not only does inflation affect many costs over which regulated companies have little or no control, but providing automatic adjustments reduces regulatory lag.[2] However, while there is general agreement on the *purpose* of an inflation adjustment, determining the most appropriate form of the adjustment in any particular application can be difficult. The most common adjustment is known as *RPI-X*, where "RPI" is a retail (consumer) price inflation index and "X" is an efficiency factor designed to encourage the regulated firm to improve its productive efficiency. However, using the consumer retail price index may not provide an accurate estimate of changes to industry factor costs for the simple reason that changes in the cost of a firm's inputs (e.g., fuel, labor, iron pipe, etc.,) may be quite different than changes to the prices of the consumer's market basket of goods and services, of which energy may be only a small, although crucial, component.[3]

Although using producer-specific measures of inflation generally will be more accurate than using retail price measures, producer measures are often subject to greater volatility. One has merely to follow the rapid ups and downs on crude oil and natural gas prices to see just how volatile these prices are. This raises a regulatory concern because, even if a given inflation measure is accurate over the long run, if that measure experiences significant short-term volatility, retail consumers can see wide swings in the prices they pay. Not only does this contravene a regulatory goal of rate stability, large price swings make it difficult for consumers, especially large industrial and commercial ones, to optimize how they produce

---

[2]   The company may be able to hedge commodity or exchange rate costs over a limited period and may have certain buying power based on the volume of its purchases, but it cannot shield itself from general inflation.

[3]   In the U.S., the Dept. of Labor, Bureau of Labor Statistics, publishes inflation indices for specific producer (input) prices. *See*, www.bls.gov/ppi.

goods and services. As a result, it is not uncommon for regulators to use RPI measures as the basis for inflation adjustments, since price changes in an overall "market basket" will tend to be less volatile than the individual bits that make it up. A good deal of work has been performed to justify the credibility and objectivity of indices, as well as their suitability as proxies for the general rise in the cost of providing service to customers.

Internationally, different regulators have adopted diverse inflation indices. For example, British regulators tend to use retail price indices, while regulators in the United States use wholesale price indices for oil pipelines. Ontario regulators use input (i.e., producer) price indices, whereas Mexican regulators use a combination of wholesale and consumer price indices. Moreover, some countries have relied on U.S. price indices. For example, until the beginning of 2002, Argentina had dollarized utility tariffs, whereas Mexico, in addition to using a combination of indices, incorporates the percentage of costs whose services or goods are procured abroad.

8.4 An Alphabet Soup of Adjustment Factors

Economists love to use different letters in adjustment formulas to denote the many factors, in addition to inflation adjustments, that are used to adjust tariffs. The best known of these adjustment factors is the X factor, which, as we discussed in the previous section, is used to encourage firms to improve their operating efficiency. However, in addition to the X factor, regulators employ K factors to account for changes in a firm's capital investment, Q factors to account for service quality, and Z factors that exclude price changes of specific inputs.[4] Whatever letters of the alphabet are assigned, to work well, automatic price adjustment mechanisms require reliable and objective methods for determining all of the elements of the price-change formulas.

The Productivity (X) Factor

The productivity, or X factor, in a PBR formula accounts for the expected change in industry productivity that will be passed through to consumers in prices. All other things being equal, improved productivity will result in lower prices to consumers, which is why X factors tend to be positive and "RPI-X" indices lower than just the rate of inflation. In theory, the X factor can be negative, reflecting an expected *decrease* in relative productivity. In prac-

---

[4] As mentioned in Chapter 4, some countries also use different letters to represent these adjustments.

tice, however, regulators apply other factors to ensure that regulated firms cannot raise their prices more than the inflation rate. Various patterns have been applied in practice, such as X starting at zero and rising or X starting high and then falling to a lower long-term rate.

Wherever possible, the productivity trend should be based on the relevant industry, rather than the specific company itself. Using an X factor based on a company's own productivity can either penalize a company for being highly productive in the past or reward it for past inefficiency. In either case, this practice violates the competitive standard that lies at the heart of PBR.[5] Moreover, the value of efficiency incentives for regulated companies will be tied directly to a long-term regulatory commitment to those incentives, which in turn depends on the reasonableness and objectivity of the data and analysis used to develop those incentives. Thus, accurate and objective measures of underlying productivity growth in the subject industry are crucial to developing effective incentive regulation plans.

Any rate adjustment formula containing an X factor will itself provide short-term incentives (depending on how often prices are adjusted). Yet, setting the X factor at each tariff review must incorporate long-term incentives. Hence, whatever method is used to set the X factor must be objective and replicable (i.e., be capable of being used at subsequent reviews). To meet these criteria, the method of setting X should, where possible:

1. Use publicly available data that are expected to be available at subsequent reviews;

2. Use an understandable and transparent methodology that will not be continually challenged or changed;

3. Ensure that any judgmental adjustments are consistent with defined principles or productivity measurement; and

4. Provide a reasonably reliable measure of likely future productivity growth of the industry compared to the productivity of the economy as a whole.

---

[5] Some regulators have applied a company-specific adjustment to the industry trend. For example, the natural gas regulator in Argentina applied separate X factors to each of the 10 regulated distribution companies in 1997. *See*, Andres Gómez-Lobo and Vivien Foster, "The 1996–97 Gas Price Review in Argentina," *Private Sector*, Note No. 181, April 1999, 5.

Methods to Calculate the X Factor

The most popular and well-researched method used to calculate X factors is called *total factor productivity* (TFP) analysis.[6] In order to measure productivity using the TFP approach, historical indices for the major inputs into the production process are analyzed in precise ways. For example, a TFP analysis of the electric industry will compare the quantities of labor, fuel, capital, etc. used as *inputs* to production with the *outputs* from production (i.e., sales of electricity). Simply put, if the industry produces more output over time relative to the inputs used, the industry is becoming more productive. A robust TFP study requires a reasonably lengthy time series of data for the industry in question to smooth out short-term fluctuations into stable trends.

The other common method for determining X factors is based on forecasting.[7] Unlike TFP analysis, forecasting is a highly subjective process. Under this approach, the X factor is used in conjunction with a base price (P_0) to ensure that a price cap (i.e., how much prices are allowed to increase from year to year) will allow the company to earn the net present value (NPV) of its annual projected revenue requirement in each year of the plan period. Thus, rather than the X factor determining how much prices can increase each year, an administratively determined price cap determines the X factor.

For example, suppose Company X is expected to have revenues of $100 million this year. Suppose that prices are expected to increase 10% next year and 10% the following year. (In other words, RPI = 10%.) In that case, the company's revenue requirement would, all else equal, need to increase to $110 million next year and $121 million in the second year. Now suppose that regulators do not wish prices to increase more than 5% each year, implying a revenue requirement of $105 million in year one and $110.25 million in year two. To determine the X factor, they adjust the NPV of the revenue requirement and set it equal to the NPV of the proposed tariff increase. In our simple example, the X factor would be set to 5%. However, when prices are not expected to increase at the same rate each year, the present values are compared and a "smoothed" adjustment is calculated. Thus, suppose that the RPI was expected to be 5% this year and 10% next year. If regulators wanted to limit the tariff price increases to no more than 5% each year, they would calculate an X factor such that the NPV of the revenue requirement was the same as the NPV assuming 5% annual increases. Given the expected RPI changes of 5% and 10%, respectively, the calculated X factor would be about 2.5%.

---

[6] In addition, data envelope analysis (DEA) and other so-called "frontier" analyses, which we discussed in Chapter 5, have been used to determine the efficiency of a number of firms and to calculate a specific X for each regulated company. *See, e.g.*, Netherlands Competition Authority, *Addendum B BIJ to the Method Decision No. 102106-89*, Netherlands Government Gazette of 27 June 2006, no. 122, 19.

[7] This method is used in Great Britain, for example.

X Factors Across the World

Different countries have determined the X factors using a combination of methods and add-ons. Although a simple comparison of X factor values across countries is not entirely accurate—since each method has a different rationale, and the particular circumstances of each industry may justify a different result in each setting—it is nevertheless interesting to examine different X factors that regulators have adopted. These are summarized in Table 8-1.

Table 8-1: X Factors in Values and Methods in Selected Countries

Country	Area	Company	Market	Sector	X Factor Value	X Factor Method	Stretch Factor?
Argentina	National	All 2 in sector	Gas	T	2.38% + company-specific factors	TFP + reduction for yr 1 rates	N, but yr 1 rate reduction
Argentina	National	All 9 in sector	Gas	D	2.12% + company factors	TFP + company factors	N, but yr 1 rate reduction
Argentina	National	All 5 in sector	Elec	T	0.20% to 1.00%	Benchmarking	N
Australia	Victoria	All 4 in sector	Gas	D	Varies by co.	Forecasting	Implicit
Australia	Victoria	All 5 in sector	Elec	D	12.40%–28.10% yr one; 1.00% following years	Forecasting	Implicit
Australia	Victoria	SPI Powernet	Elec	T	0.77%	Forecasting	Implicit
Australia	Victoria	GasNet	Gas	T	0.00%–3.00%	Forecasting	Implicit
Australia	NSW	All 5 in sector	Elec	D	-3.16%–1.47%	Forecasting	Implicit
Australia	National	Telstra	Telco	N/A	5%	TFP; DEA and MFP studies also considered	Y
GB	UK	All 14 in sector	Elec	D	3.00%	Forecasting	Implicit
GB	UK	NGC	Elec	T	1.50%	Forecasting	Implicit
GB	UK	Transco	Gas	T&D	2.00%	Forecasting	Implicit
Mexico	National	TelMex	Telco	N/A	3.00%	Forecasting	N
Mexico	National	7 in sector	Gas	D	Relative: 0.11%–4.12%; Internal: 2.77%–13.69%.	Forecasting, stochastic frontier	N
Netherlands	National	All 10 in sector	Elec	D	3.20%	DEA + frontier	Y
US	Mass.	Boston Gas	Gas	T	0.41%	TFP + stretch	Y
US	California	SDG&E	Gas	D	1.08%, 1.23%, 1.38%	TFP + stretch	Y
US	California	SoCal Gas	Gas	T&D	2.10%, 2.20%, 2.30%, 2.40%, 2.50%	TFP + stretch + rate base adjustment	Y
US	California	SoCal Ed	Elec	D	1.60%	TFP + stretch	Y
US	California	SDG&E	Elec	D	0.92%, 1.32%, 1.62%	TFP + stretch	Y
US	Maine	CMP	Elec	D	0%, 2.0%, 2.25%, 2.75%, 2.75%, 2.75%, 2.9%	TFP + stretch	Y
US	Illinois	SBC Illinois	Telco	N/A	4.30%	TFP	Y
US	National	Local Ex. Cos.	Telco	N/A	6.50%	TFP	Y

T: Transmission in electricity and transportation for natural gas
D: Distribution

As the table demonstrates, stretch factors normally accompany TFP-based X factors. In addition, the table demonstrates the prevalence of TFP and forecast-based X factors above any other methods.

The glaring problem with this approach is that it uses one model to determine both initial prices and the X factor at the same time. Recall from basic algebra that, if an equation has two unknowns and one solution, there are an infinite number of values that will solve the equation. Thus, if regulators use one measure as the basis for determining two sets of variables, infinite combinations of P_0 and X values can be specified. This, however, makes it impossible for regulated companies to receive a fair shake.

Subjective Add-Ons to the X Factor

While the best PBR plans use TFP as the starting point in designing the X factor, they rarely use TFP alone. In fact, many regulators have made X factors slightly larger than the TFP productivity factor alone. The (shaky) regulatory rationale for this is that TFP captures historical productivity growth, whereas PBR is designed to provide regulated firms with incentives to become more efficient in the future. As such, regulators argue that industry productivity should grow at a faster rate in the future, and they thus typically add a "stretch factor" or a "consumer dividend" to the productivity offset.[8] Because of the unpredictability of future productivity changes, however, determining stretch factors is subjective and introduces the same sort of "two unknowns/one solution" problem we discussed earlier.

The Investment (K) Factor

Although much less common than the X factor, several countries also incorporate an investment factor (called the K factor) into their price adjustment formulae.[9] The rationale for the K factor is that the cost of investments that cannot be made under existing tariffs (because of too little revenue to cover their costs) can be incorporated into the rate base by increasing the current tariff by the K factor. In other words, the K factor is essentially an *ad hoc* way of rolling the costs associated with a larger rate base—additional annual depreciation and a larger total return on investment—into tariffs.

---

[8] Regulators have also decided to increase the X factor by arguing that the regulated company had "accumulated inefficiencies," and, therefore, a higher X would provide the incentive to eliminate those inefficiencies.

[9] For example, regulators in Great Britain have used a K factor in regulating water utility tariffs, while regulators in Argentina have used a K factor to adjust natural gas distribution and transportation tariffs. For a discussion of K factor application in Great Britain, see, Mark Armstrong, Simon Cowan, and John Vickers, *Regulatory Reform: Economic Analysis and British Experience*, (Cambridge, MA: MIT Press, 1994), 344. In Argentina, the natural gas regulator calculated K factors in much the same way as British regulators calculate X factors, using NPV equivalents and adjusting tariffs to be consistent with a given forecast of future revenue requirements. *See*, Gómez-Lobo and Foster, *supra* note 5.

The Service Quality (Q) Factor

A potential, but easily remedied, drawback to incentive regulation in all its forms is that companies given a profit incentive to reduce costs may do so in ways that run counter to consumer interests or other regulatory policy goals. For example, an electric distribution company that reduced costs solely through redundancies of line workers available to restore electricity after outages would almost surely have reduced service quality, perhaps dangerously so. And, whereas in competitive industries customers can switch suppliers if they object to low service quality, a monopolist faces no such risk (but does risk customers choosing not to take service at all or to take less of it). Fortunately, such potential drawbacks of incentive regulation are easily addressed.

The solution to regulated companies reducing costs by reducing product or service quality is simply to require the company to maintain (or improve, where appropriate) the quality of service it provides. (The intent of service quality measures is generally to *preserve* rather than *increase* current levels of service quality, unless there is demonstrable evidence that current service quality levels are unsatisfactory.) In many rate adjustment mechanisms, such requirements are designed as another formula component, called the *Q factor*.

Two basic issues must be confronted when designing service quality measures. First, what are the appropriate measures to monitor quality of service? Second, what is required to ensure that quality of service is preserved?

Answering the first question requires two separate efforts. The first is that service quality measures should address those areas of greatest importance to customers. The second is that, whatever measures are selected, they must be conducive to objective measurement. Thus, when monitored, service quality can be compared fairly to benchmarks established in advance, rewarded where appropriate, and penalized where inadequate. Answering the second question is more a policy matter to establish measurable service standards. For example, one standard could be, and often has been, ensuring service availability to rural customers.[10]

The inclusion of incentives for improving quality of service is a relatively recent regulatory development that has been applied under both price-cap and revenue-cap schemes. Most price adjustment schemes incorporating Q factors last from three to five years. Typically, they coincide with the regulatory tariff period. Moreover, service quality standards, and sometimes the components of the Q factor, are typically reset at each tariff review, just like the inflation and productivity factors.

---

[10] In the United States, the Rural Electrification Act of 1936, which we discussed in Chapter 1, can really be thought of as a service quality measure.

There are about the same number of service quality approaches that use both carrots and sticks as there are schemes that solely use one or the other. All of the incentive schemes rely on multiple service quality indicators, since any one indicator can be quite volatile. For example, an electric distribution company indicator based solely on the duration of outages could be skewed by a single weather event, such as a hurricane. When two or more service quality indicators are combined, they also tend not to be given the same weights.[11] Moreover, most such indicators are "technical," such as specific measures of reliability (of which there are many, as we discuss in Chapter 12), rather than commercial indicators, such as response time to phone inquiries. Moreover, service quality indicators are usually calculated annually.[12]

The level of the indicators is compared against a standard that generally is negotiated between the regulator and the regulated company and/or set using historical data. The standards for each indicator are set using historical data, projected improvement, negotiation, and values from other jurisdictions and/or other companies (in many cases a combination of two of these alternatives is used).

The Exclusion (Z) Factor

Z factors (known also as *exogenous adjustment factors*) are specific items that are wholly or partly excluded from price and revenue adjustment formulae.[13] Z factors typically control for nonrecurring and exogenous items, such as changes in financial accounting standards, changes in tax rates, or even changes in environmental or other laws. The Z factor isolates the risk from the regulated company and passes through the incurred costs to ratepayers. If, for example, the income tax is changed, affecting either the amount of taxes or the rate of return used on the revenue requirement, the monetary impact can be passed through to ratepayers using a Z factor.

The exogenous adjustment factor is an important component of a price regulation plan that allows the regulated company to treat costs the same way that companies in a competitive market would. Exogenous cost changes represent any changes in the company's costs—up or down—that are beyond the company's control. In a competitive industry, if these costs

---

[11] Weights alone do not determine the relationship between changes in performance and changes in allowed revenues. The way performance changes translate into service quality indices, and indices into revenue changes, is important. Since the weights assigned to different attributes will almost always be subjective, there is, potentially, room for mischief by both regulators and regulated companies.

[12] There are, of course, exceptions. For example, Argentina calculated service quality on transmission systems every month. In California, on the other hand, distribution service quality is calculated only once a year.

[13] Mexico calls this factor in the natural gas industry "Y."

were reasonably and prudently required to provide service, changes in these costs would alter the long-run marginal and average cost curves of the industry; and they would directly affect the market price prevailing in that industry. Because the costs are not under the company's control, automatically passing such cost changes through to customers does not affect the company's incentive to behave efficiently. Thus, changes in these costs: (1) should be passed directly through to customers, because that is what would occur in a competitive industry; and (2) can be passed through to customers without affecting the company's incentive to reduce costs.

Some exogenous factors may have economy-wide effects and thus appear reflected in the evolution of the inflation measure or X factor. For this reason, exogenous events that adversely affect just the regulated firm—as opposed to the entire economy—are good candidates for Z factors.

Z factors can be established either by specifying the *types* of events in advance that will be considered exogenous (e.g., hurricanes, tax law changes, plagues of locusts, etc.) or by specifying the *set of criteria* that extraordinary events must satisfy to be included in the Z factor (e.g., exogenous events cause cost increases of 10% or more, locusts eat all of the distribution poles, etc.). In practice, there may not be much difference between the two, and both can reduce uncertainty and subsequent contention over Z factor issues.

8.5 Shared-Savings and Off-Ramps

As we discussed in Chapter 4, adjustment plans typically include *off-ramp* provisions under which a new tariff review gets triggered. These provisions are designed such that both shareholders and customers are shielded from excessive risk. Off-ramp provisions are necessary when the adjustment formulae are not tracking costs accurately.

Most shared-savings and off-ramps are triggered when the rate of return (ROR) is above or below certain predetermined levels. For example, if actual costs have been way below the forecast costs used to calculate the initial prices, the adjusted prices that are collected by the regulated company will give a ROR above the maximum ROR determined as a trigger mechanism. However they are triggered, the design and use of shared-savings mechanisms and off-ramps, especially the underlying conditions that trigger them, must be thought through carefully. Otherwise, they can either introduce too much regulatory risk to the firm or fail to provide the firm with sufficient incentives to improve its performance.

8.6 Chapter Summary

Today, performance-based regulation is the most popular regulatory regime in the world. PBR has reduced the time and resources needed to regulate prices, while offering firms incentives to improve their efficiency. Typically, PBR regimes require major regulatory efforts to reset key parameters only every four or five years. In between, rates are adjusted using well-defined formulae.

Like most other aspects of rate regulation, however, PBR is not a panacea, nor is it immune to regulatory fudges. Almost all regulatory jurisdictions apply their own unique formulae containing different sets of components and estimating key parameters using methods of varying sophistication, accuracy, and objectivity. As a consequence, actual PBR regimes that have been put into effect worldwide are often eye poppingly different.

Of all the different components used in PBR formulae, the X factor is the component for which economists, engineers, and other professionals working in regulated industries have devised innumerable and "creative" ways to determine. While this is, in part, a result of regulatory and political expediency, it also stems from the basic difficulty of defining and measuring "productivity" itself. No doubt, the methods we have summarized above will be displaced by newer methods in the medium term.

CHAPTER 9
MARKET POWER IN THE ELECTRIC AND NATURAL GAS INDUSTRIES

9.1 Introduction

In the previous eight chapters, we have reviewed many of the theoretical aspects of rate regulation, as well as the mechanics. Rate regulation applies to local natural gas and electric utilities and is the purview of state regulators. With restructuring and competition in the electric and natural gas industries, the detection of *market power* and the prevention of anticompetitive behavior has become an increasingly important component of the federal regulatory toolbox. Indeed, it is perhaps ironic that deregulation of these two industries has increased the importance of other forms of regulation designed to ensure that wholesale markets are truly competitive.

That a firm has market power simply means it has the ability to affect market prices (or competition in other dimensions).[1] Firms with excessive market power can increase prices and harm consumers, raising regulators' concerns that deregulating previously regulated activities will not improve consumers' welfare and, indeed, may make consumers worse off. This is of particular concern because once a market is deregulated, reregulation is impractical—like stuffing a genie back into the bottle.

Today, many of the independent transmission system operators (ISOs) in the United States,[2] such as ISO-NE, PJM, Midwest ISO, and others, have full-time *market monitors* who constantly evaluate the competitiveness of wholesale electric markets. Moreover, each of these ISOs has specific rules governing price setting in situations where market power is detected.

State and federal regulators need to assess whether generation spun off by previously vertically integrated electric utilities will have market power in wholesale electric markets. These evaluations can be complex because they hinge not only on a generator's absolute size in the

---

[1] A more comprehensive definition and discussion of market power follows in Section 9.2.

[2] In some cases, ISOs have been supplanted, in part, by regional transmission organizations (RTOs), whose structure was established by FERC, as discussed in its Order 2000, 89 FERC ¶ 61,285 (1999).

market, but also on its control of local transmission facilities and the way electric transmission systems operate. For those who continue to be regulated, rates typically are based on the COS principles we discussed in Chapters 4 and 5.

The repeal of the Public Utility Holding Company Act (PUHCA) in the United States in 2005 led to a new wave of proposed utility mergers. The purpose of these mergers is to exploit—depending on whom you ask—either economies of scale and scope or market power. This means that, at both the state and federal levels, regulators must evaluate whether the merging entities will be able to exercise market power, both in wholesale electric markets and, in some cases, in upstream natural gas markets.

At the federal level, FERC has a legal mandate under the Federal Power Act to ensure that wholesale rates are "just and reasonable." Accordingly, FERC has the authority to challenge energy transactions to the extent that those transactions may reflect the exercise of market power and/or anticompetitive behavior. Similarly, state public utility commissions have jurisdiction over both retail sales of electricity and wholesale sales that do not cross state lines. For example, under the Federal Power Act, all firms selling electricity at wholesale must have their rates accepted for filing at FERC in the form of a rate schedule or tariff. In order to sell electricity at market-based rates (i.e., at whatever price the market will bear), an entity must file a market-based rate application demonstrating that it does not have market power.

FERC also intends to ensure that mergers and acquisitions in the energy industry are consistent with the public interest. In addition to allowing far-flung utility mergers, the repeal of PUHCA expanded FERC's authority to review and approve those mergers.[3] In analyzing the competitive effects of a proposed merger, applicants have to demonstrate that the merger passes the market power screen established by the Commission. Similarly, with restructuring resulting in electric and natural gas utilities now operating in both the regulated and the deregulated sides of the business, there are new concerns regarding *affiliate abuse*, *reciprocal dealing*, and *foreclosure* of competitors' access to the market by means of raising barriers to entry. In all these scenarios, all regulators have a legitimate concern and a legal mandate to ensure that consumers are not left unprotected from the exercise of market power.

---

[3] As we mentioned in Chapter 1, PUHCA allowed mergers only between utilities whose service territories were contiguous.

At the state level, regulators are concerned not only with pure market power, but often also with the allocation of benefits in mergers involving out-of-state firms.[4] We discussed the complexities of cost allocation in Chapter 6. However, allocating costs and benefits among different firms can be even more contentious and fraught with uncertainty, because merging firms may use different, but legitimate, accounting practices.

9.2 Defining Market Power

What is *market power*? Market power just means that a firm is able to affect market prices, that is, the firm is not a price taker. Economic textbooks define market power as the ability to raise prices profitably above marginal cost. (You might want to review Figure 2-4, where we showed how a monopolist could increase profits by restricting output and raising prices.) In 1992, the Department of Justice (DOJ) and the Federal Trade Commission (FTC) published their *Merger Guidelines*,[5] which define seller market power as the ability to profitably maintain prices above the competitive level for a significant period of time. The *Merger Guidelines* acknowledge that market power may also affect competition on other dimensions, such as product quality, service, or technological innovation. Symmetrically, buyers can exercise market power by reducing prices below competitive levels. This is called buyer market power, or *monopsony* power.

As was shown in Figure 2-4, market power creates welfare losses. However, market power does not necessarily imply that firms are making abnormal profits. After all, firms have to recover investment costs, which might not be possible by setting prices at marginal cost. This is not unusual in energy markets in which large, up-front capital investments are necessary to enter the market. For example, consider a software development firm for which, once a new product is created, the cost of providing a copy to an additional customer (the marginal cost) is virtually zero. However, the developer still needs to recover its investment in research and development. Obviously, it cannot charge marginal cost for its product. Only by exercising some degree of market power would the developer be able to stay in business.

Sometimes lawyers and regulators define market power differently than economists: as anticompetitive or manipulative conduct that is not acceptable under legal norms. Although market power can result from illegal practices, e.g., price-fixing or anticompetitive conduct

---

[4] Regulators have also expressed concern when public utilities are purchased by private firms, such as investment banks. Those concerns stem from regulators' fears that they will not be able to oversee those firms' operations.

[5] U.S. Department of Justice and Federal Trade Commission, *Horizontal Merger Guidelines*, 57 Fed. Reg. 41,552 (April 2, 1992).

(such as creating artificial barriers to entry), market power can often exist without any legal violations. In fact, the economist's definition of market power assumes neither the violation of legal norms, nor anticompetitive conduct. Pricing above marginal cost is not evidence, by itself, of anticompetitive behavior. Nor is it evidence that markets require regulatory intervention. In most real-world markets, this is not only inevitable, but also necessary for prices to provide signals to market participants that new investment is needed. It is this behavior by individual market participants that steers Adam Smith's "invisible hand" and leads to efficient market outcomes and technological breakthroughs.

In light of technological and other factors that make any approximation to pure competition unattainable, economists have long developed a more realistic concept of *"workable competition."*[6] The workable competition concept focuses on whether the results from the market process would improve welfare relative to the regulated status quo, whether the allocation of resources—including opportunities for innovation—is reasonably efficient, and whether profits are sufficient to reward the investments made. In other words, can a deregulated market realistically provide sustainable benefits for both consumers and firms?

What constitutes "workable" competition in specific markets is, not surprisingly, a matter of great dispute. A number of competition measures and presumed competitive thresholds have been developed by the DOJ and FTC to address the issue. Similarly, FERC requires a "just and reasonable price" standard for energy products. While there clearly is some ambiguity in the interpretation of just and reasonable, as we discussed in Chapter 3, the legal standard that emerged for just and reasonable prices is interpreted as wholesale prices that recover production costs, including a "fair" rate of return on capital investment.

So why do economists care about market power? The obvious reason is that firms with excessive market power can increase prices and harm consumers. This is the *distributional* consequence of market power. As shown in Figure 2-4, market power transfers wealth from consumers to suppliers. But there is another consequence of market power. Firms with market power generally restrict production, reducing economic efficiency. The welfare loss is also shown in Figure 2-4. When the market price is above marginal cost, both the seller and the buyer would be better off if an extra unit were produced and sold at some price below the market price but above marginal cost. Market inefficiency suggests that resources are not dedicated to their best use, and to the extent possible, everybody could be better off if a different market mechanism were developed.

---

[6] *See, e.g.,* Joe Bain, "Workable Competition in Oligopoly: Theoretical Considerations and Some Empirical Evidence," *The American Economic Review* 40, no. 2 (1950): 35–47.

In all cases, market power cannot exist without *barriers to entry* (or *market barriers.*) Recall from Chapter 2 that we defined barriers to entry as costs borne by new market entrants that are not borne by incumbent firms. Additionally, we discussed the strategic implications of market barriers and how incumbent firms may act to increase those barriers by increasing the likelihood that new entrants will suffer unsustainable losses if they enter.

Evaluating barriers to entry is a crucial component in analyzing market structure. In markets where entry is relatively easy, market power is less of a concern, because market participants cannot sustain prices above the competitive norm. Both the DOJ/FTC's *Merger Guidelines* and FERC consider that a merger would not raise antitrust concerns when entry is *timely, likely, and sufficient* in its magnitude. A similar transaction would raise competitive concerns if entry is not likely, or worse, if the transaction itself leads to or is the result of the incumbent firms creating barriers to entry.

9.3 Dominant Firms

An ability to increase prices above competitive levels is not limited to monopolists. Indeed, when regulators are evaluating market power concerns, it is rare that they are confronting pure monopolies. Instead, regulators most often address the competitiveness of markets when there are a limited number of firms in the market (e.g., the automobile industry) or when one firm in the market is far larger than all of the others. The latter situation describes a market with a *dominant firm*. Understanding dominant firm behavior is important because regulators must determine whether the firm is so dominant as to prevent sufficient, or "workable," competition when dealing with market power issues.

A dominant firm has market power because all of the other "fringe" firms in the industry cannot meet market demand by themselves. Essentially, a dominant firm sets the price it charges based on the *residual demand*, i.e., the remaining market demand that is not served by the small, fringe firms. The dominant firm uses the residual demand curve in the same way a monopolist uses the market demand curve, setting its price based on marginal revenue and marginal cost. After the market leader sets the price, the followers supply the market with all they can at the given price. This situation exists in many markets where a firm or a group of firms sets prices and a competitive fringe of small firms takes such price as given.

The important thing to note is that a dominant firm can exert market power because it knows that its output is required to meet market demand. In a purely competitive market, market price would be determined by the intersection of the market demand and supply curves. Instead, the dominant firm is able to set a price based on the residual demand curve and above competitive levels. Oddly enough, fringe firms benefit from the dominant firm's behavior. At the competitive price, the fringe firms would supply very little of the market. By restricting its output and raising the market price, however, the dominant firm provides an "umbrella" for the fringe firms to raise their prices and sell more output.

In electric and natural gas markets, which are characterized by periods of time when demand peaks noticeably, dominant firm behavior can emerge because one or more large suppliers become *pivotal*. Without their output, there is insufficient supply to meet demand. Thus, a *pivotal supplier* finds itself with market power.

9.4 Horizontal and Vertical Market Power

Market power is classified as either *horizontal* or *vertical*. The examples we have discussed so far refer to *horizontal market power*, that is, a firm's ability to influence price in a single market. For example, a natural gas pipeline company that controlled 80% of the pipeline capacity in the eastern United States would likely have horizontal market power. If the pipeline company decided to unilaterally raise prices above competitive levels, other firms in the market would not be able to step in and cover all the market such that prices are brought back to competitive levels, especially at times of peak demand.

The terms *market share* and *market concentration* are used interchangeably to represent horizontal market power, although they are not quite the same thing. Both are taken to mean an ability to raise prices above competitive levels, although that may not always be true. Nevertheless, it is a good starting point for markets with high barriers to entry, where new entrants are not likely to discipline the incumbent firms' pricing behavior. Market share is straightforward: it represents the total share a firm has of market demand. Market concentration, on the other hand, typically refers to an overall measure of the market, specifically the relative size of large and small firms.[7]

---

[7] If market barriers are low, neither market share nor market concentration indicates market power, because all attempts to raise prices above the competitive level will meet with new entry.

> **Measuring Market Concentration**
>
> The most common measure of market concentration is the Herfindahl-Hirschman Index (HHI), which is the sum of the squared market shares of each firm in a given market. Thus, a market having just one firm, or a 100% market share, has an HHI of $100 \times 100 = 10,000$, while a market of five equally sized firms (each having a 20% market share) has an HHI of $5 \times 20 \times 20 = 2,000$. An HHI analysis has long been at the heart of the DOJ/FTC *Horizontal Merger Guidelines*, which were adopted in FERC's 1996 Merger Policy Statement. In evaluating a proposed transaction, a market with an HHI of 1800 is considered highly concentrated, and a transaction that increases the HHI by 50 points or more in such a market is expected to give rise to market power concerns. In market-based rate proceedings, by contrast, FERC has established (as part of its interim generation market power screens) that an HHI of 2500 is the threshold above which a market may raise market power concerns.

Small competitors can benefit from the (horizontal) market power of a larger firm. As in the case of a dominant firm discussed above, this is called the *price umbrella*. If a large firm increases prices, small competitors may not be able to capture all the large firm's customers, but they would at least be able to charge a higher price to their customers, since the alternative—the large firm—is now more costly. In the absence of high barriers to entry or barriers for existing competitors to expand their market share, horizontal market power is considered to be self-correcting. If a firm increases its prices, both its competitors and new entrants can step in to serve demand by charging lower prices. New entry and competition would in turn contribute to reduce the large firm's market share and market power.

Vertical market power refers to the ability of a firm to use its market power in one market in order to exercise market power in another distinct, but vertically related, market. For example, a firm with "upstream" market power in an input market, such as transmission services, may attempt to use its market power in order to either *foreclose* competition or increase prices in a "downstream" market, such as a regional wholesale market. An electric generating company that owns transmission capacity connecting its generating plants to local distribution companies could ensure that electricity from its plants gets preferential access to the transmission system, and, thus, sell that electricity to the local distribution companies.

This type of *market foreclosure* is a way firms can exercise vertical market power, and it has long been recognized by economists (and the courts) as a form of anticompetitive behavior.[8] One of the most famous cases that showed how vertical market foreclosure applies to regu-

---

[8] *See, e.g., United States v. Terminal Railroad Association of St. Louis*, 224 U.S. 383 (1912) (requiring a group of railroads owning the railroad bridges across the Mississippi River at St. Louis to provide reasonable access to competing railroads who were previously denied access).

lated industries was *AT&T*.[9] In that case, regulation of AT&T's regulated "downstream" business (i.e., the local telephone exchanges) provided the means to monopolize the "upstream" equipment market.

> **Sorry, Wrong Number! Vertical Market Foreclosure in *United States v. AT&T Co.***
>
> One of the most famous cases of vertical foreclosure involved AT&T. Prior to its divestiture, AT&T's local phone rates were set under COS regulation, based on the same methods we discussed in Chapters 4–6. The company paid high prices for equipment purchased from its affiliate, Western Electric, and cross-subsidized markets. By buying telephone equipment from Western Electric at an inflated price, AT&T was able to increase its rate base, since telephone equipment was considered a capital investment. AT&T could then point to the high equipment prices as justification for raising local exchange rates. This affiliate abuse was coupled with other "bad acts" towards competitors, including refusing to buy competitors' telephone products, not allowing retail customers to use other manufacturers' equipment, and refusing to provide rivals with interconnections.

One might argue that regulatory oversight ought to be sufficient to prevent companies from misbehaving. However, natural gas and electric utilities may evade the regulatory constraints in ways that are difficult for regulators to detect. This regulatory "arms race" perhaps explains why, despite increasingly sophisticated monitoring of firm behavior, firms continue to find ways to exercise market power.

Figure 9-1 shows a conceptual diagram of the transactions in a typical electricity market and highlights the ways utilities can exercise market power. The left-hand side of Figure 9-1 identifies two ways a utility is able to exercise vertical market power. First, the dashed lines indicate the potential for the utility to exercise market power though its monopoly over transmission service. Control over transmission facilities may give a utility the ability to (1) exclude competitors from markets for wholesale generation, and (2) leverage its market power to the wholesale generation market. Second, the crossed-out lines indicate the potential exercise of *monopsony* power though the utility's monopoly over retail distribution as the *load serving entity* (LSE). A utility can use its position as a dominant buyer of wholesale power to discriminate in favor of its own generation and raise entry barriers for competing wholesale generators. Much as a dominant seller can dictate prices to increase its profits, a dominant buyer can dictate terms more favorable to itself than would be expected under competitive conditions (or it can simply refuse to buy power from certain sellers).

---

[9] *United States v. AT&T Co.*, 552 F. Supp. 131 (D.D.C. 1982), *aff'd sub nom. Maryland v. United States*, 460 U.S. 1001 (1983).

Figure 9-1: Diagram of Market Power in the Electric Industry

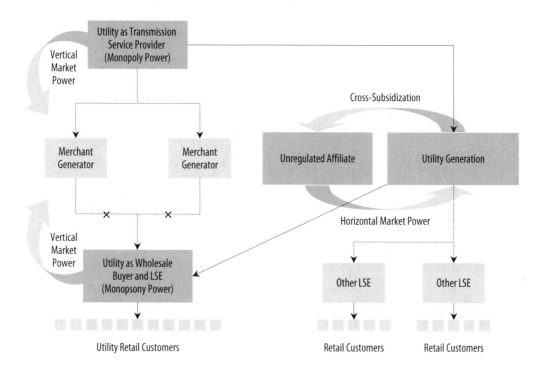

The right-hand side of Figure 9-1 indicates the utility's ability to exercise horizontal market power through its owned generation, as well as the utility's ability to engage in *affiliate abuse* and *cross-subsidization* through transactions with its unregulated affiliates. The most obvious form of cross-subsidization occurs when a vertically integrated utility inappropriately shifts costs that are incurred by its unregulated operations onto its regulated captive customers—or alternatively, shifts revenues from its regulated business to its unregulated business. This is achieved, for example, by having the affiliate increase the price of the energy purchased. Apart from harming customers, by cross-subsidizing its wholesale business, the utility is able to provide its unregulated affiliates with an artificial market advantage over competitors.

Cross-subsidization may also involve more subtle ways of shifting risks rather than direct costs from unregulated affiliates to the regulated retail business. During unfavorable market conditions, a franchised utility would have the incentive to incorporate its unregulated affiliates into the rate base, thereby providing the deregulated affiliate with a "safety net." This strategy gives the utility a competitive advantage that is not available to independent market participants and harms the competitive process. In addition, by incorporating a "failed" merchant asset back into the rate base, ratepayers are forced to take on losses that should be borne by shareholders and creditors.

Finally, cross-subsidization can occur when a utility uses a common pool of generation resources in order to serve its *captive* (cost-of-service) customers and wholesale (market-based rate) customers. As the utility needs to dispatch less efficient resources, this practice may force captive customers to bear increased generation costs that subsidize the utility's unregulated business. Consistent with the economic premise of the "regulatory compact" and the requirement that the rates be "just and reasonable," captive customers should not suffer economic losses that are the result of a utility's incremental wholesale sales unless they are afforded equivalent opportunities to benefit from such sales. In other words, as we discussed in Chapter 6, economic efficiency requires that deregulated sales be allocated the *incremental* costs associated with such sales.

Detecting Horizontal Market Power

Traditionally, economists and regulators have assessed the competitiveness of markets using a structural approach—and more specifically, using a "structure-conduct-performance" (SCP) paradigm.[10] Under this approach, market structure (i.e., the number of active buyers and sellers and the relative concentration of activity among those buyers and sellers) is expected to have a strong impact on the conduct of individual market participants (i.e., their individual pricing behavior) and ultimately their performance (i.e., their profitability). This approach recognizes that market participants' conduct and performance can also affect market structure, e.g., by using profits to invest in activities that ultimately create barriers to entry to potential new entrants, or by setting prices and output at levels that will discourage new entry or hasten market exit by existing competitors.

In order to assess the competitiveness of a particular market, the traditional SCP approach typically focuses on measuring individual firms' market shares or overall market concentration. Economic theory predicts that as concentration increases, prices are more likely to increase above a competitive level if there are significant barriers to entry. Thus, for example, if a proposed transaction were to increase concentration in an already highly concentrated market, economists and regulators likely would oppose the transaction unless adequate mitigation measures were put in place to prevent the transaction from increasing prices in

---

[10] For a detailed discussion, see Frederick Scherer and David Ross, *Industrial Market Structure and Economic Performance*, 3rd ed. (Boston: Houghton Mifflin, 1990).

the future. A high level of market concentration is also expected to increase the ability and incentives of the dominant market participants to engage in various forms of anticompetitive behavior, such as creating artificial barriers to entry.

The DOJ/FTC's *Merger Guidelines* and FERC's Order 592 both focus on horizontal market power and rely on different measures of market concentration to test for it. Simple measures based on the market share of the largest firms, such as C1 (largest firm's share) and C4 (sum of four largest firms), have been used extensively in economics. In connection with market-based rate applications, FERC also considers the applicant's market share of uncommitted capacity, which is the applicant's available capacity to serve wholesale customers after subtracting its retail load obligations, operating reserves, and other long-term commitments. The applicant fails FERC's market share test when it owns or controls more than 20% of the uncommitted capacity in the market in any season.[11] FERC also uses the HHI index, which continues to be the most common measure of market concentration and takes into account all market participants in calculating market concentration. Under fairly broad assumptions, the industry average price-cost margin is directly related to the HHI. In other words, a change in the HHI reflects the expected change in market prices (relative to average costs) due to changes in industry market structure—such as a change resulting from a merger.

More recently, the *pivotal supplier test* has become a crucial indicator of market power in the electric industry, especially as FERC has sought to establish competitive wholesale power markets. The pivotal supplier test examines whether at least some of the firm's capacity must be used to meet the market's peak demand. When a supplier is pivotal, it is in a position to demand a price above competitive levels and be assured of selling at least some of its capacity. A market can "pass" the market share test, yet there can be a pivotal supplier during many hours of the year. For example, in a market with seven suppliers, each with 1000 MW of installed capacity, each supplier would have just over a 14% market share.[12] The HHI value for this market (1,429) would also suggest that the market is not highly concentrated.[13] However, if peak demand were 6,100 MW, at least some of each supplier's capacity would be necessary to meet peak demand (because six suppliers with 6,000 MW of capacity cannot serve 6,100 MW of demand). Then, all the firms in this hypothetical market would be considered pivotal.

---

[11] All market power tests begin by defining the relevant *geographic* and *product markets*.

[12] $100\% \div 7 \approx 14.29\%$.

[13] The HHI = $7 \times (100 \div 7)^2 = 1429$.

A more sophisticated test of market power used in wholesale energy markets is FERC's *delivered price test* (DPT). The DPT simulates the competitive environment at different market prices that represent seasonal demand conditions. By incorporating transmission constraints and generation costs, the DPT only takes into account those suppliers that can physically and economically serve the market at a given price. Then, it applies the other tests (market share, HHI, or pivotal supplier tests) to the suppliers in question.

A Market-Based Rate Application Example

Under the Federal Power Act, any firm wishing to sell electricity into the wholesale market at unregulated prices must demonstrate that it does not have market power in its control area. FERC may require a DPT analysis to simulate the competitive environment at different seasonal demand conditions by incorporating transmission constraints and generation costs. Then, it applies the market share test, HHI test, and pivotal supplier test. The table below shows a hypothetical market, using the market share threshold of 20%.

In the first scenario, all the "economic capacity" (EC) is considered for the winter season. EC is just the total amount of generating capacity controlled by the utility. The utility has a 30% market share and fails the test. In the second scenario, only the available economic capacity (AEC) is considered. AEC subtracts from EC so-called "native load" and long-term contract obligations. For example, a vertically integrated utility having 3,000 MW of EC and a retail peak summer load of 2,000 MW will have only 1,000 MW of AEC.

Since the utility has a larger share of committed capacity than IPPs and importers, it passes the test. The next two scenarios consider the same control area in the summer. Because of tighter transmission constraints, imports are only 1,000 MW in the third scenario, and, because electricity is not easily stored, the utility would have market power. Finally, the last scenario considers expected transmission upgrades and new generation entry—*timely, likely, and sufficient,* that would lower the utility's market share to 15%. Ease of entry would limit the ability of the utility to exercise market power.

Table 9-1: Delivered Price Test

Test – Season	Utility Capacity (MW)	IPP Capacity (MW)	Imports (MW)	Utility Market Share	Pass/Fail
I) EC – Winter	3,000	3,000	4,000	30%	Fail
II) AEC – Winter	1,000	2,000	3,000	17%	Pass
III) AEC – Summer	1,000	2,000	1,000	25%	Fail
IV) AEC – Summer	1,000	3,000	2,500	15%	Pass

Similarly, FERC would consider historical data and structural market conditions, such as the existence of market institutions (ISOs, RTOs) that would limit the exercise of transmission market power, control of fuel resources and generation sites, historical generation dispatch, transmission services and wholesale sales data, opportunities for affiliate abuse, whether the utility would be pivotal during peak-load conditions, etc. These considerations can make all the difference between granting market-based rate authority and the need to impose structural market power mitigation measures.

Detecting Vertical Market Power

Although there have been high-profile cases in other regulated industries, vertical market power has tended to be ignored in electric and natural gas markets. Vertical market power has been studied most often in the context of whether market power in the natural gas market would affect downstream electric markets, but not so much in the context of Figure 9-1, where electric utilities that control transmission access have a privileged market position stemming from a large retail customer base and from deregulated affiliates competing in wholesale markets.

Vertical market power is more difficult to address than horizontal market power for a number of reasons. First, there is a long list of beneficial reasons for firms to participate in vertically related markets, unrelated to the exercise of market power. Firms may vertically integrate in order to reduce transaction costs, to improve quality controls, or to ensure adequate input supplies, among other reasons. Second, determining whether a firm's behavior in one market has anticompetitive effects in another vertically related market requires the regulator to evaluate both upstream and downstream markets. Finally, vertical market power is more difficult to measure. There are no straightforward measures of vertical market power that are similar to measures of market concentration for horizontal market power, although some concentration in the upstream market is clearly required.[14] The consequence of vertical market power is not an immediate price increase from the incumbent's market share; it is the foreclosure of competitors in vertically related markets or the transfer of costs from unregulated affiliates to the regulated business. Vertical market power could be implicit in a firm's dispatch decisions, as affiliates get preferential access to transmission services or a firm favors its own higher-cost generation, despite the availability of lower-cost alternatives. Finally, vertical market power in the upstream natural gas market could affect downstream wholesale electric markets, raising overall market-clearing prices, even if the downstream market was fully competitive. The reason is that, by raising the price of natural gas (an input to electric production), the market price of electricity will increase.

It is sometimes difficult for regulatory authorities to detect whether a local utility is discriminating against competing firms. However, it is important to note that market monitors have generally focused on the exercise of horizontal market power through such quantitative measures as capacity concentration ratios and prices. These measures do not attempt to assess the extent to which market participants are able to leverage their market power into adjacent markets. In that context, the failure to identify vertical market power stems

---

[14] FERC established a two-pronged test for vertical market power. *See*, Revised Filing Requirements Under Part 33 of the Commission's Regulations, Final Rule, 93 FERC ¶ 61,164, Order No. 642, (2000).

not only from the complexity of the analysis required, but also from the lack of a conceptual framework that comprises the full extent of regulated utilities' ability to exercise market power.

Unfortunately, unlike horizontal market power, vertical market power is not "self-correcting." Horizontal market power may be corrected through new entry, but vertical market power may involve incumbent firms raising barriers to entry in order to foreclose competitors first and then increasing prices. In other words, since small competitors and potential new entrants generally do not benefit from vertical market power exercised by a dominant firm, vertical market power is more likely to withstand competitive market forces. Thus, Adam Smith's "invisible hand" will not necessarily correct an anticompetitive situation.

Some measures of vertical market power may be readily available for regulators and market monitors, although a thorough analysis of market structure and incentives in an industry characterized by vertical linkages is necessarily more complex and time-consuming. Looking at historical generation data rather than capacity ownership may provide a better picture of the market reality. Buyer market power can also be assessed through market concentration indices, similar to those used to assess sellers' horizontal market power. Detecting discriminatory practices through transmission services is more difficult and requires individualized analysis of transmission-related costs, transmission reservations, refusal rates, etc.

The structural characteristics of a market are important considerations in assessing vertical market power, since those structural characteristics provide firms with the incentive to engage in anticompetitive practices. The absence of market institutions, such as RTOs and ISOs, as well as procurement processes or marketwide auction processes, tends to limit market transparency and facilitates the exercise of market power. In this context, incumbent firms' reluctance to implement or support these institutions can also be interpreted as evidence that they attempt to preserve their ability to exercise market power.

9.5 Remedies for Market Power

Regulatory agencies use *structural* and *behavioral* remedies to address market power and to mitigate the competitive concerns arising from a particular change in market structure, such as a merger. The common characteristic of structural remedies is that they directly address the incentives and/or ability of a market participant to exercise market power. Under the SCP paradigm, a change in market structure affects firms' conduct and ultimately their performance. Structural remedies may include divestitures that change the relative market shares of the existing participants. They may also involve a change in participants' access to other assets, such as through the sale or sharing of intellectual property among participants, or some other change in how the market operates. For example, FERC emphasized the need for a change in the rules governing wholesale electric markets through the formation of RTOs.

A structural remedy is distinguished from a behavioral remedy, which generally restricts specific activities and requires that a market participant be actively monitored to ensure against prohibited behavior. A frequent example of a behavioral remedy is the appointment of a "market monitor" to ensure that firms do not engage in specific activities, such as the creation of artificial transmission congestion, in order to increase prices. COS regulation is another example of a behavioral remedy used by FERC when a company is denied a market-based rate application. These remedies do not, however, change the participant's underlying incentives to engage in such behavior.

Antitrust enforcement agencies have concluded that behavioral rules alone are not an effective constraint against the exercise of market power in energy markets. Remedies that change ownership of assets may be more effective and less costly to enforce. The FTC and the courts have also suggested divestiture as a "natural remedy" to mitigate market power from structural market changes. Structural remedies are often superior because they directly remove the incentive to "misbehave." Monitoring and enforcing regulations may be particularly difficult in such intricate markets where the conditions that allow firms to exercise market power can shift over the course of each day, as is the case in energy markets. If there are no structural impediments preventing companies from acting on their incentives, it should not be surprising that at least some will get "creative" and act on those incentives through whatever means are at their disposal. Behavioral remedies also create indirect costs from firms attempting to evade the spirit of the remedy while adhering to the letter. Moreover, overzealous monitoring may restrain firms from adjusting to changing market conditions through procompetitive activities, because of their fear of penalties.

Withholding of Generation Resources

In reaction to various electricity market crises, such as the "meltdown" of California's wholesale electric market in 2000, much attention has been focused on whether wholesale suppliers violated competitive norms by bidding resources at prices in excess of their marginal costs. In the context of electricity markets, such behavior is called *economic withholding*, but such a label does not make the conduct anticompetitive. Similarly, *physical withholding*—not offering all available capacity when the price is above a supplier's marginal cost—is another variant of exercising market power, but such conduct is likewise not anticompetitive *per se*.

As a matter of economic theory, the lack of marginal cost bidding is not evidence of anticompetitive or manipulative behavior by market participants, nor is it evidence even that competition is failing or that markets are broken. In real-world markets operating under a range of supply and demand conditions, bidding above marginal cost should be viewed as an inevitable and desirable response of independent, profit-maximizing decisions where the ideal conditions of a perfectly competitive market do not prevail.

As explained earlier, this profit-maximizing behavior by individual market participants attracts new competition and leads to efficient outcomes for the market as a whole. In particular, pricing above marginal cost does not necessarily imply: (1) collusion among suppliers, (2) the presence of dominant suppliers, (3) demand that is unresponsive to price, or (4) chronic supply scarcity. A supplier that charges prices above marginal cost does not have unlimited power to set whatever price it wants. The supplier is limited by the competitive response of other suppliers as well as by any response of demand. As the supplier raises its price, it runs an increasing risk that either another supplier will step in to serve demand or that buyers will curtail demand.

The incentive to bid above marginal cost is shown in Figure 9-2. Imperfect competition—which is the reality of most markets—implies that the supplier's residual demand curve is not entirely horizontal. By raising its supply curve above marginal cost, the supplier achieves a higher price on all of its quantity. To maximize profits, the seller continues to increase its supply curve above its marginal cost curve until an equilibrium point is reached. At the equilibrium point, a slight increase in price leads to a marginal gain (a higher price on the quantity sold) that balances with the marginal loss (the profit lost as a result of the reduced quantity). In Figure 9-2, the marginal gain is represented by the light gray rectangle, and the marginal loss is given by the dark gray rectangle. Clearly, this incentive to price above marginal cost is not the result of collusion among suppliers. Rather, whenever the residual demand curve is not horizontal, there would be a marginal gain from raising price above marginal cost. It is up to regulators to determine whether the extent of this practice is "just and reasonable" or the result of anticompetitive practices. Moreover, regulators must determine whether intervention will improve overall customer welfare.

Figure 9-2: Optimal Supply Curve Under Imperfect Competition

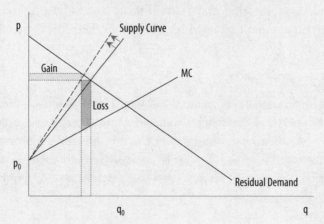

9.6 The Essential Facilities Doctrine

For electric and natural gas markets to function well, generators and natural gas producers must have access to markets. For electric generators, transportation takes place over high-voltage transmission lines. In the past, the majority of those lines were owned by electric utilities. In the natural gas market, FERC addressed many access concerns when it restructured the industry in a series of orders that separated out production, transmission, and distribution and guaranteed producers equal access to transmission pipelines.[15] Both in electric and natural gas markets, transmission facilities can be thought of as "essential facilities" that allow regulatory agencies such as FERC to require access to be shared with competitors.

The essential facility doctrine (EFD) originated in a 1912 U.S. Supreme Court decision, *United States v. Terminal Railroad Association of St. Louis*,[16] a case brought under the 1898 Sherman Antitrust Act—the first piece of federal legislation designed to control market power abuse. The difficulty with the EFD, however, has always been the tension between the legitimate property rights of facilities owners and the desire of regulators to prevent market power abuse. After all, market competition does not generally require that one competitor must give a break to another or that a successful firm be prevented from competing aggressively. Nevertheless, the Court found that there is not an absolute right to refuse to deal with competitors, stating, "It is true that as a general matter a firm can refuse to deal with its competitors. But such a right is not absolute; it exists only if there are legitimate competitive reasons for the refusal."[17]

Over time, case law has developed four criteria, all of which must hold, to determine whether a facility is "essential." These are:

1. The facility must be controlled by a dominant firm.
2. Competing firms must lack a realistic ability to reproduce the facility.
3. Access to the facility is necessary in order to compete in the related market.
4. It must be feasible to provide access to the facility.

For electric and natural gas transmission, these criteria often apply. First, historically these facilities have been controlled by dominant firms, whether individual electric utilities or consortia. Indeed, because retail utilities are awarded exclusive local distribution franchises, they are dominant in their geographic markets. Second, because it can be extremely difficult

---

[15] See Chapter 1 for a discussion of those FERC orders.
[16] 224 U.S. 383 (1912), *supra* note 8.
[17] *Eastman Kodak Co. v. Image Technical Servs., Inc.*, 504 U.S. 451, 483 n.32 (1992).

to site new facilities, reproducing existing facilities is often infeasible. Moreover, thinking back to the origin of regulation in the electric industry, economies of scale made duplication of facilities, such as multiple distribution lines running through neighborhoods, unwarranted. Third, transmission system access is a necessary component of a competitive wholesale generation market. And, fourth, providing equitable access to others is generally straightforward.

9.7 Chapter Summary

Monitoring markets is costly. Thus, it is important to determine how susceptible wholesale electric and natural gas markets are to market power abuses; the degree of susceptibility should guide decisions on how vigilant market oversight should be. Moreover, regulation itself is never perfect, and overly onerous regulation can reduce market efficiency and impose costs on the very consumers it is supposed to protect.

The susceptibility of a market to anticompetitive abuse depends on its structure. For example, exerting market power in agricultural commodities markets is difficult, because there are low entry barriers, thousands of suppliers, and the products can be easily stored and transported. On the other hand, the diamond market has been run for decades by a successful cartel that controls output and maintains high prices.

Electric markets are especially susceptible to horizontal market abuse and warrant close oversight. Because electricity cannot yet be cheaply stored, demand pressures cannot be addressed by taking supplies from inventories in the way one might respond to an increase in the demand for corn. Moreover, market barriers in electric generation are substantial. Decades of "not-in-my backyard" environmental regulations have made it virtually impossible to build new generation and transmission facilities in some states; the permitting processes that generation and transmission developers must endure are not for the faint of heart, or wallet. This has created a situation in which generation developers are often confronted with two chicken-egg dilemmas: an inability to obtain financing for new projects without signed long-term contracts with local utilities and an inability to obtain long-term contracts without guaranteed financing. Additionally, for wholesale markets to be competitive, generators must have competitive access to the electric transmission grid. Without an ability to transmit low-cost electricity to customers, wholesale markets cannot be competitive. Such transmission market access continues to be a concern.

Electricity markets are also susceptible to vertical market power abuse to the extent that there is market manipulation of upstream fuel markets. If electric generators cannot obtain competitively priced fuel, such as natural gas and coal, then wholesale electric markets will be overpriced, regardless of their competitiveness. Not surprisingly, the likelihood of such upstream market power abuse is disputed. Some contend that vertical market abuse is possible, such as by manipulating access to upstream pipeline and other transportation facilities. Others contend that such manipulation is not possible. An example shows how these considerations may interact in determining whether an electric utility has market power.

Our own view can be expressed as the old Russian saying, *Doveryay, no proveryay*, which means "Trust, but verify." Regulators should remain vigilant, but avoid allowing regulation to become so onerous that it stifles competition. Well-functioning markets do not mean that prices will never spike or increase. Competitive markets must be allowed to respond to changing market conditions. In the case of electric generation and transmission, those responses require consumers to experience price changes. Competitiveness requires a reduction in regulatory barriers that prevent the development of new infrastructure. And, it requires that regulators provide a set of rules that provides certainty to investors.

PART II:
EXTENSIONS AND APPLICATIONS

If you have survived reading through Part I, you should have a strong regulatory and economic foundation upon which to base further investigation of the electric and natural gas industries. In Part II, we address a number of topics that have been the focus of more recent regulatory and policy efforts and which we expect to remain prominent for many years.

We begin in Chapter 10 by introducing readers to the treatment of uncertainty. Uncertainty about energy markets has taken on new importance as price volatility in electric and natural gas markets has increased, the electric industry continues to be restructured, and environmental policy considerations, such as global climate change, have become more prominent. We will describe an economic framework that, by addressing these market and nonmarket uncertainties directly, can help lead to better decisions. Next, in Chapter 11, we will review some basic tenets of environmental economics and examine several key environmental regulatory policies that are affecting strategic decisions in the energy industry. In Chapter 12, we switch from environmental issues to those of electric reliability. As electric systems have come under increasing stress, which is the combined result of an aging and inadequate infrastructure and steady increases in electric demand, the provision of "reliable" electric service has taken on greater importance. However, developing a workable definition of a "reliable" electric system is difficult, to say nothing of deciding how much reliability is enough.

In Chapter 13, we provide an overview of key international market and regulatory reforms in energy industries. Finally, Chapter 14 presents what our—no doubt clouded—crystal ball reveals regarding future regulatory issues and explores how continuing conflicts between politics and economics will likely affect the future structure of the electric and natural gas industries.

CHAPTER 10
DEALING WITH UNCERTAINTY

10.1 Introduction

The electric and natural gas industries have changed markedly since their beginnings. As energy markets have evolved and become global in scope, market complexity has increased. Market uncertainty has been exacerbated by regulatory and environmental uncertainty. Restructuring of the electric industry, for example, has proven more complex than initially imagined. In the early days of restructuring, regulators and politicians focused on implementing retail competition and divesting utilities' generating assets; they rather ignored the more complex issues surrounding transmission and distribution. As those issues have been tackled more recently, policies have been changed and rules have been revised, and this has increased uncertainty. For investors, such uncertainty can be an anathema because of the long lead times for new generating and transmission investments. Uncertainty has also increased in the natural gas industry as its traditional links to the oil market have loosened, and natural gas has become a key feedstock for electric generation.

For regulated natural gas and electric companies and their regulators, dealing effectively with uncertainty is crucial. How much insurance should the local natural gas company purchase, if any, to avoid price spikes, since insurance is never free? What is a prudent insurance decision? How should the local electric distribution utility balance its *obligation to serve* against its *obligation to build* new distribution facilities to meet uncertain future load growth in different parts of its service territory? What should the utility build and when should it build it? How should an integrated electric utility factor the potential for new environmental laws into its decisions to build new generating plants and refurbish existing ones?

10.2 Key Issues

The only certainty about the future is its uncertainty. We can imagine what it will be like, we may even be able to assign probabilities to some future events, but we do not know what will happen. Moreover, while we can estimate the riskiness of different policies or investments, the public's evaluation of those same risks may be markedly different.[1] And, even if everyone agrees on the underlying risks and uncertainty, they may react very differently to it, much as some investors prefer high-risk investments, while others are comfortable only with risk-free government bonds.

In addressing risk and uncertainty in the electric and natural gas industries, we need to address several issues. First, how can we make economic decisions in the face of market and nonmarket uncertainties? For example, how does the owner of an electric generating plant decide whether buying new pollution control equipment for a coal-fired power plant is preferable to shutting the plant down? How does a utility regulator determine whether it is prudent for a utility to enter into a long-term power supply contract with the owner of that coal-fired power plant? How does the regulator determine whether the local natural gas distribution company's price hedging efforts, in response to increasing market volatility, are reasonable? Second, how do we measure uncertainty, especially uncertainty about nonmarket issues like global climate change? Third, how do we determine the value of new information that might help reduce uncertainty?

From a regulatory standpoint, uncertainty also has critical impacts. As we discussed in Chapter 1, restructuring of the electric industry was accompanied by numerous political and policy compromises, such as extended rate caps for small customers. Price volatility in United States electric and fossil fuels markets increased, especially after 2002. By late 2005, a confluence of events, notably the damage to the natural gas collection and gathering infrastructure along the U.S. Gulf Coast caused by Hurricanes Katrina and Rita, led to a subsequent spike in natural gas prices and much higher electric prices. This created a regulatory and political backlash, with many calling for reregulation of the electric industry. Not coincidentally, a number of studies appeared analyzing the benefits (or lack thereof) of electric industry restructuring.[2]

---

[1] Most people use the terms "risk" and "uncertainty" interchangeably. Technically, however, they are not the same thing. Risk deals with known probabilities, such as flipping a fair coin. Uncertainty refers to events whose probabilities are not yet known. For a more detailed discussion, the classic reference is Frank H. Knight, *Risk, Uncertainty, and Profit* (Boston: Houghton-Mifflin, 1933).

[2] *See, e.g.*, Paul Joskow, "Markets for Power in the United States: An Interim Assessment," *The Energy Journal* 27 (2006): 1–36. *See also*, Howard Axelrod, David DeRamus, and Collin Cain, "The Fallacy of High Prices," *Public Utilities Fortnightly* 144 (November 2006): 55–60. For an "indictment" of electric industry restructuring, see, e.g., John Kwoka, "Restructuring the U.S. Electric Power Sector: A Review of Recent Studies," study prepared for the American Public Power Association, Nov. 2006, http://www.appanet.org.

As we write this in mid-2007, how the future of electric industry restructuring will resolve itself is uncertain. In part, this uncertainty is the result of conflicting policy objectives and a misunderstanding of basic economics. Market competition is not a guarantee of low electricity prices. Rather, competition is a means for efficiently allocating scarce resources, sending appropriate price signals to guide investment and consumption decisions, and providing incentives for various market participants to act in ways that maximize social welfare. On the other hand, the complexities of electric industry restructuring were underestimated. Moreover, simply deeming a market "competitive" does nothing to address underlying regulatory and planning issues that have made new resource and infrastructure development more difficult.

If regulators and politicians move the electric industry back towards a more regulated path, especially regarding acquiring supplies for smaller customers, the methodologies local utilities use to assemble resource portfolios will no doubt be questioned. In the 1980s and 1990s, for example, *integrated resource planning*, or IRP, was the rage. That approach required utilities to develop long-term resource plans—for as long as 20 to 30 years in some cases. These plans evaluated all sources of supply (including energy conservation) on what was euphemistically called a "level playing field," and were, ironically, based on *cost-effectiveness* rather than *least-cost*.[3] However, because the planning methodologies tended either to address future uncertainty only rudimentarily or to ignore uncertainty entirely, these central planning exercises tended to have little practical value, except as ways for some advocates to flog their particular resource choices with little regard for the underlying economics. Moreover, IRP methodologies were expanded to encompass not only meeting customers' demand for electricity, but also to address needs for expanding transmission and local distribution infrastructure under the rubric of *distributed utility* (DU) planning.[4] It is perhaps ironic that, years later, there is once again a call to use these same methodologies, despite their underlying economic flaws.

---

[3] The difference between *cost-effective* and *least-cost* can be discerned from our discussion in Chapter 2. Essentially, cost-effectiveness is based in a comparison of average costs. For example, suppose the price of electricity in the market is $100 per MWh. We would conclude that an alternative resource is cost-effective as long as its average cost is less than or equal to $100 per MWh. This is how most utility or government-sponsored *demand-side management* programs have always been evaluated. A least-cost approach, however, looks at the marginal cost of resource alternatives, with the goal of selecting a portfolio of resources that truly minimizes overall costs. Under this framework, we would select alternative resources in the order of their marginal costs, up to $100 per MWh, since that value is the marginal cost of additional supply. For a discussion, see, e.g., Charles Feinstein and Jonathan Lesser, "Defining Distributed Utility Planning," in "Distributed Resources: Toward a New Paradigm of the Electricity Business," special issue, *The Energy Journal* (1997): 41–62.

[4] For a discussion, see Feinstein and Lesser, *id.*

10.3 Making Investment Decisions Under Uncertainty[5]

Having just criticized some resource planning methodologies for their failure to address uncertainty appropriately, in this section we review several methodologies that can be used. To motivate the discussion, we begin by illustrating the potential failures of several commonly used approaches, notably *sensitivity analysis* and *scenario analysis*. Next, we introduce the notion of real options, which are similar to financial options except they are applied to physical assets. Finally, we discuss the value of new information, which, in an increasingly uncertain world, can take on much greater importance.

Many readers are already familiar with how uncertainty affects investment decisions. If you are saving for retirement, you must decide how to allocate those savings. Should you put more money into high-yield, but high-risk stocks, or stick to lower-risk, lower-return investments? Similarly, if you have ever bought or sold stock options or dabbled in commodities futures, you probably understand the effects of uncertainty on investment value, perhaps painfully so.

In dealing with electric and natural gas companies, similar risk-versus-returns issues arise. The question is how best to deal with those uncertainties. What is the best way of making decisions when confronted with uncertainty? Traditionally, most utilities ignored the issue entirely. In the 1950s and 1960s, growth was steady, and adding new infrastructure was uncontroversial. Utilities could merely draw a straight line to forecast future growth. Things began to change, of course, as the oil price shocks of the 1970s and new environmental regulations began affecting growth in demand.

In response, most companies dealt with uncertainty using sensitivity analysis and scenario analysis. Sensitivity analysis begins with a "base case" model and then adjusts inputs individually to determine the impact on the "base case" decision, such as a higher wholesale electric price or higher interest rates. Scenario analysis starts with the same base case, but constructs specific "scenarios" that can include multiple changes. So, an analyst might construct an "environmental" scenario that included more stringent environmental laws and higher fuel prices.

The problem with both approaches is that they do not provide any information on the likelihood of different events or scenarios, yet those likelihoods will have the most impact on decisions. As a result, both approaches ignore information and can fail to identify "least-

---

[5] For a comprehensive treatment of this subject, see Avinash Dixit and Robert Pindyck, *Investment Under Uncertainty* (Princeton: Princeton University Press, 1994). While the mathematics used is frequently complex, Chapter 2 of that text has an excellent introduction to the subject using a number of simple examples.

cost" choices. Consider, for example, a local electric utility that must decide whether to build new infrastructure to meet peak load growth driven by planned industrial growth in the area. The timing of that growth is not clear, however, and depends on the strength of the economy. We can define three load growth levels, Low, Medium, and High, and three investment strategies for each, I_A, I_B, and I_C. Table 10-1 shows the costs for each strategy and load growth level.

Table 10-1: Distribution Planning Costs

Strategy	Low	Medium	High
I_A	$12	$20	$52
I_B	$14	$24	$36
I_C	$20	$28	$32

If we only consider "Medium" load growth, strategy I_A would be chosen because it has the lowest cost. Moreover, strategy I_A is the lowest cost if load growth is "Low," and strategy I_C has the lowest cost if load growth is "High." Strategy I_B is never selected. As a result, we might select Strategy I_A because it is "robust," in the sense that it is the least-cost choice for two of the three strategies.

What happens, however, if we start assigning probabilities to each of the load growth levels? For example, suppose we have determined there is a 30% probability that load growth will be Low, a 40% probability that it will be Medium, and a 30% probability load growth will be High. The results are shown in Table 10-2.

Table 10-2: Expected Costs of Alternative Investment Strategies

Probability:	30%	40%	30%	
Strategy	Low	Medium	High	Exp. Cost
I_A	$12	$20	$52	$27.20
I_B	$14	$24	$36	**$24.60**
I_C	$20	$28	$32	$26.80

As the table shows, Strategy I_B, which is never the preferred choice for any of the three strategies, is actually the least-cost choice, at $24.60. Moreover, Strategy I_A, the most "robust" strategy because it has the lowest cost under both the Low and Medium load growth scenarios, has the highest expected cost, $27.20. Thus, this simple (and, admittedly, contrived) example shows that uncertainty matters and that evaluating the probability of different events can be crucial. In general, sensitivity and scenario analyses are unreliable because they fail to examine the <u>likelihood</u> of different events. In essence, those two planning methods simply discard valuable information.

Real Options

The previous example showed how uncertainty matters when making decisions. Next, we consider typical discounted cash flow analysis and the impacts of uncertainty and flexibility on investment choices. Suppose an investor is considering whether to build a new electric generating plant whose output will be sold in the wholesale market. The cost of the plant is $500 million. If built, the plant will produce one million megawatt-hours (MWh) of electricity each year forever. (We ignore the potential for the plant to fail, and we assume, for simplicity's sake, that there are no fuel costs to worry about.) Suppose it is equally likely that the price of electricity will be either $40 per MWh or $80 per MWh and will never change. The expected price will equal the probability-weighted average of the two prices, (0.5) × $40 per MWh + (0.5) × $80 per MWh, or $60 per MWh.

We can calculate the *net present value* (NPV) of building the plant under both price scenarios, as well as at the expected price. The NPV can be written as

$$NPV = -C + \sum_{t=0}^{\infty} \frac{P \times Q}{(1+r)^t} \qquad (10\text{-}1)$$

where C is the cost of the plant, P is the price of electricity, Q is the quantity of electricity produced, and r is the discount rate. So, at the expected price of $60 per MWh, the NPV of building today (in millions of dollars) is just

$$NPV = -C + \sum_{t=0}^{\infty} \frac{P \times Q}{(1+r)^t} = -\$500 + \sum_{t=0}^{\infty} \frac{\$60}{(1.1)^t} = \$100$$

It appears that, since the NPV is positive, the investor should go ahead and build the plant. That conclusion, however, may be wrong. If the price turns out to be $40 per MWh, then the NPV will equal

$$NPV = -\$500 + \sum_{t=0}^{\infty} \frac{\$40}{(1.1)^t} = -\$60$$

If the investor knew the price would be only $40 per MWh, he would not invest in the plant. So, suppose the investor does not need to commit to building the plant in the current year and can wait until the next. At that time, the price uncertainty will be resolved, and the investor can make a build/no-build decision knowing the price with certainty and knowing that he will build <u>only</u> if the price is $80 per MWh. We can calculate the expected NPV of waiting one year as

$$NPV_W = 0 + 0.5 \times \left\{ -\frac{C}{1.1} + \sum_{t=1}^{\infty} \frac{P \times Q}{(1+i)^t} \right\} = 0.5 \times \left\{ -\frac{\$500}{1.1} + \sum_{t=1}^{\infty} \frac{\$80}{(1.1)^t} \right\} = \$273 \qquad (10\text{-}2)$$

where NPV_W refers to the NPV of waiting. The first term of equation (10-2) is just $0 since, if the price turns out to be $40, there will be no investment. Thus, by waiting one year, the investor's gain in expected value equals $173 million ($273 million minus $100 million).

This example resembles a *call option* on a common stock. A call option gives an investor the right, but not the obligation, to make an investment, in this case at the end of one year. An option can never have negative value.[6] But it is not always valuable. Specifically, it does not always pay to wait. In fact, using this example, we can determine when it makes sense to wait and when it makes sense to invest immediately. Intuitively, the value of waiting is the additional information we gain, in this case knowing the future market price with certainty. The cost of waiting is forgone revenues if the future turns out well.

Suppose the future price follows a simple pattern shown in Figure 10-1.[7]

Figure 10-1: The Future Price of Electricity

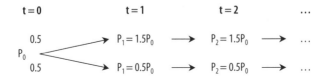

In other words, next year the price will either rise with 50% probability to 1.5 times the current price or it will fall with equal probability to 0.5 times the current price. In both cases, the price will remain at that level forever. By examining the current price, we can establish a rule for when to invest. We want to invest today if the opportunity cost of waiting is greater than the option value of waiting. First, we can calculate the minimum price next year for the investment to have a positive NPV if we wait. So, we set equation (10-2) to zero, and solve for P_1. Thus,

---

[6] Strictly speaking, the minimum value of any option is the price that is paid for it. So, if you pay $10 for a call option on a stock that provides you with the right to buy the stock at $50 per share, then you cannot lose more than the $10.

[7] This example is adapted from Dixit and Pindyck, *supra* note 5.

$$NPV_W = -\frac{500}{1.1} + \sum_{t=1}^{\infty} \frac{P_1}{(1.1)^t} = 0 \tag{10-3}$$

Simplifying equation (10-3), we have

$$-\frac{500}{1.1} + 10P_1 = 0 \Rightarrow P_1 = \$45$$

If P_1 is $45 in the high case, that means the initial price, P_0, equals $P_1 \div 1.5$, or $30. So, if $P_0 < \$30$, we will never wait to invest in the plant, because there is no chance the investment will be profitable.

Next, we can determine when the expected NPV of investing today is greater than the expected NPV_W of waiting. To do that, we can set equations (10-1) and (10-2) equal to one another, and solve for P_0. Thus, we have

$$-500 + \sum_{t=0}^{\infty} \frac{P_0}{1.1^t} = 0.5 \times \left\{ \frac{-500}{1.1} + \sum_{t=1}^{\infty} \frac{1.5 P_0}{1.1^t} \right\} \tag{10-4}$$

Equation (10-4) simplifies to

$$-500 + 11 P_0 = \frac{250}{1.1} + 7.5 P_0 \tag{10-5}$$

or $P_0 = \$78$. Thus, if today's price is $78 per MWh or higher, the opportunity cost of waiting will be greater than the value of the option to wait.[8] Figure 10-2 graphs the value of waiting and not waiting, respectively, as a function of the initial price, P_0. As shown, below $30 per MWh, there would be no investment at all, so neither waiting nor proceeding immediately has value. Between $30 and $45, the expected NPV of proceeding immediately is actually less than zero, which means that the minimum price at which investment today has a positive NPV is $45 per MWh. However, between $30 and $78, the NPV of waiting is greater than the NPV of investing today. Specifically, the option value of waiting is positive, and equal to max $[0, NPV_W - NPV]$.

---

[8] Dixit and Pindyck, *supra* note 5, demonstrate how this approach can be recast in the language of options and asset portfolios to arrive at the same results.

Chapter 10: Dealing With Uncertainty

Figure 10-2: Value of Option to Invest

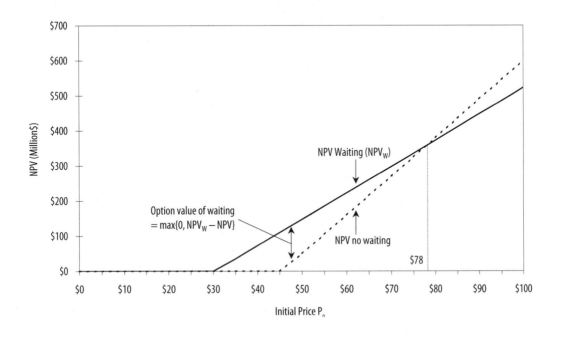

Intuitively, we tend to view uncertainty as something "bad." It turns out, however, that from the standpoint of flexibility and option value, greater uncertainty leads to higher real option values. This is why traders tend to lament those times when the stock market is calm.

Next, suppose the price can move up or down as shown in Figure 10-3.

Figure 10-3: Increased Price Uncertainty

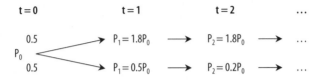

Now, the price will either be 80% higher than the original price or 80% lower. Under these conditions, it turns out that the initial price would have to increase to over $136 per MWh for it to make sense to invest immediately.[9] Moreover, the initial price would have to be less

---

[9] To see this, solve equation (10-4) once again, substituting $1.8P_0$ in the right-hand side instead of $1.5P_0$.

than or equal to $25 per MWh ($45 ÷ 1.8) for the investor to walk away from the investment immediately. What this means is that the value of the option to wait increases, and the value of investing immediately decreases, as shown in Figure 10-3.

Decision Trees and the Value of Information[10]

In George Orwell's bleak novel of the future, *1984,* one of the sayings in the government's language "Newspeak" was "Ignorance is Strength." Yet, intuitively, we know that more information is usually preferred to less. For example, as we will discuss in Chapter 11, information, or the lack of it, can be a crucial component affecting environmental policies and regulation. For example, knowing more about the precise economic impacts of global warming can help policymakers develop more appropriate policy instruments. It may also reduce the temptation for well-intentioned, but ill-considered, "we must do something" regulatory responses, such as a state legislature ordering the immediate closure of all coal-fired power plants to reduce greenhouse gas emissions without first considering the costs of blackouts.

Decision trees are useful tools for making good decisions and determining the value of new information. As an aside, good decisions are often equated with good outcomes. Alas, in the presence of uncertainty, good decisions can still have bad outcomes, a situation that can have important regulatory impacts.[11] Insuring yourself against accidental death may be a very good financial decision, but you will probably not consider your dying a good outcome. Rather than focusing on such a macabre subject, we illustrate the concepts with a gentler example.

Suppose you are deciding whether to walk to work tomorrow or ride the bus. You prefer walking in good weather, but you do not relish walking or, unlike Gene Kelly, singing in the rain. Suppose the local weather forecaster, with typical assertiveness, states there is a 50:50 chance of rain tomorrow. Now, since the cherry blossoms are in bloom, if you walk tomorrow and it does not rain, you will greatly enjoy yourself. So, on a scale of 1 to 10 points, we can assign that outcome as a "10." On the other hand, if you walk and it rains, your new suit will be ruined. We can assign that outcome a "0." Finally, if you take the bus, you will arrive to work safe, dry, and bored. So, let's assign that outcome a value of "6."

---

[10] For an introduction to decision trees and the broader field of "decision analysis," see Robert T. Clemen, *Making Hard Decisions: An Introduction to Decision Analysis*, 2nd ed. (New York: Duxbury Press, 1996).

[11] Recall from Chapter 5 our discussion on prudence and used and usefulness that regulatory prudence reviews are supposed to be based solely on what was known at the time. Whereas prudence is not an *ex post* concept, used and usefulness is. Thus, it is possible for a regulated firm to make a prudent decision that, because of a bad outcome, is not deemed used and useful.

Chapter 10: Dealing With Uncertainty

We can summarize this information together in Table 10-3 in a simple matrix.

Table 10-3: Decision Matrix

		Decision	
		Walk	Ride Bus
State of the World	Rain	0	6
	No Rain	10	6

To determine what you should do, we can represent your choices and the uncertainties you face with a decision tree, as shown in Figure 10-4. In the figure, we represent decision "nodes" with a square, uncertainties with a circle, and outcomes with a triangle. There are two decision "branches" and two uncertainty branches off each decision branch. We determine the highest value outcome by working backwards from the right-most point of the tree. So, taking the upper "walk" branch first, we determine the expected value of the outcome, E(Walk). Thus,

$$E(Walk) = (0.5) \times 10 + (0.5) \times 0 = 5.0$$

The expected value of the bottom branch, E(Bus), is just

$$E(Bus) = (0.5) \times 6 + (0.5) \times 6 = 6.0$$

Thus, unless you like to gamble on the weather, you should take the boring bus, since it has a higher expected value than walking.

Figure 10-4: A Decision Tree and Outcomes

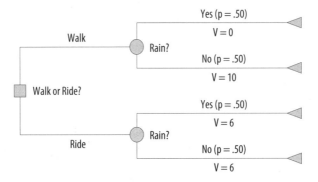

Now suppose you have another option. Tonight's weather forecast reported that there is a cold front 100 miles to the west. There is a 90% probability of rain if the cold front moves through overnight and a 10% probability of rain if the cold front stalls. If you set your alarm 15 minutes earlier than usual and listen to the weather report in the morning, you will know which of these events has taken place. Of course, waking up earlier has a cost, which we assume reduces the value of all outcomes by one point. We can illustrate this new situation with the expanded decision tree in Figure 10-5.

Figure 10-5: Extended Decision Tree with Additional Information

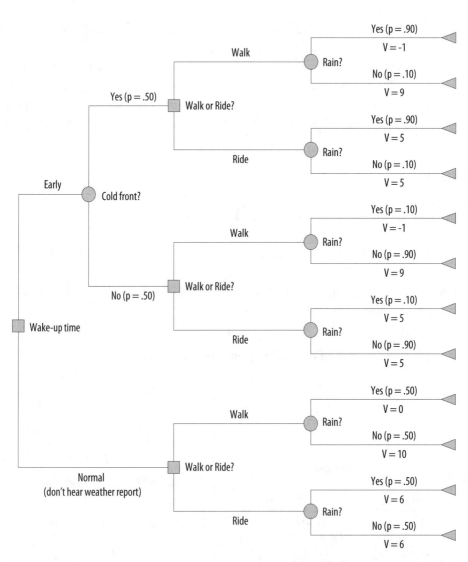

The left-most branch of the decision tree is whether or not to wake up early. If you do not wake up early, the bottom branch of that first decision node duplicates the decision tree of Figure 10-4. Without listening to the weather report, the probability of rain (as far as you are concerned) is still .5.[12] So, if you choose not to wake up early, your best decision will still be to ride the bus, since that decision has an expected value of 6.0 points. If you decide to wake up early and listen to the weather report, you will have additional information about the cold front. So, we can again work backwards from the right-most outcomes along the upper branch and determine the expected values. For example, if the cold front has moved through overnight and you still decide to walk, your expected value will be

$$E(\text{Front} \mid \text{Walk}) = (0.1) \times (9) + (0.9) \times (-1) = 0$$

If the front has passed through and you ride the bus, your expected value will be

$$E(\text{Front} \mid \text{Ride}) = (0.1) \times 5 + (0.9) \times 5 = 5$$

Clearly, if you wake up early and hear that the front has passed, you will want to ride the bus. If, however, the front has stalled, your expected value if you walk will be

$$E(\text{No Front} \mid \text{Walk}) = (0.9) \times (9) + (0.1) \times (-1) = 8$$

If the front has stalled and you ride the bus, your expected value will be

$$E(\text{No Front} \mid \text{Ride}) = (0.9) \times 5 + (0.1) \times 5 = 5$$

So, if the front has stalled, you will definitely want to walk and enjoy the cherry blossoms.

Tonight, you know what decisions you will make in the morning for each of the two possible weather reports. However, you do not have to make your actual decision tonight. Instead, you just have to decide whether to wake up early and listen to the weather report. If you decide not to listen, your expected value will equal 6, because you will want to ride the bus as before. If you do decide to wake up early, your expected value is

$$E(\text{Wake Up Early}) = (0.5) \times E(\text{Front} \mid \text{Ride}) + (0.5) \times E(\text{No Front} \mid \text{Walk})$$
$$= (0.5) \times 5 + (0.5) \times 8 = 6.5$$

---

[12] This may seem counterintuitive, but you can perform a simple experiment to convince yourself. Toss a coin in the air and catch it in your hand. (Do not look at the coin.) While the coin was in the air, the probability of heads was .5. Now that you have caught the coin, it is either heads or tails, but you still do not know which. Thus, you have no more relevant information until you look at the coin. Until you look at the coin, the probability to *you* is still .5.

Thus, your best option is to decide to wake up early and decide whether or not to walk to work based on the weather report. The value you gain will be greater than the cost (in terms of lost sleep). The reason is that the additional information allows you to make a higher-value decision. If you listen to the weather report and it says rain is likely, you will take the bus and be slightly worse off than if you had slept later (because you woke up earlier). However, if you hear the report say rain is unlikely, you will be much better off than if you had slept later. In essence, by waking up early, you are buying an option. The insurance "premium" is forgone sleep. The benefit is the opportunity to enjoy a walk in the sunshine.

The Role of Emotions

Traditional economics assumes rational decision-makers.[13] Yet, all of us have probably made decisions based on emotions, rather than dispassionate considerations of probability and expected values. In many cases, this is reasonable. After all, confronted with the example above, we doubt that many individuals will systematically develop a decision tree to determine how they should travel to work on a given day. In some cases, the information necessary to make a "rational" decision is not available. In other cases, the parameters involved in making a decision (e.g., Coke or Pepsi?) are either purely subjective or poorly defined (e.g., "Tastes great, less filling"). Finally, some decisions are emotional or political (e.g., decisions to marry or have children; decisions on how to vote on a complex issue, etc.).[14] However, when it comes to major investment decisions and regulatory evaluation of those decisions, ideally the role of emotions and politics will be limited. Not only does relying on an emotional or political evaluation standard violate regulatory tenets, it tends to increase the perception of regulatory uncertainty, which leads to real increases in costs.

---

[13] A more recent branch of economics has developed that focuses on seemingly "irrational" decisions, and why we make such decisions. *See, e.g.,* Richard H. Thaler, *Quasi-Rational Economics*, (New York: Russell Sage Foundation Publications, 1994).

[14] However, Nobel Prize-winning economist Gary Becker developed sophisticated theories that helped understand such decisions in the context of standard economic models. *See, A Treatise on the Family,* (Cambridge, MA: Harvard University Press, 2005).

Applying Decision Analysis Techniques to the Electric Industry

How might this type of analysis apply to a company confronting market uncertainties (including electric price volatility) and nonmarket uncertainties, such as whether regulators will change air pollution regulations? Suppose the owners of a coal-fired power plant are concerned about the potential for a new environmental regulation that will require them to reduce carbon emissions by 50% starting five years from now. If the regulation is implemented, there will be three ways to reduce the plant's emissions: (1) shut down the plant, (2) purchase emissions allowances at an unknown future price,[15] or (3) invest in a new, experimental technology that is designed to capture 80% of the carbon emissions and inject it (called "sequestration") deep underground. If the owners choose option 3, they will be able to sell their surplus carbon allowances. Of course, there is also a chance that the regulation will never take effect.

Initially, it would seem that the obvious solution is to wait and see whether the regulation is implemented. However, if the new technology works as planned, the demand for it will increase rapidly, as will its cost. So, if the owners wait too long, they risk having to pay much more for the technology, having to buy very expensive emissions allowances, or being forced to shut down the plant. Figure 10-6 presents the decision tree.

The first thing to notice about Figure 10-6 is that, as we start adding alternatives and uncertainties, the number of branches multiplies rapidly. (If the new regulations do not come into force, then we assume the plant will continue to operate as usual.) Let's examine the upper portion of the decision tree first. The upper branch traces the outcomes of installing the new carbon reduction technology today. The advantage of doing so is that the cost of the technology is known today, although whether the technology will work remains uncertain.

The first uncertainty we encounter moving towards the right is whether the technology works. If it does, uncertainties remain as to whether the new carbon regulations will be put into place, what the price of the excess emissions allowances sold by the plant will be, and what the price of electricity produced by the plant will be. Next, we can trace the "technology does not work" branch. In that case, and if the new emissions regulations are put into place, the plant's owners will have to decide whether or not to shut down the plant. If not, then the total value of the plant will depend on the future price of electricity and the price of carbon allowances that the plant's owners will have to purchase.

---

[15] Today, emissions allowances are bought and sold in the United States to regulate emissions of sulfur dioxide and oxides of nitrogen as part of the Clean Air Act. We discuss that Act, and other environmental regulations affecting the electric and natural gas industries, in the next chapter.

Fundamentals of Energy Regulation

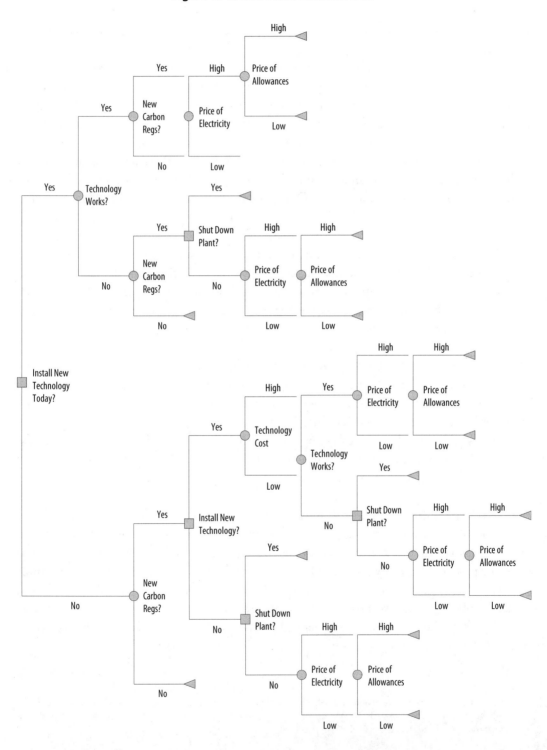

Figure 10-6: Coal Plant Decision Tree

Next, we can consider the lower half of the tree. Along this path, before they make any decisions, the plant owners decide to pursue a wait-and-see strategy to resolve the uncertainty over whether the new regulations will be put into place. This strategy has its own risks, of course, if the regulations are put into place. Moving rightward from the "yes" branch of "New Carbon Regs," the owners must once again decide whether or not to install the technology. However, there is now a new uncertainty about the cost of the technology, in addition to the uncertainty as to whether the technology works. If it does not work, the owners will face the same decision they would have faced if they had installed the technology immediately and it had not worked: whether or not to shut down the plant. If the technology does work, there is still a question as to its value, which will depend on the future price of electricity and the price of carbon allowances.

In reality, most decision trees will be even more complex. In Figure 10-6, we have made several simplifying assumptions, notably that there are only two time periods: "today" and "the future." Additionally, uncertainties can affect, or influence, one another. The future price of electricity, for example, is likely to be affected if the new regulation is put into effect. The price of carbon allowances will be affected by whether or not the new technology works and by its eventual cost. If the technology works and is cheap, then the price of carbon allowances is likely to be low. If the technology does not work—or works, but is expensive—the price of carbon allowances is likely to be high. Those outcomes will affect the plant owners' decision to continue running the plant or not.

Regulatory Impacts

This type of analysis can also be crucial from a regulatory standpoint. For a vertically integrated and still regulated utility, regulators will want to ensure that management makes prudent investment decisions that account for the uncertainties and do not place an unnecessary cost burden on captive ratepayers. Utility regulators may also be concerned about unregulated wholesale generators bidding into "provider of last resort" (POLR) auctions to provide electricity to retail customers, or generally in what are called "competitive procurements" for electricity. In a competitive procurement, a local distribution utility issues a request for bids from wholesale generators to provide generation for all of its customers. The wholesale generators are scrutinized by regulators to make sure that in providing generation to retail customers, they meet their contractual obligations. Not only is this important from the standpoint of meeting customers' daily electric needs, it can be a critical issue for maintaining the overall reliability of the electric system.[16]

---

[16] We discuss electric system reliability in Chapter 12.

10.4 Measuring Price Volatility

We have already discussed how electric and natural gas prices have become increasingly *volatile* in recent years. We have also discussed how market prices for electricity and natural gas (ignoring issues such as market power) are determined by the interaction of supply and demand. A hot and humid day, for example, will cause air conditioning loads to increase, raising overall electric demand. So, if tomorrow is expected to be much hotter than today, we would predict the demand for electricity to increase. As demand increases, so will market clearing prices, because more peaking units will have to be switched on.

Most transmission system operators use sophisticated econometric models to forecast these changes in demand and supply, most importantly to ensure that enough electricity is available to avoid blackouts, but in some cases also to evaluate whether market power concerns are likely to emerge. However, no matter how sophisticated the econometric models, forecasters will almost always guess wrong, because no model can account for <u>all</u> of the factors that affect electric demand. As a result, some of the response will be uncertain or, to use the technical term, *stochastic*.

Volatility is one measure of risk. It is similar to standard deviation, but is normalized to a specific time period. Thus, one can think of volatility as standard deviation per unit of time.[17] As an example, consider the daily closing prices for natural gas at Henry Hub, as shown in Figure 10-7. As the chart shows, for the first six months of 2005, the price remained within a range between $6.00 per MMBtu and $8.00 per MMBtu. Then, in August 2005, prices started increasing steadily as the damage to the natural gas gathering pipeline infrastructure from Hurricanes Katrina and Rita caused fears about supply shortages for the upcoming winter. However, prices fell dramatically in December 2005, from a high price of $15.39/MMBtu on December 14, 2005, to just over $10 per MMBtu on December 31. The fall in price was in large part the result of the mild winter that had been experienced up until then. Clearly, Figure 10-7 shows that natural gas prices were highly volatile during 2005.

---

[17] For readers who wish to learn more about basic statistical concepts, an excellent introductory book is David Freedman, Robert Pisani, and Roger Purves, *Statistics* (New York: W.W. Norton, 1998).

Chapter 10: Dealing With Uncertainty

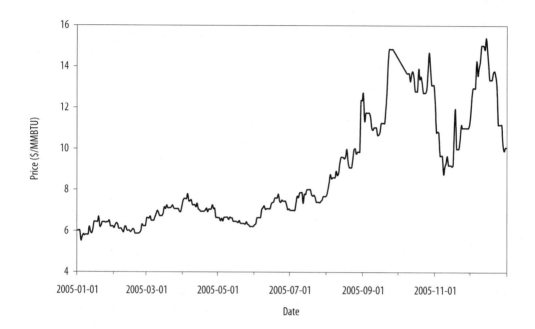

Figure 10-7: Henry Hub Daily Average Closing Natural Gas Prices (2005)

Measuring volatility is critical for determining the value of hedging and the cost of reducing exposure to uncertain market prices. For example, to use the Black-Scholes option pricing model,[18] one must enter the estimated volatility of the underlying security. Volatility can also be a critical component of capital investment decisions, such as determining whether to build a new generating plant. In financial markets, volatility underlies the value of all financial instruments, from a basic hedge that "locks in" a fixed price at a certain time (such as a *call* option), to the most sophisticated trading strategies in what are called *exotics*.[19]

---

[18] The Black-Scholes model is the most famous of all financial options models. For those who would like to delve into the details, see, e.g., Thomas E. Copeland and J. Fred Weston, *Financial Theory and Corporate Policy*, 3d ed. (New York: Addison-Wesley, 1988), Chapter 8.

[19] For a thorough introduction, see John Hull, *Options, Futures, and Other Derivatives*, 6th ed. (New York: Prentice-Hall, 2005). *See also,* Philippe Jorion, *Value at Risk*, 2nd ed. (New York: McGraw-Hill, 2001).

Using the daily data, the easiest way to calculate historic volatility for the entire year is as follows:

1. Calculate the logarithm of day-to-day price changes for the entire year.

2. Calculate the standard deviation of those price changes.

3. Multiply the standard deviation by the square root of the average number of trading days per year, usually defined as 252.[20]

These calculations show that natural gas price volatility for 2005 was about 56%.

One of the potentially annoying characteristics of volatility calculations is that they are, well, volatile.[21] Moreover, in this example, we made some simplifying assumptions about natural gas prices that are not entirely correct. Specifically, we assumed that natural gas prices follow a pattern called a *random walk*.[22] This pattern assumes there are no underlying trends or seasonality factors. Yet, we know that natural gas prices are seasonal. They increase in peak weather periods (hot and cold) and decrease in the spring and fall. Because we might want to calculate different volatilities, such as for each season, we need to plot the volatility for each quarter of 2005. For the first two quarters, the volatility averaged about 40% on an annualized basis. It increased to over 60% in the third quarter, and to over 80% in the fourth quarter of 2005.

Estimating future volatility is trickier. Typically, an analyst will assume either that historic volatility will continue into the future or that volatility can be estimated by assuming that prices follow a specific stochastic pattern. A random walk is one of many such patterns. More often, analysts will develop models that incorporate both known (or *deterministic*) economic fundamentals (e.g., supply and demand conditions, seasonality, etc.,) along with random (or *stochastic*) changes.[23]

---

[20] The number that the standard deviation is multiplied by depends on the frequency of the data. For monthly data, the standard deviation is multiplied by the square root of 12 to estimate an annualized volatility. For weekly data, the multiple is the square root of 52.

[21] In financial options modeling, *vega* measures the sensitivity of option value to change in volatility. Vega equals the absolute change in option value relative to a 1% change in volatility. In addition to vega, options traders will often estimate the *delta*, *gamma*, and *theta* of their option positions. Collectively, these four terms are known as the "Greeks." They measure the sensitivity of an option's price to quantifiable factors.

[22] A random walk is technically called *Brownian motion*.

[23] For a discussion, see Sheldon M. Ross, *Introduction to Probability Models*, 6th ed. (New York: Academic Press, 1997). For a more advanced discussion, see, Dragana Pilipović, *Energy Risk: Valuing and Managing Energy Derivatives* (New York: McGraw-Hill, 1997).

10.5 Nonmarket Uncertainties

In making decisions about hedging, as well as capital investment decisions, we often confront multiple uncertainties that are linked, or *correlated*. For example, volatility of natural gas prices is correlated with volatility in electric market prices, because natural gas-fired generation tends to be the marginal resource in times of peak demand. Moreover, volatile electric prices can affect prices in natural gas markets as traders seek to lock in future natural gas supplies for generating units or, in the case of natural gas local distribution companies, for their customers. Thus, it is important to understand the underlying economic structure of key uncertainties.[24]

However, not all uncertainties are market-based. We cannot estimate the "volatility" of regulatory and political structures.[25] Nor can we always use standard options pricing models like Black-Scholes to estimate the value of a generating plant or a natural gas pipeline accurately. There can be too many uncertainties whose structure is indeterminate. Nonmarket issues, therefore, can complicate attempts to address uncertainty. So what can be done? And what approaches should be avoided?

First, ignoring nonmarket uncertainties or addressing them crudely, such as with sensitivity or scenario analyses, should probably be avoided, because crude approaches to address nonmarket uncertainties will be as potentially misleading as using those approaches to deal with market uncertainties. Fortunately, there are several structured approaches that can be used.

To do so, we return to the difference between *risk* and *uncertainty*. As we discussed, risk refers to events with known probabilities. For example, engineers routinely measure failure rates for equipment and develop specific probability distributions that describe when equipment failure will occur. So, if we wish to evaluate the costs and benefits of upgrading a nuclear power plant, we may be able to use reasonable probability distributions of key component failures that affect future availability and cost.[26]

---

[24] A natural question that also arises is how to identify the uncertainties that "matter" and those that do not. It is surprising how often what "common sense" tells us should and should not be important is not always correct. There are several structured approaches to assessing the importance of different uncertainties, such as "tornado diagrams," which can be used in conjunction with decision tree and Monte Carlo models. For more information, see Clemen, *supra* note 10.

[25] For example, while it may be possible to handicap the next election, how does one predict changes in political majorities over the long term? Moreover, how can one predict whether the positions taken by political parties today will remain constant over time, or whether they will evolve in a specific way?

[26] *See, e.g.,* Norman J. McCormack, *Reliability and Risk Analysis: Methods and Nuclear Power Applications* (New York: Academic Press, 1981).

Suppose, however, we wish instead to address the economic value of refurbishing a coal-fired power plant. The benefits of refurbishment likely will depend on the types of environmental regulations that are in place over the expected lifetime of the plant (both with and without refurbishment). However, it is difficult (at least for us) to ascribe specific probability functions to regulatory actions. For example, we could say that the imposition of a specific dollar-value carbon tax is associated with a log-normal probability distribution function. That is as accurate a statement as saying that the likelihood of our encountering 20-foot tall creatures with rotating eyes on Mars can be estimated using the same probability distribution function. We simply do not know, because there is no information we can use to base an estimate on. Moreover, the timing of new environmental regulations may be correlated with their severity. For example, it is more likely that a smaller carbon tax would be imposed sooner than a larger tax would.

In considering these tough-to-model uncertainties and their affects on capital investment decisions, therefore, one approach is to determine *event thresholds*, i.e., the levels at which the uncertainty changes the optimal decision that is made today. This is also why using real options and decision tree approaches can be crucial. By structuring investment decisions to include "off-ramps," we can identify critical values for key parameters that can be monitored.

Table 10-4, for example, shows combinations of carbon tax timing and magnitude that could affect the decision to refurbish.

Table 10-4: Critical Event Matrix—Joint Probability Thresholds

CO_2 Tax ($ per ton)	Years Until Tax Imposed									
	1	2	3	4	5	6	7	8	9	10
3.00	1.000	1.000	1.000	1.000	1.000	1.000	1.000	1.000	1.000	1.000
6.00	1.000	1.000	1.000	1.000	1.000	1.000	1.000	1.000	1.000	1.000
9.00	0.850	1.000	1.000	1.000	1.000	1.000	1.000	1.000	1.000	1.000
12.00	0.720	0.780	0.830	1.000	1.000	1.000	1.000	1.000	1.000	1.000
15.00	0.590	0.650	0.700	0.740	1.000	1.000	1.000	1.000	1.000	1.000
18.00	0.440	0.500	0.550	0.590	0.620	0.644	1.000	1.000	1.000	1.000
21.00	0.270	0.330	0.380	0.420	0.450	0.474	0.489	0.502	0.513	1.000
24.00	0.080	0.140	0.190	0.230	0.260	0.284	0.299	0.310	0.317	1.000
27.00	0.000	0.000	0.050	0.090	0.120	0.144	0.159	0.168	0.175	0.180
30.00	0.000	0.000	0.000	0.010	0.020	0.025	0.029	0.032	0.034	0.035

Table 10-4 presents a hypothetical matrix of (tax level, timing) pairs that affect a decision made today to refurbish. The table shows that the sooner we believe the carbon tax will be imposed, the smaller the magnitude of carbon tax that will affect the refurbishment decision. This matrix can be calculated by developing a cash-flow model that assesses the present value of refurbishment as a function of carbon tax level and timing. Thus, if we knew with certainty that a carbon tax of no more than $12 per ton would be imposed no sooner than five years from now, we would go ahead and refurbish. Next, we can add uncertainty to the decision framework. Essentially, we can determine critical probability thresholds that determine at what point the decision to refurbish "flips" for each combination.[27]

The table shows that, for certain combinations of tax level and timing, the decision to refurbish today is unaffected. (These are the unshaded cells with probability values of 1.000.) On the other hand, the probability values in the shaded cells show the joint probability values where the decision "flips." For example, in Table 10-4 we have highlighted the cell combining a tax of $24 per ton beginning seven years from today. The value shown, 0.299, indicates that if we believe there is just under a 1-in-3 probability that a tax of at least $24 per ton will be imposed no later than seven years from now, then refurbishing the plant should not be undertaken.

Clearly, decision-makers must still use their judgment in these sorts of cases to assess the likelihood of different events. Another potential complication is that decision-makers must decide how much risk is acceptable. Moreover, they may have to weigh the risks of different investment strategies. An example is shown in Figure 10-8. In this figure, we compare the NPVs of two alternative, and mutually exclusive, investments, A and B. As shown, investment A has a lower expected NPV than investment B, but it also has a less risky distribution of returns. Moreover, A's *value-at-risk* ("VaR"), which equals the probability that its NPV will be negative, is also lower than the VaR for investment B.[28] The choice of A or B ultimately depends on how well decision-makers can define the maximum losses they can potentially absorb, as well as their overall aversion to risk.

---

[27] Technically, we are estimating a *joint probability* of two dependent events (magnitude and timing).

[28] Similar to VaR measures, one can also calculate *cash-flow-at-risk* (CFaR), *earnings-at-risk* (EaR), and so forth.

Figure 10-8: Comparing Multiple Projects— Probability Distribution of NPV

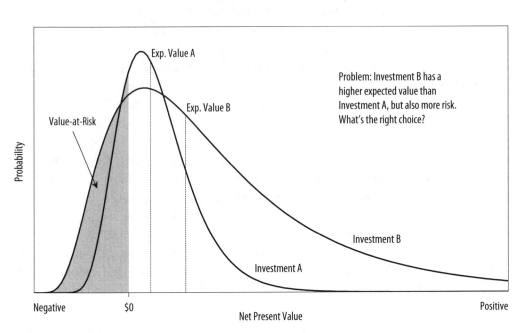

10.6 Chapter Summary

This chapter has provided an admittedly whirlwind tour of how uncertainty can complicate regulatory aspects of the electric and natural gas industries, as well as how uncertainty can affect investment decisions. In the electric industry, which remains in the throes of restructuring efforts, market and nonmarket uncertainties will continue to be crucial. Regulatory uncertainty, both in terms of the continued nature of market competition, the development of new markets, and uncertainty about future environmental regulations, likely will exert a significant influence on firms' generation and infrastructure investment decisions. The natural gas industry, while more completely restructured, faces complications of its own, not only in terms of future supplies, but also in terms of greater price volatility and development of the necessary infrastructure to transport natural gas to customers in the face of opposition to siting new pipelines and storage facilities.

Whatever the uncertainty, the worst way to deal with it is to ignore it. Deterministic models, especially those assessing the costs and benefits of long-lived assets or regulatory policies with long-term implications, will always be wrong. Simplistic planning methods, such as sensitivity and scenario analysis, will be unreliable because they fail to examine the likelihood of different events. In essence, all three methods consign valuable information, which is readily available, to the dustbin. That approach makes no economic sense.

CHAPTER 11
ENVIRONMENTAL REGULATION OF THE ENERGY INDUSTRY

11.1 Introduction

In the previous chapter, we discussed how *regulatory uncertainty*, our euphemistic term for fears (realized or not) that politicians and regulators will change existing rules midstream, can derail resource development and investment decisions. We considered several examples, such as a coal plant owner deciding whether to refurbish an aging power plant in the face of a possible future carbon tax or to invest in new (but untested) pollution control technology. Our goal was to demonstrate that uncertainty and risk have real economic consequences for investment decisions and that these decisions affect supply, demand, and market price, as well as—in the case of electricity—the overall reliability of the electric grid.

To that regulatory uncertainty, we can add the growing role of environmental regulation, which has become more pervasive over time, both in the United States and other countries. Energy use, unfortunately, has been targeted by some as the major cause of worldwide environmental degradation. Debating whether environmental quality is, in fact, decreasing worldwide is a topic far beyond this book.[1] But no one can refute the fact that we need energy to live and work, and that energy is a crucial component in environmental and health solutions. Thus, energy and environmental regulators need to understand the impacts of environmental policies on energy supplies, demand, market prices, and regulated rates.

With that in mind, we have three goals for this chapter: first, to provide a brief overview of several important economic concepts involved in making those trade-offs; second, to provide an overview of key regulatory concepts, which often conflict with those economic

---

[1] One of the more controversial books on this subject, precisely because it challenges the conventional wisdom of ever-declining environmental quality, is Bjorn Lomborg, *The Skeptical Environmentalist* (Cambridge: Cambridge University Press, 2001).

concepts; and, third, to provide an overview of key environmental legislation that affects the energy industry and regulated rates.[2]

We begin by discussing *environmental costs* in comparison to what economists call *externalities*. These two are not the same, although the differences between them are not well understood. This misperception may be one reason that environmental and energy regulators continue to adopt a confusing smorgasbord of conflicting regulations designed to either directly or indirectly incorporate environmental costs into the prices of energy.

We then provide a brief description of how environmental costs actually can be estimated. This is itself controversial, as some environmentalists believe that placing a monetary value on environmental quality is morally repugnant.[3] Although we understand the sentiment, moral or not, explicitly or no, societies can, and do, place monetary values on the environment. It thus makes sense to understand how those values are developed and how such values can be used to make appropriate economic trade-offs.

Next, we evaluate different regulatory approaches and their impacts on both environmental quality and energy prices. We focus on the differences between *market-based* regulation and *command-and-control* regulation. While the latter was historically the most common approach to improving environmental quality and reducing pollution, market-based approaches, where feasible, are far more efficient: they can achieve the same environmental goals at a lower cost.

We conclude by discussing two currently expanding areas for regulatory policy: *renewable portfolio standards* and, more broadly, policies to address global climate change. At the state level, many energy regulators have developed independent, and sometimes conflicting, policies to encourage renewable resource development and reduce carbon emissions. While well-intentioned, these policies represent an "eat-your-spinach" approach that imposes significant costs on local ratepayers but exports the vast majority of the benefits to others.

---

[2] For readers interested in a deeper understanding of environmental economics, there are many textbooks available. A favorite is one of the author's own, which, alas, is out of print. *See* Jonathan A. Lesser, Daniel E. Dodds, and Richard O. Zerbe, *Environmental Economics and Policy* (New York: Addison-Wesley, 1997) (LDZ 1997). A good introductory book that is in print, at least as we write this, is Thomas H. Tietenberg, *Environmental and Natural Resource Economics*, 7th ed. (New York: Addison-Wesley, 2005).

[3] *See, e.g.*, Douglas E. Booth, *Valuing Nature: The Decline and Preservation of Old-Growth Forests* (Lanham, MD: Rowman and Littlefield, 1994).

11.2 Environmental Costs and Environmental Externalities

Living means interacting with the environment around us—the air, water, land, oceans, plants, and animals. Thousands of years ago the environment generally controlled us. Today we control, though not entirely, our environment. The environmental issues that confront us today, from localized impacts of urban "sprawl," to global climate change, are testament to that lack of complete control.

All of our actions affect the environment. That is neither "bad" *per se*, nor is it unique. Nevertheless, as our overall economic well-being has improved, we have become far more cognizant of our unintentional impacts on the environment. Since it is doubtful that any rational person wants to foul the air we breathe or the water we drink simply for the sake of doing so, adverse impacts on the environment can most accurately be viewed as unintended side effects that impose costs on society. Those unintended side effects are, in essence, what we mean by *externalities*. As such, they are a type of *social cost*, which is defined as a cost that falls outside private, market transactions.

What is critical to understand, however, is that not all environmental impacts are externalities. If your neighbor's trash blows into your yard, it is an environmental externality. If your neighbor purposefully dumps his trash into your yard without your consent, it is a criminal act. Most importantly, if your neighbor pays you to <u>allow</u> him to dump his trash in your yard, it is no longer an externality. Instead, it becomes a market transaction, no different than buying something from the store. In such a case, the externality and its attendant social costs will have been *internalized* by creating a private, market-based transaction.

The difference between most goods and services and the environment is that the environment is a *public good*. In other words, nobody owns or has a *property right* to the environment at large. You simply cannot go outside and point to the air you own. Nor, if I live next door, is there a way to improve the quality of "your" air without improving the quality of mine. That ambiguity of rights often leads to externalities.[4] Economists call this characteristic *nonexclusivity*, and it is what makes dealing with environmental problems complex. The challenge of developing policies to combat global climate change is, for example, that for those policies to be effective, everyone must reduce emissions. Otherwise, another classic problem associated with public goods arises: *free riders*. Free riders are those who obtain benefits without paying for them.

---

[4] A classic description is Garrett Hardin, "The Tragedy of the Commons," *Science* 162 (1968): 1243–48.

> **Externalities and the Coase Theorem**
>
> Internalizing externalities can take place only if two conditions are met. First, there must be potential economic gains to be had from a voluntary transaction. All of the parties to the transaction must be able to provide something the others want at a lower cost than they can provide on their own. For example, presumably it is cheaper, from my neighbor's perspective, for him to dump his garbage in my yard than to dump it elsewhere. In theory, such gains always exist with an externality, since externalities exist only if there are unintended side effects that are not part of a transaction. Second, the transaction must be feasible in a practical sense. It may be easy for me and my neighbor to reach an agreement about where he dumps his garbage. With air and water pollution, however, it is probably not feasible to reach agreements between all polluters and all of the polluted, since, in many cases, these will be the same parties. The *transactions costs* will be too high to make a deal practical.
>
> These two conditions were formalized by Ronald Coase in what has come to be known as the *Coase Theorem*.[5] The Coase Theorem states that, if property rights are all well-defined and there are no transactions costs, there will be no externalities. The Coase Theorem is important because it essentially asks us to determine if, through better institutional arrangements, we can reduce transactions costs and, therefore, improve overall economic well-being. Indeed, it was the Coase Theorem that inspired the development of the market-based "cap-and-trade" system adopted in the United States as part of the 1990 Clean Air Act Amendments to address sulfur dioxide and nitrogen oxide pollution spewed, primarily, by coal-fired power plants.
>
> Moreover, the Coase Theorem addresses one of the most common mistakes concerning how environmental policies are implemented: the assumption that <u>any</u> amount of pollution, no matter how small, represents an environmental externality that not only must be eliminated, but also must be paid for by the polluter. This is false. First, it is only economically efficient to reduce pollution to a level where the marginal cost of further pollution reductions equals the marginal benefit. Second, that equilibrium point can be reached <u>regardless</u> of who pays.

Regulatory responses to environmental issues often confound economists, because the costs to comply with some environmental regulations often appear to exceed the benefits. Although this is sometimes the result of the "law of unintended consequences," it is also frequently the result of differing philosophies.

Whereas economists like to measure costs and benefits, environmentalists often decry such accounting exercises as wrongheaded, because they view the preservation of the environment as an almost sacred trust. What this means is that many environmentalists view pollution in terms of morality, i.e., "wicked" polluters harming the virtuous. Hence, they see "polluter pays" regulations as the only possible policies. While this may be a noble position to take, it is less virtuous than it may seem.

---

5   Ronald Coase, "The Problem of Social Cost," *Journal of Law and Economics* 3 (1960): 1–44.

One can certainly argue that environmental protection ought to be provided to specific groups or individuals even if it is not "economically efficient" to do so. For example, in *Lead Industries Association, Inc. v. EPA*,[6] a U.S. court of appeals specifically prohibited any cost-benefit analysis for certain pollutants, in this case lead, which is regulated under the Clean Air Act. In its decision, the court said that "the absence of consideration of [economic] factors was no accident; it was the result of a deliberate decision by Congress to subordinate such concerns to the achievement of health goals." Presumably, Congress's concern for the health and welfare of children, the group most affected by airborne lead emissions, outweighed considerations of whether the cost of protecting children was "worth" the benefit.

However, even if regulations are designed based on something besides economic efficiency, such as protecting children, there will always be an *optimal* level of pollution and an optimal level of environmental risk. Not surprisingly, this is a sorely misunderstood economic concept, because it is both counterintuitive and, for some, abhorrent. How can there be "optimal" levels of pollution and environmental risk other than none whatsoever, since both are "bad"? The reason is simple: eliminating all pollution and environmental risk means eliminating all of the valuable goods and services associated with that pollution and risk. Because of this fact, regulations are not written to "zero-out" pollution. Moreover, the entire concept of "zero-pollution" technologies is impossible. From the day they emerged from the primordial ooze, our human ancestors changed the environment, whether by starting fires to keep warm or clubbing their prey. Our technology has changed, but the underlying dynamic has not. If we are to exist, we will have an impact on the environment.

11.3 Regulatory Responses[7]

To understand the menu of regulatory responses to environmental costs, we need to expand a bit further on social costs. Consider a coal-fired power plant that is generating electricity and which has no pollution control measures installed whatsoever. Each megawatt-hour (MWh) of generation produced by the plant is accompanied by emissions of sulfur dioxide (SO_2), which is associated with "acid rain;" oxides of nitrogen (NO_X), which is associated with "smog;" carbon dioxide (CO_2), which is associated with global warming; and an assortment of other pollutants, including particulates ("soot"), mercury, and so forth.[8]

---

[6] 647 F.2d 1130 (D.C. Cir. 1980), *cert. denied*, 101 S.Ct. 621 (1980).

[7] This section is adapted from LDZ 1997, Chapter 7. See, *supra* note 2. .

[8] We ignore the pollution caused by mining and transporting the coal to the plant. Such *fuel-cycle* impacts, while important, will needlessly complicate the example.

Each MWh of electricity generated has an associated marginal cost, including the cost of the coal itself and the accompanying nonfuel operation and maintenance (O&M) costs. Let's suppose those costs are constant, and equal to $50 per MWh. To distinguish this marginal generation cost from the associated pollution costs, we refer to it as the *marginal private cost* (MPC) of generating electricity. That MPC is the horizontal line in Figure 11-1.

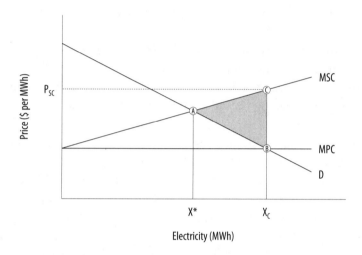

Figure 11-1: Inefficiency in Private Production

As we generate more electricity at the plant, the amount of pollution emitted increases. Each MWh of generation, therefore, has an associated *marginal social cost* (MSC). The MSC equals MPC plus the cost of using the atmosphere as the plant's dustbin. In Figure 11-1, we have drawn the MSC as increasing. We are assuming the total costs of additional pollution will increase as the aggregate emissions increase: One molecule of pollution will likely have no impact on health and well-being; ton after ton will.

In Figure 11-1, we have also drawn the demand for electricity, shown as the downward sloping curve D. The coal plant owner will produce a quantity of electricity equal to X_c, where the marginal cost (the supply curve in our example) intersects the demand curve (Point B). At this level of output, however, MSC (Point C) is greater than MPC. The social cost of generating electricity from the coal plant equals P_{SC}. By failing to incorporate the social costs of his generation production, the coal plant owner produces too much electricity. Production beyond X* MWh imposes costs on society that are greater than the overall market value of the production itself.[9] The additional social costs equal the shaded area ABC.

From a policy standpoint, society would like to reduce the coal plant's output from X_c to X*. Therefore, the key regulatory question is: what is the best way to do so?[10] This is where things get a bit more complicated, because the tools regulators use will affect how the coal plant owner responds, as well as the overall costs and benefits of reducing the pollution, including the specific costs incurred to enforce the regulations themselves.[11]

There are at least seven different types of regulatory policy instruments. These fall into two broad categories: *market-enhancing* mechanisms and *market-substituting* mechanisms.[12] Table 11-1 lists these instruments and shows into which category they fall.

Table 11-1: Types of Environmental Policy Instruments

Market-Enhancing Mechanisms	Market-Substituting Mechanisms
Output taxes on polluting activities	Imposition of prescribed technologies
Direct taxes on pollutants	Limits on the quantity of pollutants
Tradable emissions permits	Payments to reduce pollutants
	Subsidies for pollution control measures

As we discuss in the sections that follow, these policy instruments differ in their capacity to achieve the desired level of environmental quality at the least cost, which, from the standpoint of economic efficiency, is the desired outcome.[13]

---

[9] Externalities can also be positive. In that case, too little production will occur.

[10] This is where difficulties in measuring those environmental costs come into play. In Figure 11-1, we assume that the costs associated with pollution are known. In reality, regulators would ideally estimate those costs so as to determine an appropriate reduction in emissions.

[11] In some cases, *common law* remedies, i.e., the law made by judges, can be used to address some externalities. For example, *private nuisance* and *public nuisance* actions can be taken to address unreasonable interference with the use of private and public lands, respectively. The problem with common law remedies, however, is their high administrative cost, a consequence of the fact that they are almost always applied to single individuals or firms.

[12] Another tool is to impose emergency restrictions on polluters.

[13] Even when regulations are not based on economics but on the rights of individuals (e.g., children) not to be exposed to certain types of pollution (e.g., lead), the regulations should accomplish the goal as efficiently as possible. After all, why spend two dollars to achieve a goal when you could spend just one dollar to achieve it?

Command-and-Control Policies

The most common form of environmental policy instruments are known collectively as *command-and-control* instruments. It is unfortunate that such policy instruments are the least likely to reduce pollution at the least cost. Moreover, it is ironic that some state regulators and politicians are reintroducing command-and-control policies, even though market-based approaches have won over even skeptical environmentalists.

Command-and-control policies fall into three general categories. The most common are prescribed-technology policies that regulate the types of pollution control measures that must be used. The second group of policies regulates emissions quantities themselves by restricting either *allowed emissions per unit of output* (e.g., mercury per MWh of electricity generated) or *allowed emissions per unit of time* (e.g., maximum allowable concentrations of carbon monoxide in a 24-hour period). The last and least common category is emergency restrictions that can ban certain activities (e.g., operation of certain industries, driving, etc.) during periods of extremely high pollution levels.

Prescribed-technology policies require polluters to adopt the identical technological solutions regardless of whether those technologies are the most efficient, the polluters have equal costs of pollution reduction, or the costs of the reductions exceed the benefits. This means that a command-and-control policy will yield the most efficient outcomes only by accident.

Quotas are another common command-and-control approach. Emissions quotas can take two forms: (1) they can impose an emissions limit per unit of time (e.g., tons per year), or (2) they can impose an emissions limit per unit of output (e.g., pounds per MWh). An emissions limit per unit can achieve the same emissions levels as an emissions tax, since the marginal cost of production will increase to account for the cost of pollution control equipment. However, this type of emission restriction does not account for environmental damage. In other words, a polluter is simply given a specific pollution limit. The polluter will thus invest in emissions controls to keep total emissions below the prescribed maximum point, but he will not take into account the external costs of those emissions. If a policy that limits emissions per unit of output is established, then the same problem arises as if regulators had imposed a tax on output: the allocation of emissions among different plants with different efficiencies will not be least-cost.

Market-Based Policies

As Figure 11-1 showed, if production of a good has external costs, its competitive market price will not reflect the full social cost of its production. Suppose, therefore, that we tax each MWh of electricity, setting the tax, T^*, equal to the difference between MSC and MPC. Since the coal plant owner now pays a tax of $\$T^*$ per MWh, the owner's MPC curve shifts upwards by that amount, as shown in Figure 11-2. Since MPC increases, the price increases to P^*. The number of MWh generated by the plant decreases to X^*, and we will have achieved the "right" level of generation from the coal plant.

Figure 11-2: Effects of an Output Tax

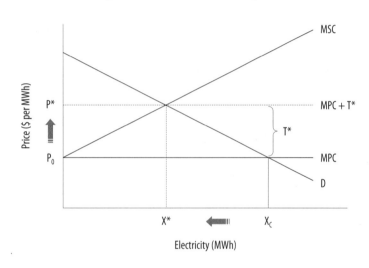

The total revenues collected by imposing this tax on output represent a transfer of wealth from electricity buyers to the government. What the government does with those tax revenues can also affect the overall well-being of the economy. For example, there are a number of proposals to combat global warming through a carbon tax in which the revenues collected would be used to lower income tax rates.

Although an output tax can eliminate one source of economic inefficiency arising from an externality—overproduction—by forcing buyers to pay the true social cost of electricity, an output tax provides no incentive whatsoever for the coal plant owner to install efficient pollution control measures and, thus, generate electricity with the most efficient technology.[14]

---

[14] If the coal plant owner, in fact, owns multiple plants with different emissions levels, then imposing a uniform tax per MWh will not achieve the efficient outcome, because the "dirty" plants will tend to produce too much electricity, while the "clean" plants will produce too little.

The owner simply pays the tax per MWh and sells less electricity. On the other hand, output taxes have low administrative and enforcement costs. An output tax will not require monitoring of emissions at the plant and can be administered much like any other tax.

Emissions Taxes

The effects of an emissions tax differ from those of an output tax, because an emissions tax imposes specific market prices on the pollutants themselves. Thus, it forces the coal plant owner to pay the costs associated with emitting pollution into the atmosphere. As a result, the owner will have an economic incentive to reduce those emissions as long as the marginal cost of controlling emissions is less than the tax. Second, because the coal plant owner will want to maximize profits and minimize costs, a correctly set emissions tax will lead to the optimal level of generation and the optimal set of inputs. Third, the emissions tax will increase the cost of production and raise the plant's MPC, which will be reflected in the final price of electricity. This will reduce the amount of electricity purchased by consumers to the correct level, X^*.

How is the correct emissions tax determined? In principle, the emissions tax rate should be set where the marginal benefit (MB) of additional pollution reduction (or *abatement*) just equals the marginal cost (MC) of control. This is shown in Figure 11-3.

Figure 11-3: Determination of the Optimal Emissions Tax

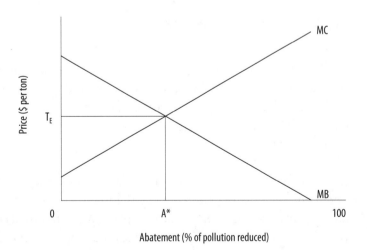

Tradable Emissions Permits

As its name implies, a *tradable emissions permit* is a permit that allows polluters to pollute for a price. Such permits can be bought and sold in a well-defined market, and such an arrangement is known as a *cap-and-trade* system. Several such markets exist. The most successful markets have been those created for SO_2 and NO_X emissions. These markets were established by the 1990 Clean Air Act Amendments (1990 CAAA).[15] Under the emissions trading approach, the goal is to achieve the desired reduction in pollution at the lowest possible cost by providing industry participants with the right monetary incentives to reduce pollution.

To understand how cap-and-trade systems work, recall our discussion of how, in the case of multiple coal plants having different clean-up costs, an output tax would not lead to an economically efficient level of production at each plant. The reason is that the same total emissions reduction can be achieved at a lower cost. For example, if plant A can reduce one ton of SO_2 at a cost of $5, and plant B can reduce one ton of SO_2 at a cost of $10, society can save $5 by allowing plant B to emit one additional ton, while having plant A emit two fewer tons.

One way around this limitation is to allow polluters to buy and sell rights to pollute and to let them exchange those rights among themselves. This is the logic behind tradable emissions permits.[16] The 1990 CAAA established a nationwide market for SO_2 emissions and a regional market for NO_X emissions in the eastern United States.[17]

Under the emissions cap-and-trade approach, the goal was to achieve the same reduction in pollution, but at a lower cost, by providing industry participants with the right monetary incentives to reduce pollution. By providing a carrot-and-stick approach instead of just a stick, Congress realized it could achieve much better results with far fewer adverse consequences for the economy and, ultimately, for consumers.

The idea was to set a specific emissions goal, called an emissions cap, and then let the market decide the best way to reach that goal. In other words, rather than using "command-and-control" policies to specify what each and every plant must achieve, Congress established an overall limit on air pollution and told industry, "You decide how best to achieve it." In that

---

[15] More recently, new cap-and-trade markets have been established for carbon dioxide in Europe.

[16] For a more detailed explanation and analysis, see Thomas Tietenberg, "Transferable Discharge Permits and the Control of Stationary Source Air Pollution," *Land Economics* 55, no. 3 (1979): 391–416.

[17] In 2005, the Clean Air Interstate Rule (CAIR) went into effect. Under CAIR, SO_2 emissions, and NO_X emissions in a number of eastern states, will be further reduced.

way, the power of the market is harnessed; individual polluters determine the lowest-cost approaches to achieving the emissions cap. With a market price for emissions allowances established, those who can reduce emissions at a lower per-unit cost will do so, selling their "excess" allowances to those for whom the cost of reducing pollution is higher.

With a system of tradable emissions permits, such as the ones that exist for SO_2 and NO_X in the United States, regulators first determine the total amount of pollution that will be permitted. This is usually called an emissions *ceiling*. Ideally, the total amount of pollution will be set at the optimal level (i.e., where the marginal benefit of abatement equals the marginal cost of control), as shown in Figure 11-3. For example, under the CAAA, SO_2 emissions from almost all U.S. electric generating plants with generating capacities greater than 25 MW were capped at 8.9 million tons beginning in the year 2000. The government issues permits, or allowances, equal to this cap to major polluters, including coal-fired power plants and major industrial polluters such as oil refineries and cement plants. Polluters with high control costs will have an incentive to purchase additional permits from polluters with low control costs, and vice versa. The trading of permits should lead to a point where polluters all have the same marginal control cost and total control costs are minimized.[18] The administrative costs of tradable permits are not excessive, because trades are made in observed markets.[19]

Cap-and-trade systems work best when the affected pollutants are widely dispersed. This is one reason that such systems have been proposed to control greenhouse gas emissions, whose impacts are global by definition. A problem arises, however, if the targeted pollutants do not disperse sufficiently and, as a result, have more localized impacts. For example, EPA has proposed to establish a cap-and-trade system for mercury emissions from coal-fired power plants. However, because mercury disperses less widely than NO_X, SO_2, and CO_2, the suitability of a cap-and-trade system for it continues to be disputed. Localized impacts, especially those for which the degree of localization is disputed, can create a conundrum for regulators: balancing the efficiency gains of reducing emissions at the lowest possible cost against the potential for local emissions levels to remain constant, or even increase.

Many environmentalists were initially skeptical of a market-based approach because they thought it would allow some electric generators an opportunity to "pay to pollute." Well, it did. Some generators chose to pay, because it was much less costly than installing new equipment. Other generators invested in emissions reduction technology because that al-

---

[18] One problem with cap-and-trade systems is the restriction on eligible market participants. For example, some utility regulators do not allow regulated utilities to sell allowances to upwind facilities. As such restrictions multiply, however, the efficiency of emissions markets decreases, short-circuiting their very purpose.

[19] For example, EPA holds an annual auction of "reserved" allowances for the current year and for emissions seven years into the future.

lowed them to sell their emissions "credits" to generators who chose not to invest in such equipment. The emissions reductions were still achieved, but without mandating which specific generating units had to install which type of emissions control technology. The market—not the government—provided that direction. Not only were emissions reductions achieved, but it turned out that the cost of achieving those emissions reductions was much lower than expected.

11.4 Measuring Environmental Costs and Benefits[20]

We cannot go to the market to purchase clean air or more wilderness. This makes developing appropriate environmental policies and regulations difficult. For example, to establish a truly economically efficient cap on SO_2 emissions, we would have to: (1) estimate the environmental damages caused by SO_2, such as acid rain; (2) estimate when those damages would occur and how long they would continue; and (3) perhaps even deal with the potential benefits of SO_2 emissions to reduce global warming. (Estimating an efficient level of greenhouse gas emissions is likely to be more problematic.)

Since we cannot directly observe the prices individuals are willing to pay for improved environmental quality, economists resort to alternative approaches. In some cases, it is possible to estimate the value of environmental goods indirectly. For example, homes with sweeping views of the mountains or ocean usually have higher prices than similar homes without those views. By identifying the different attributes of homes and comparing their sales prices, we can estimate the market value of the view.

In many cases, however, the estimation process is more complex. For example, in the Four Corners region of the southwestern United States, where Utah, Colorado, Arizona, and New Mexico meet, several large coal-fired power plants were built in the late 1960s and early 1970s. The air pollution from those plants reduced visibility at Grand Canyon National Park. Precisely how much visibility was reduced and what other sources were contributing to that reduction were disputed. Nevertheless, from an economic standpoint, it would be good to know whether the benefits of improving clear views across (say) the Grand Canyon were worth the additional expense of reducing air pollution from whatever the sources were.

---

[20] For a far more detailed exposition, see A. Myrick Freeman, *The Measurement of Environmental and Resource Values* (Washington, DC: Resources for the Future, 1993).

Unlike estimating the value of a view from a home, however, views at the Grand Canyon are public goods, since no individual owns the park. Moreover, there is the question of value to whom, since even people who have never visited the Grand Canyon may value a pristine view, either because they intend to visit in the future or even if they never intend to visit. Finally, there is the problem of defining the view itself.

Typically, issues relating to recreation-related environmental quality are based on individuals' willingness to pay to travel to recreational facilities, whether national parks, lakes, or fishing streams.[21] These recreational use values, however, will not always capture all of the value of a public good. The reason is that individuals can value places they never intend to visit. Such passive use or *existence values* are quite real. For example, in 1989, the Exxon Valdez ran aground in Prince William Sound, Alaska, spilling millions of gallons of crude oil and setting off a protracted legal battle. Although the environmental damages to fishermen whose livelihoods were destroyed were a major component of those litigated damages, it was argued that the damages to individuals who had never even seen Prince William Sound were also of major significance.[22]

Preserving Health and Well-Being

Health-related pollution issues are arguably the most common type of environmental issue encountered, and they are the most problematic. Not only is there the issue of determining the physical effects of increased exposure to pollutants, there is much controversy over how, or even whether, to compare the costs of environmental regulations with the cost of premature death and increased incidence of disease. Some people consider such comparisons to be reprehensible. How, they argue, can we "put a price tag" on lives in order to decide whether environmental regulations are worthwhile?

The arguments are vehement because they involve the *statistical value of life*, which is an economic concept that is much misunderstood. The controversy arises because many mistakenly believe that economists are placing values on other people's lives, such as Grandma or Uncle Joe. In fact, economists measure the value of life individuals place on their own lives. People constantly make choices about their life and health. We decide whether to smoke or not. We decide whether to step into the crosswalk early or wait until the light turns red. We send our children to school on the bus because we believe that the benefits of

---

[21] *Id.* Freeman discusses these travel cost models.

[22] *See*, Richard Carson et al., "A Contingent Valuation Study of Lost Passive Use Values Resulting from the Exxon Valdez Oil Spill: Report to the Attorney General of the State of Alaska" (La Jolla, CA: Natural Resource Damage Assessment, Inc., 1993). Exxon settled the damages litigation for a total of $1.1 billion before all of the studies were completed.

an education far outweigh the potential risks of riding in the school bus. In estimating the statistical value of life, economists examine the value individuals place on <u>marginal</u> changes in risk.

Logically, one might believe that environmental regulations enacted to improve health and well-being should be based on their relative costs and benefits, and only regulations for which the benefits exceed the costs should be enacted. This is not always the case, because noneconomic goals, such as policies designed to protect children from exposure to damaging pollutants, may take priority over costs and benefits.[23] For example, the 1977 Clean Air Act Amendments specifically recognized multiple goals of cleaner air, including health, welfare, economic, and social effects.[24]

> **Perceived vs. Actual Risk**
>
> One problem that often appears when developing environmental regulations is the difference between the risks that individuals <u>perceive</u> they face from environmental impacts and the <u>actual</u> statistical risks they face. Economic losses can occur when regulators act based on perceived risks that differ greatly from actual risks. Thus, the individual who thinks nothing of driving off without fastening his seatbelt may be terrified of his potential cancer risk from higher electromagnetic fields near high-voltage transmission lines, even though there is no statistical evidence whatsoever for the latter. In fact, The U.S. Supreme Court addressed a similar issue in a 1983 case, *Metropolitan Edison v. People vs. Nuclear Energy,*[25] in which the defendants opposed operation of a nuclear power plant because of the alleged psychological harm it would cause, such harm stemming from the fact that many people were frightened of nuclear power. But the Court held that the Nuclear Regulatory Commission, which regulates nuclear plant operations, did not need to consider psychological harm derived from unsubstantiated fears and things that go bump in the night.
>
> A more recent, and unfortunate, development for the nuclear power industry concerns terrorism. Many individuals fear that terrorists will target and attack operating nuclear plants and cause huge releases of radioactive debris. While the likelihood of such attacks succeeding is undoubtedly small, the perception of the risk is almost certainly much higher. This creates a significant policy dilemma, especially for those who see global climate change as the most important environmental challenge of our time. Whether the benefits derived from nuclear plants that emit no greenhouse gases can outweigh fears of nuclear catastrophe remains to be seen.

---

[23] *See, e.g., Lead Industries, supra* note 6.
[24] Pub.L. No. 95-95, 91 Stat. 747.
[25] 460 U.S. 766 (1983).

11.5 Environmental Costs and Energy Prices

In the United States, federal and state environmental laws have increased natural gas and electric prices in a number of ways. For example, the U.S. government has restricted natural gas exploration and drilling offshore and on federal lands. This has impeded the search for new natural gas supplies and contributed to higher natural gas prices. Imposing air pollution emissions caps, even using a market-based cap-and-trade system, obviously internalizes external environmental costs and raises the price of electricity.

The first two examples can be considered as internalizing environmental costs, although whether the trade-off is appropriate is another matter. However, a third example provides a glimpse into the adverse economic impacts of conflicting regulations and regulatory uncertainty. Although the 1990 CAAA introduced market-based solutions to address SO_2 and NO_X emissions, it also perpetuated high-cost command-and-control regulations covering new sources of pollution. The Act requires newly built coal-fired power plants to install state-of-the-art pollution control equipment under a section of the Clean Air Act called *New Source Review* (NSR).

The most controversial issue surrounding NSR has been whether routine maintenance upgrades constitute "new" sources. From an economic standpoint, maintenance upgrades that improve operating efficiency would benefit plant owners and reduce emissions per unit of output. However, because maintenance upgrades could also increase a generator's output (because of lower marginal production costs), it would be possible for total emissions to increase. This led to a dilemma. The EPA could impose NSR requirements even for routine maintenance, and firms would simply avoid upgrades entirely, perpetuating inefficiency and possibly increasing emissions of some pollutants. Or the EPA could allow firms to improve operating efficiency and reduce emissions per unit of output, but at the risk of higher total pollution levels.

For a number of years, EPA evaluated NSR requirements on a case-by-case basis, thus perpetuating regulatory uncertainty. Then, EPA developed an *Equipment Replacement Provision* that would have allowed power plants, refineries, and factories to upgrade existing equipment without being subject to NSR, notwithstanding an increase in emissions, so long as the upgrades amounted to less than 20% of the replacement cost of the equipment. However, in a 2006 decision, a U.S. court of appeals found that the Equipment Replacement Provisions were contrary to the Clean Air Act and excluded changes that should be regulated under the NSR program, thus recreating the case-by-case uncertainty.[26]

11.6 Externality Adders

In the late 1980s, in response to what they believed to be inadequate consideration of the environmental costs of new power plants, many state utility regulators began examining ways of reducing those costs further without having to amend environmental laws like the Clean Air Act. The most commonly adopted (and least sensible) approach equated the marginal benefits of pollution reductions with the highest marginal cost control measures. Under this fundamentally flawed approach, utility regulators would impose externality cost "adders" on a utility's generation resources based on the marginal cost of control measures that were required by environmental regulators. Rather than require consumers to pay these environmental costs directly as an output tax, utility regulators required utilities to incorporate those costs into *integrated resource planning* (IRP) exercises that compared these incorrect estimates of the social cost of electric generation to the cost of nonpolluting resources, especially energy conservation.[27]

For example, suppose the cost of controlling SO_2 emissions from a typical coal plant was $500 per ton. If the plant emitted one ton of SO_2 per 10 MWh of electricity generated, then utility regulators would "add" $50 per MWh, or 5¢ per kWh, of generation to the plant's other operating costs. So, if the coal plant produced one kWh of electricity for 6¢, utility regulators would set the "social" cost of generation from the plant at 11¢ per kWh. These regulators would then determine that reducing (or avoiding) each kWh of generation from the coal plant had a social value of 11¢, since, if society requires coal plants to install scrubbers, then society must value SO_2 emissions reductions at $500 per ton or more.[28] Thus, they reasoned, the utility could afford to spend up to 11¢ per kWh on nonpolluting energy sources, especially energy conservation measures, and customers would be better off.

---

[26] *New York v. EPA*, 443 F.3d 880 (D.C. Cir. 2006). In a still more recent case, the U.S. Supreme Court ruled that investments that reduced hourly emissions rates could still fall under NSR if total annual emissions increase. *See, Environmental Defense v. Duke Energy Corp.*, No. 05-848 (U.S. April 2, 2007).

[27] As we mentioned in Chapter 7, note 26, some regulators and politicians are promoting "integrated portfolio management," which is simply a new name for IRP.

[28] This has sometimes been (wrongly) called the "revealed preference of regulators."

Compelling as the "logic" of this argument may be, it is completely wrong.[29] First, control costs often have little relationship to damage costs. Environmental laws and regulations can tell us a lot about the values legislators and regulators are willing to impose on society to reduce pollution, but such policies are often imposed, rightly or wrongly, for reasons having little to do with economics, such as the rights granted to children in the *Lead Industries* case. Moreover, they tell us nothing about the trade-offs individuals would make.

Second, energy regulators who impose additional costs on firms above and beyond what environmental regulators have imposed will improve overall economic well-being only if marginal social costs and marginal social benefits differ. For example, suppose the marginal social cost of reducing pollution equaled the $500 per ton cost of the scrubber, but economists estimated the marginal social benefit at $450 per ton. The appropriate response for utility regulators would be to reduce the regulated price of electricity by the equivalent of $50 per ton of SO_2 or, using our coal plant example, by ½¢ per kWh.

Third, choices between alternative electric production (or savings) technologies should be based on total social costs, rather than marginal costs. After all, if the choice is between two different technologies, society will want to choose the one with the lowest total social cost, regardless of the marginal costs.

In the United States, the "externality adder" phase generally ended once electric industry restructuring began in the mid-1990s, although several states that never restructured their electric industries, such as Vermont, still employ them for purposes of comparing energy efficiency and renewable resources. More recently, however, and in spite of the proven benefits of using market-based approaches to reduce air pollution, some states are beginning to reimpose command-and-control regulations that are more stringent than federal regulations. Not only do some of these regulations address pollutants covered under the Clean Air Act, they also regulate carbon dioxide emissions, as we discuss in more detail in the next section.[30] One unanticipated side effect of these policies, however, may be to force generators to shut plants down, rather than invest in needed environmental upgrades. This may lead to problems with overall electric system reliability and higher electric rates, a subject we address in the next chapter.

---

[29] For a detailed explanation, see Daniel Dodds and Jonathan Lesser, "Can Utility Commissions Improve on Environmental Regulations?" *Land Economics* 70, no. 1 (1994): 63–76.

[30] *See, e.g.,* the Maryland Healthy Air Act, MD. Code Ann., Environment, Title 2, Subtitle 10, §§ 2-1001–2-1005.

11.7 Current Regulatory Policies: Renewable Energy and Global Climate Change

In this section, we briefly address two emerging environmental policy areas that have the potential to affect energy prices significantly. The first is the emergence of *renewable portfolio standards* (RPS), which have been implemented by a number of U.S. state energy regulators and by regulators in a number of other countries. The second area concerns state, federal, and international policies to address global warming and climate change.

Renewable Portfolio Standards

In 2005, renewable energy sources, primarily generation from hydroelectric dams, provided about 9% of the total electricity generation in the United States. The percentage supplied by other forms of renewable energy—wind, solar, and biomass—was just over 2%.[31] According to the International Energy Agency, hydropower contributed 16% of electricity supply, and other renewable sources supplied another 2% worldwide. Energy and environmental policymakers wish to increase these production levels significantly. For example, the European Union has a target to produce over 22% of its electricity from renewable energy by 2011. Many U.S. state governments—some with regulated and some with restructured electric industries—want to rapidly increase reliance on renewables, although the types of generation that are deemed renewable vary, primarily for political reasons.[32]

The most frequently advanced policy for supporting renewable energy sources in electricity generation is the renewable portfolio standard (RPS).[33] Also known as renewable obligations, green credits/certificates, and the like, these market share requirements mandate that either producers or users derive a certain percentage of their electricity from renewable sources. Currently, the District of Columbia and nearly half of the U.S. states have established an RPS or a state-mandated target for renewables. Several other countries—including Australia, Austria, Belgium, Brazil, the Czech Republic, Denmark, Finland, Italy, Japan, the Netherlands, South Korea, Sweden, and the United Kingdom—have planned or established their own programs.

---

[31] U.S. Energy Information Administration (EIA), *Electric Power Annual* (October 2006).

[32] For example, the state of Pennsylvania, which has a large coal mining industry, classifies as renewable integrated gasification combined cycle (IGCC) plants that use coal, while in Vermont, only hydropower development below 80 MW of capacity is considered renewable.

[33] In the U.S., the federal government also provides a specific subsidy for wind energy. In 2006, that subsidy was 1.8¢ per kWh generated.

An RPS combines a subsidy to producers of energy from renewable generating resources (i.e., the value of the credit) with a tax to producers of energy from nonrenewable sources (i.e., the cost of buying needed credits). From the standpoint of overall price impacts, the question is whether an RPS will increase or decrease the prices of electricity (and natural gas, to the extent that it is the marginal fuel for electric generation). In the true economist's fashion, the answer depends on a number of factors, including the magnitude of the renewable requirement, the responsiveness (called *elasticity*) of electric and natural gas prices to changes in demand and supply, and the types of renewable resources developed.[34]

Policies that Address Climate Change

Regardless of whether one believes that global warming is occurring because of human activity and has already put the world on a dead-end road to perdition or whether it is just the Earth's natural climate variability,[35] climate change is today a key focus of environmental and energy regulators worldwide. We will not delve into the scientific controversies in this book.[36] However, from the standpoint of energy regulation, the impacts of climate change policies may be extensive, depending on what policies (if any) are implemented and when.

First, as we discussed in the previous chapter, there are real costs to regulatory uncertainty. Generating companies face uncertainty over the costs and benefits of new investments, including investments in pollution control measures, types of generating facilities, and so forth. Additionally, climate change policies that increase the cost of fossil fuels will affect overall demand. Changes in forecast growth rates will also affect other investment decisions, such as drilling for natural gas, development of new gas pipelines and related facilities, and construction of new electric transmission lines.

Approaches to regulated greenhouse gas emissions have taken several forms that may affect electric and natural gas prices. At the broadest level, there is the Kyoto Treaty, which sets specific emissions reductions targets. Should the United States ultimately participate in Kyoto or other climate change treaties, mechanisms to reduce overall CO_2 emissions would have to be put into place. Given the "global" nature of global warming, a cap-and-trade ap-

---

[34] *See, e.g.,* Karen Palmer and Dallas Burtraw, "Cost-Effectiveness of Renewable Electricity Policies," *Energy Economics* 27, no. 6 (2005): 873–94.

[35] In the mid-1970s, there were predictions that the Earth was cooling and mankind would soon have to deal with a new ice age. *See, e.g.,* "The Cooling World," *Newsweek,* April 28, 1975. *See also,* Dennis T. Avery and S. Fred Singer, *Unstoppable Global Warming: Every 1,500 Years* (New York: Rowman and Littlefield, 2007).

[36] There are many, many books on the subject. The United Nations Environment Programme Intergovernmental Panel on Climate Change (IPCC) reports are comprehensive and detailed collaboration by many scientists. The IPCC Fourth Assessment will be published in 2007. For an interesting dissent regarding the economic importance of climate change, see Lomborg, note 1, *supra*.

proach would be appropriate. However, because of a lack of direct federal policy action on climate change, a number of states and environmental groups have taken several approaches on their own. As we discussed previously, Maryland imposed direct CO_2 emissions limits on coal-fired power plants.[37] Other states have pursued lawsuits against some of the country's largest electric utilities, alleging that their citizens are directly harmed by greenhouse gas emissions from those utilities' generating plants.

Although the magnitude, timing, and ultimate consequences of global climate change remain uncertain, a reasonable economic argument can be made for undertaking *some* policies that begin reducing CO_2 emissions today, especially if such policies provide other, more immediate benefits. To the extent that both the costs and the benefits of reducing CO_2 (and other greenhouse gas) emissions are uncertain, emissions reductions can be thought of as a sort of financial "option" that acts like an insurance policy. It may provide large benefits in the future or turn out not to have been needed. What is critical is to determine the quantity of insurance that should be purchased (i.e., how much of a reduction in CO_2 to target) and the lowest-cost methods of achieving such a target.

Climate Change Policies and Fairness

In choosing regulatory policies to address climate change, any economist will tell you that you should choose the policies that provide the greatest return for a given cost. While some engineering solutions have been developed and tested that sequester carbon underground, the most likely policy candidates will be emissions and output taxes, coupled with nationwide emissions quotas and a cap-and-trade system.

In some cases, emissions and output taxes on carbon will produce identical results. This is different than in the case of other pollutants. If you burn a ton of coal to generate electricity, you get a certain amount of carbon, even though the amount of electricity produced from that ton of coal will vary, depending on the efficiency (*heat rate*) of the coal plant. By contrast, an emissions tax on carbon and an output tax on electricity would have different impacts, because different generating technologies produce different levels of emissions. Thus, imposing a carbon tax would encourage substitution away from high-carbon fuels like coal towards lower-carbon fuels like natural gas. On the other hand, uniform taxes on energy (e.g., dollars per Btu) would not provide that incentive, and so would be less effective. Moreover, strict emissions quotas would be even less effective.

---

[37] Maryland HAA, *supra*, note 30.

Strictly from the standpoint of economic efficiency, emissions quotas on carbon will be less valuable than emissions taxes, because quotas do not require polluters to take into account the full social cost of their pollution. Another benefit of carbon taxes over quotas is that the revenues collected from a carbon tax could be "recycled" to reduce other taxes. A final disadvantage of quotas—and in the case of carbon emissions quotas on specific nations—is the difficulty of measurement and enforcement. For example, a number of countries that signed the Kyoto Treaty in 1999 and pledged to reduce their emissions have not done so. Moreover, the emissions they claim are estimates. The principal disadvantage of a carbon tax is the uncertainty over the extent to which emissions taxes would actually reduce emissions. Another potential disadvantage is that emissions taxes on carbon could be regressive, imposing relatively larger costs on the poorer members of society.

Even though emissions taxes are likely more efficient, it may make sense to enforce emissions limits that are not fully tradable. The reason is that rich countries with a set of fully tradable emissions permits might be able to bid for a greater share of worldwide emissions. As a result, poorer countries could find themselves worse off, with fewer options for improving their economies. There would also be the minor issue of allocating permits among different countries in the first place. Awarding emissions quotas on the basis of past emissions (called *grandfathering*) rewards past inefficiency. It also penalizes developing countries, whose total emissions would be expected to increase as their economies and populations grow. These conflicts have already reared up as ratification and enforcement of the Kyoto Treaty has been debated.

CO_2 Litigation: The Worst Possible Approach?

In 2004, a coalition of states filed suit against five of the largest U.S. electric utilities to force those utilities to reduce CO_2 emissions.[38] The states lost. In 1999, several environmental groups sued the EPA, arguing that the agency was *required* to regulate CO_2 emissions from automobiles under the Clean Air Act. EPA responded that, although the Clean Air Act does not prohibit regulating CO_2 emissions, an absence of prohibition is not the same thing as a requirement to regulate. A federal court of appeals denied the environmental groups' request, ruling that the petitioners lacked *standing* because they could not show they had suffered specific injury because of EPA's failure to regulate CO_2 emissions from automobiles *Massachusetts v. Environmental Protection Agency*, 415 F.3d 50 (D.C. Cir. 2005). However, in April 2007, the U.S. Supreme Court sided with the states and determined that CO_2 emissions fall under the Clean Air Act's definition of "pollution." *Massachusetts v. Environmental Protection Agency*, No. 05-1120, April 2, 2007 (U.S.).

---

[38] *Connecticut v. American Electric Power Company, Inc.*, 406 F. Supp. 2d 265 (S.D.N.Y. 2005), appeals pending, No. 05-5104-CV (2d Cir., argued June 7, 2006). Since the Supreme Court has now determined that CO_2 emissions from automobiles are covered under the Clean Air Act, it is reasonable to conclude that power plant emissions are covered as well.

> From an economic and regulatory standpoint, it is difficult to see how lawsuits, or litigation generally, represent a prudent approach to environmental regulation, because lawsuits are unlikely to provide any appreciable benefits to individual plaintiffs. For example, successful lawsuits mandating CO_2 emissions reductions at specific power plants—a command-and-control approach—would marginally reduce greenhouse gas emissions, but at an unnecessarily high cost. Moreover, it would force those utilities' ratepayers or other power purchasers to bear disproportionate costs with little or no real environmental benefits. And, if successful, such lawsuits would have a chilling effect on the financial community, exacerbating the financial uncertainty felt by regulated and nonregulated generators alike. That would lead to higher costs of capital and, ultimately, higher electric prices.

Gains and Losses

From an economic standpoint, state-level mandates for renewable resources and greenhouse gas emission reductions represent a new type of regulatory approach. As we first discussed in Chapter 3, the traditional regulatory approach is designed so that captive ratepayers pay for only those costs deemed prudent and known and measurable. Moreover, those costs are generally allocated among different classes of ratepayers based on causation.

RPS requirements and greenhouse gas regulations turn this traditional regulatory approach on its head. These policies force utility ratepayers to bear all of the costs, while exporting the vast majority of the benefits elsewhere. In essence, rather than reducing free ridership, these regulations create free riders by replacing the known-and-measurable standard with a paternalistic "eat-your-spinach" regulatory approach.[39]

The economic reasons for this are straightforward. In general, renewable resources, such as wind, have greater direct monetary costs than their fossil fuel counterparts.[40] If this were not the case, then developers would build these resources without various subsidies and tax credits. Thus, to induce additional supply, regulators create an artificial demand for renewable generation with RPS requirements. Retail electric utilities and other retail electric providers must prove they have met the RPS, either by contracting directly with generation owners or by purchasing green credits. In either case, their supply costs increase, which in turn increases the costs paid by their retail customers. The additional costs paid by retail customers are transferred to renewable generation developers.

---

[39] Another approach that is common in European countries is the use of "feed-in-tariffs" (FIT) that provide renewable plant developers with a known set of (above-market) energy prices for a specified number of years. For a discussion, see, e.g., Philippe Menanteau, Dominique Finon, and Marie-Laure Lamy, "Price Versus Quantities: Choosing Policies for Promoting the Development of Renewable Energy," *Energy Policy* 31, no. 8 (2003): 799–812.

[40] Direct comparisons of the cost of (say) wind and solar generation with fossil-fueled generation are complicated by the nature of the former's output. Wind turbines generate power only when the wind blows. They cannot be turned on and off as changes in demand dictate without some form of "firming" resource. This reduces the monetary value of their output.

Similarly, enforcing specific greenhouse gas limits at the state level increases the cost of electricity. However, in the absence of coordinated worldwide actions, the benefits accruing to local customers from these local greenhouse gas reductions will be negligible, since by definition climate change is a global phenomenon. Thus, everyone outside the local area free rides on the backs of local customers. Whether this "eat-your-spinach" approach is an effective policy strategy depends on one's point of view. It is clearly not an economically efficient one.

11.8 Chapter Summary

In this chapter, we have touched on only a few of the many environmental issues affecting the electric and natural gas industries. Whereas environmental regulations currently affect the natural gas industry primarily by restricting exploration and drilling areas, the electric industry continues to be the focus of extensive environmental laws and policies.

While great strides have been made towards adopting efficient, market-based approaches to reduce environmental damages from electric generation over rigid command-and-control policies, there remain a number of inconsistencies that impose excessive costs on industry and, ultimately, consumers. Moreover, energy regulators, especially at the state or local level, are increasingly acting as environmental regulators. In doing so, they have often implemented counterproductive policies. Regardless of whether one believes economic efficiency should trump other environmental goals, such as fairness, regulations that operate at cross-purposes will generally achieve little. Moreover, environmental regulations to "right" real or perceived environmental "wrongs" should be designed to accomplish their objectives in ways that are as economically efficient as possible.

CHAPTER 12
REGULATING ELECTRIC SYSTEM RELIABILITY

12.1 Introduction

Ensuring the reliability of the electric system is a complex undertaking because, unlike other commodities, electricity cannot be stored cost-effectively. This means that total electric supply must always match demand at each and every moment in time. The complex physics of electricity dictate that an integrated electric system must be composed of precisely coordinated networks that have built-in, multiple redundancies to ensure the system operates even if individual components fail.

Electric system reliability is itself difficult to define, because *reliability* means different things to different people; for example, a computer chip manufacturer will be most concerned about power quality, such as small changes in voltages that can ruin fiercely expensive machinery. A residential customer, on the other hand, might be completely unaware of small voltage changes, but he will be affected by frequent power outages that cause his electronic clocks to reset. If you ask two economists to define reliability, you may receive three different answers; if you ask two engineers, the answers may include an alphabet soup of acronyms, such as CAIDI, CAIFI, MAIFI, SAIFI, and SAIDI.[1] Thus, to effectively measure and regulate reliability, regulators and power system operators must first agree on what reliability means.

Our goal in this chapter is threefold. First, we provide a brief introduction to how a typical integrated electric system works, from a central-station generating plant, to the lamp you are using to read this book. Second, we examine the characteristics of reliability over different time dimensions, because it turns out that reliability when considered over the next minute is quite different than reliability when considered over the next decade. As we discuss, a crucial attribute of reliability over any time frame is that it has characteristics of a *public good*. Third, we discuss the development of regulated markets for reliability and their different attributes, including how those markets interact with other generation markets. As we show, the overall complexity of an integrated electric system increases the complexity of developing reliability markets. Moreover, some of these markets have been created using costing concepts we discussed in Chapters 4 and 5.

---

[1] For descriptions of each of these reliability indices and their use, see H. Lee Willis, *Power Distribution Planning Reference Book* (New York: Marcel Dekker, 1997), 164–83.

12.2 Direct Current Circuits[2]

An integrated electric system consists of generating plants, high-voltage transmission, and local distribution facilities. For consumers, the most obvious characteristic of such systems is how much instantaneous power these systems supply (called *watts*) over time. Hence, most electric bills report consumption in *kilowatt-hours* (kWh). Like water flowing through a garden hose, the amount of power delivered depends on how much pressure is applied (by opening the faucet) and the diameter of the hose.[3] For electricity, the pressure applied is measured by voltage *(volts)*. The electric equivalent to the amount of water that flows through the hose per second is called *current*, which is measured by amperage *(amperes)*. The greater the pressure, the more water can be pushed through.

Power is equivalent to the flow of water through the hose at any moment. If your house catches fire, you will no doubt prefer the fire department arrive with its powerful high-pressure hoses to being left alone to put the flames out with your own garden hose. It is obvious why—the fire department can douse the flames with many more gallons of water per second than you can. Thus, power can be expressed as

$$\text{Power } (W) = I \text{ (current)} \times V \text{ (voltage)} \tag{12-1}$$

where V = volts and I = amperes (amps).[4] The amount of electric energy we consume is based on the amount of power supplied over time. Energy is just the ability to do work, whether it is raising an elevator, pumping water, or driving a car. For example, suppose you have a 20-amp circuit in your home and the voltage on the circuit is 110 volts. Then, the circuit can supply up to $20 \times 110 = 2200$ watts of power. Now suppose you plug in your electric stove, which has a 2400-watt burner. If you turn on the burner, the circuit will not be able to handle the entire load placed on it. The result will be either a "blown" fuse or a "tripped" circuit breaker, both of which are preferable to melting the wire. Continuing our hose analogy, fuses and circuit breakers are the equivalent of a pressure limiter that prevents so much water pushing through that the hose bursts.

---

[2] A basic understanding of how an electric system works provides some context for defining system reliability and in understanding the development of markets to provide it. Parts of this section are based on the following sources: H Wayne Beatty, *Electric Power Distribution Systems: A Nontechnical Guide* (Tulsa, OK: PennWell Publishing, 1998); Frank Graves, *A Primer on Electric Power Flow for Economists and Utility Planners*, Electric Power Research Institute, Report TR-104604, 1995; and Steven Stoft, *Power System Economics: Designing Markets for Electricity* (Piscataway, NJ: IEEE Press/Wiley, 2002).

[3] When we say we apply pressure, we are really discussing a difference in pressure between the two ends of the hose. Unless you happen to live in a vacuum, the pressure on the end of the hose just equals normal atmospheric pressure. Thus, to push water through, the pressure at the faucet must be increased. The difference in pressure between the faucet and the end of the hose is the equivalent of the voltage applied.

[4] The symbol "*W*" is typically used for power, since power is measured in watts.

Another crucial component of the electric power system is *resistance*. Turning once again to the water hose analogy, resistance is the friction of the water moving along the inside of the hose. The greater the friction inside the hose, the larger the hose's resistance to water flow will be. If you increase the pressure too much, the hose will burst. Similarly, resistance in electric circuits creates heat. An incandescent bulb, for example, is a large resistor. If you apply a voltage to it, the filament emits light and heat. But apply too much voltage, and the filament melts. In fact, incandescent bulbs are often lamented because most of the electric energy they use is converted to heat rather than actual visible light. Along any transmission line, some electricity will also be lost in the form of heat. In fact, this is why the earliest power systems did not extend far from generating sources. The power losses were too large if electricity was transferred more than a few miles.

Engineers and physicists are always in search of better *conductors* in which resistance is minimal. A good conductor, such as copper wire, is one in which electrons flow easily.[5] Gold is an excellent conductor, but because of its expense, it obviously is not used in electric wires. Air and rubber, on the other hand, are terrible conductors. For electric systems, the Holy Grail is high-temperature *superconductivity*, in which resistance is zero at ambient temperature. Although much progress has been made toward manufacturing high-temperature superconducting wires, to our knowledge, the technology to maintain superconductivity with significant power flows over long distances does not yet exist.

The simplest type of power is called *direct current* (DC). Figure 12-1 presents a simple representation of a DC electric system, with one generator and one light bulb.

Figure 12-1: A Simple Electric System

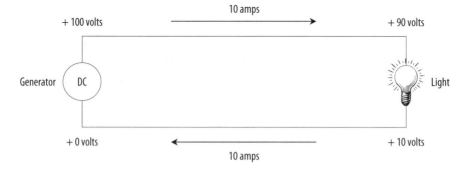

---

[5] Electrons do not really move along a circuit, they simply oscillate in place, jostling their neighbors. The oscillations are propagated along a circuit at close to the speed of light.

The electric system is a closed loop. The generator produces pressure in the form of voltage, which excites the electrons in the conducting wire. The 100 volts applied to the conductor causes a current of 10 amps to flow in a clockwise direction through the wire. Because of resistance along the wire, the voltage at the light bulb falls to 90 volts.[6] The light bulb, being a pure resistor, causes the voltage to drop even further, to just 10 volts. Finally, the voltage drops to zero at the generator site, again because of resistance along the return path to the generator.[7]

It turns out that the amount of current that flows through any electric circuit is directly proportional to how hard the electrons are pushed, and that amount is inversely proportional to how much resistance the electrons face. Mathematically, this can be written as

$$I = V \div R \tag{12-2}$$

where R is resistance. This equation is called *Ohm's Law*, after its creator, Georg Simon Ohm. In his honor, electrical resistance is measured in *ohms*. Recalling our stove example above, if the wire for the circuit is sized too small, the resistance along it will be so great that the heat generated will melt the wire. Circuit breakers and fuses prevent this from happening.[8]

By solving equation (12-2) for V, and substituting into equation (12-1), we can write power W as a function of current and resistance:

$$W = I \times (I \times R) = I^2 R \tag{12-3}$$

Equation (12-3), in fact, explains why electric power is transmitted using large, high-voltage lines. For example, consider our simple electric system in Figure 12-1. Using equation (12-1), we can calculate the power output of the generator. It equals (10 amps) × 100 volts = 1,000 watts, or 1 kW. We can calculate the resistance, R, along the line between the generator and the light bulb using equation (12-2). Thus, $V = I \times R$, or 10 volts = 10 amps × R, implying R

---

[6] One can think of the resistance along the wire as "consuming" part of the generator's output. The power consumption associated with the resistance in the wire is given by equation (12-1). The decrease in voltage from 100 at the generator to 90 at the light bulb is called the *voltage drop*.

[7] Figure 12-1 illustrates *Kirchoff's Laws*. Kirchoff's First Law is that the current flow into any point on a circuit equals the current flow out. (All of the water that goes in one end of the garden hose comes out the other end.) Kirchoff's Second Law is that the voltage drops around any loop sum to zero.

[8] In your home, different circuits may have different amperage limits, called *ratings*. This explains why, when installing a new circuit breaker or fuse, it is important to have a properly rated one. For example, a 20-amp circuit breaker installed on a circuit rated at only 15 amps will allow too much power to flow before "tripping," which could result in melting wires and fire.

= 10 ÷ 10 = 1.0 ohm (Ω). Using equation (12-1), the total power loss between the generator and the light bulb equals 10 volts × 10 amps = 100 watts. So, 10% of the total output of the generator is lost even before it reaches the light bulb.

Next, we modify the generator to produce the same 1 kW amount of power by lowering the current to one amp and increasing the voltage to 1,000 volts as shown in Figure 12-2. Applying Ohm's Law, we can calculate the voltage drop between the generator and the light bulb. Thus, V = 1 amp × 1.0 Ω = 1 volt. So, the voltage drop between the generator and the light bulb in the circuit falls by a factor of 10.

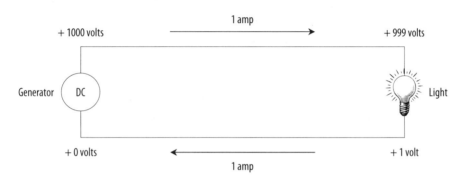

Figure 12-2: Impact of Higher Voltage

The total power loss between the generator and the light bulb was initially 10%. The new power loss is just (1 volt) × (1 amp) = 1 watt. Thus, by increasing the voltage by a factor of 10, the power loss decreases by a factor of 100. In other words, losses decrease by the square of the voltage increase. This is why engineers want to transmit power from generators to local distribution facilities using the highest possible voltages. It also explains why power must be transformed back to a lower voltage level for household use. If we actually put 999 volts through the light bulb, the filament would burn out almost instantly.[9]

There are actually three different types of resistance: *pure resistance* (e.g., the type of resistance that lights an incandescent bulb), *capacitive resistance* (capacitance, i.e., resistance arising from capacitor-like features of wire), and *inductive resistance* (inductance, i.e., resis-

---

[9] Higher voltage is also more dangerous when there is lots of current flowing. Static electricity, such as the little shock you receive touching the doorknob, is actually delivered at levels above 10,000 volts. But the amperage is so small that you are not hurt. Contrast this with a bolt of lighting, with voltage levels in the hundred of millions and amperes of current in the thousands.

tance arising from coil-like features of wire).[10] The latter two forms of resistance play an important role in maintaining electric system reliability, because most electric transmission and distribution systems operate on alternating current (AC).

12.3 Alternating Current Circuits

Edison's initial electric system used DC to distribute power (see Figure 12-1). Because current flows in only one direction, DC is conceptually simple. The problem with DC systems, however, is that they are difficult to manipulate, as, for example, in the case where you would want to change voltages to reduce power system losses. In an AC system, the current switches direction. For example, in the United States, AC switches direction 120 times per second. A complete *cycle* consists of switching direction and then switching back. So, in the United States, the *frequency* of the electric system is 120 ÷ 2 = 60 cycles per second or 60 Hertz.[11]

AC is particularly useful because, unlike DC power, it is easy to change voltages using a simple device called a *transformer*. A transformer is just an iron ring wrapped in two sets of unconnected wires. The reason transformers work can be traced back to the British scientist Michael Faraday, who discovered the relationship between electricity and magnetism. Faraday showed how passing a current through a wire wrapped around an iron bar induces a magnetic field (hence, the term *electromagnet*). Moreover, the reverse holds true as well: placing a conductor in a magnetic field induces a current to flow. The first wire (such as the one coming from the generator) induces a magnetic field in the iron ring, which then induces a current in the second wire. It turns out that the voltage in the second wire is directly proportional to how tightly the second wire is wound around the iron ring relative to the first wire. Using the example in Figures 12-1 and 12-2, to increase (step up) the voltage to 1,000 volts from 100 volts, the second wire needs to be wound 10 times more tightly around the iron ring than the first wire.

---

[10] *Capacitors* are pairs of parallel metal plates that sandwich an insulating material called a *dielectric*. Electric charge accumulates on these plates until, when fully charged, the capacitor discharges much like a dam bursting. The ability to hold charge is called *capacitance*. *Inductors* are coils of wire that create magnetic fields when current passes through them. Remove the current and the magnetic field disintegrates. As it does so, however, it "induces" a brief current in the opposite direction of the original. Thus *induction* is caused by the opening and closing of a DC circuit or the continuous changing of current directions in an AC circuit. A common surge protector that homeowners use to protect computers, televisions, etc., is a type of inductor. Whereas resistors always oppose the flow of electrons through them, inductors oppose *changes* in current through them.

[11] Named after the German physicist, Heinrich Hertz, not the eponymous car-leasing firm. European electric systems typically operate at 50 Hertz.

The difficulty with AC power systems is that, while voltage and current both vary depending on the frequency of the system, they do not vary at the same phase. Thus, current will either "lag" or "lead" voltage, depending on the type of circuit.[12] This can create problems for maintaining the reliability and stability of the electric system, which in turn increases the complexity of ensuring that generators and transmission grid operators are not at cross-purposes.

12.4 Defining Reliability[13]

We turn next to how reliability is defined. The electric industry has been moving steadily toward providing reliability in wholesale (or *bulk power*) electric markets. In particular, wholesale and retail deregulation has led to the creation in the United States of *independent system operators* (ISOs) and *regional transmission organizations* (RTOs). Both types of entities were established in conjunction with FERC's so-called "Standard Market Design" (SMD) efforts. SMD is a set of nationwide rules for market operation. These rules encompass, for example, locational marginal pricing to manage transmission congestion.[14]

The 1965 Northeast blackout prompted the formation of the North American Electric Reliability Council (NERC) in 1968, as well as 10 regional reliability councils whose mission was to coordinate the operations of the many independent electric utilities and, thus, reduce the risk of future blackouts. A few of those regions encompass "power pools," such as one in New England that fully coordinates and dispatches generation. The others oper-

---

[12] Technically, voltage and current are *out of phase*. This occurs because the motors that generate electricity (by moving an aperture arm in and out of a magnetic field) have a property called *reactance*. Moreover, it creates something called *reactive power*. Reactive power does not provide useful work with which to run a motor or light a lamp. But it is quite real, and increases overall energy losses. On the positive side, however, reactive power can provide what is called *voltage support*. As loads draw more power, voltage tends to decrease, which is called *voltage sag*. If voltage and current get too far out of phase, system voltage can collapse, which Stoft describes as, "one of the worst calamities that can befall a power system." See Steven Stoft, *Power System Economics: Designing Markets for Electricity*, supra note 2, 388. For a complete discussion on reactive power, including sample calculations, see Frank Graves, *A Primer on Electric Power Flow for Economists and Utility Planners*, supra note 2.

[13] Portions of this section are adapted from Jonathan Lesser and Guillermo Israilevich, "The Capacity Market Enigma," *Public Utilities Fortnightly* 147 (December 2005), 38–42.

[14] FERC issued its so-called SMD Rule in August 2002. *Remedying Undue Discrimination through Open Access Transmission Service and Standard Electricity Market Design, Notice of Proposed Rulemaking*, Docket No. RM01-12-000, 67 Fed. Reg. 55,452 (Aug. 29, 2002), FERC Stats. & Regs. ¶ 32,563 (2002). By 2005, however, with the development of regional transmission organizations and the concerns expressed by many state regulators, FERC abandoned its national effort. However, as discussed in Section 12.5, *infra*, SMD concepts led to development of competitive markets for installed generating capacity.

ated more loosely. They allowed individual utilities to determine how they dispatched their generating plants, but the pools coordinated operations to ensure the overall system functioned smoothly.

The need for coordinated regional operation of generation gives us insight into the challenges of designing "reliability markets" and helps us to define reliability. In our nonengineering way, we define reliability as <u>the ability to meet the demand for electricity over time, whether during the next 10 minutes or the next 10 years</u>. Typically, the ability to ensure that the electric system can respond to sudden changes in demand or sudden disturbances (such as generator outages or short circuits) is called *system security*. System security requires generating units that can instantaneously increase or decrease their output, be brought on-line, and so forth. These units are generally referred to as *operating reserves*.

Providing reliability also requires *system adequacy*, which is a longer-term planning concept. System adequacy refers to the ability of the electric system to meet the overall demand for electricity at all times in the future, taking into account planned and unplanned outages. Ensuring system adequacy requires sufficient *planning reserves*.

Reliability Standards

As part of its mission in response to the Northeast blackout of 1965, NERC developed voluntary standards for operating and planning the North American Bulk Power System. That system appeared to work well for many years. However, in 1998, two major outages on the west coast of the United States spurred calls for more stringent, and mandatory, reliability standards. Then, on August 14, 2003, a blackout occurred over significant portions of the Midwest, Northeast, and Ontario, Canada. This blackout affected an estimated 50 million people and 61,800 megawatts of electric load. It was caused by several entities' failures to follow NERC's existing operating policies.[15]

It was not until passage of the Energy Policy Act of 2005 (EPAct 2005), however, that mandatory reliability standards were required to be developed and applied to the operators of the nation's bulk power transmission system. In July 2006, NERC was certified by

---

[15] A discussion of the causes of the 2003 blackout, as well as recommendations to improve system reliability and prevent future blackouts, can be found in *Final Report on the August 14, 2003 Blackout in the United States and Canada: Causes and Recommendations*, U.S.-Canada Power System Outage Task Force, April 5, 2004.

FERC to be the Electric Reliability Organization (ERO). ERO will be responsible for developing and enforcing these mandatory reliability standards in the United States, and FERC will be required to approve those standards.[16]

Ancillary Services

Ensuring reliability also requires that power system operators provide a host of services in addition to actual power. Several of these services, including some which ensure that power systems maintain stable frequency and voltages, arise from the purely physical and engineering requirements that are necessary to provide consumers with electricity on demand. Frequency and voltage control are moment-to-moment services that are required at all times.

Another important engineering service is *transmission security*. Recalling our garden hose analogy in Section 12.2, if too much water pressure is applied, the hose will burst. Similarly, too much electrical pressure, in other words, voltage, can cause a transmission line to overheat and sag. A transmission line that sags too much can create havoc if it encounters another line or a nearby tree.[17] Moreover, overused lines can melt. Transmission security measures ensure that, should such events occur, the affected lines are immediately removed from service.

In addition to these purely engineering-based ancillary services, system operators provide several economic services. Among these are *economic dispatch* and *trading enforcement*. Economic dispatch minimizes the overall cost of providing power to consumers by using (dispatching) those generators with the lowest marginal production costs to meet consumer demand. Trading enforcement is an accounting service. It is needed because electrons cannot be tagged like salmon. Once a generator injects power onto the grid, that electricity obeys the laws of physics, not legal contracts. As a consequence, there is no physical way to trace whose generation went where. To address this problem and ensure that markets function, system operators trace all of the injections and withdrawals from the power grid and match them with contract agreements.[18]

---

[16] In 2006, FERC issued a Notice of Proposed Rulemaking (NOPR) accepting many of the reliability standards proposed by ERO. *See Mandatory Reliability Standards for the Bulk-Power System*, Docket No. RM06-16-000. On March 16, 2007, FERC finalized 83 reliability standards in this docket.

[17] In fact, inadequate tree trimming near transmission lines was a major cause of the August 2003 blackout.

[18] For example, suppose you contract with a generator to deliver 100 MW of power around-the-clock next week. Unless you are physically unplugged from the electric system, or the entire system is not operating, you will receive that power. However, the generator may only inject 50 MW of power onto the grid. The only way to determine that is through after-the-fact evaluation.

Reliability as a Public Good

As the previous discussion illustrates, there are a number of services the transmission system operator provides to ensure system reliability. Given all of the coordination required to ensure the electric system operates well, or even operates whatsoever, we can ask whether it even makes sense to discuss a "market" for reliability. Our answer is "yes," but with some qualification. After all, system reliability is not simply a tradable commodity like wheat; it is, instead, a *public good*.

First, reliability has two characteristics in common with public goods. These are *nonexclusivity* and *nonrivalry* in consumption. Nonexclusivity in consumption means that reliability for one is reliability for all. Nonrivalry in consumption means that the operating decisions made for an individual generating unit may create *spillovers* that have both good and bad effects on others. By his activity, the transmission line owner who diligently trims trees produces benefits for all users on interconnected transmission system, not just those whose electricity flows through that one owner's line. More importantly, as was the case with the northeastern U.S./Canada blackout of August 2003, the transmission line owner who fails to trim trees adequately can impose significant costs on others. As with all public goods, left to their own, individual suppliers will not provide enough system reliability, because they cannot reap the full economic benefits of doing so. They would rather "free ride" on other suppliers' investments. This is a typical characteristic of public goods: nonexclusivity means that someone who does not pay can still consume the public good just as much as someone who does. As a result, no one has an incentive to invest; after all, why invest when you can "free ride" on the good deeds of others?

12.5 Reliability and Installed Capacity Markets

One of the most controversial elements associated with deregulation of wholesale electric markets has been the need to ensure there is sufficient generating capacity to meet customer demand in peak hours, both from the standpoint of short-term system security and, in the long term, from the standpoint of system adequacy. To understand the controversy, we must first distinguish between electric *capacity* and electric *energy*. Capacity is the ability to instantaneously supply energy. Thus, it is the same as power. Energy, as we discussed above, is the ability to do work. Assuming a generator is connected to the power grid, it provides both capacity and energy. To ensure reliable electric service, transmission planners want to ensure that there are sufficient quantities of both at all times. Thus, planners want to ensure the electrical equivalent of sufficient fire hoses (capacity) that can pump enough water (energy) to put out as many fires as might burn simultaneously (demand). Moreover, planners want to have redundancies in the system in case a hose or two bursts unexpectedly.

In theory, in a fully deregulated wholesale electric market, generators ought to provide sufficient energy to meet customer demand at all times. In practice, however, the public good nature of reliability makes this unlikely. To understand why, consider Figure 12-3, which presents a stylized load-duration curve.

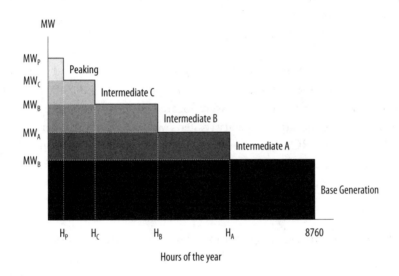

Figure 12-3: Load Duration Curve and Generating Resources

Over the 8,760 hours of the year, loads vary. For a very few hours, H_P hours in Figure 12-3, the demand for electricity is extremely high, at MW_P. During those few hours, it is necessary to run peaking units, such as combustion turbines and diesel engines. These generators have very high operating costs, since they are typically older, less fuel-efficient units that require significant maintenance. For a total of ($H_C - H_P$) hours, total demand is MW_C. During these hours of the year, a number of "Intermediate C" units are operating. Even though they are less costly than peaking units, these generators are still fairly expensive to operate. Similarly, we have drawn two additional classes of intermediate generators and, lastly, baseload generators. These supply energy round-the-clock for the entire year.

Maintaining system reliability means having sufficient generation and reserves (in case of unplanned generator outages, short circuits caused by squirrels or other fierce creatures gnawing at wires, and so forth) during every hour of the year. That is unlikely to be a challenge when demand is quite low, such as in the middle of the night. This requires that the owners of the least-used generators be kept financially whole so that their capacity is available. However, in some years, loads may never reach the levels where those peaking units are needed to run. Still, those units provide a valuable service in reserve, much like an insurance policy. Thus, the question arises as to what price owners ought to be paid.

Before electric industry restructuring in the United States, the costs of these plants were folded into utilities' cost of service. But, with industry restructuring, many of these units became components of unregulated wholesale generators. Because transmission systems typically span multiple states, the prices at which wholesale generators can sell energy and capacity in the United States are governed by FERC. As we discussed in Chapter 9, FERC established a procedure by which generators could apply to sell *energy* at market-based rates. Capacity, however, continued to be priced based on cost-of-service standards.

As wholesale energy markets developed, some generation owners found they could not earn enough revenue to justify maintaining a number of older, less-efficient generating plants. However, because some of these plants were located in areas that were woefully short of transmission and local generating capacity (called *load pockets*), they could not be allowed to shut down. Therefore, FERC created a contractual mechanism called a *reliability must run* (RMR) agreement to keep those generators needed to maintain system reliability. RMR agreements provide a guaranteed revenue base, much like a price floor in an agricultural support policy.

An RMR designation prevents a generation owner from shutting down generating units needed to maintain the integrity—the reliability—of the entire regional power grid. RMR ensures such owners are adequately compensated for providing that regional benefit. Rather than being compensated based on the dictates of supply and demand, however, the prices paid to generators under RMR agreements are based on cost of service in much the same way as regulated local utilities' cost-of-service filings are made with their state regulators.

This began to change as part of FERC's (ultimately failed) push for Standard Market Design (SMD). SMD was based on the view that market solutions could provide resource adequacy and security more efficiently than traditional cost-of-service arrangements. The goal was to ensure both system security and system adequacy by providing opportunities for existing generators to earn enough money to remain in the market and for new generation to enter the market, especially in areas where there was insufficient local transmission capacity. FERC wished to create localized markets within power pools to further enhance the incentives of generators to locate in constrained areas. This objective led to regulatory efforts to create *locational installed capacity markets* (LICAP) and address short-term and long-term *Reliability Compensation Issues*. Short-term Reliability Compensation Issues relate to the appropriate compensation for units that are needed for reliability, but they are subject to mitigation in the energy market and, therefore, may not earn enough money to continue operating. Long-term Reliability Compensation Issues relate to local capacity shortages identified in the relevant market's reliability-based planning process.

When energy prices are capped, something regulators have argued is necessary to combat market power, generation developers wishing to build new peaking capacity may be reluctant to invest, and the price spikes they count on will be reduced, increasing the financial risk of such projects. More importantly, banks that are asked to finance such investments will be less likely to provide the necessary capital and, if they do agree to provide financing, will charge higher interest rates. As a result, if new peaking units are not built at all, overall prices paid by retail customers in the energy market may increase.[19] Moreover, regulatory changes to wholesale market structures can increase uncertainty and retard new investment.[20] Finally, the "lumpy" nature of capacity investments, especially in capacity-constrained areas, can create additional revenue uncertainty. If the generator builds new capacity, energy prices in the local area may decline so far that the generator will be unable to recover its costs, thus creating a Catch-22 situation.[21]

Thus, short of a guaranteed schedule of sabotage, generation developers are likely to avoid such a constrained region, even though, from a broader market perspective, that is precisely where they ought to build. The answer to this paradox lies in the inability of generators to rely on high energy prices to finance investments. In other words, you cannot rely on a lack of reliability. It is just too risky given the inherent volatility of electric markets, the often-occurring phenomena of regulatory and political intervention, and other market imperfections.

---

[19] Of course, price caps are not the only risk facing potential generation developers. Many state regulators have become increasingly concerned about who will build new baseload generation. Continued industry restructuring, market uncertainties, and changing environmental regulations have increased risk and created an investment climate where developers and banks want signed, long-term contracts with utilities before breaking ground. In this environment, utilities and other retail providers are reluctant to enter into long-term contracts because of the regulatory and market risks such contracts pose.

[20] This is another reason why regulatory certainty is critical when establishing any new market, whether for generating capacity or air pollution permits: investors need to know the market rules that will apply and be confident that those rules will not change in a way that increases their downside financial risk.

[21] From an economic standpoint, the generator is facing a downward sloping demand curve, rather than a single price, as in a purely competitive market.

The solution to these dilemmas has been to provide distinct installed capacity payments, or their equivalent, to generators.[22] Because installed capacity provides reliability (both short-term and long-term), which is a public good, market forces alone will provide too little of it, regardless of whether generation markets are fully deregulated or fully regulated.

FERC's market-based solution for installed capacity markets has been to encourage transmission system operators to create such markets. Different regional transmission operators in New England, New York, and the Midwest have all adopted slightly different approaches. For example, starting in 2003, the New York ISO began developing a set of three downward sloping demand curves for installed capacity in separate transmission zones: New York City, Long Island, and the Rest of State (ROS). The parameters of each demand curve are determined by the target level of installed capacity, which is based on a forecast of peak loads during the year and the projected cost to construct a new peaking generator in that transmission zone.[23]

Figure 12-4, for example, presents the demand curves for the winter 2006 period. The dollar values for each demand curve at the point equal to 100% of the capacity requirement are based on an estimate of the capital cost of building new peaking generation, as levelized over the expected lifetime of such a plant.[24] (The levelization calculation is similar to a typical fixed mortgage payment calculation.) The capacity level itself is based on forecast peak demand plus a specified operating reserve of capacity. This operating reserve is determined by the NYISO's engineering boffins using complex transmission models that determine whether a breakdown of generating units or loss of certain transmission circuits will lead to an inability to meet customer demand (and, hence, a blackout).[25] Beyond this level, the marginal value of new capacity decreases, since a surfeit of existing capacity means the marginal value of additional capacity, from the standpoint of further reducing the likelihood of outages, decreases. For New York City and Long Island, the NYISO determines that once

---

[22] Some regional transmission organizations (RTOs) have developed what are called *forward capacity markets* to ensure sufficient reliability. These markets are similar to forward markets for other commodities; they provide guaranteed capacity at contracted-for times in the future.

[23] Details of the market, including how the NYISO estimates the need for installed capacity, and the rules for the auction that determine the market-clearing prices, can be found at the NYISO Website: www.nyiso.org/public/products/icap/index.jsp. NYISO adjusts the capacity slightly to account for forced outages. Thus, a generator that proffers a 100-MW plant with a forced outage rate of 5% is deemed to provide $100 \times (1 - 0.05) = 95$ MW of *unforced capacity* (UCAP).

[24] The cost estimate is developed based on a set of assumptions, including the cost of siting, turbines, fixed O&M costs, and so forth. Most importantly, the levelized cost depends on project financing assumptions, including both capital structure, the cost of debt and, most controversially, the required return on equity for the hypothetical plant's owners.

[25] Typically, planners adopt a standard of one outage every 10 years, called a *loss of load probability*. This standard is ad hoc, because it is extremely difficult to measure how much consumers value a reduced likelihood of power outages.

existing generating capacity increases more than 18% over the amount needed to meet its reliability standard, additional capacity has no additional value. For the ROS, the value of capacity beyond a 12% surplus has no additional value. The difference in these two threshold values is the result of more transmission paths that can provide electricity to customers in the ROS, versus the limited avenues available into New York City and Long Island.

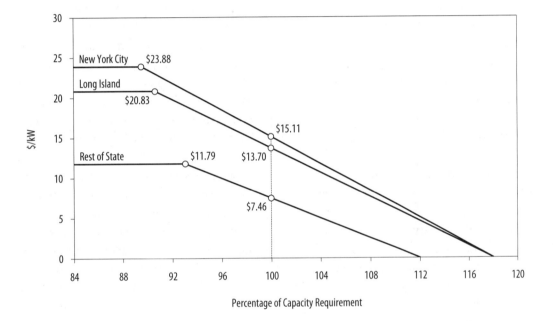

Figure 12-4: NYISO Locational Capacity Demand Curves

Source: NYISO.

The price ceilings shown in Figure 12-4 are the result of several factors. In theory, the price ceilings are set such that the ebb and flow of capacity over time will provide the owner of new generation with just the level of compensation required to earn a return comparable with the business and financial risks of development, much as under a standard cost-of-service rate regime. In practice, these ceilings are a political compromise between reluctant generators and wary consumers.[26]

---

[26] The development of similar demand curves in New England was the subject of intense litigation, in which one of the authors provided testimony. The litigation ultimately resulted in rejection of the entire approach and adoption of a forward capacity market. That market is set to emerge fully in 2010. Interested readers may wish to consult the FERC Website, www.ferc.gov, and search through the voluminous materials in *Devon Power, LLC, et al.*, Docket No. ER03-563-030.

12.6 International Capacity Markets

Capacity markets have also been developed internationally; some exist in countries that restructured their electricity markets long before the first restructuring efforts in the United States. The electricity markets of Chile, England and Wales (E&W), and Argentina included capacity payments by the early 1990s.

Restructuring in E&W resulted in a virtual duopoly between National Power and PowerGen, with a competitive fringe of state-owned nuclear power plants, Scottish companies, Electricité de France, and other IPPs. National Power and PowerGen took over most of the existing fossil fuel power stations and set market prices more than 80% of the time. The price paid to all generators included the system marginal price and a capacity payment. The capacity payment was expected to provide a market signal to generators for new generation capacity. Generators had to declare capacity available for each half-hour period. The system operator calculated the capacity payment based on the probability of supply interruptions. The more capacity declared available, the lower the capacity payment.

Generators, however, exploited a loophole in this market design. By reducing the amount of capacity they declared to be "available capacity," they were able to raise prices. Since that additional capacity was actually available, the calculated capacity payments did not reflect actual supply scarcity. Electricity prices proved to be volatile, and in March 2001, the pool was abandoned in favor of the New Electricity Trading Arrangements (NETA). National Power and PowerGen reduced their installed capacity, while electricity sales kept growing year after year. The Office of Electricity Regulation charged National Power and PowerGen with manipulating prices through the capacity payment. PowerGen admitted manipulating the capacity payment by reducing the declared capacity available, and then, after the capacity payment was calculated, by reoffering additional capacity.

Many Latin American countries, including Chile, Argentina, Peru, and Bolivia, successfully restructured their electricity markets and attracted new investments by adding fixed capacity charges to the revenues generators obtained from energy prices. In these markets, energy prices are basically determined by the fuel cost of the marginal unit (not by suppliers' bids). Without the opportunity to obtain meaningful energy revenues above their variable costs, capacity payments are necessary so that peaking units can recover their fixed capital expenditures. These payments are generally based on the estimated replacement cost of an efficient peaking unit, and they are added to energy prices during peak hours. In some cases, capacity charges were meant to attract sufficient investment. In Argentina, for example, generous capacity charges attracted surplus capacity and reduced energy prices—sometimes below fuel costs.[27]

Wholesale electricity markets in Australia and the Nordic countries do not rely on capacity markets. Australia's national wholesale market opened in 1998 with just New South Wales and Victoria; other regions have joined since then. This market relies on a spot energy market with an AU$10,000 bid cap and an integrated financial forward market.[28] In addition, the system operator, the National Electricity Market Management Company (NEMMCO), performs medium-term and short-term projected assessments of system adequacy processes. This program of information collection and disclosure of security prospects is designed to help market participants make decisions about supply, demand, and outages of transmission networks. However, NEMMCO is also entitled to implement an escalating series of market interventions, mostly though reserve contracts, in order to guarantee power system security.

The reforms in Australia are widely considered to have delivered considerable economic benefits. With stable forward prices and new investments in capacity, Australia has not experienced the wholesale price volatility observed in regional U.S. markets. In this context, political and regulatory intervention has not been necessary. The million dollar question is whether intervention will surface when sustained prices reach AU$10,000. Similarly, regulators in South America understand that system reliability is a public good and that capacity payments are necessary because capped energy revenues do not attract sufficient investment. Whether these models will provide sufficient incentives for new generation investment remains to be seen.

---

[27] *See, e.g.*, Robert Wilson, "Architecture of Power Markets," *Econometrica* 70, no. 4 (July 2002); and Pedro J. Ferreira, "On the Efficiency of the Argentinean Electricity Wholesale Market" (Ph.D. dissertation, University of Chicago, 2002).

[28] Approximately 7,700 U.S. dollars at 2006 exchange rates.

12.7 Chapter Summary

Because electricity cannot be stored cost-effectively, highly complex, integrated power systems have been developed to meet the needs of consumers. These systems are designed to adapt instantaneously to constantly fluctuating demand, and they incorporate multiple redundancies to minimize the likelihood of blackouts. Those design attributes ultimately define electric reliability. Although reliability has multiple dimensions, it hinges on short-term system security and long-term system adequacy. Most importantly, reliability is a public good. As a result, even wholly unregulated energy markets will provide too little reliability, and separate mechanisms are needed, whether cost- or market-based, especially for installed capacity.

CHAPTER 13
REGULATION AND REFORM IN INTERNATIONAL MARKETS

13.1 Introduction

An extensive worldwide privatization movement began in the 1980s. Many governments that had failed dismally to efficiently manage their utilities decided to relinquish this responsibility to private companies. The United Kingdom led the way early in the decade. The Thatcher government realized that Britain's state-owned industries, created in a wave of nationalization after World War II, were hemorrhaging money because of bloated payrolls and the absence of any market incentives whatsoever. After the government determined its control was neither desirable nor necessary to the provision of reliable utility services, it privatized the industry. The government created 39 new UK companies by floating shares between 1979 and 1992.[1] Facing similar problems, many other countries privatized their utility industries as well. Between 1988 and 1993, roughly 2,700 state-owned enterprises were privatized in more than 95 countries, raising over $270 billion in private capital.[2]

Today, privatization is generally recognized as a crucial component of efforts to improve economic development and utility services—and to improve government balance sheets. Privatization has raised funds for governments, increased capital investment, created competitive markets, and reduced the government's role in the industry. In turn, those efforts have improved operating efficiencies, widened share ownership, and made use of market forces to improve the availability and reliability of electric and natural gas services.

The form of privatization varies in different countries and is defined in major part by the particular legal system that is in place. In some countries, such as Argentina, the federal government completely removed itself from the operation of the utility industry but retained ownership of the assets by giving private firms the concession of those assets for a

---

[1] David M. Newberry, *Privatization, Restructuring, and Regulation of Network Utilities* (Cambridge, MA: MIT Press, 1999), 13.

[2] U.S. Energy Information Administration, *Privatization and the Globalization of Energy Markets*, October 1996, 4.

certain period of time. In other countries, such as Guatemala, the government continues to share ownership with private companies and forms private-public partnerships and other arrangements.

13.2 Transition Mechanisms

Transforming state-owned utilities into well-functioning private companies is not for the faint of heart. Typically, governments need to enact legislation setting up the necessary regulatory frameworks. Recall that, as we discussed in Chapter 4, regulated utilities in the United States operate under a so-called *regulatory compact*, which has been developed and defined over many decades by a body of laws, rules, orders, and contracts, rather than any one piece of legislation. Imagine, then, the difficulty of suddenly having to develop an entirely new regulatory framework without the benefit of past legislation and case law. Moreover, creating such frameworks from scratch also requires educating new regulators, who will require a solid grounding in potentially arcane concepts, such as those we discussed in previous chapters. Not for nothing, therefore, has the regulatory process in some countries where privatization has taken place been erratic and error-prone. For example, the natural gas regulator in Argentina missed the deadline to come up with a uniform system of accounts for the regulated companies in 1995. The regulator thought that existing Argentine GAAP was enough. This lack of regulatory accounting caused problems a year later during the first tariff review. The regulator then enacted a new system of regulatory accounts in 2000, potentially correcting the problems for the next tariff review.[3, 4]

To achieve privatization, new legislation was implemented at the same time that the industry in which one or more state-owned companies providing services was restructured. The electric industry was typically segmented into generation, transmission, and distribution. Power plants were privatized as stand-alone companies or in generation companies. In some cases, such as Great Britain, transmission functions were spun off into one or more companies. In other cases, such as Panama, the government has continued its ownership. Finally, in most countries, electric distribution companies have been regionalized. A

---

[3] Ente Nacional Regulador del Gas (Enargas), Resolution N° 1660/2000 (March 31, 2000), Argentina.

[4] We use the word "potentially" because "Emergency" legislation enacted by the new government in Argentina on January 6, 2002, unilaterally eliminated the existing regulatory compact and imposed a price freeze in all regulated activities. *See* Ley de Emergencia Pública y Reforma del Régimen Cambiario, Law N° 25,561 (January 6, 2002), Argentina. As a result, numerous lawsuits against the government of Argentina were filed in international arbitration courts. Most of these suits are still ongoing as of the date of printing of this book. Very few concession contracts have been renegotiated, and only a few selected tariffs have been allowed to increase from their frozen peso levels (even though between January of 2002 and December of 2006 the currency depreciated to one-third of its value and accumulated inflation was 50%).

similar pattern has been observed in the natural gas industry where, with a few exceptions in those countries that have privatized that industry, transportation and distribution have been separated into distinct companies.

Once legislation was enacted and state-owned companies restructured, the private sector was allowed either to own or operate those companies through different mechanisms. In some countries, this was accomplished by floating shares in the state-owned companies. Other countries sold blocks of shares in tenders to prequalified bidders. In still others, the government signed direct contracts with private operators.[5] This step sometimes created havoc because the conditions of the state-owned companies were far better known by the government that sold them than by potential buyers. Thus, the specter of buying a pig-in-the-poke has always been real, leading to lower sale prices.[6] For example, some of the less desirable power plants offered for sale in Argentina received bids below the government minimums.[7] At the same time, the lack of complete information, in addition to other factors such as the different perceptions of bidders as to how many efficiencies can be adopted, allowed some governments to reap very profitable sales prices.

13.3 Alternative Privatization Arrangements

The participation of the private sector in regulated industries has been made possible not only through formal privatization efforts (drafting laws, restructuring the industry, tendering assets, etc.), but also through a number of alternative approaches, including public-private partnerships (PPPs). Under a PPP, a private company signs a contract with the government to variously build, operate, lease, transfer, and/or own certain assets. Regulation, therefore, is by contract. The government and the private company enter into an agreement establishing a set of rules that determines the tariffs or regulated prices to be paid either by the government or customers. Thus, companies that are regulated by contract also operate under a type of regulatory compact with the government. This compact allowed companies to recover "prudently incurred" operating and capital costs while serving the public.

---

[5] While governments tried to achieve efficiency by bringing private operators into public services, and one of the most widely used justifications for this was that state-owned companies could not achieve those efficiencies on their own, it was ironic that state-owned companies from abroad were allowed to participate in the tender process and were awarded concessions in some countries.

[6] There are rumors that there have been "sweetheart" deals between the government and favored private investors in which the government appears to remain a "silent" partner. For example, a number of commentators have suggested this has been the case in Russia. (Timothy L. O'Brien and Steven Lee Myers, "Kremlin and Russia Inc Realign after Yukos Trial," *New York Times*, June 14, 2005.)

[7] Carlos Bastos and Manuel Abdala, "Reform of the Electric Power Sector in Argentina," *Buenos Aires* (1993): 113.

Unlike private contracts, a public-private partnership is a risk-sharing business model in which the government and one or more private companies jointly provide services or goods. PPPs often form when a project requires a massive investment to establish the necessary infrastructure and because either the government or private firms (or both) lack the expertise, financial resources, and incentives to undertake such projects by themselves. Typically, the private sector participates in the construction of infrastructure, and the government provides financial guarantees and operating expertise.

Over the last few decades, there has been a significant increase in PPPs all over the world for new motorways, bridges, power and water plants, and airports.[8] PPPs themselves can take many forms, including Build, Lease and Transfer (BLT); Build, Operate and Transfer (BOT); Build, Own and Operate (BOO); and so forth. For example, under a BOT arrangement, the infrastructure asset is designed, financed, operated, and maintained by the private body for a predetermined period of time. At the end of this period, the ownership of the infrastructure asset is transferred to the government. Under a BOT arrangement, the private owners earn a rate of return for assuming the financial risks of building and operating the facility. However, the rate of return will not necessarily be fixed. Instead, similar to price-cap regulation, although the private firm that signed the BOT agreement might have a cap on expenses and a fixed rate of return, such companies typically sign an operating agreement with their holding companies abroad at the same capped expenses, and the overall rate of return for the consolidated entity will depend on its economic efficiency throughout the whole BOT process (operating the BOT company and operating the holding company abroad providing services to the BOT company).

> **Incentives from the Bidding Process in the Natural Gas Industry in Mexico**
>
> Until 1995, transport, storage, and distribution of natural gas in Mexico were provided only by the state-owned company, Petróleos Mexicanos (Pemex). With privatization, the government regulator, the Comisión Reguladora de Energía (CRE) introduced a series of laws and orders (called *Directivas*). Under these regulations, natural gas transmission and distribution tariffs are set using a revenue yield mechanism. This mechanism calculates the maximum average rate at the beginning of the five-year regulatory period. Each year, the maximum rate is modified through a revenue cap formula that includes a measure of inflation and an efficiency factor.
>
> As of 2006, there were a total of 21 regional natural gas distribution companies with permits to operate. Most of these companies had obtained their permits through a tender process in which the amount paid by the winner was determined by the regulator beforehand. Companies would then submit their offers with the average maximum rate they would be willing to accept. The company bidding the lowest average maximum rate was selected as the best offer.

---

[8] The first known example of a BOT contract was signed in 1834 for construction of the Suez Canal. *See, e.g.,* Sidney M. Levy, *Build Operate Transfer* (New York: John Wiley & Sons, 1996), 19.

The average maximum rates used to select the winning bidders were calculated with projected cost data for that company's first five years of operation. At the end of the fifth year, a new average maximum rate is calculated, using projected cost data for the next five-year period. Additionally, the regulators estimate a K factor that adjusts the average tariffs to increase (decrease) revenues if the revenues in the previous five-year period were below (above) the expected revenues.

This regulatory approach created a tremendous incentive for bidders to underestimate the average maximum rates they would accept for the first five years of operation. Additionally, a bidder could expect that its new average maximum rate after years 2 and 4 would be adjusted for an average revenue shortfall (or windfall) based on the K factor the regulators estimated if average revenues were below (above) initial expectations.

Once the first tariff review was finished, in fact, there were substantial increases in the average maximum tariffs. Table 13-1 shows the increases for each of the distributors (only one shows a decrease) that were obtained by dividing the new average maximum tariff by the previous average maximum tariff adjusted by inflation. The average increase was 88%.

Table 13-1: Increase in Average Maximum Tariffs for Mexican Natural Gas Distributors

Company	Region	Increase (%)
Repsol México, S.A. de C.V.	Saltillo-Ramos Arizpe-Arteaga	52.44
Repsol México, S.A. de C.V.	Región Metropolitana de Toluca	526.70
México, S.A. de C.V.	Nuevo Laredo	75.12
DGN de Chihuahua S.R.L. de C.V.	Chihuahua	298.89
DGN de Mexicali, S.R.L. de C.V.	Mexicali	582.77
Gas Natural de México (GNM-Repsol)	Monterrey	-5.28
Compañía Mexicana de Gas, S.A. de C.V.	Monterrey	91.02
Compañía Nacional de Gas, S.A. de C.V.	Piedras Negras	-17.15
Gas Natural de Juárez, S.A. de C.V	Ciudad Juárez	76.76
Tamauligas, S.A. de C.V	Norte de Tamauligas	442.58
NORAM-GUSTA	Rio Pánuco	123.90
Consorcio Mexi-Gas, S.A. de C.V	Valle Cuautitlán - Texcoco	184.28
Distribuidora de Gas Querétaro	Querétaro	249.36
Distribuidora de Gas Natural de Jalisco	Guadalajara	871.27
Distribuidora de Gas de Occidente	Cananea	51.33

Source: Authors' calculations based on data from CRE Resolutions.

13.4 Establishing the Regulatory Framework

As we noted earlier, one of the most vexing problems associated with privatizing government-owned and operated electric and natural gas companies has been establishing entirely new regulatory frameworks. To do this, countries generally have adopted an intermediate position between two different approaches for setting regulated rates. One of these has been the U.S. approach, which uses historical costs and known and measurable changes for the next regulatory period. The other has been the British approach, which uses cost projections. Regardless of the types of regulatory frameworks adopted, however, the new regulatory agencies and regulated companies have relied on legal precedents established under both systems and have later used precedents from other countries that followed the UK in the privatization wave.[9]

Although the new regulatory frameworks were established with high hopes of success, many failed to include or even anticipate all of the provisions needed to ensure that success. Moreover, some countries created conflicting provisions in their new regulatory frameworks that inevitably led to regulatory disputes. And, in many cases, because they lacked both the experience and the preparation to resolve disputes fairly and efficiently, regulators often wrongly decided against their newly created private companies.[10]

As we discussed in Chapter 3 and Chapter 10, regulatory uncertainty can harm any private company's financial well-being by lowering credit ratings, raising its cost of debt, and reducing the incentive for new capital investment. In countries with newly established regulatory mechanisms, however, the adverse impacts of poor regulatory decisions are magnified, especially in countries with dodgy legal systems and weak or nonindependent avenues of appeal. Regulatory uncertainty and its impacts have been especially severe in countries where regulators have not been truly independent or where regulators have viewed themselves more as consumer advocates, rather than as independent judicial bodies.

13.5 Renegotiation and Change

In a number of countries that privatized their electric and natural gas industries, the initial years of euphoria gave way to grievance and recrimination, both on the part of private entities and the governments that created them. Private companies, for example, have often complained that their contracts needed renegotiation, because of lack of results, changes in forecast conditions, or claims that other parties (chiefly, governments) did not comply with certain commitments.[11] In some cases, negotiations effectively changed the entire regulatory framework that was first envisioned. In other cases, governments themselves initiated changes to the regimes they created. For example, in some countries, newly privatized firms' promises of infrastructure investments never materialized, prompting review by regulatory authorities and renegotiation of contracts. In other cases, governments initiated changes

---

[9] Unlike the U.S., British legal precedent extends back only to the early 1980s, when privatization began.

[10] Many of these failures occurred in Latin America, where countries typically follow civil code procedures, in contrast to countries like the U.S., where common law procedures and respect for private property rights are the rule.

[11] We are not providing an opinion if the private operators' claims were reasonable.

because of a desire to enact broader structural or macroeconomic reforms. Most, but not all, of these cases have been settled amicably. For instance, some of the conditions demanded by the government of Argentina in its long renegotiation process after enacting unilateral changes at the beginning of 2002 (which is still ongoing as we write this in 2007) are of the "take it or leave it" nature. In such cases, the likelihood of adequate compensation for the affected firms is slight.

Another common problem has been disputes arising after the initial regulatory honeymoon. In many countries, these disputes have typically arisen in conjunction with rate reviews. Whereas some countries have used American and British regulatory precedents to resolve these disputes, others have either negotiated settlements with regulated companies or unilaterally imposed their own solutions. Not surprisingly, the latter approach has resulted in additional appeals. Of course, the success of such appeals has often hinged on the underlying legal frameworks in which they have been made; the more mercurial the government, the less likely it is that the appeals have succeeded.

Still another problem that has arisen with privatization has been the emergence, by election or otherwise, of new governments that have felt no obligation to honor agreements reached by their predecessors. In some cases, the new governments brought new ideas they wished to implement in regulated markets, or they believed that previous governments had implemented reforms incorrectly. More frequently, however, governments have resorted to populist appeals, unilaterally implementing new regulatory frameworks to "protect" citizens from "rapacious" utilities accused of reaping windfall profits.[12] Changes were implemented by negotiating with regulated companies through new legislation and regulatory orders and, in the most extreme cases, renationalization. Not surprisingly, such populist moves further damaged the electric and natural gas industries by increasing the wariness of new firms to enter markets, as well as the ability of existing firms to finance new investment or even continue operations.

13.6 International Arbitration

While a country's domestic investors can fall victim to the whims of government-imposed regulatory changes, foreign investors have other avenues of appeal when a government lacks an independent, or even functioning, judiciary. Countries that have undertaken privatization in order to gain access to foreign capital typically have been required to sign Bilateral

---

[12] One does not need to look at a developing country for an example of this type of unilateral government measure. The British government implemented a windfall profits tax in 1997, clawing back £5.2 billion on past profits achieved by privatized utilities. Lucy Chennells, "The Windfall Tax," *Fiscal Studies* 18 (1997): 284.

Investment Treaties (BITs). BITs provide additional guarantees to foreign investors, who can lodge appeals in a number of international venues.[13] Litigation typically starts with the private investor requesting remedy (either for expropriation, unfair treatment, or other claims).[14]

> **Argentina's Currency Devaluation**
>
> In January 2002, Argentina passed the Economic Emergency Law, which de-dollarized rates and prices in existing utility concession contracts and froze those rates at their peso levels. Next, the country allowed the exchange rate of the peso to float against the dollar, rather than maintaining its previous fixed exchange rate. As the peso's value crumbled, the dollar revenues of the utilities declined by 33%, and this caused the utilities to default on their debt obligations—the majority of which were in U.S. dollars.
>
> Many investment banks that lent funds to the Argentine utilities had purchased Political Risk Insurance (PRI) policies in case of expropriation or other government actions that caused just such defaults. As a result of the peso devaluation and rate freeze, they filed claims with those insurance companies to collect the defaulted amounts. The insurance companies demurred, claiming that the defaults were simply normal business risks resulting from currency devaluation. The cases have been extensively litigated, mainly at the London Courts of International Arbitration (LCIA).

13.7 Chapter Summary

The privatization wave in the 1980s and 1990s, as well as alternative private-public partnerships, reformed international energy markets and created a diverse set of regulatory regimes. In their infancy, however, many of these regimes were ill-defined. That, together with the inexperience of newly minted regulators, led to numerous regulatory disputes whose outcome has, in some cases, refined the regulatory compact, and in others, thoroughly undermined faith in the regulated industries. In countries where the latter occurred, a collapse in new infrastructure investment soon followed.

The robustness and success of any regulatory reform, and the new economic and regulatory frameworks that emerge, can be judged only in the long term. Whether such judgments are made based on a series of tariff reviews or operation of newly competitive markets,

---

[13] Even without BITs, contracts that have awarded regulator concessions and infrastructure projects awarded by contracts often contain specific clauses allowing referees or international tribunals to solve disputes. These international courts include the International Court for Settlement of Investment Disputes (ICSID) and the International Chamber of Commerce (ICC), and tribunals formed under the auspices of the United Nations Commission on International Trade Law (UNCITRAL).

[14] Governments typically dispute the jurisdiction, claiming that domestic courts should handle all disputes.

spot judgments can undo, and unfortunately have undone, new regimes. However, whereas there are many examples of international problems that have led to extensive legal disputes (which in some cases have been resolved only through international arbitration),[15] the overall pattern has been one of success. In numerous countries, significant benefits have been realized because the private sector has been able to achieve market efficiencies that state-owned companies could not. Yet, even some of these successful regimes have suffered from the waning commitments of diverse political parties that have reached power. That, unfortunately, has increased regulatory risk and harmed consumers.

---

[15] Additional disputes among countries have heightened concerns over the security of natural gas supplies in Europe. For example, the clash between Russia and Ukraine in 2006 over natural gas supplies delivered by Gazprom has preoccupied governments across Europe. While the political ramifications are dodgy, Russian saber rattling has opened the door to other potential LNG developments that may provide cost-effective alternatives to Russian natural gas.

CHAPTER 14
THE FUTURE OF ECONOMIC REGULATION IN THE ELECTRIC AND NATURAL GAS INDUSTRIES

14.1 Introduction

In an oft-cited case, *Nebbia v. New York*,[1] the U.S. Supreme Court upheld regulation of the retail price of milk because the industry was "affected with a public interest." The Court reached that conclusion, even though the dairy industry was not a public utility like electricity or natural gas. Although retail milk prices are no longer regulated in most of the continental United States, dairy farmers continue to benefit from a system of price supports. The Court's statement is still applied to natural gas transmission and distribution. And it is applied even more so to all aspects of the electric industry, even though the industry has been restructured. Despite the success of deregulation in other industries, many observers remain convinced that utility services—water, natural gas, and especially electricity—ought to remain firmly under government control. Others disagree, arguing that regulation is neither necessary nor effective.[2]

This book was not intended to support philosophical or political arguments either for or against regulation per se. In the same way energy regulators approach the prudence of utility decisions, i.e., with a presumption of prudence unless proven otherwise, so we approach competition.

Of course, competitive *liberty* ought not to be confused with competitive *license*. Abusive and anticompetitive practices that exploit firms' market power must be checked. Moreover, because of their nature as a public good, some industry services, such as providing electric system reliability, require coordination and regulation. In addition, the essential facilities doctrine, which guarantees equitable access to important infrastructure "bottlenecks," still applies in many cases. There are simply no reasonable and cost-effective substitutes for transporting natural gas through some (but probably not all) interstate pipelines or for

---

[1] 291 U.S. 502 (1934).

[2] A more detailed discussion can be found in Charles F. Phillips, *The Regulation of Public Utilities*, 3d ed. (Arlington, VA: Public Utilities Reports, 1993), Chapter 17. Phillips's discussion on federal-state jurisdiction is particularly interesting because it was written in the early 1990s, prior to electric industry restructuring. The conclusions he reached were quite prescient.

delivering electricity via high-voltage transmission lines. Moreover, electric and natural gas local distribution services effectively remain natural monopolies that require continued regulatory oversight.[3]

14.2 The Regulatory Clash of Politics and Economics

Both in the United States and internationally, regulation and restructuring continue to be affected by political and economic considerations that are often at odds. This is nothing new, of course. Beginning in the 1970s, regulation and economics began to diverge in the U.S. electric industry. This was the result of a volatile combination of industry hubris regarding the cost of nuclear power and the economic tailspin the economy entered as a result of the 1973 OPEC oil embargo. The rate increases that resulted from these events incited a backlash from consumers and politicians that led to the development of a new regulatory structure. This structure focused less on after-the-fact cost review and more on before-the-fact planning requirements.[4] The National Energy Legislation of 1978 expanded the role of state utility regulators, many of whom became energy and environmental policy advocates rather than independent judicial arbiters of "just and reasonable" rates. Some regulators continue to function in this way today in the electric industry, in spite of restructuring, wholesale competition, and, in some states, retail competition.[5]

In part, this was to be expected. Neither consumers nor electric utility investors benefited from cost overruns and poor management. However, this transformation came with a high price. Not only has it jeopardized regulators' independence from political pressure, it has also substituted regulatory judgment and fiat for the discipline of the marketplace. For example, a number of states have passed legislation mandating that electric supplies must be met with minimum percentages of renewable resources. Different states have imposed

---

[3] For economic purists, we should technically refer to these markets as not *contestable*, since a market may not be contestable, even though a monopolist is not a natural monopolist. For a thorough introduction to the theory of contestable markets, see William J. Baumol, John C. Panzar, and Robert D. Willig, *Contestable Markets and the Theory of Industry Structure*, rev. ed. (New York: Harcourt, 1988).

[4] We believe this transformation is consistent with what is known as the *interest group theory* of regulation. For a discussion, see Phillips, *supra* note 2, at 185–86, and references therein. The interest group theory of regulation is one of four broad (and overlapping) theories of regulation. Phillips summarizes these four theories, drawing from Barry Mitnick, *The Political Economy of Regulation: Creating, Designing, and Removing Regulatory Forms* (New York: Columbia University Press, 1980), Chapter III.

[5] Phillips, *supra* note 2, at 208, fn. 70, argues that none of the four theories of regulation he reviews—Public Interest Theory, Capture Theory, Interest Group Theory, or Equity-Stability Theory—can explain restructuring and deregulation of public utilities. With regard to electric industry restructuring, we disagree, because we believe that the first three theories could explain restructuring.

different requirements, both in terms of the percentages of renewable supplies required by dates certain, and in terms of what resources qualify as "renewable." As we discussed in Chapter 11, this has resulted in curious sets of rules, where burning garbage, waste coal, and integrated coal gasification all count as "renewable" and some hydroelectric plants do not.

Proponents argue that by assuming greater advocacy roles in addition to their judicial roles, state regulators help spur needed changes in the electric industry that address important environmental issues, including global climate change and reducing the United States' dependence on foreign oil. This may be so, but as we discussed in Chapter 11, doing something is not preferable to doing nothing if the "something" results in higher costs without commensurate benefits. More to the point, however, is that *advocacy* is incompatible with *oversight*.

Regulators who become policy advocates, whether by choice or because politicians thrust that role upon them, cannot effectively serve as independent overseers of regulated markets. Moreover, when different regulators employ different standards, regulatory uncertainty results, and firms and captive ratepayers lose owing to the adverse financial impacts. Electric industry restructuring, for example, became embroiled with political considerations after the "California debacle" that took place in 2000–2001. As a result, two of the state's three large, investor-owned utilities became insolvent, and one, Pacific Gas & Electric Company, declared bankruptcy.[6]

Under California's restructuring law, utilities were required to purchase all of their generation needs from a wholesale power exchange for the first four years of restructuring. However, retail prices were capped. When wholesale prices spiked, the utilities began to hemorrhage money, and their credit rankings sank. As the utilities moved closer to bankruptcy, power producers were, understandably, less willing to sell them electricity. Both the U.S. government and the state intervened. A federal judge ruled that power producers were required to sell to utilities, and the California legislature authorized the Department of Water Resources (DWR) to sign long-term bilateral contracts with producers. When market prices subsequently fell, the contracts themselves became controversial. The state also petitioned FERC in an unsuccessful attempt to abrogate those contracts.[7]

---

[6] For a detailed discussion, see Timothy Brennan, "The California Electricity Experience, 2000-01: Education or Diversion?" Resources for the Future, Oct. 2001.

[7] *Public Utilities Commission of the State of California v. Sellers of Long-Term Contracts to the California Department of Water Resources*, Docket Nos. EL02-60-000, EL02-60-003 and EL02-60-004; *California Electricity Oversight Board v. Sellers of Energy and Capacity Under Long-Term Contracts with the California Department of Water Resources*, Docket Nos. EL02-60-000, EL02-60-003 and EL02-60-004 (Consolidated), Order on Rehearing and Clarification, 105 FERC ¶ 61,182 (2003).

Not only did the experience in California lead to an almost complete halt in further restructuring efforts by other states and other countries, it drove some politicians to call for reregulation. Those efforts were further reinforced when a large run-up in natural gas and electricity prices caused wholesale electric prices to spike after Hurricanes Katrina and Rita in 2005. As we write this in 2007, some politicians and regulators are seeking to reregulate the electric industry and return to the central planning dictates of the 1980s. As the philosopher George Santayana famously said: "Those who cannot remember the past are condemned to repeat it."[8]

14.3 The Future of U.S. Regulation

We do not know whether the trend of increased politicization of regulation will continue. We hope, perhaps naïvely, that the trend will halt or even reverse itself, since politicizing regulation, especially rate regulation and creation of new market structures, perpetuates inefficiency and often postpones much needed change. The increasing turmoil in international energy markets (which has accelerated during this decade) and the continued upheaval in the U.S. electric market do not lend themselves to political faith in the efficiency of markets. Politics, we observe, is often about short-term change, whereas new market structures are long-term investments. Given the challenges that await, we can only hope that new regulatory directions include a nod towards true economic efficiency. U.S. regulation of the electric and natural gas industries has stood out because of its long legal pedigree. Yet, that pedigree seems at risk at the very time when economic and technical change in both industries requires as much regulatory certainty as possible.

How will this regulatory future evolve? We do not know. However, if past is also prologue, we can hazard some assumptions about key regulatory issues forthcoming in both industries.

Natural Gas

From the standpoint of supplies, the success of deregulating the natural gas industry is self-evident. After declarations in the 1970s that the U.S. natural gas spigot would run dry within a decade, market forces unleashed huge investments in exploration, development, and new technology. Today, natural gas regulation takes the form of regulating interstate pipeline rates and local distribution charges. This is unlikely to change (although the regulatory regimes applied may evolve), and it is especially true at the local distribution

---

[8] *Life of Reason, Reason in Common Sense* (New York: Scribners, 1905), 264.

level, where increased price volatility created a political backlash and has inspired calls for greater price stability. A greater need for more sophisticated, low-cost hedging strategies has complicated the tasks of assessing the prudence of firms' hedging activities and estimating revenue requirements—either under traditional cost-of-service or, as is becoming more common in the United States, performance-based regimes. Since there is no uniquely "correct" quantity of insurance one ought to buy, regulators must weigh the costs and benefits for those consumers who cannot directly hedge their natural gas purchases.

At the interstate pipeline level, FERC's deregulation efforts have been hugely successful. The natural gas pipeline industry is competitive, even if most individual pipelines can be considered essential facilities. Although FERC allows pipelines to charge market-based rates in the same way that it allows wholesale electric generators to do so, the proportion of pipelines that qualify is likely to remain low.

A more critical issue for interstate pipelines, as well as retail customers and electric generators that use natural gas, is future natural gas supplies. With more areas off-limits to new exploration and development, domestic supplies will inevitably tighten. How much of that decrease can be met by increased imports of liquefied natural gas (LNG) is a matter of speculation. Although the economics of LNG are favorable, there has been extensive opposition to siting LNG terminals. Many pipelines use this fact to argue for shorter "economic lifetimes" and higher depreciation rates, which, if you recall from Chapter 5, we defined as the time beyond which a pipeline could not operate profitably. Moreover, some pipelines have linked supply uncertainty to their overall investment risk. To the extent that FERC sets allowed rates of return for interstate pipelines, the link between supply risk and overall investment risk will need to be developed further. Moreover, as we also discussed in Chapter 5, the changing structure of the interstate pipeline industry has made FERC's reliance on its traditional discounted cash flow approach problematic and will require developing new rate-of-return methodologies.[9]

Electricity

With apologies to Winston Churchill, who was speaking of Russia, the electric industry in the United States will likely remain "a riddle wrapped in a mystery inside an enigma." Many underestimated the complexity of deregulating some aspects of electric markets (especially the transmission sector) and of creating new market institutions to provide electric

---

[9] Some pipelines have also cited the financial risks faced by their customers as a reason to increase their allowed rate of return, and are seeking to revamp the discounted cash flow approach traditionally used by FERC. *See, e.g., Kern River Gas Transmission Company*, Request for Rehearing of Kern River Gas Transmission Company, Docket No. RP04-274-000, November 20, 2006, 46–68.

services. Perhaps because electricity is considered a basic necessity of life, if not one of the key drivers of the economy, upheavals in the industry have historically been met with political overreach and hyperbole. In the 1930s, it was PUHCA. In the 1970s, it was nuclear power plant cost overruns and the aforementioned vanishing natural gas supplies that led to PURPA and a generation of costly qualifying facilities. In the 1990s, it was the drive to break up the industry and vacuum up the benefits of low natural gas prices caused by an enduring surplus natural gas "bubble," while imposing price caps as the *quid pro quo* for utilities to be able to recover "stranded" generating costs. Most recently, we have seen calls to reregulate the electric industry, extend retail price caps, and impose increasingly stringent renewable resource supply requirements on retail providers.

The electric industry has been hamstrung by the impact of local environmental issues, especially the reluctance of communities to allow new infrastructure development nearby, even if that development is designed to "keep the lights on." Although the advent of restructuring and wholesale competition unleashed a boom of new generating supplies, the boom itself was narrow. It was manifest almost exclusively in the development of natural gas-fired generating plants that were predicated on the low gas prices that prevailed in the 1990s. With the September 11, 2001, attacks on the United States, however, the world energy dynamic changed rapidly. World energy demand has increased, led by China's voracious appetite for growth. As prices have risen, so has the volume of the chorus of politicians, regulators, and consumer advocates calling for reregulation, in the mistaken view that regulation can somehow negate the forces of supply and demand.

Regulation of the electric industry has also been made more complex, because, as we discussed in Chapter 12, a reliable electric system is a public good. FERC's continued push towards the use of market mechanisms to provide reliability, while admirable, has required the creation of new markets for capacity and reserves. These new markets have sparked new controversies. We will have to wait to see how these controversies will ultimately be resolved to find out if the reliability standards required under the Energy Policy Act of 2005 (which will be developed and enforced by the Electric Reliability Organization) will result in a more reliable electric system. One thing seems clear—unless the growing resistance to new infrastructure can be overcome so that developers can build needed facilities efficiently (and with a minimum of regulatory uncertainty), enforceable reliability standards are likely to have only a marginal impact.

Finally, we expect the role of environmental regulation to continue to grow at both the state and federal levels. The clash of politics and economics will further transform utility regulators into environmental policy advocates, especially regarding global climate change. However, as we argued in Chapter 11, while these state-level policies are unlikely to provide any tangible environmental benefits to ratepayers, they will impose real costs. More states are also likely to introduce command-and-control regulations explicitly directed towards coal-fired power plants. This will further exacerbate pressure to maintain needed base-load generating supplies and aggravate conflicts between environmental quality and system reliability.

Regional transmission organizations and FERC will need to intervene to ensure that newly developed reliability standards are maintained. We also expect that coalitions of states and environmental advocates will continue to pursue "regulation by lawsuit" with respect to both greenhouse gases and pollutants directly covered under the Clean Air Act, even though this is the most costly and inefficient approach to the development of environmental policy. While these actions may be well-intentioned, consumers are likely to be the biggest losers.

14.4 Concluding Thoughts

As we wrote in our preface, one of our primary goals was to explain the economic underpinnings of rate regulation so readers would better understand its often arcane mechanics and grasp the implications of rate regulation on the broader economic decisions regulated firms must make. We hope readers have developed such an understanding, whether because of our efforts or in spite of them.

Regardless of the changes that the electric and natural gas industries undergo in the future, and they undoubtedly will change in ways we cannot even speculate about, rate regulation will continue to play an important role in these industries. We can only hope that future approaches to rate regulation (in the United States and elsewhere) will be crafted to be both pragmatic and sound, and that they will benefit industry participants and consumers alike. For example, the electric industry in the United States should be allowed to return to its original mission—providing safe, reliable, and affordable supplies—rather than continue its role as tax collector and environmental policy instrument. The electric industry has, in many ways, been knotted up by regulatory policies. To meet the demands of the future, the knots ought to be untied. Another opportunity for regulators is to improve the sophistication of the economic models used to evaluate utility decisions. In an era of increasing market uncertainty, regulators and regulated firms should rely on economic models that can address uncertainty in more comprehensive ways. Finally, if regulators insist on pursuing noneconomic policy goals, be it renewable portfolio requirements, energy-efficiency funds, or new environmental regulations, their decisions would benefit from the use of economic tools that can identify truly "least-cost" approaches. We do not know if regulators will adopt our suggestions, but as economists, we can always assume they do.

SELECT BIBLIOGRAPHY

Books and Articles

Alexander, Ian, Colin Mayer, and Helen Weeds. "Regulatory Structure and Risk: An International Comparison." World Bank Policy Research Working Paper No. 1698, December 1996.

Armstrong, Mark, Simon Cowan, and John Vickers. *Regulatory Reform: Economic Analysis and British Experience.* Cambridge, MA: MIT Press, 1994.

L'Autorità per l'Energia Elettrica e il Gas, Deliberazione n. 166/05, July 29, 2005.

Averch, Harvey, and Leland Johnson. "Behavior of the Firm under Regulatory Constraint." *American Economic Review,* December 1962, 1052–1069.

Avery, Dennis T., and S. Fred Singer. *Unstoppable Global Warming: Every 1,500 Years.* New York: Rowman and Littlefield, 2007.

Axelrod, Howard, David DeRamus, and Collin Cain. "The Fallacy of High Prices." *Public Utilities Fortnightly* 144 (November 2006): 55–60.

Bain, Joe S. *Barriers to New Competition.* Cambridge, MA: Harvard University Press, 1956.

———. "Workable Competition in Oligopoly: Theoretical Considerations and Some Empirical Evidence." *The American Economic Review* 40, no. 2 (1950): 35–47.

Bastos, Carlos, and Manuel Abdala. "Reform of the Electric Power Sector in Argentina." *Buenos Aires,* (1993): 113.

Baumol, William J., John C. Panzar, and Robert D. Willig. *Contestable Markets and the Theory of Industry Structure.* Rev. ed. New York: Harcourt, 1988.

———. *Contestable Markets and the Theory of Industry Structure.* New York: Harcourt Brace Jovanovich, 1982.

Beatty, H. Wayne. *Electric Power Distribution Systems: A Nontechnical Guide.* Tulsa, OK: PennWell Publishing, 1998.

Becker, Gary. *A Treatise on the Family.* Cambridge, MA: Harvard University Press, 2005.

Bernstein, Jeffrey. "X-Factor Updating and Total Factor Productivity Growth: The Case of Peruvian Telecommunications, 1996–2003." *Journal of Regulatory Economics* 30, no. 3 (2006): 316–342.

Bonbright, James C. *Principles of Public Utility Rates.* Arlington, VA: Public Utilities Reports, 1961.

———. *Principles of Public Utility Rates.* 2d ed. Arlington, VA: Public Utilities Reports, 1988.

Booth, Douglas E. *Valuing Nature: The Decline and Preservation of Old-Growth Forests.* Lanham, MD: Rowman and Littlefield, 1994.

Brennan, Timothy. "The California Electricity Experience, 2000-01: Education or Diversion?" Resources for the Future, October 2001.

Brigham, Eugene F., and Louis C. Gapenski. *Financial Management: Theory and Practice.* 6th ed. Chicago: Dryden Press, 1991.

Carlton, Dennis W., and Jeffrey M. Perloff. *Modern Industrial Organization.* 2d. ed. New York: Harper Collins, 1994.

Carson, Richard, et al. "A Contingent Valuation Study of Lost Passive Use Values Resulting from the Exxon Valdez Oil Spill: Report to the Attorney General of the State of Alaska." La Jolla, CA: Natural Resource Damage Assessment, Inc., 1993.

Chennells, Lucy. "The Windfall Tax." *Fiscal Studies* 18 (1997): 284.

Clemen, Robert T. *Making Hard Decisions: An Introduction to Decision Analysis.* 2nd ed. New York: Duxbury Press, 1996.

Coase, Ronald. "The Problem of Social Cost." *Journal of Law and Economics* 3 (1960): 1–44.

Copeland, Thomas E., and J. Fred Weston. *Financial Theory and Corporate Policy.* 3rd ed. New York: Addison-Wesley, 1988.

———. *Financial Theory and Corporate Policy.* 2nd ed. Reading, MA: Addison-Wesley, 1983.

Dixit, Avinash, and Robert Pindyck. *Investment Under Uncertainty.* Princeton, NJ: Princeton University Press, 1994.

Dodds, Daniel, and Jonathan Lesser. "Can Utility Commissions Improve on Environmental Regulations?" *Land Economics* 70, no. 1 (February 1994): 63–76.

Edison Electric Institute and the American Gas Association. *Introduction to Depreciation and Net Salvage of Public Utility Plant and Equipment.* May 2003 (EEI/AGA 2003).

Fama, Eugene F. *Foundations of Finance.* New York: Basic Books, 1976.

Fama, Eugene F., and Kenneth R. French. "Multifactor Explanations of Asset Pricing Anomalies." *Journal of Finance* 51, no. 1 (1996): 55–84.

Feinstein, Charles, and Jonathan Lesser. "Defining Distributed Utility Planning." *The Energy Journal*, "Distributed Resources: Toward a New Paradigm of the Electricity Business," Special Issue (1997): 41–62.

Ferreira, Pedro J. "On the Efficiency of the Argentinean Electricity Wholesale Market." Ph.D. dissertation, University of Chicago, 2002.

Financial Accounting Standards Board. *Statement of Financial Accounting Concepts No. 2*, (May 1980).

Freedman, David, Robert Pisani, and Roger Purves. *Statistics*. 3d ed. New York: W.W. Norton, 1998.

Freeman, A. Myrick. *The Measurement of Environmental and Resource Values*. Washington, DC: Resources for the Future, 1993.

Gaynor, Patricia E., and Rickey C. Kirkpatrick. *Introduction to Time-Series Modeling and Forecasting in Business and Economics*. New York: McGraw-Hill, 1994.

Gómez-Lobo, Andres, and Vivien Foster. "The 1996-97 Gas Price Review in Argentina." *Private Sector*, Note No. 181, April 1999.

Goodman, Leonard S. *The Process of Ratemaking*. Vienna, VA: Public Utilities Reports, 1998.

Graves, Frank. *A Primer on Electric Power Flow for Economists and Utility Planners*, Report No. TR-104604. Palo Alto, CA: Electric Power Research Institute, 1995.

Green, Richard, and Martín Rodríguez Pardina. "Resetting Price Controls for Privatized Utilities: A Manual for Regulators." *EDI Development Studies*, Economic Development Institute (World Bank), 1999, 64–67.

Gwynne, Peter. "The Cooling World," *Newsweek*, April 28, 1975.

Hamada, Robert S. "The Effect of the Firm's Capital Structure on the Systematic Risk of Common Stocks." *Journal of Finance* 25 (May 1972): 435–52.

Hardin, Garrett. "The Tragedy of the Commons." *Science* 162 (1968): 1243–48.

Harvey, Campbell. "12 Ways to Calculate the International Cost of Capital." National Bureau of Economic Research, unpublished paper, December 2005.

Hull, John. *Options, Futures, and Other Derivatives*. 6th ed. New York: Prentice-Hall, 2005.

Jorion, Philippe. *Value at Risk*. 2nd ed. New York: McGraw-Hill, 2001.

Joskow, Paul. "Markets for Power in the United States: An Interim Assessment." *The Energy Journal* 27 (2006): 1–36.

Kahn, Alfred. *The Economics of Regulation: Principles and Institutions*. New York: Wiley, 1970.

———. *The Economics of Regulation*. Cambridge, MA: MIT Press, 1988.

Knight, Frank H. *Risk, Uncertainty, and Profit*. Boston: Houghton-Mifflin, 1933.

Kolbe, Lawrence, and William Tye. "The Duquesne Opinion: How Much 'Hope' is There for Investors in Regulated Firms?" *Yale J. Reg.* 8 (1990), 113.

Kwoka, John E. "Restructuring the U.S. Electric Power Sector: A Review of Recent Studies." Study prepared for the American Public Power Association, Nov. 2006, www.appanet.org.

Lesser, Jonathan A. "The Economic Used and Useful Test: Implications for a Restructured Electric Industry." *Energy Law Journal* 23, no. 2 (2002): 349–81.

———. "ROE: The Gorilla is Still at the Door." *Public Utilities Fortnightly* 145 (July 2004): 19–23.

Lesser, Jonathan A., Daniel E. Dodds, and Richard O. Zerbe. *Environmental Economics and Policy.* New York: Addison Wesley, 1997.

Lesser, Jonathan A., and Guillermo Israilevich. "The Capacity Market Enigma." *Public Utilities Fortnightly* 147 (December 2005), 38–42.

Levy, Sidney M. *Build Operate Transfer.* New York: John Wiley & Sons, 1996.

Lomborg, Bjorn. *The Skeptical Environmentalist.* Cambridge: Cambridge University Press, 2001.

Mankiw, N. Gregory. *Principles of Economics.* 4th ed. Mason, OH: South-Western College Publishing, 2006.

McCormack, Norman J. *Reliability and Risk Analysis: Methods and Nuclear Power Applications.* New York: Academic Press, 1981.

Menanteau, Philippe, Dominique Finon, and Marie-Laure Lamy. "Prices versus Quantities: Choosing Policies for Promoting the Development of Renewable Energy." *Energy Policy* 31, no. 8 (2003): 799–812.

Mitnick, Barry. *The Political Economy of Regulation: Creating, Designing, and Removing Regulatory Forms.* New York: Columbia University Press, 1980.

Modigliani, Franco, and Merton Miller. "The Cost of Capital, Corporation Finance, and the Theory of Investment." *American Economic Review* 48, no. 3 (June 1958): 261-297.

Morin, Roger A. *New Regulatory Finance.* Vienna, VA: Public Utilities Reports, 2006.

National Association of Regulatory Utility Commissioners (NARUC). *Electric Utility Cost Allocation Manual.* Washington, DC: NARUC, 1992.

National Association of Regulatory Utility Commissioners (NARUC), Staff Subcommittee on Gas. *Gas Distribution Rate Design Manual.* Washington, DC: NARUC, 1989.

National Grid. *The Statement of the Connection Charge Methodology*, Issue 2, Revision 1, Effective from April 1, 2006.

———. *The Statement of the Use of System Charging Methodology*, Issue 2, Revision 1, Effective from April 1, 2006.

Newberry, David M. *Privatization, Restructuring, and Regulation of Network Utilities.* Cambridge, MA: MIT Press, 1999.

New York ISO Installed Capacity Manual, Appendix J, www.nyiso.com/public/webdocs/products/icap/icap_manual/app_a_attach_icapmnl.pdf.

O'Brien, Timothy L., and Steven Lee Myers. "Kremlin and Russia Inc Realign after Yukos Trial." *New York Times,* June 14, 2005.

Officer, Robert. *The Cost of Capital of a Company under an Imputation Tax System.* Victoria, Australia: Parkville, 1991.

Palmer, Karen, and Dallas Burtraw. "Cost-Effectiveness of Renewable Electricity Policies." *Energy Economics* 27, no. 6 (2005): 873–94.

Peirson, C. Graham, R. G. Bird, R. Brown, and P. Howard. *Business Finance.* 6th ed. Sydney: McGraw-Hill, 1995.

Phillips, Charles F. *The Regulation of Public Utilities.* 3d ed. Arlington, VA: Public Utilities Reports, 1993.

Pilipović, Dragana. *Energy Risk: Valuing and Managing Energy Derivatives.* New York: McGraw-Hill, 1997.

Potential Supply of Natural Gas in the United States, Report to the Potential Gas Committee, December 31, 2004. Golden, CO: Potential Gas Agency, Mineral Resources Institute, Colorado School of Mines Foundation, 2005.

Ross, Sheldon M. *Introduction to Probability Models.* 6th ed. New York: Academic Press, 1997.

Scherer, Frederick, and David Ross. *Industrial Market Structure and Economic Performance.* 3d ed. Boston: Houghton Mifflin, 1990.

Schleifer, Andrei. "A Theory of Yardstick Competition." *Rand Journal of Economics* 16, no. 3 (1985): 319–27.

Spinner, Howard. "Choosing an Efficient Energy Assistance Program." *Public Utilities Fortnightly* 126 (December 1990), 27–31.

Stigler, George. *The Organization of Industry.* Chicago: University of Chicago Press, 1968.

Stoft, Steven. *Power System Economics: Designing Markets for Electricity.* Piscataway, NJ: IEEE/Wiley Press, 2002.

Suelflow, James E. *Public Utility Accounting: Theory and Practice.* Lansing, MI: Michigan State University, Institute of Public Utilities, 1973.

Sykes, Alan. "An Introduction to Regression Analysis." Working Paper 020, John M. Olin Program in Law and Economics (University of Chicago), October 1993.

Thaler, Richard H. *Quasi-Rational Economics*. New York: Russell Sage Foundation Publications, 1994.

Tietenberg, Thomas H. *Environmental and Natural Resource Economics*. 7th ed. New York: Addison-Wesley, 2005.

Tietenberg, Thomas H. "Transferable Discharge Permits and the Control of Stationary Source Air Pollution." *Land Economics* 55, no. 3 (1979): 391-416.

U.S.-Canada Power System Outage Task Force. *Final Report on the August 14, 2003 Blackout in the United States and Canada: Causes and Recommendations.* April 5, 2004.

U.S. Department of Justice and Federal Trade Commission. *Horizontal Merger Guidelines*. 57 Fed. Reg. 41,552 (April 2, 1992).

U.S. Energy Information Administration. *Electric Power Annual.* October 2006.

———. *Privatization and the Globalization of Energy Markets*. October 1996.

U.S. Securities and Exchange Commission. "Final Data Quality Assurance Guidelines," http://www.sec.gov/about/dataqualityguide.htm, last accessed on February 19, 2007.

Wellisz, Stanislaw. "Regulation of Natural Gas Pipeline Companies: An Economic Analysis." *Journal of Political Economy*, February 1963, 30–43.

Westley, Glenn D. *New Directions in Econometric Modeling of Energy Demand. With Applications to Latin America*. Washington, DC: Inter-American Development Bank, 1992.

Willis, H. Lee. *Power Distribution Planning Reference Book*. New York: Marcel Dekker, 1997.

Wilson, Robert. "Architecture of Power Markets." *Econometrica* 70, no. 4 (July 2002).

Winfrey, Robley. *Statistical Analyses of Industrial Property Retirements*. Bulletin 125, Engineering Research Institute (formerly Iowa Engineering Experiment Station), Iowa State University, 1935.

Winfrey, Robley, and Edwin Kurtz. "Life Characteristics of Physical Property." *Iowa Engineering Exp. Sta. Bul.* 103 (1921).

Wirick, David, and John Gibbons. "Generally Accepted Accounting Principles for Regulated Utilities: Evolution and Impacts." National Regulatory Research Institute, NRRI 95-07, 1994.

Cases

Associated Gas Distributors v. FERC, 824 F.2d 981 (D.C. Cir. 1987).

California Electricity Oversight Board v. Sellers of Energy and Capacity Under Long-Term Contracts with the California Department of Water Resources, Nos. EL02-60-000, EL02-60-003 and EL02-60-004 (Consolidated), Order on Rehearing and Clarification, 105 FERC ¶ 61,182 (2003).

Colorado Interstate Gas Co. v. F.P.C., 324 U.S. 581 (1945).

Columbus Southern Power Co., 133 PUR4th 525 (Ohio P.U.C., 1992).

Connecticut v. American Electric Power Co. Inc., 406 F. Supp. 2d 265 (S.D.N.Y. 2005), *appeals pending*, No. 05-5104-CV (2d Cir., argued June 7, 2006).

Denver Union Stockyard Co. v. United States, 304 U.S. 470 (1938).

Devon Power, LLC, et al., FERC Docket No. ER03-563-030.

Duquesne Light Co. v. Barasch, 488 U.S. 299 (1989).

Eastman Kodak Co. v. Image Technical Servs., Inc., 504 U.S. 451 (1992).

Environmental Defense v. Duke Energy Corp., No. 05-848 (U.S. April 2, 2007).

Federal Power Comm'n v. Hope Natural Gas Co., 320 U.S. 591 (1944).

Groesbeck v. Duluth, S.S. & A.Ry, 250 U.S. 607 (1919).

Jersey Central Power & Light v. FERC, 810 F.2d. 1168 (D.C. Cir. 1987).

Kern River Gas Transmission Company, Docket No. RP04-274-000, Opinion No. 486, 117 FERC ¶ 61, 077, October 19, 2006 (appeal filed November 20, 2006).

Lead Industries Association, Inc. v. EPA, 647 F.2d 1130 (D.C. Cir. 1980), *cert. denied*, 101 S.Ct. 621 (1980).

Mandatory Reliability Standards for the Bulk-Power System, Notice of Proposed Rulemaking, FERC Docket No. RM06-16-000, October 20, 2006.

Massachusetts v. Environmental Protection Agency, 415 F. 3d 50 (D.C. Cir. 2005).

Massachusetts et al. v. Environmental Protection Agency, No. 05-1120, __U.S.__, April 2, 2007 (U.S.).

Metropolitan Edison v. People vs. Nuclear Energy, 460 U.S. 766 (1983).

Missouri ex rel. Southwestern Bell Tel. Co. v. Missouri Pub. Serv. Comm'n, 262 U.S. 276 (1923).

Munn v. Illinois, 94 U.S. 113 (1877).

Nebbia v. New York, 291 U.S. 502 (1934).

New York v. EPA, 443 F. 3d. 880 (D.C. Cir. 2006).

Open Access Same-Time Information System (formerly Real-Time Information Networks) and Standards of Conduct, Final Rule, Docket No. RM95-9-000, Order No. 889, 75 FERC ¶ 61,078, April 24, 1996.

Phillips Petroleum Co. v. Wisconsin, 347 U.S. 672 (1954).

Pipeline Service Obligations and Revisions to Regulations Governing Self-Implementing Transportation, Final Rule, Docket Nos. RM91-11-000, RM87-34-065, Order No. 636, 59 FERC ¶ 61,030, April 8, 1992.

Preventing Undue Discrimination and Preference in Transmission Service (OATT Reform), Notice of Proposed Rulemaking (NOPR), Docket Nos. RM05-25-000 and RM05-17-000, May 19, 2006. Appendix B, Pro-Forma Open Access Transmission Tariff, www.ferc.gov/industries/electric/indus-act/oatt-reform/nopr/pro-forma.pdf, accessed February 19, 2007.

Promoting Transmission Investment Through Pricing Reform, Final Rule, Docket No. RM06-4-000, Order No. 679, 116 FERC ¶ 61,057, July 20, 2006.

Promoting Wholesale Competition Through Open Access Non-Discriminatory Transmission Services by Public Utilities, Docket Nos. RM95-8-000, RM94-7-001, Order No. 888, 75 FERC ¶ 61,080, April 24, 1996.

Public Utilities Commission of the State of California v. Sellers of Long Term Contracts to the California Department of Water Resources, FERC Docket Nos. EL02-60-000, EL02-60-003 and EL02-60-004.

Regional Transmission Organizations, Final Rule, Docket No. RM99-2-000, Order No. 2000, 89 FERC ¶ 61,285, December 20, 1999.

Remedying Undue Discrimination through Open Access Transmission Service and Standard Electricity Market Design, Notice of Proposed Rulemaking, Docket No. RM01-12-000, 67 Fed. Reg. 55,452 (Aug. 29, 2002), FERC Stats. & Regs. ¶ 32,563 (2002).

Revised Filing Requirements Under Part 33 of the Commission's Regulations, Final Rule, Docket No. RM98-4-000, Order No. 642, 93 FERC ¶ 61,164, November 15, 2000.

Smyth v. Ames, 169 U.S. 466 (1898).

U.S. v. AT&T Co., 552 F. Supp. 131 (D.D.C. 1982).

U.S. v. Terminal Rail Road Ass'n of St. Louis, 224 U.S. 383 (1912).

Western Mass. Elec. Co., 80 PUR4th 479 (Mass. D.P.U. 1986).

Wilcox v. Consolidated Gas Co., 212 U.S. 19 (1909).

Williams Pipeline Co, Docket Nos. OR79-1-000 and 022 (Phase I), Opinion No. 154-B, 31 FERC ¶61,377 (1985).

International Sources

Autoridad Nacional de los Servicios Públicos (ANSP). Resolution AN No. 435-ELEC, December 1, 2006 (Pan.).

Comisión Reguladora de Energía (CRE). PGPB Permit G/061/TRA/99, given by CRE, June 2, 1999 (Mex.).

———. Resolution 138/97, September 19, 1997 (Mex.).

———. Resolution 089/99, June 2, 1999 (Mex.).

Decreto Supremo No. 08438 (the "Electricity Code"), July 31, 1968 (Bol.).

Ente Nacional Regulador del Gas (ENARGAS). Resolution No. 1660/2000, March 31, 2000 (Arg.).

———. Resolution No. 469, June 30, 1997 (Arg.).

Ente Nacional Regulador de la Electricidad (ENRE). Resolution ENRE No. 1619/1998, November 13, 1998 (Arg.).

Law No. 1604, December 21, 1994 (Bol.).

Law No. 24,065, "The Electricity Law," January 16, 1992 (Arg.).

Ley de Emergencia Pública y Reforma del Régimen Cambiario, Law No. 25,561, January 6, 2002 (Arg.).

Luis E. Cintron & Co. "Independent Auditor's Report," prepared for ORIL, 2005 (Puerto Rico).

Netherlands Competition Authority. *Addendum B BIJ to the Method Decision No. 102106-89*, Netherlands Government Gazette, no. 122, June 27, 2006.

Organismo Supervisor de la Inversión en Infraestructura de Transporte de Servicio Público (OSITRAN). Resolution Nô. 010-2004-CD-OSITRAN, March 31, 2004 (Peru).

Productivity Commission Inquiry Report. "Review of the Gas Access Regime, Report No. 31, June 11, 2004 (Austl.).

Superintendencia de Electricidad (SSDE). Resolution SSDE Nô. 288/2006, October 10, 2006 (Bol.).

INDEX

A

above-the-line expenses, 41, 52, 68n16
accounting, regulatory, 60
actuarial methods, 96–97
administrative and general (A&G) costs, 39, 51, 52, 138
affiliate abuse, 198, 205
Affiliated Retail Electric Providers (AREPs), 183–84
air pollution, 35
Alaska Power Administration, 5n6
allocative efficiency
    capital markets, 111, 112
    competitive markets, 77
    and input prices, 186n
    marginal cost approaches, 170–72
allowed emissions per unit of output, 252
allowed emissions per unit of time, 252
alternating current, 274–75
American Institute of Certified Public Accountants (AICPA), 83
amperage, 270, 272n8
ancillary services, 12, 176–77, 277
Annual Rate Method, 126, 127
anticompetitive practices
    generation resources, withholding of, 211–12
    natural gas industry, 13
    regulations generally, 3
    See also affiliate abuse; barriers to entry; collusion; foreclosure; market concentration; market power; monopolies; reciprocal dealing
Arbitrage Pricing Model (APM), 116n70
Argentina
    capacity payments, 178, 284, 285
    devaluation of the peso, 294
    inflation indices, 188
    K factor, 173n29, 192n9
    privatization, 287, 288
    provider of last resort (POLR) service, 182–83
    regulatory disputes, 293
    service quality calculations, 194n12
    transmission tariffs, electric, 177–78
    X factor, 189n
Arizona, 257
Associated Gas Distributors v. FERC, 8n12
asymmetric regulation, 71
Atlantic-Seaboard Method, 141
auctions
    book value, 107
    decision tree analysis, 235
    tradable emissions permits, 256n19
    of tranches, 184
    valuation of assets, 106
Australia
    Capital Asset Pricing Model (CAPM), 116n70
    deregulation, 3
    provider of last resort (POLR) service, 182–83
    renewable sources, 263
    wholesale electricity market reforms, 285
Austria, renewable sources, 263
average cost pricing, 30–32
average remaining life (ARL), 93–94, 96, 125, 127
average service life (ASL), 93, 124–25

B

bankruptcy
    Pacific Gas & Electric, 299
    and yardstick competition, 74

barriers to entry
   competitive markets, 21
   defined, 25–26
   and market power, 199–200, 201, 202
   and subsidies, 25n11
   and welfare loss, 200
behavioral remedies, 211–12
Belgium, renewable sources, 263
below-the-line expenses, 41, 68n16
benchmarking
   among companies, 74–76
   dangers of, 66
   service quality, 193–94
   tariffs, 173
   See also yardstick competition
Beta measures, 116–17, 120
Bilateral Investment Treaties (BIT), 293–94
billing determinants, 79, 153, 154–56. *See also* weather normalization
blackouts
   Northeast U.S. (1965), 275, 276
   U.S./Canada (2003), 276, 277n17, 278
Black-Scholes pricing model, 237
block tariffs, 164–65
Bolivia
   capacity payments, 177n41, 284
   net asset base, 67n11
   operating costs, 85n
   working capital allowance formula estimate, 58
bond covenants, 119
Bonneville Power Administration, 5n6
book reserve, 92. *See also* depreciation
book value, 107
book value capitalization, 120–21
Brazil, renewable sources, 263
Build, Lease and Transfer (BLT), 290
Build, Operate and Transfer (BOT), 290
Build, Own and Operate (BOO), 290

C

CAIDI, 269
CAIFI, 269
California
   electric industry restructuring, 10, 36, 211–12, 299–300
   service quality calculations, 194n12
call options, 225
Canada
   blackouts, 276, 277n17, 278
   inflation indices, 188
   natural gas importation, 7, 12
   open access, 174
   shareholder risk, 120
capacitive resistance, 273
capacitors, 274n10
capacity, electric, 278–79
capacity markets
   Australia, 285
   non-U.S., 284–85
   Nordic countries, 285
capacity payments
   England and Wales restructuring, 284
   installed capacity payments, 282
   locational installed capacity markets (LICAP), 282
   peaking units, 177
capacity rights, 174, 175
cap-and-trade, 255, 256, 260, 264
Capital Asset Pricing Model (CAPM), 113, 115–18
capital costs
   defined, 40, 51
   peak demand, 169
   variables among firms, 66
   See also working capital
capital markets, types, 111–12
carbon dioxide
   cap-and-trade, 255n15, 264

climate change, 249
    command-and-control regulation, 262
    defined as pollution, 266
    litigation over power plant emissions, 266–67
    Maryland, 265
carbon tax. *See* taxes: carbon
cash flow analysis, 224
Chile
    capacity markets, 284
    cost estimation, bottom-up approach, 87
China, 302
Clean Air Act, 249
Clean Air Act Amendments (1977), 259
Clean Air Act Amendments (1990)
    and carbon dioxide emissions, 266
    Equipment Replacement Provision, 261
    New Source Review (NSR), 260
    tradable emissions permits, 35, 255
Clean Air Interstate Rule (CAIR), 255n17
climate change
    clash of economics and politics, 302
    heat island effects, 161
    policies, 246, 264
    state policies, 265
cluster analysis, 108n53
coal-bed methane (CBM), 12
Coase Theorem, 142n11, 248
coincident peak loads, 147, 155
collusion, yardstick competition, 73
Colorado, 257
Comisión Reguladora de Energía (CRE), 50n26, 290
command-and-control regulation, 87, 246, 252, 303
competition, workable, 200
competitive equilibrium, 18–21
conductors, electric, 271
Connecticut v. American Electric Power Co., 266
consumer's surplus, 20, 27

consumption allocation factors, 146
consumption forecasts, 153, 156–57. *See also* weather normalization
contestable markets, 28, 29, 298n3
contract carriage, 174, 175
cooling degree day (CDD), 160
Corrected Ordinary Least Squares (COLS), 86, 89–90
    Panama, 89
cost adjustment mechanisms, 67, 71, 188
cost allocation
    cross-subsidies, 142
    generally, 123, 141, 144
    joint costs, 33
    pipelines, natural gas, 175–76
    rate cases, 68
    tariff design, 151
    and utility mergers, 199
    See also consumption allocation factors; customer allocation factors; demand allocators; ring-fencing; *specific types of costs*
cost-benefit analysis, 10, 249, 259
cost classification
    defined, 139
    Latin America, 141
    See also Atlantic-Seaboard Method; Seaboard Method
cost-effectiveness, 10, 221
cost frontiers, 87–89
cost functionalization, 136–39. *See also* Kansas-Nebraska Method; Massachusetts Method
cost measurement
    generally, 38
    regression models, 89–90
    See also test year
cost of capital
    defined, 110
    measuring, generally, 38

317

cost of capital *(continued)*
    return on rate base, 81, 109
    See also various types of risk
cost of common equity, proxy firms, 113
cost of debt, 109, 111
cost of service (COS)
    cost-of-service model, 135
    cost-of-service studies, 67–69, 81
    incentive to disguise costs, 34
    and performance-based regulation (PBR), 67n12
    and privatization, 63
    reliability must run (RMR) agreements, 280
    short-run and long-run costs, 49, 50
    social costs, 48
    top-down vs. bottom-up approaches, 68
cost-of-service regulation (COSR)
    advantages of, 76
    and capacity pricing, 280
    and cost allocation, 142
    cost-of-service studies, 67–69
    as "low-powered" regime, 120
    price adjustments, automatic, 186
    regulatory lag, 69
cost projections (regulatory framework), 292
costs
    accrued, 52
    avoided, 9–10
    common, 52–53, 136n2, 145
    of debt, 56
    deferred, 52, 68n17, 122 *(see also* regulatory assets)
    direct, 52–53, 70
    environmental, 47–48
    external, 165
    fixed, 144, 145
    future, 54–55
    historical, 54
    indirect, 52–53, 70

    international variables, 74–75
    long-run, 47, 49–50
    marginal, 18, 33
    nonrecurrent, 46, 54
    opportunity to recover, 39
    private, 47
    recurrent, 54
    short-run, 47, 49–50
    social, 47, 261
    transformation into prices, 77–80
    variable, 142, 144, 169–70
    See also administrative and general (A&G) costs; cost classification; cost functionalization; fuel costs; joint costs; marginal private cost (MPC); marginal social cost (MSC); operation and maintenance (O&M) costs; original costs; replacement costs
cost structures, 66
    and Data Envelope Analysis, 88
country risk premiums, 76, 119, 120
cross-subsidies
    cost allocation, 142
    cost functionalization, 136
    and market foreclosure, 204, 205–6
    and market power, 23
    and ring-fencing, 59
current, electric, 270, 275
customer allocation factors, 146
customer classes. *See* rate classes
cycling (electricity), 274
the Czech Republic, renewable sources, 263

D

Data Envelope Analysis (DEA), 86, 87–89
    X factor, 190n6
debt equivalency, 81
debt financing, 111
decision trees, 228–31, 233–35

default service, 182–83
degree-day, 160
delivered price test (DPT), 208
demand allocators, 146–47
demand forecasts, 157. *See also* consumption forecasts; peak demand studies
Denmark, renewable sources, 263
depreciation
    and capital expenses, 51
    cost recovery, 31
    defined, 55, 91–92
    operating costs, 40–41
    and revenue requirements, 97–98
    and taxes, 98
    See also Annual Rate Method; average remaining life (ARL); average service life (ASL); net asset base; net present value (NPV); Original Group Method; retirement ratio; survivor curves; survivor ratio; Trended Original Cost (TOC)
depreciation, calculations of, 91–92, 93–95, 96–97, 124–33. *See also* average remaining life (ARL); average service life (ASL)
deregulation
    of distribution, 3
    electric industry, 301–2
    general history, 3
    natural gas industry, 8
    outside of the United States, 3
    pipelines, natural gas, 8
    success factors, 16
    of transmission, 3
    See also default service
direct current, 270–74
Discounted Cash Flow (DCF) Model
    drawbacks of, 172
    example, 114–15
    indicative values (privatization), 106–7

pipelines, natural gas, 301
and proxy firms, 113, 118–19
distributed utility planning (DU), 221
distribution, deregulation, 3
Dividend Growth Model. *See* Discounted Cash Flow (DCF) Model
dominant firms, 201–2
Dominican Republic, subsidies, 181n55
Due Process clause, 15
Duquesne Light Co. v. Barasch, 104–5

E

earnings-sharing mechanisms, 71, 72
economic dispatch, 277. *See also* reliability: electric
Economic Emergency Law (Argentina), 294
economic life, 93, 94
economies of scale
    pipelines, natural gas, 22
    and regulation, 24
    and the regulatory compact, 44
    tariff design, 180–81
    utility mergers, 198
economies of scope, 22, 23, 198
Edison, Thomas, 4, 6, 274
efficiency frontiers, 90
efficiency incentives, 187, 189
efficient market, 21
Efficient Market Hypothesis (EMH), 112, 114
electric cooperatives, 26
electric industry
    environmental regulation, generally, 268
    FERC Form 1 (Annual Report of Major Electric Utilities), 60
    gas-fired generation, 13
    generation resources, 10–11
    nationalization of, 26
    reregulation, 221, 222

electric industry *(continued)*
    subsidization of rural service, 17
    See also default service; reliability: electric; renewable generation resources; restructuring: electric industry
Electricité de France, 284
Electric Reliability Organization (ERO), 277, 302
electric system security, 276. *See also* reliability: electric
embedded cost methods, 168, 169–70, 171–72
emissions caps, 257. *See also* cap-and-trade; New Source Review (NSR); quotas
emissions taxes. *See* taxes: emissions
energy, electric, 278–79
Energy Policy Act of 1992. *See* EPAct
Energy Policy Act of 2005, 302
Energy Tax Act, 7
England & Wales, capacity markets, 284–85
Entergy New Orleans, 46, 54
entry-exit scheme, 166, 174, 176
environmental regulation
    command-and-control regulation, 252
    cost-benefit analysis, 248–49, 259, 265
    and demand, 222
    externalities, 35, 247
    externality adders, 261–62
    as impediment to new generation and transmission facilities, 214, 302
    output taxes, 253
    psychological harm, 259
    and uncertainty, 38
    See also costs: environmental; EPA; New Source Review (NSR); taxes: emissions; taxes: output taxes; tradable emissions permits
EPA, 5n9, 260. *See also* environmental regulation
EPAct, 10, 36, 180, 276

Equal Proportion of Marginal Cost (EPMC), 171
Equipment Replacement Provision, 260–61
essential facilities doctrine (EFD), 213–14, 297
Europe
    feed-in-tariffs (FIT), 267n39
    pipelines, natural gas, 176
    shareholder risk, 120
    supplier of last resort service, 182n59
    See also specific countries
event thresholds, 240–41
EWG. *See* Exempt Wholesale Generator
excess capacity, 25
exchange efficiency, capital markets, 111, 112
Exempt Wholesale Generator (EWG), 10, 36, 178
exogenous adjustment factors. *See* Z factor
externalities
    environmental costs, 35–36, 246, 247
    examples of, 47
    positive, 251n9
    See also Coase Theorem
externality adders, 261–63
extraordinary rate reviews, 59
Exxon Valdez, 258

F

fair rate of return (regulatory policy), 80, 109
Fair Value Doctrine, 100n31
fair value regulation, 173
Fama, Eugene, 112
Faraday, Michael, 274
Federal Power Commission (FPC), 5, 6
Federal Power Commission v. Hope Natural Gas, 102, 104–5, 109, 113
Federal Reserve Open Market Committee (FOMC), 118
federal/state regulatory conflicts, 17, 38

Federal Water Power Act, 5
feed-in-tariffs (FIT), 267n39
FERC (Federal Energy Regulatory
   Commission)
   creation of, 5n5
   delivered price test (DPT), 208
   market share test, 207, 208
   natural gas pipeline deregulation, 8
   pipeline tariffs, 61
   pivotal supplier test, 207, 208
   regulatory accounting, 60
   reliability must run (RMR) agreements,
      280
   Standard Market Design (SMD), 275, 280
   valuation of assets, 100n32
   wholesale energy markets, 280
   and wholesale natural gas market, 8
   working capital allowance formula, 58
   See also Good Utility Practice; Trended
      Original Cost (TOC)
FERC Form 1 (Annual Report of Major
   Electric Utilities), 60
FERC Form 2 (Major Natural Gas Pipeline
   Annual Report), 60
FERC Form 6 (Annual Report of Oil
   Pipeline Companies), 60
FERC Order 380, 8
FERC Order 436, 8
FERC Order 500, 8
FERC Order 592, 207
FERC Order 636, 8
FERC Order 637, 9
FERC Order 836, 36
FERC Order 888, 9, 178–79
FERC Order 2000, 197n2
"Final Data Quality Assurance Guidelines"
   (SEC), 83
Financial Accounting Standards Board
   (FASB), 83
Finland, renewable sources, 263

foreclosure, 198, 203–4
Forked River nuclear plant, 104
formula-based pricing mechanisms, 70, 72
forward capacity markets, 282n22
Four Corners region (U.S.), 257
4-CP method, 148
FPA (Federal Power Act), 198, 208
free cash flow, 172
free riders, 12, 247, 278
fringe firms, 201–2
fuel costs
   cost adjustment mechanisms, 67, 186
   cost allocation, 142
   and market power, 215
   operating costs, 39
   in revenue requirement studies, 54
   See also pass-through mechanisms

G

Generally Accepted Accounting Principles
   (GAAP), 122
generation capacity, gas-fired, 9
generation resources, withholding of, 211–12
gold-plating, 42, 44
Good Utility Practice, 41–42, 43
Grand Canyon National Park, 257–58
Great Britain. *See* United Kingdom
Green Mountain Power Company, 71–72
green tags, 35. *See also* renewable portfolio
   standards
Groesbeck v. Duluth, 141
Guatemala
   cluster analysis, 108n53
   cost estimation, top-down approach,
      86n14
   privatization, 288
   subsidies, 181n55

H

heating degree day (HDD), 160
hedging strategies, natural gas, 301
Henry Hub, 186, 236–37
HHI (Herfindahl-Hirschman Index) analysis, 203, 207, 208
holding companies, electricity, 4. *See also* PUHCA
Hope Natural Gas. See *Federal Power Commission v. Hope Natural Gas*
Horizontal Merger Guidelines (DOJ/FTC), 199, 201, 203, 207
Hurricane Katrina, 11, 46, 54, 220, 300
Hurricane Rita, 11, 46, 220, 300
hydroelectric power, 5n6, 37

I

incentive rate tariff structures, 166
incentive regulation, 34, 193. *See also* performance-based regulation (PBR)
increasing block price tariff structures, 165
incremental cost methods, 168, 206
independent transmission system operators (ISOs), 197, 210, 275
index funds, 110
inductive resistance, 273–74
inflation, 101
inflation adjustments, 187–88
inflation indices
    Argentina, 188
    Canada, 188
    Mexico, 188
    United Kingdom, 188
information asymmetry, 72, 73–74
installed capacity payments, 282
integrated portfolio management, 170n26
integrated resource plans (IRPs), 170, 221, 261
interest group theory of regulation, 298n4

intergenerational equity, 31, 68
international arbitration, 293–94, 295
International Energy Agency, 263
interruptible rates, 166–67
Inverse Elasticity Method. *See* Ramsey Pricing
Iowa Curves, 96, 132–33
ISO-NE, 197
Italy, renewable sources, 263

J

Japan, renewable sources, 263
Jersey Central Power & Light v. FERC, 104–5
joint costs, 52, 53, 136, 142, 145
just and reasonable (regulatory principle)
    cross-subsidies, 142
    first reference to, 4n2
    and Good Utility Practice, 41n
    historical context, 63
    just price doctrine, 44
    National Energy Legislation, 9
    peak demand forecasts, 157
    regulators as policy advocates, 298
    tariff design, 162–63
    variable operating environments, 66
    and workable competition, 200
    See also *Federal Power Commission v. Hope Natural Gas*
just price doctrine, 44

K

Kansas-Nebraska Method, 138
K factor, 188, 192
    Mexican tariffs, 291
kilowatt-hours (kWH), defined, 270
Kirchoff's Laws, 272n7
known and measurable (regulatory principle)
    cost functionalization, 135
    and future costs, 54
    Good Utility Practice, 41

in justification of costs, 43, 80–81
Mexico, 85
operation and maintenance (O&M) costs, 85
variations in application of, 46
Kyoto Treaty, 264, 266

L

Latin America
    capacity payments, 284
    failure of regulatory mechanisms, 292
    open access, 174
    shareholder risk, 120
    social tariffs, 181n55
    See also specific countries
Lead Industries, Inc. v. EPA, 249
lead-lag study, 57–58
least-cost, 221
least-squares approach, 133
lifeline rates, 165, 181
light bulbs, 4, 271, 272
liquefied natural gas (LNG), 12, 301
load factor, 142n12, 147, 148, 155. *See also* coincident peaks; noncoincident peaks
load pockets, 280
load serving entity (LSE), 204
local distribution companies (LDCs), 8, 45, 69
locational capacity demand curves, 283
locational installed capacity markets (LICAP), 280
London Courts of International Arbitration (LCIA), 294
Long Island Lighting, Shoreham plant, 104
long-run incremental cost studies, 54
low-income rate structures, 34

M

MAIFI, 269
manufactured gas, 5–6

marginal cost approaches, 170–72, 176
marginal private cost (MPC), 250
marginal social cost (MSC), 250
market barriers. *See* barriers to entry
market-based rate applications, 37
market concentration
    vs. market share, 202
    measurement of, 29n, 203
    relation to prices, 28
    and structure-conduct-performance (SCP) paradigm, 206–7
    See also HHI (Herfindahl-Hirschman Index) analysis
market design, 11–12
market-enhancing mechanisms, 252
market monitors, 197
market participants' conduct and performance, 28–29, 206
market power
    barriers to entry, 25–26, 28, 201
    and cross-subsidies, 23
    defined, 199
    and deregulation, 3
    distributional consequences, 200
    FERC Order 637, 9
    generally, 197
    horizontal, example, 202
    natural gas industry, 13
    preventing abuses of, 38, 297
    rate applications, 198
    remedies, 210–12
    self-correction, 203, 210
    vertical, 203–6, 209–10, 215
    wholesale generating markets, 37
    See also delivered price test; dominant firms; market share test; monopsony power; pivotal supplier test
market share, defined, 202
market share test, 207, 208
market structure, 28, 206

market-substituting mechanisms, 252
market value capitalization, 120–21
Maryland, 184, 265
Massachusetts Method, 138
Massachusetts v. EPA, 266
maximum daily quantity (MDQ), 174
Mcf-mile method, 175–76
mercury, 249
Merger Guidelines. See *Horizontal Merger Guidelines* (DOJ/FTC)
mergers and acquisitions
    market concentration, 29n
    PUHCA, 4
    utility mergers, 198
    See also market concentration
Metropolitan Edison v. People vs. Nuclear Energy, 259
Mexico
    estimation of operating costs, 85
    inflation indices, 188
    natural gas industry, 290–91
    pipelines, natural gas, 50n26
    provider of last resort (POLR) service, 182–83
    time value of money, 168n22
    valuation of assets, 106n
    working capital allowance formula, 58
Midwest ISO, 197
Missouri ex rel. Southwestern Bell Tel. Co. v. Missouri Pub. Serv. Comm'n, 103
model company approach
    Chile, 87
    Latin America, 108
    Peru, 173
    and uncertainty, 86
    X factor, 87
Modified Fixed Variable (MFV) rate, 164
monopolies
    competitive equilibrium, 19, 21
    government-owned, 3
    impetus for regulation, 40
    natural monopolies, 21–22, 23–24, 38
    and pricesetting, 29–31
    production decisions, 26–28
    service quality, 193
monopsony power, 199, 204
Montana, 11n
multifactor models, 116n70
multipart tariffs, 31, 32, 182
Munn v. Illinois, 4n2, 15

N

naïve forecasts. *See* billing determinants
NARUC (National Association of Regulatory Utility Commissioners), 53, 61, 145
National Electricity Market Management Company (NEMMCO) (Australia), 285
National Energy Conservation Policy Act, 7
National Energy Legislation, 7, 9, 298
nationalization, 26, 293
National Power (company), 284
Natural Gas Act, 6
natural gas industry
    consolidation, 6
    deregulation, 8
    distribution plant and expense accounts, 139
    drilling, 12
    drilling restrictions, 260
    entry-exit scheme, 176
    hedging strategies, 301
    joint costs, 53
    market power, 13
    Mexico, 290–91
    open access, 213–14
    predictions, 300–1
    price volatility, 236–38
    reregulation, 12

Russia, 295n
two-part tariffs, 174
vertical market power, 209
wholesale market, 8
See also liquefied natural gas (LNG); pipelines, natural gas
Natural Gas Policy Act (NGPA), 7, 8
Natural Gas Wellhead Decontrol Act of 1989, 8
Nebbia v. New York, 297
NERC. *See* North American Electric Reliability Council
net asset base, 57
    Bolivia, 67n11
    the Netherlands, renewable sources, 263
net present value (NPV), 98, 190, 224, 241–42
net salvage, 93, 95
New Electricity Trading Agreements (NETA), 284
New Jersey, 184
New Mexico, 257
New Replacement Value (NRV), 108
New Source Review (NSR), 260, 261
New York City, 4
New York ISO (NYISO), 282
New Zealand, 3, 107, 116n70
NGPA, 7, 8
nitrogen, oxides of, 249, 255, 260
noncoincident peaks, 155
nonexclusivity, 247, 278
nonrivalry, 278
Nordic countries, capacity markets, 285
North American Bulk Power System, 276
North American Electric Reliability Council (NERC), 275–77
Northwestern Corp., 11n
nuclear power
    curtailments on, 10–11
    decommissioning costs, 52
    plant construction, 5, 9, 103–6
    relicensing, 37
    used and useful (regulatory principle), 103–6
nuisance lawsuits, 251n11
NYMEX, 186

O

obligation to build (regulatory principle), 229
obligation to connect (regulatory principle), 37
obligation to serve (regulatory principle), 15, 36, 157, 219
Office of Electricity Generation, 284
off-ramps, 71, 72, 76, 196
Ohm's Law, 272, 273
oil pipelines, 60–61, 101–2
oil spills, 258
one-factor models, 116
one-part tariffs, 163
OPEC oil embargoes, 6, 9, 104, 298
open access
    Open Access Transmission Tariff (OATT), 178–80
    pipelines, natural gas, 8, 174, 213–14
    Standard Market Design (SMD), 277n14
    transmission, electric, 9
    See also Third Party Access (TPA)
Open Access Transmission Tariff (OATT), 178–80
operating efficiency
    and performance-based regulation, 69, 70
    and yardstick competition, 73
operating environments. *See* cost structures
operating reserves, electric, 276. *See also* reliability: electric
operation and maintenance (O&M) costs
    Bolivia, 85n
    defined, 51
    Good Utility Practice, 41

operation and maintenance (O&M) costs *(continued)*
   known and measurable (regulatory principle), 85–86
   lack of return on, 81
   projections of, 85–86
   prudence of, 84
   regulatory disallowance of, 85
   top-down vs. bottom-up approaches, 86, 87
   types, 84
   variables among firms, 66
   and working capital allowance, 58
   See also administrative and general costs; Data Envelope Analysis (DEA); depreciation; fuel costs; model company approach
opportunity costs, 56–58, 108
optimized depreciated replacement cost (ODRC), 107–8
Optimized Derived Value (ODV), 107–8
Ordinary Least Squares (OLS), 86, 89–90
original cost
   original book cost, 101
   privatization, 106, 107
   rate base calculations, 92
   vs. replacement costs, 48–49
   valuation of assets, 57, 99, 100
   See also Trended Original Cost (TOC)
Original Group Method, 126

P

Pacific Gas & Electric (PG&E), 299
Panama
   Corrected Ordinary Least Squares (COLS), 89
   privatization, 288
pass-through mechanisms, 185–87
peak demand studies, 155–56, 157–59

peaker method, 173–74, 176–77
peaking capacity
   billing determinants, 154
   cost allocation, 145, 146–47
   and cost of service (COS), 280
   idle resources, 24–25
   maximum, 158–59
   and price volatility, 236
   short-run vs. long-run costs, 49
   See also coincident peaks
peaking units, 279–80, 281
Pennsylvania Public Utility Commission, 104
performance-based regulation (PBR)
   advantages of, 76
   and cost of service (COS), 67n12
   effects on labor force, 73
   forms and advantages of, 69–70
   price adjustments, automatic, 186
   privatization, 63
   and regulatory cost reduction, 70
   total factor productivity (TFP) analysis, 70, 192
   United Kingdom, 73
   variety of regimes, 196
   X factor, 188–89
   See also shared-savings mechanisms
Peru
   capacity payments, 178, 284
   cost estimation, bottom-up approach, 86n
   discount rates, 169
   efficient company basis for revenue requirement, 45
   model company approach, 173
Petróleos Mexicanos (Pemex), 106n, 145, 290–91
pipelines, natural gas
   construction, 12, 22–23, 93
   deregulation, 8
   economic life, 93
   essential facilities, 37

FERC deregulation orders, 8–9
FERC Form 2 (Major Natural Gas Pipeline Annual Report), 60
future gas supplies, 301
infrastructure, 12
net salvage costs, 95
open access, 8
replacement cost calculations, 48–49
straight-fixed-variable rule, 52n30, 164
tariff methods, 174–76
two-part tariffs, 163–64
pivotal supplier test, 207, 208
PJM (ISO), 197
point-to-point transmission service, 180
Political Risk Insurance (PRI), 294
politics
    currency devaluation and political risk, 293
    and decision-making, 232
    infrastructure development, 37
    political-economic conflicts, 298
    political expediency, 16
    and regulatory certainty, 300
pollution controls, 48, 249, 253, 261–62
POLR. *See* provider of last resort
populism and renegotiation, 293
Portugal
    peer companies, 45
    yardstick competition, 74
PowerGen, 284
power marketing agencies, 5n6
Powerplant and Industrial Fuel Use Act, 7
power pools, 275–76, 280
prescribed technology policies, 252
price adjustments, automatic, 186–87. *See also* K factor; off-ramps; Q factor; shared-savings mechanisms; X factor; Z factor
price caps
    formulae, 65
    and peaking capacity investment, 281
    and performance-based regulation (PBR), 69
    regulation, 120
    restructuring, electric industry, 11, 220
    X factor, 192
price discrimination, 27n
price elasticity of demand, 153n3, 171, 263
price-fixing, 199
prices, regulated, 64–65
price setters, 26
pricesetting, and monopolies, 29–31
price structure, 77
price takers, 23
price-to-beat (PTB) service, 183–84
price umbrella, 203
price volatility, 236–38. *See also* Black-Scholes pricing model
Prince William Sound, 258
privatization
    Argentina, 287, 288
    Discounted Cash Flow (DCF) Model, 106–7
    Guatemala, 288
    negotiation, 292–93
    Panama, 288
    and rate base, 106
    Russia, 289n7
    United Kingdom, 63, 287, 288
    See also international arbitration; public-private partnerships
producer's surplus, 20–21
provider of last resort (POLR) service, 36, 182–83, 186
proxy firms, 113, 119
prudent investment (regulatory principle)
    basic concept, 39
    and cost recovery, 80
    and *Federal Power Commission v. Hope Natural Gas,* 102–3
    Good Utility Practice, 41–42

prudent investment (regulatory principle) *(continued)*
   and net asset base, 57
   return on investment, 81
   used and useful (regulatory principle), 228n11
   See also *Federal Power Commission v. Hope Natural Gas*
psychological harm, 259
public good, 247, 278, 279. *See also* reliability: electric
public interest (regulatory principle)
   dairy industry, 297
   and electric reliability, 37
   impetus for regulation, 40
   industries affected, 15–16
   and monopolies, 19
   nationalization, 26
   universal electric service, 17
public-private partnerships (PPPs), 288–89
Public Service of New Hampshire, Seabrook facility, 104
public utilities, definition, 15–16
Public Utility Act, 4
Public Utility Regulatory Policies Act. *See* PURPA
Puerto Rico, revenue requirement, 59n
PUHCA (Public Utility Holding Company Act), 4, 40, 198, 302
purchased power agreements (PPAs), 81
pure resistance, 273
PURPA (Public Utility Regulatory Policies Act)
   avoided costs, 9
   goals of, 7
   and long-term contracts, 10
   qualifying facilities (QFs), 302
   sales of privately generated electricity, 167
   wholesale competition, 179

Q

Q factor, 195–96
qualifying facilities (QFs), 9, 179, 304
quotas, 252, 265–66

R

Ramsey Pricing, 171
random walk, 238
rate base
   defined, 68
   depreciation in calculating, 92
   internationally, 106–7
   just and reasonable (regulatory principle), 99
   original cost approach, 106
   return on, 81, 99
   used and useful (regulatory principle), 104
   See also revenue requirement
rate cases, 68, 109, 185
rate classes, 52, 144, 147–48
rate-of-return regulation, 301. *See also* cost-of-service regulation (COSR)
rate reviews, 70
rates, 166–67, 168
rate year, 50, 80
reasonable rate of return (regulatory principle), 31
reciprocal dealing, 198
recovery of costs (regulatory principle), 31
regional transmission organizations (RTOs)
   establishment of, 197n2, 211
   installed capacity markets, 282
   market transparency, 212
   predictions, 305
   reliability, electric, 282n22
   Standard Market Design (SMD), 275–76
regulated prices, five-step procedure, 77–80
regulation
   defined, 16

and economies of scale, 24, 44
and economies of scope, 22, 23
goals of, 17, 21, 32, 162
and monopolies, 29–31
noneconomic factors, 17
and price stability, 186
regulators, as policy advocates, 298–99, 302
regulatory accounting
    Argentina, 288
    fixed and variable cost mixes, 140
    generally, 82–84
    three sets of books, 82
regulatory assets, 122
regulatory compact
    and cross-subsidies, 206
    defined, 43–44
    historical basis, 16
    historical context, 63
    obligation to serve, 36–37
    and privatization, 288
regulatory cost reduction, 70
regulatory lag, 69, 185, 186
regulatory reform, 294
regulatory structures. *See* cost of service (COS); performance-based regulation (PBR); yardstick competition
regulatory structures, common elements, 64–65
reliability, electric
    capacity payments, 177
    defined, 269, 275, 276
    installed capacity markets, 278–81
    Latin America, 285
    Long-term Reliability Compensation Issues, 280–81
    predictions, 302
    public good, 278, 285
    and risk, 239
    Short-term Reliability Compensation Issues, 280–81
    standards, 276–77, 303
    supply, 36
    See also alternating current; direct current
reliability must run (RMR) agreements, 280
renewable generation resources, 17, 35, 262
renewable portfolio standards (RPS), 35, 246, 263–64, 267 *See also* green tags
renewable sources
    feed-in-tariffs (FIT), 267n39
    state mandates, 298–99
replacement costs
    pipelines, natural gas, 48–49
    valuation of assets, 57, 100, 107, 108
reregulation
    Montana, 11n
    natural gas industry, 12
    retail price increases, 302
    uncertainty and, 220, 221
residual demand, 201–2
resistance, 271, 272–74. *See also* Ohm's Law
restructuring, electric industry
    competitive procurement, 184
    and excess capacity, 25
    externality adders, 262
    inception of (1994), 10
    Latin America, 284
    and peaking capacity, 280
    policy changes, 220
    See also California: electric industry restructuring
retail price index (RPI), 187, 188
retirement ratio, 130
return on equity
    automatic adjustments, 71–72
    book vs. market value, 120–21
    and cost-of-service regulation (COSR), 67
    developing countries, 119–20
    Latin America, 76
    measurement of, 56–57

return on equity *(continued)*
    and performance-based regulation (PBR), 70
    See also Capital Asset Pricing Model (CAPM); Discounted Cash Flow (DCF) Model; Risk Premium Model (RPM)

revenue, total. *See* revenue requirement
revenue caps, 69–70
revenue checks, 168, 169
revenue differential, 171
revenue reconciliation, 171
revenue requirement
    alternative terms for, 39
    calculations of, 55–56, 65
    cost of capital in, 101
    defined, 39
    effect of depreciation rates on, 97–98
    exogenous impacts, 59
    fair rate of return (regulatory principle), 80, 81
    generally, 44
    industry considerations, 58–59
    inflation in, 101
    levelizing of, 50
    mathematical expression of, 51–52
    Puerto Rico, 59n
    rules for determining, 65
    setting of, 80
    and X factor, 190
    See also above-the-line expenses; below-the-line expenses; capital costs; depreciation; known and measurable (regulatory principle); operation and maintenance (O&M) costs; rate year; revenue checks; taxes; test year
revenues, allowed. *See* revenue requirement
revenues, permissible. *See* revenue requirement
revenues, regulated. *See* revenue requirement
revenue-sharing mechanisms, 71

ring-fencing, 59, 149
risk
    business, 111
    diversifiable, 110, 118
    equity risk premium, 118
    financial, 111
    interest rate, 118n74
    nondiversifiable, 110, 111, 118
    and personal choices, 259–60
    portfolio, 110
    public-private partnerships, 290
    shareholder risk, 120
    systematic, 110, 118
    vs. uncertainty, 220n1, 239
    unsystematic, 118
    value-at-risk, 241
    See also price volatility
Risk Premium Model (RPM), 113, 118
RPI factor, 65
RPI-X adjustment, 187, 188
RPI-X regulation. *See* performance-based regulation (PBR)
Rural Electrification Act of 1936, 17, 77n1
Russia, 295n

S

SAIDI, 269
SAIFI, 269
San Francisco, 4
scenario analysis, 222–24, 243
Seaboard Method, 141
security-market line, 116
sensitivity analysis, 222–24, 243
service quality. *See* Q factor
service quality standards, 194
shared-savings mechanisms, 71, 72, 76, 196. *See also* earnings-sharing mechanisms; revenue-sharing mechanisms
simultaneous equations, 153

single-issue ratemaking, 186
Smyth v. Ames, 49, 103, 105
social policy goals, 180–81
Southeastern Power Administration, 5n6
South Korea, renewable sources, 263
Southwestern Power Administration, 5n6
Standard Market Design (SMD), 275, 280
standard offer service (SOS), 182
Statement of Financial Accounting Concepts No. 2 (FASB), 83
Stochastic Frontier Analysis (SFA), 86, 91–92
Straight Fixed Variable (SFV) rule, 164
straight-line method, 93, 95
stranded costs, 11, 182, 302
structural remedies, 210–11
structure-conduct-performance (SCP) paradigm, 28, 206, 210
subsidies
    and barriers to entry, 25n11
    rural electric service, 17
    social policy goals, 181
    wind energy, 263n33
    See also cross-subsidies; low-income rate structures
sulfur dioxide
    cap-and-trade, 255
    Clean Air Act Amendments (1990), 260
    emissions caps, 257
    externality adders, 261
    power plant emissions, 249
superconductivity, 271
Superfund sites, 5n9
suppliers, pivotal, 202, 207
survivor curves, 125–26, 131, 133. *See also* Iowa Curves
survivor ratio, 130
Sweden, renewable sources, 263

T

take-or-pay contracts, 8, 174
tariff base. *See* revenue requirement
tariff design
    complexity, 184
    consumption and, 151–52
    correct output/correct price, 162
    social policy goals, 180–81
    See also entry-exit scheme; peaker method
tariff levelization, 168–69
tariff reviews
    valuation of assets, 108
    X factor, 189
tariffs. *See* multipart tariffs; Open Access Transmission Tariff (OATT); transmission tariffs, electric; two-part tariffs
tariff-setting methods, 168, 173
tariff structures, 65, 77–78, 162–63. *See also* block tariffs; incentive rate tariff structures
taxes
    carbon, 242–43, 266
    and depreciation rates, 98
    emissions, 254, 265
    interest synchronization, 56
    known and measurable (regulatory principle), 81
    output taxes, 251–52, 265
    revenue requirement calculations, 51, 55–56
    tax normalization, 56
    tax shields, 111
test year
    future, 45–46, 80
    historic, 80, 170
    and net asset base, 57
    partial, 45
Texas, 183–84

Third Party Access (TPA), 176
Three Mile Island, 104
timely, likely, sufficient standard, 201, 208
time series of data, 156
time value of money, 50, 168
total factor productivity (TFP) analysis, 70, 189n, 190
tradable emissions permits, 255–56, 266. *See also* cap-and-trade
trading enforcement, 277. *See also* reliability: electric
tranches, 184
transformers (electricity), 274
transmission
    deregulation, 3
    electric, 9
    essential facilities, 37
    interstate, 4, 6
transmission security, 277. *See also* reliability: electric
transmission tariffs, electric, 177–79
Trended Original Cost (TOC), 101
two-part tariffs, 162, 163, 174

U

uncertainty
    advantages, 227
    costs of, 264
    countries with newly established regulatory mechanisms, 293
    and investment, 220, 224–28, 281
    nonmarket, 239–41
    political expediency, 61
    probability, 224, 225, 239
    regulatory conflicts, 38
    and Z factor, 195
    See also decision trees; environmental regulation; scenario analysis; sensitivity analysis

Uniform System of Accounts, 5n7, 61, 83, 137
United Kingdom
    deregulation, 3
    Discounted Cash Flow (DCF) Model, 172n30
    entry-exit tariffs, 171n27
    inflation indices, 188
    K factor, 192n9
    performance-based regulation (PBR), 73
    privatization, 63, 287, 288, 292
    provider of last resort (POLR) service, 183
    renewable sources, 263
    transmission tariffs, electric, 178
    X factor forecasting, 190n7
United States Constitution
    Fifth Amendment, 44
    Fourteenth Amendment, 15
United States. Department of Energy (DOE), 5n5
United States. Federal Energy Regulatory Commission. *See* FERC
United States. Securities and Exchange Commission (SEC), 4, 83
United States v. AT&T, 203–4
United States v. Terminal Railroad Association of St. Louis, 203, 213
universal service, 77n1
used and useful (regulatory principle)
    defined, 42–43
    disallowance of generation supply costs, 105
    Duquesne Light Co. v. Barasch, 104–5
    ex post concept, 228n11
    and *Federal Power Commission v. Hope Natural Gas,* 102
    Good Utility Practice, 41
    and net asset base, 57
    return on investment, 81
Use of System charge, 178
Utah, 257

utility mergers, 198–99, 201

V

valuation of assets, 99-100, 106, 107, 108n53
value added of the regulated activity. *See* revenue requirement
value-at-risk (VaR), 241
value of life, statistical, 258
value of service, 57
values, existence, 258
Vermont, 262
voltage sag, 257n12
volts, defined, 270

W

Washington, D.C., 263
Washington Public Power Supply System, 104
water pollution, 35
weather normalization, 153, 160–61
weighted average cost of capital (WACC)
    calculations of, 110–11, 120–21
    and cost-of-service regulation (COSR), 67
    return on capital assets, 57
    in revenue requirement calculations, 51
welfare loss
    and market power, 199, 200
    monopolies, 27, 31
    tariff design, 161, 163
wellhead prices, 6, 7, 12, 36
Western Power Administration, 5n6
Westinghouse, George, 4, 6
wheeling, 178
whole-life technique, 94–95
wholesale power rates, 5
widow-and-orphan investments, 5, 110
Wilcox v. Consolidated Gas, 109
wind energy, 267n39
workable competition, 200

working capital
    Bolivia, 58
    in capital costs, 40
    defined, 51, 57
    Mexico, 58
working capital allowance, 57–58
World Trade Center attacks (Sept. 11, 2001), 302

X

x-efficiency, 77
X factor
    calculations of, 188–92
    difficulty of measuring productivity, 196
    exogenous effects, 195
    in model company approach, 87
    in performance-based regulation (PBR), 70
    in price cap formulae, 65
    in RPI-X inflation adjustments, 187
    See also total factor productivity (TFP) analysis

Y

yardstick competition, 63, 66, 73–74, 76

Z

Z factor, 65, 188, 195
zone-gate method, 175